"*Between Hitler and Churchill* is a groundbreaking historical study that is both original and revelatory. With the acumen of a seasoned detective, Yaacov Falkov masterfully assembles new sources, shedding light on a crucial and long-forgotten episode from WWII. His work reveals obscured tensions among Poland, Soviet Russia, and Britain during the early years of the war, and crucially, it exposes secret negotiations with the Nazis that might have ended the war as early as 1940. Written with the gripping allure of a thriller, this book not only captivates but also challenges us to fundamentally reconsider much of what we thought we knew about the Second World War."

— Danny Orbach, Hebrew University of Jerusalem, author of *The Plots against Hitler and Fugitives: A History of Nazi Mercenaries During the Cold War*.

"In his fascinating and immensely readable account of World War II diplomacy, espionage, and everything in between, historian Yaacov Falkov paints a detailed picture of an attempt to reach a secret agreement between the Polish Government in Exile and Nazi Intelligence Services. Weaving a tale that is hard to put down, he describes the activities of Samson Mikiciński and Edward Szarkiewicz, two Jewish-born businessmen, the first who carried out clandestine operations in occupied Poland and elsewhere, and the second, who orchestrated the arrest of the first, claiming that he collaborated with Nazi spy agencies. While the reader may not agree with the author's conclusions regarding the feasibility of the Polish government coming to terms with a Nazi occupation similar to France, and how to regard Polish leaders who tried to establish a relationship with the Germans during the first phase of occupation, it still makes for a fascinating and thought-provoking read."

— Judy Baumel-Schwartz, Director, Finkler Institute for Holocaust Research, Bar-Ilan University, Ramat Gan Israel.

"The story you are about to read possesses all elements of a thriller, but it is based on painstaking archival research. Falkov recreates the tangled web of relationships in the Polish-German-British geopolitical triangle, from the Nazi invasion of Poland to Churchill's political marginalization of Sikorski and his government in the autumn of 1942. Questioning a black-and-white picture of this period in historiography and popular culture, Falkov depicts the actions and fates of two Polish Jews, Samson Mikiciński and Edward Szarkiewicz to demonstrate that history is much more complex and enigmatic than we could ever imagine."

— Bojan Aleksov, author of *Jewish Refugees in the Balkans, 1933-1945* (Brill, 2023)

"In the field of intelligence history, fact is often stranger and more surprising than fiction. Falkov's book exceeds that and shows how fragile history is at key points of decision-making and how World War II may have taken a radically different course than it did. The book is about two people, adventurers, secret agents, men of the world, working for different sides but with quite similar traits, undertaking perilous covert missions that could change the destiny of Europe. Falkov's book is a must read not only for WWII fans but to anyone interested in intelligence and history. The reverberations of the events examined in this book shape conflicts in Europe even today."

— Shlomo Shapiro, Paterson Professor in Security and Intelligence, Bar-Ilan University, and Chairman of the International Intelligence History Association (IIHA)

BETWEEN HITLER AND CHURCHILL

TWO JEWISH AGENTS AND THE ATTEMPT
BY THE BRITISH COUNTERINTELLIGENCE
SERVICE TO PREVENT A SECRET
AGREEMENT BETWEEN THE POLISH
GOVERNMENT-IN-EXILE AND NAZI GERMANY

Jews of Russia & Eastern Europe and Their Legacy

Series Editor

Maxim D. Shrayer (Boston College)

Editorial Board

Karel Berkhoff (NIOD Institute for War, Holocaust and Genocide Studies)
Jeremy Hicks (Queen Mary University of London)
Brian Horowitz (Tulane University)
Luba Jurgenson (Universite Paris IV—Sorbonne)
Roman Katsman (Bar-Ilan University)
Dov-Ber Kerler (Indiana University)
Vladimir Khazan (Hebrew University of Jerusalem)
Alice Nakhimovsky (Colgate University)
Antony Polonsky (Brandeis University)
Jonathan D. Sarna (Brandeis University)
David Shneer (University of Colorado at Boulder) (deceased)
Anna Shternshis (University of Toronto)
Leona Toker (Hebrew University of Jerusalem)
Mark Tolts (Hebrew University of Jerusalem)

Other Titles in this Series

Babel' in Context: A Study in Cultural Identity
Efraim Sicher

Jews in the East European Borderlands: Essays in Honor of John D. Klier
Edited by Eugene M. Avrutin & Harriet Murav

Jacob's Ladder: Kabbalistic Allegory in Russian Literature
Marina Aptekman

*"I am to be read not from left to right, but in Jewish: from right to left":
The Poetics of Boris Slutsky*
Marat Grinberg

Exemplary Bodies: Constructing the Jew in Russian Culture, 1880s to 2008
Henrietta Mondry

For more information on this series, please visit:
https://www.academicstudiespress.com/jews-of-russia-eastern-europe-and-their-legacy-series/

BETWEEN HITLER AND CHURCHILL

TWO JEWISH AGENTS AND THE ATTEMPT
BY THE BRITISH COUNTERINTELLIGENCE
SERVICE TO PREVENT A SECRET
AGREEMENT BETWEEN THE POLISH
GOVERNMENT-IN-EXILE AND NAZI GERMANY

YAACOV
FALKOV

ACADEMIC STUDIES PRESS
BOSTON
2025

Library of Congress Cataloging-in-Publication Data

Names: Falkov, Yaacov, author. | Sigal, Michael, translator.
Title: Between Hitler and Churchill : two Jewish agents and the attempt by the British counterintelligence service to prevent a secret agreement between the Polish government-in-exile and Nazi Germany / Yaacov Falkov; [translated by Michael Sigal].
Other titles: Ben Hiṭler le-Tsʹertsʹil. English
Description: Boston : Academic Studies Press, 2025. | Series: Jews of Russia & Eastern Europe and their legacy | Includes bibliographical references and index. | Translation of Ben Hiṭler le-Tsʹertsʹil : shene sokhnim Yehudim u-maʹamats ha-biyun ha-Briṭi le-manoʹa heskem ḥashaʹi ben memshelet Polin ha-golah le-Germanyah ha-Natsit, 2022.
Identifiers: LCCN 2024033493 (print) | LCCN 2024033494 (ebook) | ISBN 9798887196848 (hardback) | ISBN 9798897830053 (paperback) | ISBN 9798887196855 (adobe pdf) | ISBN 9798887196862 (epub)
Subjects: LCSH: World War, 1939-1945--Secret service--Great Britain. | World War, 1939-1945--Diplomatic history. | Great Britain--Foreign relations--Poland. | Great Britain--Foreign relations--Germany. | Germany--Foreign relations--Great Britain. | Poland--Foreign relations--Great Britain. | Jews, Polish--Great Britain. | World War, 1939-1945--Collaborationists--Poland. | World War, 1939-1945--Participation, Jewish.
Classification: LCC D750 .F3613 2025 (print) | LCC D750 (ebook) | DDC 940.54/8641--dc23/eng/20240923
LC record available at https://lccn.loc.gov/2024033493
LC ebook record available at https://lccn.loc.gov/2024033494

Copyright © English Translation, Academic Studies Press, 2025.
Published in Hebrew by Magnes Press in 2022.
ISBN 9798897830053 (paperback)
ISBN 9798887196855 (adobe pdf)
ISBN 9798887196862 (epub)

Book design by Lapiz Digital Services
Cover design by Ivan Grave

Published by Academic Studies Press
1007 Chestnut Street
Newton, MA 02464
press@academicstudiespress.com
www.academicstudiespress.com

Contents

Important Background Events	ix
Officer Ranks of the Polish Armed Forces during World War II	xii
Major and Minor Dramatis Personae	xiv
Glossary of Terms, Abbreviations, and Acronyms	xvii
Acknowledgments	xxii
Introduction. A Chance Encounter at the Warsaw International Airport and Its Surprising Ramifications	1
Preamble: Talking with the Enemy	10
A Common Destiny, with Limited Liability	10
The Kingdom's Most Important Prisoner	18
The Enemy of My Friend Is My Friend	20
The Führer Wishes to Strike a Deal	28
The Reich's Key Bargaining Chip	36
An Unexpected Short-Term Symbiosis	41
Offers of Friendship amid a Bloody Bacchanal	44
The Loyal Professor's Double Game	52
Part One. A VILE TRAITOR OR A SUPERHERO?	55
Chapter 1. From Provincial Polish Jew to Chilean Diplomat	57
Obscure Origins	57
Renouncing His Roots	58
Getting Acquainted with Berlin	60
The Fiasco in Paris and the Return to Poland	61
Rescuing Jews and Reaching out to the Nazis	65
In the Frock Coat of a Diplomat	69
Chapter 2. The Miracle Worker of Occupied Warsaw	73
The Escape from Hell as a Pleasure Trip	73
The Great Comeback in France	75
The Office on Frascati Street	79
The Road to Freedom through the Enemy Lair	82

Gestapo Officers Thrown Into the Street	89
The Birth of the Wondrous Union of the "Tiger" and the "Fox"	91
"I Have Done Something for Poland"	94

Chapter 3. The Top Player of Fascist Bucharest — 96

The Polish War on Romanian Soil	96
No More Trips to the General Government	103
The Polish Rival and His Bulgarian Connections	106
The End of the Fragile Partnership	111
The Move to Turkey	114
The Polish Desk at the Chilean Embassy	115

Chapter 4. A Base of Operations and Secret Negotiations on the Banks of the Bosporus — 122

In the Backyard of the World War	122
An Open and Cynical Struggle	125
Among Criminals and Nazi Spies	132
Acting at the Behest of the Polish Government	134

Chapter 5. Suspicions, Preparations for Neutralization, and an Abduction in Istanbul — 138

The Beginning of the Great Hunt	138
The Object of Surveillance from the Ambassador Hotel	142
A Partner in the Crosshairs	145
"A Little, Cunning Jew"	147
The Odd Inmates of the Latrun Prison Camp	153
The Last Stage in the Struggle for the Fate of "Lis"	157
A Belated Alibi from the Gestapo Files	164
The Failure of the Game of Prevention	165
The Most Sensitive Undertaking	168
"The Turks Have Given an Outstanding Performance!"	170
Hints in the Ambassador's Diary	173
A Noble Flight	175

Chapter 6. Publicity, Investigation, and a Mysterious Death in the Sands of Haifa — 179

A Worldwide Sensation	179
The Mysterious Inmate P.	182
The Invention of a Nazi Superspy	186
The Intelligence Analyst Crying out in the Wilderness	192
Futile Interventions	194
An Anonymous Grave in the Land of the Forefathers	198
A Polish Domestic Affair	201

Part Two. A COUNTERINTELLIGENCE ACE OR
A DESPICABLE SADIST? — 207

Chapter 7. A Plot Hatched in London under the Auspices of MI5 — 209
   Terrified Poles in Palestine — 209
   The Mystery of Room B at the Westminster Hospital — 212
   The Grey Eminence of the Polish Army in Exile — 218
   Cast Down from the London Olympus — 222

Chapter 8. Egyptian Exile, Professional Fiasco, and Disappearance
in the Mists of History — 229
   The Best Investigator in the Middle East — 229
   The Survivor from the KMF 25-A Convoy — 233
   Captain Dunlop Refuses to Rewrite Reports — 235
   "A Super-Intriguer Who Has Fallen out with This Department" — 239
   A Life without Aspirations — 241

Part Three. THE WORLD AFTER SAMSON AND EDWARD — 247

Chapter 9. The Battle Over the Legacy of "Lis" — 249
   A Tiny Army in a Large Leather Suitcase — 249
   A Polish-Turkish Diplomatic Crisis around the Division of Jewish Property — 251
   The Lawyer Florin Writes to General Gürsel — 255

Chapter 10. The Fates of the Secondary Characters in this Drama,
against the Backdrop of the Processes That Shaped Its Course — 258
   The Chronicle of a National, Political, and Personal Fiasco — 258
   The Desperate Search for a Polish Quisling — 267
   The Betrayers Betrayed — 275
   Keeping a Low Profile — 279

Afterword — 285
   A Perfect Tragedy of Imperfect Heroes — 285
   Open Ranks — 291
   Sane Realists in the "European Jungle" — 292
   The Legacy of Thucydides — 299

Sources and Bibliography — 302
Index of Names — 327

I formed a close alliance with these two rulers to destroy Chao and equally divide its territory into three. Because of the basis of our alliance, they would never violate it. Our armies have been exposed here at Chin-yang for three years. Now that we are about to seize it [Chao] and enjoy the profits, how could they have any intent to betray me? It's certainly not possible...

—*Han Fei (c. 325–250 or 280–233 BCE), The Treatise Han Feizi*[1]

---

1 Quoted from: Sawyer, The Tao of Spycraft, 320.

Important Background Events

1795–1918. The territory of Poland is partitioned among three powers: Prussia (later, the German Empire), the Austro-Hungarian Empire, and the Russian Empire.

November 22, 1918. The recreation of an independent Polish state under the name Rzeczpospolita Polska, also known as the Second Polish Republic.

May 12–14, 1926. The May Coup (przewrót majowy in Polish) under the leadership of Józef Piłsudski; the beginning of the gradual elimination of parliamentarism in Poland.

May 12, 1935. The death of Polish leader Józef Piłsudski.

August 23, 1939. The signing of a nonaggression pact between the Soviet Union and Nazi Germany. This document, which has gone down in history as the Molotov-Ribbentrop Pact (named after the German and the Soviet foreign ministers who signed it), enabled the two signatory states to partition the territory of Poland between them in September 1939.

September 1, 1939. The beginning of the German military invasion of Poland, also regarded as the beginning of World War II.

September 17, 1939. Soviet troops move into the eastern part of Poland, in coordination with their German counterparts.

September 28, 1939. The signing of the German-Soviet Boundary and Friendship Treaty, which finalized the borders between the German and the Soviet zones of the occupied Polish Republic.

September 30, 1939. The Polish government-in-exile, under the leadership of Władysław Sikorski, is formed in France.

October 26, 1939. A change of regime in the German-occupied Polish territories that had not been annexed to the Reich: the military administration hands over the reins of power to a civilian administration under Hans Frank; this territory becomes known officially as the Generalgouvernement (General Government).

May 10, 1940. Winston Churchill becomes prime minister of the United Kingdom.

June 19–25, 1940. In the aftermath of the Fall of France, the Polish government-in-exile and its armed forces relocate to Britain.

July 10, 1940–May 11, 1941. An air war begins in the skies over the United Kingdom. Western historians will divide it into two stages: the Battle of Britain (July 10–October 31, 1940) and the Blitz (September 7, 1940–May 11, 1941).

July 30, 1940. The Polish government-in-exile and the Soviet leadership sign an agreement and resume diplomatic ties.

November 4, 1940. Romania's new fascist, pro-German government expels all Polish diplomats.

June 22, 1941. The German military invades the Soviet Union (Operation Barbarossa).

March 18, 1942. With Churchill's consent, Joseph Stalin authorizes the evacuation of a Polish military force under the command of General Władysław Anders from the Soviet Union to the Middle East.

April 13, 1943. The Germans announce the discovery of a mass grave of Polish officers massacred by Soviets in the Katyn Forest (in Smolensk Oblast, Russia) in the spring of 1940.

July 4, 1943. General Władysław Sikorski, head of the Polish government-in-exile, dies in an airplane crash near Gibraltar.

January 17–May 18, 1944. The Battle of Monte Cassino, also known as the Battle for Rome, begins when the Allied troops break through a line of German fortifications on their way to the Italian capital. Polish Allied troops suffer heavy casualties, with more than a thousand killed in action; around 2,500 soldiers were injured.

August 1–October 2, 1944. The London-based Polish government-in-exile and its loyalists in German-occupied Poland stage the Warsaw Uprising, a failed attempt to drive the Nazis out of the Polish capital before it is captured by Soviet forces.

March 31, 1945. The Red Army suppresses the last pockets of German resistance in the territory of Upper Silesia. This day is considered the date of the final liberation of Poland from the Nazis.

May 8–9, 1945. The Third Reich surrenders unconditionally to the Allies.

June 28, 1945. The Provisional Government of National Unity (Tymczasowy Rząd Jedności Narodowej) takes power in Poland under the aegis of the Soviet Union.

Officer Ranks of the Polish Armed Forces during World War II

Some of the characters in this book were officers in the Polish army in exile and intelligence and counterintelligence organs. The English version of this book uses the British equivalents of their Polish ranks.

Petty officers

Second Lieutenant—*podporucznik*. In the period described here, this was the lowest officer rank in the Polish army, equivalent to the rank of *podporuchik* in the Imperial Russian army and roughly equivalent to the rank of second lieutenant in the militaries of English-speaking countries.

Lieutenant—*porucznik*. It is equivalent to the rank of *poruchik* in the Imperial Russian army, and to that of first lieutenant in the militaries of English-speaking countries.

Captain—*kapitan*.

Staff officers

Major—*major*.
Lieutenant Colonel—*podpułkownik*.
Colonel—*pułkownik*.

Generals

Major General—*generał brygady*. The lowest general rank in the Polish army, with no equivalent in the Russian army.
Lieutenant General—originally, *generał dywizji*.
General—originally, *generał broni*. The highest officer rank in the Polish army in the period described here.

Major and Minor Dramatis Personae

Samson Mikiciński—the first protagonist. A wealthy businessman of Jewish origin and native of the Polish town of Boćki in the Russian Empire. Starting in 1938, he smuggled well-off Jews from the territory of the Third Reich into Latin America. A year later, he was recruited by the Polish government-in-exile, then based in France, to carry out highly sensitive, clandestine operations in the territory of occupied Poland and other European countries.

Edward Szarkiewicz—the second protagonist. A Jewish businessman, who was born near Lwów (present-day Lviv in western Ukraine) at a time when the city was still part of Austria-Hungary. In the 1930s, as a citizen of independent Poland, he became very close to the highest circles of power in Warsaw and officially converted to Catholicism. Following the outbreak of World War II, he joined the Polish military intelligence, and went on to serve in Romania, Palestine, and the United Kingdom. He orchestrated the arrest of Mikiciński, whom he accused of collaborating with the Nazi spy agencies.

Viktor Kutten—a successful Polish businessman of Jewish or German origin. After the defeat and occupation of his country in September 1939, he fled to neighboring Romania, where he quickly became a major cross-border smuggler, eventually partnering with Mikiciński and aiding the latter in both his business dealings in occupied Poland and in carrying out secret assignments from the government-in-exile. He was arrested by Szarkiewicz in Palestine on charges of collaborating with the Nazis and assisting Mikiciński in his criminal activities.

Hector Briones Luco—a veteran, pro-German Chilean diplomat and member of a wealthy and highly influential family in Chile. On the eve of World War II, he made the acquaintance of Samson Mikiciński under unclear circumstances and supplied him with a Chilean diplomatic passport. He went on to employ Samson in the Chilean representations in Paris, Bucharest, and Istanbul, thereby shielding the protagonist of this book from persecution by the Nazis and the Romanian fascists and giving him freedom of movement throughout a European continent hurtling toward the abyss of war. In exchange, he received generous, regular payments.

Dr. Scholz, also known as *Heinz Fabian*—an officer of the Abwehr, the Nazi military intelligence service, active in the German city of Breslau (present-day Wrocław in western Poland). About a year before Germany invaded Poland, Scholz initiated contact with Mikiciński, aiding him in smuggling wealthy Jews out of the Reich and later in carrying out secret assignments for the exiled Polish elite in exchange for money. He may have acted at the behest of the chief of the Abwehr, Admiral Wilhelm Canaris, who wished to set up a secret channel of communication with the West.

Stanisław Kot—a professor at Jagiellonian University in Kraków, one of the foremost contemporary experts on the history of Polish culture and an influential politician. After the establishment of the Polish government-in-exile in French territory, he held several key posts and was regarded as Sikorski's right-hand man. After Mikiciński's first successful trip into occupied Poland as a Chilean diplomat, Kot recruited him as an agent for special assignments in the General Government and in Romania. A highly ambitious person, Kot did his utmost to secure a senior political position in postwar Poland.

Władysław Sikorski—a hero of the struggle for Polish independence at the end of World War I, prime minister of Poland in 1922–1923, lieutenant general of the Polish army. After the defeat in September 1939, he fled to Paris, where he was proclaimed head of the Polish government-in-exile and its armed forces. He sponsored the activities of Prof. Kot in the territory of occupied Poland, and Mikiciński himself smuggled his wife and daughter out of occupied Warsaw.

Kazimierz Iranek-Osmecki—an officer of the Dwójka, the Polish military intelligence service, who in the autumn of 1939 found himself in France. He was assigned to the Polish intelligence station in Bucharest when Edward Szarkiewicz served there, and later went on to have a remarkable career in occupied Poland, in charge of the intelligence and counterintelligence of the famous Home Army (Armia Krajowa), a clandestine organization answerable to Sikorski. As an influential figure in the camp of the political opponents to Sikorski and Kot, he aided Szarkiewicz in his attempts to neutralize Mikiciński and Kutten.

Izydor Modelski—a major general of the Polish army, who joined the government-in-exile in the autumn of 1939 as second deputy minister of war. Hoping to realize his dream of climbing to the top of the Polish military hierarchy, he entered into a secret pact with the British (who were dissatisfied with Sikorski) to sponsor Szarkiewicz's attempts to neutralize Mikiciński, apparently with the goal of compromising and politically weakening Sikorski and Kot.

Sir David Petrie—a British aristocrat and former high-ranking official in British India. In 1941–1946, he was director general of MI5, the British internal security service. In this capacity, he constantly monitored the activities of the Polish government-in-exile, both in the territory of the United Kingdom and beyond its borders. He sponsored Modelski's attempts to undermine the authority of Sikorski, and had personal meetings with the rebellious general and with his protégé, Szarkiewicz.

Raymund John Maunsell—a high-ranking officer in the British army. From 1939–1944, he was head of SIME (Security Intelligence Middle East; see the Glossary of Terms, Abbreviations, and Acronyms). From his headquarters in Cairo, he controlled the activities of Edward Szarkiewicz as a Polish intelligence officer in the Middle East and likely also used him as a source of intelligence on Polish affairs. He later helped Szarkiewicz join the ranks of SIME, where the latter interrogated individuals suspected of spying for the Germans and Italians.

Glossary of Terms, Abbreviations, and Acronyms

Abwehr—literally: Defense. The intelligence and counterintelligence service of the supreme command of the German army. It was established in 1921 and remained active until February 1944, when it was partially swallowed up by the RSHA (the Reich Security Main Office, which was subordinated to Heinrich Himmler, Reichsführer-SS and chief of the German Police). The successful operations of this body facilitated the victories of the Nazi war machine in Europe and North Africa. At the same time, it was also a hotbed of opposition to the Nazi regime. Officers of the Abwehr—up to its chief, Admiral Wilhelm Canaris—carried out a number of acts of resistance, including the rescue of several Jews, both in the Reich and in the occupied territories.

CID (Criminal Investigation Department)—in the twentieth century, this term designated the criminal police departments in the United Kingdom and the territories under its control. In this book, the term refers to the CID that operated in Mandatory Palestine. It was responsible both for fighting ordinary crime and for combating the sabotage and terror activities of the Axis Powers (Germany and Italy; later: Germany, Italy, and Japan) and of local Jewish and Arab clandestine organizations.

DNB (an abbreviation of German News Agency in German)—the official news service of the Third Reich, which operated in the years 1933–1945 under the auspices of Propaganda Minister Joseph Goebbels. Its abroad offices were often used as platforms for Nazi espionage and sabotage operations.

Dwójka—the common, unofficial name of the Second (Intelligence) Department of the Polish General Staff (Sztab Generalny) in 1918–1939, and of the Staff of the Supreme Commander (Sztab Naczelnego Wódza) in 1939–1945. During World War II, the personnel of the Paris (and, later, London) headquarters of the Dwójka and its intelligence stations were nicknamed the "Dwójka people" by their compatriots.

Ekspozytura (Polish: department or branch)—in this book, the term designates the intelligence stations of the Polish Armed Forces in exile.

Free France (France libre)—the first official name of the French government-in-exile, which was led by General Charles de Gaulle and fought on the side of the Western Allies in 1940–1944. In 1942, it was officially renamed Fighting France (France combattante).

General Government for the Occupied Polish Areas (Generalgouvernement für die besetzten polnischen Gebiete or GG)—an administrative territorial entity established by the Nazis after their occupation of Poland in 1939. It comprised some of the occupied Polish territories, its capital was Kraków, and it existed until 1945.

Gestapo (a syllabic abbreviation of Secret State Police in German)—the political police of the Third Reich in the years 1933–1945. It was subordinated to the RSHA (see entry for Abwehr) and the SS (see below).

GPU (an abbreviation of State Political Directorate in Russian)—a body of the NKVD that existed in the years 1922–1923. It had wide-ranging powers in the field of state security, including political terror in Soviet territory and abroad. For its cruelty and ruthlessness in the struggle against "enemies of the Revolution," the GPU became a byword for an exceptionally brutal secret police, and this usage was common in Poland and elsewhere at the time. It is in this sense that the term was used by the protagonists of this book.

Home Army (Armia Krajowa in Polish, abbreviated AK)—the largest and most powerful Polish resistance organization in the period 1939–1945. From the moment of its creation in the autumn of 1939 (under a different name—see below), despite being formally subordinated to the Polish government-in-exile, it was under the powerful influence of the political camp that had ruled Poland before the war. For this reason, the AK was in a state of permanent conflict with Sikorski and his entourage. The most important and famous anti-German action by the AK was the Warsaw

Uprising (August–October 1944), which was brutally suppressed by the German occupying forces.

Irgun (known as Etzel in Hebrew; an abbreviation of Irgun Tzva'i Leumi, National Military Organization)—a clandestine Jewish organization that operated in Palestine in 1931–1948. It fought both the British and the Arabs.

KGB (an abbreviation of Committee for State Security in Russian)—a security agency attached to the Council of Ministers of the USSR. It existed in the years 1954–1991, and was responsible for foreign intelligence, counterintelligence, and combating dissent and terrorism, as well as protecting the Soviet leadership and guarding strategic facilities and the borders of the USSR.

Lehi (an abbreviation of Fighters for the Freedom of Israel in Hebrew)—a paramilitary Jewish organization that fought the British and the Arabs. It split from the Irgun (see above), and was active in Palestine and beyond its borders in 1940–1948.

MI5—the United Kingdom's national security agency. It was established in 1909 as Section 5 of the Directorate of Military Intelligence, and still exists today. During World War II, both the agency itself and the various counterintelligence and security organs operating under its aegis throughout the British Empire carried out a number of brilliant operations that stymied the espionage and sabotage efforts of Nazi Germany and its allies, thereby strengthening the British home front and facilitating the military successes of the Western Allies.

MI6—see SIS.

MI9—Section 9 of the British Directorate of Military Intelligence, which became a department of the British War Office during World War II. Its major goal was evacuating downed British airmen from enemy territory via neutral countries. The department relied on its own network of secret intelligence stations and individuals agents, which operated throughout Europe. It was also assisted by clandestine European resistance organizations and partisan movements.

Miecz i Pług (Polish: Sword and Plow)—a clandestine, ultranationalist, military-political Polish organization that existed in the years 1939–1944. It endorsed the idea of Slavic racial supremacy, and fought both the Germans and all the other factions of the Polish underground.

NKGB—the abbreviated name of the Soviet intelligence and counterintelligence service, which was created in February 1941 on the basis of the Main Directorate of State Security (GUGB) of the NKVD (see the following entry). It was reabsorbed by the NKVD a month after the Nazi invasion of the USSR and reestablished in April 1943, with the same areas of responsibility it had 1941. In 1946, it was renamed the Ministry of State Security (MGB).

NKVD (an abbreviation of People's Commissariat for Internal Affairs in Russian)—the Interior Ministry of the Russian Soviet Federative Socialist Republic and later of the entire Soviet Union, which existed in 1917-1946. Until February 1941, and then again from July 1941 until April 1943, the NKVD was responsible, inter alia, for: foreign intelligence, counterintelligence, protection of the leadership, the police, the border troops, and the system of camps, prisons, and penal colonies.

NOR (an abbreviation of National Radical Organization in Polish)—an ultranationalist Polish organization, which emerged shortly after the onset of the Nazi occupation and advocated ideological and military collaboration with the occupiers. It carried out an anti-Jewish pogrom in Warsaw in March 1940, before being crushed by the Germans in June that year.

RAF (the Royal Air Force)—a branch of the British Armed Forces. It was established in 1918, and still exists today.

Razvedupr (or RU)—the Intelligence Directorate of the Soviet General Staff, which was established in 1921. It was responsible for gathering strategic and field intelligence for the Red Army. After undergoing a series of structural and functional reforms during World War II, and being merged with the intelligence service of the People's Commissariat of Defense, it became the Main Intelligence Directorate of the General Staff (GRU) in 1945.

Reichstag—the building of the German parliament in 1894–1933. In the spring of 1933, following the appointment of Adolf Hitler as chancellor and the Reichstag fire (an act of arson that was blamed on the Communists and used by the Nazis as a pretext for crushing their political opponents), the building ceased to function as the seat of Germany's legislative branch and was turned into a site of propaganda exhibitions, cultural events, and speeches by Hitler.

SD (an abbreviation of Security Service in German) was the intelligence agency of the Nazi Party (NSDAP) and the SS (see below). It existed in 1931–1945 and engaged in espionage, clandestine sabotage operations, and terror against the population of the Third Reich and the German-occupied countries.

SIME (Security Intelligence Middle East)—the security service of the British Military Administration in the Middle East. It was established in 1939 and disbanded in the second half of the 1940s. It employed representatives of various British intelligence and security agencies; however, it was controlled by to the London headquarters of MI5. During World War II, the Cairo central office of SIME had branches in Egypt, North Africa, Yemen, Palestine, Syria, Iraq, Ethiopia, Turkey, and Cyprus. Its operatives were responsible for foiling the hostile activities of the secret services of Germany and its allies. After the end of the war, the organization switched to combating various anti-British liberation movements, including clandestine Jewish groups in Palestine.

SIS (Secret Intelligence Service; also known as MI6)—the foreign intelligence service of the United Kingdom. It was established in 1909 as Section 6 of the Directorate of Military Intelligence, and still exists today. The successful worldwide activities of this organization during World War II were an important factor in the Allied victory.

SO2—the operations section of SOE (see the following entry).

SOE (Special Operations Executive)—a secret British World War II organization that engaged in sabotage and reconnaissance, operating under the Ministry of Economic Warfare. It was created in 1940 and disbanded in 1946. Its activities in occupied Europe facilitated the Allied landings in France and the subsequent advance of Allied troops toward the borders of Nazi Germany in 1944–1945.

SS (an abbreviation of Protection Squadron in German)—a paramilitary organization of the NSDAP, which existed in 1929–1945 and functioned as a secret police and an intelligence and counterintelligence agency.

Union of Armed Struggle (Związek Walki Zbrojnej; ZWZ)—the major clandestine resistance organization in German-occupied Poland, which existed in 1939–1942. In February 1942, it became the Home Army (see above).

Wehrmacht—literally, Defense Force. The official name of the armed forces of the Third Reich in 1935–1945.

Acknowledgments

This book would never have been published if not for the enormous moral support and practical assistance of my wife, Lydia Mandelbaum-Falkov, and of our two children, Eliana and Ariel. It was thanks to them that I was able to devote the requisite time, spiritual and physical resources, and money to a years-long historical investigation and to actual writing. Furthermore, they accompanied me on an important scholarly field trip to Paris, where we located and photographed some of the buildings where the book's protagonists lived and worked. My beloved family is the first and most important recipient of my gratitude!

I also offer my heartfelt thanks to two of my friends and colleagues, Renée Poznanski and Dmitry Adamsky, professors of history and the social sciences. I involved them in the details of my investigation and shared my findings and conclusions with them. In return, they gave me invaluable advice on how to carry out my investigation and how to transform my findings into a book.

I also owe an exceptional debt of gratitude to my late uncle, Alexander L'vovich Dokshitser, a rare expert on history and a wonderful teacher of it. The unique library he amassed facilitated my task of setting the book in the general context of the early period of World War II.

I also extend my warm gratitude to the wonderful staff of the archival collections to which my historical quest led me: the archives of the United States Holocaust Memorial Museum (USHMM) in Washington, DC, the archives of the Yad Vashem memorial complex (YVA) in Israel, the British National Archives (TNA) in Kew, the archives of the Józef Piłsudski Institute of America (JPIA) in New York City and the archives of the Polish Institute and Sikorski Museum (PISM) in London. Their unfailing readiness to aid my research, coupled with the impeccable organization of their work, enabled me to make the discoveries that serve as the basis for this book.

Finally, I must honor all the nameless employees and archivists of the official agencies and institutions of the United Kingdom and Poland, thanks to whose painstaking efforts the information about the people and events described in this book has been meticulously written down and carefully preserved to the present day.

Introduction

A Chance Encounter at the Warsaw International Airport and Its Surprising Ramifications

---

Major international airports house not just airline companies, security personnel, fast food restaurants, and duty-free shops. Since the 1930s, they have also contained bookstores.[1] Despite the widespread belief in the declining popularity of the printed word in our digital age, these stores have been experiencing a veritable renaissance in many countries.[2] And, just like at the dawn of their lives, they still serve as a barometer of sorts of the local culture (in the apt formulation of the American scholar Prof. Franck Salameh). A foreigner entering an airport bookstore will always learn something useful about a country and its inhabitants, and upon departure, they can catch one final glimpse of the country by buying a local book or newspaper before boarding the outbound flight.[3]

I am one of those weirdos who never misses an airport bookstore, even in countries whose language is incomprehensible to me. For this reason, my encounters with colorful book covers in arrivals and departures lounges often end up weighing down my backpack. This was the case on a typical gloomy and chilly Eastern European summer day in 2012, when, on my way to yet another archival search, I found myself stranded for a couple hours at the Frederic Chopin International Airport in Warsaw. There, in a tiny bookstore whose name has since slipped my mind, my gaze was drawn to the cover of some Polish book, which sported an age-worn photograph. It bore the mysterious title *Polskie piekiełko* (The Polish Hell); below it, in smaller letters, was the subtitle: "Scenes from the Life of the Émigré Elites, 1939-1945." The name of the author, Sławomir Koper, meant nothing to me at the time, but the subject he had chosen to tackle instantly captured my attention. It was one of the greatest political and human dramas of the twentieth century: the sharp clash between different political factions and prominent individuals within the Polish leadership during World War II. This clash played out against the backdrop of the desperate attempts by this leadership to resist the brutal Nazi-Soviet (and, from June 1941, exclusively Nazi) occupation of the Second Polish Republic, and its simultaneous efforts to prevent the seemingly inevitable diplomatic betrayal of Poland by its key strategic allies—the United Kingdom and the United States of America. As is well known, London and Washington ultimately chose to sacrifice the national interests of Poland (at least as articulated by the Polish government-in-exile) in favor of military cooperation with Moscow, which they deemed more advantageous.

As I began to leaf through Koper's book, I felt the familiar urge to buy it at once, but the voice of reason ordered me to first make sure it was a worthy addition to my overflowing home library. And then, I suddenly hit upon a chapter that told of the marvelous deliverance of the families of fugitive Polish leaders from the horrors of the Nazi occupation into still-unoccupied France. It contained the following description of heroic rescuer Samson Mikiciński: "The queerest of all the queer ducks that roosted around the Sikorski government ... A Polish citizen and an ethnic Jew."[4]

This passage gave me a nasty shock mixed with disbelief. How was it possible for a Jew to repeatedly cross the borders into Nazi-occupied Poland as easily as one can cross the virtual borders of the present-day European Union and return with refugees? This seemed utterly fantastic! Any doubts about the need to buy the book evaporated at once, and I spent the flight from Warsaw absorbed in my latest acquisition.

I soon learned that Mikiciński crossed into occupied Poland from neighboring Romania; that he was in constant touch with the German military intelligence (the Abwehr), and that, in early 1941, he was abducted by the Polish secret services in Istanbul. From there, he was smuggled into Palestine (i.e., present-day Israel), imprisoned, interrogated for a time, and then (most probably) murdered in unclear circumstances. Without a doubt, this was one of the most unusual stories from the World War II period that I had ever come across. At the same time, I got the impression that my esteemed colleague, the Polish historian, had failed to ask many crucial questions regarding the person of Samson Mikiciński, his connections with the Polish government-in-exile and

---

4 Koper, *Polskie piekiełko*, 127–128.

the Nazis, his incredible activities in occupied Poland, and the circumstances of his death. I then decided to pursue these questions on my own and try to come up with answers. This was the beginning of a fascinating scholarly odyssey that lasted for years. Its results are presented in this book.

First of all, I needed to collect and read everything that had been written about my new subject in his native Poland. I soon learned that Mikiciński had been virtually ignored by Polish writers. Apart from Koper's laconic account, all I could find was an old, modestly sized book by the Polish historian and publicist Roman Buczek,[5] as well as several casual references in biographies of contemporaries, some scholarly works, and a few sensational journalistic articles from the post-Communist period. The vast majority of these sources presented Samson in a very negative light: he was as a Nazi spy, an international criminal businessman, a man of unbound avarice, a schemer, and a pathological liar. As these writers would have it, he orchestrated the rescue of the families of the Polish government-in-exile from their vanquished homeland not out of patriotic or humanistic considerations, but solely out of a desire for personal gain, and possibly even at the behest of the German intelligence organs. Mikiciński's Jewishness was not ignored by his Polish denouncers—*au contraire*, they underscored it with particular relish, sometimes even stating explicitly that the Jewish people, too, had produced traitors like Samson willing to collaborate with their German occupiers. It was obvious that virtually all publications of this kind were based on the recollections of former functionaries of the Polish government-in-exile and the clandestine Home Army (AK), and especially those of Kazimierz Iranek-Osmecki, the former chief of the AK intelligence and counterintelligence. All of them had a bone to pick with Mikiciński. Only occasionally, and then mostly in a mocking tone, did they quote Polish political, military, and other sources who offered a positive assessment of Mikiciński and his doings.[6]

---

5   Buczek, *Człowiek do złotych interesów*. Buczek's book is written in a popular style. While the author is clearly sympathetic toward Mikiciński, the scholarly value of his work is open to question. Another Polish historian, Zdzisław Kapera, criticized it for the dubiousness of the information it presents. According to Kapera, Buczek (or his editors) claims in the introduction that the book is based on Polish, British, and German intelligence documents. However, it contains not a single reference to archival sources, and for this reason the alleged facts brought up by Buczek cannot be verified by other historians. See: Kapera, "Niemieckie świadectwa": 60.
6   See, for instance: Dubicki, *Dzieje polskiej placówki dyplomatycznej w Bukareszcie*, 35; Kapera, *Niemieckie świadectwa*, 75; Koreś, "Tajemnice generała Gano," 48–53; Rutkowski, *Stanisław Kot*, 144–150; Szczepański, "Błyskotliwy agent czy zdrajca?"

Western publications about Mikiciński turned out to be less numerous and even more laconic; their authors often misspelled his first and last names and drew on the caustic testimony of Iranek-Osmecki and a few British intelligence documents from the World War II era quoting Polish sources calling Mikiciński a Nazi collaborator.[7] Only a single Western writer claiming to be a former representative of the Polish military intelligence (the *Dwójka*) in the Middle East[8] depicted Samson as a hero who had fallen victim to a plot concocted by the British secret services and the Polish government-in-exile. He used the Polish name Ladislas Michniewicz, which may have been a pseudonym, and his book *Operation Haifa*, published in Belgium in 1969, is full of fictional details and names. He did not reveal any of his sources of information about Samson's fate, thereby severely compromising the historical reliability of his work.[9] Nevertheless, his name will recur in the pages of this book.

My efforts to comb through Israeli sources for any references to Mikiciński, his activities, or his relatives proved largely fruitless. Apart from a single 1943 report by the secret service of the Jewish Irgun underground that briefly mentions the "German spy Mikociński [*sic*]," who was active in Romania; and a brief announcement in the Israeli *Maariv* daily from 1961 about the fate of the estate of the late Polish-Jewish businessman, all I found were sporadic references to Samson on Hebrew-language blogs. There, he was named "Shimshon Mikiciński" and described as a half-Jew and an agent of the British and the Nazis. He was said to have been arrested in Turkey, taken to Haifa, and killed in 1941 during an escape attempt from prison.[10]

Wishing to get to the bottom of the mystery surrounding my protagonist, I then turned to the archives. As stated above, Western historical publications implied that the British secret service had known of Samson's activities during his lifetime. I decided to try to gauge the extent of this knowledge on my own, hoping to find some obscure tidbits of information in the recently declassified document collections of MI5, SIS, and SOE, and in the analogous collections of expatriate Polish diplomats and military intelligence officers. This time, the results exceeded my boldest expectations. I made my first significant finding

---

7   See, for instance: Bines, *The Polish Country Section of the Special Operations Executive*, 34–38; Williamson, *The Polish Underground*, 49.
8   In the Polish historical literature, one can find references to Colonel Władysław Michniewicz, a former counterintelligence officer of the *Dwójka* who was actively involved in the fight against Soviet spies in the interwar period. However, we cannot be certain that this person was the author of the abovementioned book. See: Świerczek, "Władysław Michniewicz": 271–273.
9   Michniewicz, *Opération Haïfa*.
10 "Shimshon Mikichinski."

in the digital archives of the Hoover Institution, which is part of Stanford University in California. The Institution holds some unique collections of historical documents, including the papers of the Polish Foreign Ministry in exile. This collection, which comprises many thousands of pieces of unique documentary evidence, was shipped from London to Stanford immediately after the end of World War II (to prevent the possibility of these documents being handed over to the new Communist overlords of Poland). There, the documents were meticulously arranged, catalogued, and eventually digitized. Nowadays, the collection is fully accessible to both academic historians and ordinary history buffs from all over the world.

In my opinion, digital documents are deficient in one important respect: they lack that inimitable aroma of old paper, and can never be touched by human hands; this destroys the magic of the unmediated encounter between the scholar and the original document. At the same time, the digital format also has one undeniable advantage: the documents can be accessed from anywhere in the world, via a personal computer, or even a smartphone, and this greatly simplifies the scholar's task. Such was the case with my own investigation. No sooner had I entered Mikiciński's name in the "search" window of the Hoover Institution website than I saw a long list of reports by Polish diplomats and spies, describing the twists and turns of the life of my protagonist and his partners in occupied Poland. It was an amazing discovery, since, as I realized at once, none of these reports had ever been published before.

In my subsequent virtual voyages through the global digital network, I was happy to learn that additional information about the Mikiciński affair had been preserved in other American and British archives. One of these was the tiny Józef Piłsudski Institute of America, hidden on a sleepy street in Brooklyn, New York. Unlike the collections of the fabulously wealthy Hoover Institution, its archives have never been digitized, so I had to visit it in person. When I arrived at the Piłsudski Institute building, adjoined by small Polish restaurants and shops that have seemingly been directly transported to America from faraway Eastern Europe, I discovered that its unassuming facade concealed a treasure trove of documents from Polish diplomatic missions that had operated in the US from 1919–1945. While perusing them in the cozy reading room, which has carefully preserved the atmosphere of the old Polish embassy in Washington, DC, I hit upon a real historical pearl: a detailed *curriculum vitae* of Samson Mikiciński, including his relationship with his patron in the Polish government-in-exile, Prof. Stanisław Kot, a fascinating historical character in his own right, almost forgotten now, whom we will get to know in detail later on.

The author of this unique document, who obviously belonged to the circle of enemies of Mikiciński and Kot, did not bother to sign it. Thus, his name and target audience, as well as the time of writing, remain unknown. Nevertheless, numerous details in the text enable us to determine that it was composed after the end of World War II, and that its author probably drew on some earlier texts—apparently, reports of the fourth section of the Dwójka (i.e., the Polish military counterintelligence).[11]

An even bigger surprise awaited me at the British National Archives. This complex of buildings, located in Kew, a district in the London Borough of Richmond, is sometimes known simply as the "Kew Archives." In contrast to the archives in Brooklyn, this place, like many other official British institutions, exudes an imperial pomposity and is dominated by British bureaucracy. For this reason, I was able to get into the archives' reading room only after going through a fairly grueling procedure, which included filling certain forms, furnishing documentary proof of my permanent place of residence in Britain (nothing like that had ever been asked of me in any other archive in the world), and, finally, presenting a passport picture of myself, which was immediately placed on my shiny new plastic library card, which would remain valid for three years. However, when I finally walked into the reading room, I realized that all my suffering had not been in vain. As it turned out, the marvelous British archivists, using the digital request submitted by me in advance, had already plumbed the uncharted depths of the National Archives and come up with a truly legendary treasure: the personal files of Mikiciński and Kot, which had been opened and maintained by the World War II-era British secret services: MI5, the counterintelligence agency, and SOE, which engaged in sabotage and intelligence operations in wartime Europe, North Africa, and Asia. For decades, these files had been gathering dust on archival shelves, shielded from prying eyes by the label "Strictly confidential." Only relatively recently were they made accessible to scholars and the general public. And now, they lay waiting for me in the special box for visitors. I do not know if I was the first person to lay eyes on them. However, I believe myself to have been the first historian to use these files for a serious investigation of Samson Mikiciński's fate.

The results of this investigation were stunning. Filling in the blanks of Samson's life story, including his mind-boggling exploits in Nazi-occupied Poland, it also revealed the circumstances of my protagonist's untimely demise. I was surprised to discover that his frenetic activity was cut short at the very moment when, acting behind the backs of the British, he began facilitating secret contacts between Nazi Germany and a high-ranking Polish minister residing in

---

11 An undated report under the heading "Mikiciński Samson," JPIA, Archiwum Osobowe, NZ 154, Sygn. 658.

London. This is a crucial detail that did not go unnoticed by eagle-eyed British counterintelligence operatives, but has not been mentioned in any scholarly or popular work about Mikiciński or the Polish government-in-exile.

A second discovery in Kew—one no less significant and just as shocking—had to do with the biography of Edward Szarkiewicz, an officer of the Polish Armed Forces in exile. Apparently, it was he who carried out the physical liquidation of Samson in Palestine. Remarkably, the most important part of Szarkiewicz's biography was not his dramatic encounter with Mikiciński and the latter's death, but, rather, the immediate aftermath of these events. The British were very pleased with the actions of the presumed assassin, and they invited him to London shortly thereafter. There, he was to play a key role in a British plot aimed at "chastening" the Polish government-in-exile, which was acting too independently for Churchill's taste. The way to do this was by establishing strict British control over the Polish security apparatus—that is, the army and its intelligence and counterintelligence organs. I should note that this detail in the tragic history of the Sikorski government has not been mentioned anywhere, either.

Thanks to these amazing discoveries, I knew as soon as I emerged from the grandiose building of the Kew Archives that the book I was about to write would not be a mere summary of the lives of Mikiciński and Szarkiewicz, no matter how extraordinary the two men were. I now wished to tackle a much more ambitious project: rethinking the early phase of World War II, adding new strokes to the familiar picture of the transformation of the German-Polish armed conflict in the autumn of 1939 into the most terrible global slaughter in human history. Hence, the most urgent task facing me was to structure my new book in the way that would best reveal the historical value of what I had found in the archives. For this reason, I abandoned my original intention of prefacing Mikiciński's story with a brief account of the contemporary situation in Poland and in the other places where my protagonist was active. Instead, I set out to write an expanded introduction that would recreate the tangled web of relationships in the Polish-German-British geopolitical triangle, from the Nazi invasion of Poland to Churchill's political marginalization of Sikorski and his government in the autumn of 1942.

While working on the introduction, which required me to engage in new, painstaking archival searches, I became convinced that I had chosen the right track. Gradually, an utterly surprising historical picture emerged: as it turned out, Samson's attempt to facilitate a secret dialogue between the Polish government-in-exile and the Nazis was far from unique, and it did not contradict the general logic of the Polish-German-British relations in the time period I was studying. Au contraire, it was a perfectly natural link in a long chain of political efforts by Polish and the German officials to come to an agreement regarding the future of Poland with or without British involvement. The reasons that led the Poles to engage in this seemingly unnatural flirtation with the occupiers were quite weighty and logical from the Polish point of view: the bitter disillusionment in the unequal relationship with London (despite the officially declared "strategic partnership"); Churchill's increasing readiness to secretly accommodate Stalin, which included the willingness to recognize the postwar Sovietization of the eastern Polish lands occupied by the USSR in September 1939; and, finally, the suffering of Polish civilians under the brutal Nazi occupation, which the Western Allies did nothing to alleviate. The Germans, for their part, were motivated by the desire to create an autonomous Polish buffer zone under their control on the Soviet border and, if possible, to translate this step into a diplomatic breakthrough vis-à-vis the British. According to the German proponents of this scenario, it would result in the end of the war between Berlin and London, and in British recognition of the "New German Order" on the European continent.

Wishing to give the readers a maximally detailed picture of the specific diplomatic initiatives taken by both sides, I supplemented the book's introductory chapter with testimonies that had never been published before. These are accompanied by facts already known to scholars that have never been brought together and presented in the accurate historical context. I can only hope that the end result of my labors will not seem too unwieldy to my readers. Still less would I wish to be mistaken for an apologist of Hitler and the Nazi elite, since I have no intention of presenting them as advocates of a "peaceful" reordering of Europe. To reiterate: my primary goal is to provide an objective account of the relations that took place within the Polish-German-British geopolitical triangle starting in September 1939—the very relations that formed the backdrop for the actions and fates of Samson Mikiciński and Edward Szarkiewicz.

As for the rest of the book, I decided to divide it into three parts. The first two are dedicated to the lives of Mikiciński and Szarkiewicz, respectively, with some of the individual chapters prefaced with descriptions of the situations in Berlin, Bucharest, and Istanbul, where the action is set. Szarkiewicz will appear already in the first part, in the chapters that explore his tragic role in Samson's death, which foiled the secret Polish-German negotiations. At first, I had no intention to dedicate a whole section of the book to this officer, but I changed my mind after discovering the evidence of his active involvement in the British attempt to bring the "unruly" Polish leadership to heel. A careful study of his life story not only revealed the peculiarities of his relationship with the British secret services, but also furnished a vivid example of a well-known—and regrettable—phenomenon: the refusal of the British intelligence community to get involved in the fates of its numerous Polish partners and agents in the immediate postwar period. The reader will learn of the personal tragedy of Edward Szarkiewicz who, after completing his mission in London, was callously betrayed by his British co-conspirators, and forced to literally fight for his life.

The third part of the book will tell the fascinating story of Samson Mikiciński's legacy: the numerous bank deposits and suitcases crammed with valuables orphaned after his abduction and turned into the object of a diplomatic dispute between the Polish and Turkish governments. This section will also detail the subsequent fates of the secondary players in the Mikiciński affair and describe the development of the international processes that influenced Mikiciński's fate and that he himself tried to influence in the last year of his life.

The book will end in a chapter summarizing the historical significance of the contribution of the two protagonists, the Polish Jews Mikiciński and Szarkiewicz, to Polish-German-British relations in the period 1939–1942. There will be a separate discussion of the clash between the Polish and the British national interests that gave birth both to the unofficial British policy of containment vis-à-vis the Polish government-in-exile and to the ambivalent attitude of the Polish political elites (both in their occupied homeland and in exile) to Nazi Germany and the prospect of political dialogue with it. The discussion will center on the legitimacy of such a dialogue under conditions of a spreading global conflagration, coupled with the largely cynical attitude of London toward its Polish partners. In my humble opinion, even though the book cannot give a full account or analysis of these questions, the very ability to pose them is a considerable achievement of a years-long investigation that began with a chance visit to a bookstore at the Warsaw International Airport.

I sincerely envy my readers. You are about to learn the amazing details of the Samson Mikiciński Affair, the tragic fate of Edward Szarkiewicz, and the unprecedented international political context in which our two protagonists found themselves at their fateful meeting in early 1941.

Yaacov Falkov

New York—Oxford—Rishon LeZion—Jūrmala

2018–2024

Preamble

Talking with the Enemy

―――――

A Common Destiny, with Limited Liability

At the beginning of the third week of July 1940, London seemed particularly gloomy, leaden clouds dumping intermittent torrents of rain on its downtrodden. In the middle of the week, on the evening of July 16, the skies suddenly cleared.[1] This change must have lifted the spirits of the festively dressed people who were hurrying on foot or in their elegant cars to the upscale neighborhood of Kensington, near Hyde Park. There, at 55 Prince's Gate, a four-story Victorian mansion, a special event was about to take place: the official opening of a Polish cultural center: Ognisko Polskie, or the "Polish hearth."

Only a few days earlier, the German air force began its yearlong assault that future historians would divide into the Battle of Britain and the Blitz. Some Polish pilots had already enlisted in the Royal Air Force; they were among the roughly thirty thousand troops that had managed to flee Poland in September of 1939, come through the neighboring countries to France, where they faced the Wehrmacht in yet another unequal battle, and then continued to Britain in late June of 1940. Now that they had finally reached the land they called

Last Hope Island, many wanted nothing more than to meet their enemy on even ground.[2]

Ognisko Polskie was the brainchild of Count Edward Raczyński, the Polish ambassador to the United Kingdom, and supported by pro-Polish members of the British government. Meant to symbolize the common destiny of the Polish and British peoples, it celebrated their declared limitless willingness to fight Nazis hand to hand. And, indeed, the opening ceremony was a smashing success. It was attended by many high-ranking British officials, including Foreign Secretary Lord Halifax and Prince George. The latter two delivered keynote addresses, each pledging to liberate and reestablish Poland and affirming that this country would have an important place in postwar Europe.[3] But Raczyński and quite a few of his honored guests knew that the smiles and promises of wartime brotherhood "until a common victory is achieved" concealed the uncertainty between the two governments. The fugitive general Władysław Sikorski had arrived in London from France just a month earlier and was now busy establishing himself in his new sanctuary. His remaining troops which suffered two bitter defeats at the hands of the Wehrmacht in under a year, were now scattered as close as Scotland and as far away as Palestine, as they lacked sufficient equipment, ammunition, and funds to join the battle now at hand. The first Polish volunteers to the British forces, mostly pilots and naval crews, had proven themselves to be excellent fighters, and Polish military command even noted that the terrible losses they had sustained were disproportionately higher than those of their host country.[4] Nonetheless, the British quickly realized that the combat skills of most of the Polish military personnel left much to be desired and would not improve significantly any time soon. Indeed, from the autumn of 1940 to the spring of 1941, Polish land forces in the UK and the Middle East took no part in fighting the Germans or

---

2 Lipsky, an untitled memorandum without an exact date, December 1940–January 1941, PISM, A.XII.1/66a, 48–49; Kochanski, *The Eagle Unbowed*, 205–222; Koskodan, *No Greater Ally*, 42–47, 51–58, 89–97; Olson, *Last Hope Island*, 60–62, 82–97.
3 "Still keeping the home fire burning after 75 years"; the Polish ambassador to the Holy See, Kazimierz Papée, to the London Headquarters of the Polish Foreign Office in Exile, report # 240, untitled, December 3, 1941, USHMM, RG-59.036, A-12-53-37P_0122.
4 Lipsky, an untitled memorandum without an exact date, December 1940–January 1941, PISM, A.XII.1/66a, 49–50; Anthony Eden to Sikorsky, August 15, 1942, PISM, A.XII.1/52B, 17; "The key moments of the combat operations of ORP *Błyskawica* in the period September 1, 1939–June 24, 1944," an undated document, PISM, A.XII.1/82, 88; see also: Gasior, "The Polish Pilots"; Peszke, "The Polish Air Force": 54–74; Tusiewicz, *Historia Polski*, 379–380.

Italians—even though the Anglo-Polish miliary cooperation agreement was signed on August 5, 1940.[5]

Hence, in the summer and autumn of 1940, a large question mark hovered over Sikorski and his troops regarding their value as military allies of the United Kingdom; the same could be said of the political position of the Polish leader. Some of his colleagues in the Polish government-in-exile doubted both his legitimacy and his ability to wage a struggle to liberate and rebuild his enslaved homeland. On July 19, 1940, three days after the opening ceremony on Prince's Gate—Władysław Raczkiewicz, the president of Poland in exile, attempted to dismiss Sikorski from his post on legal grounds and replace him with another person. Sikorski was saved thanks only to the intervention of high-ranking Polish officers who sympathized with him and carried out a Latin American-style military coup to foil the designs of Raczkiewicz and his supporters.[6]

Worse still, the Sikorski government, because of its negligible geopolitical weight, was powerless against the Churchill government's secret diplomatic overtures to Moscow. The latter jeopardized the Poles' ability to achieve their main strategic goal of recreating an independent Polish state within the borders as set on September 1, 1939, and returning the Polish government-in-exile to liberated Warsaw. The UK, for its part, regarded its contacts with the Soviet Communist regime as fundamental to effectively combat the growing military and geopolitical threat of Nazi Germany. Naturally, Churchill did not forget that defending Poland had been the official casus belli behind the British declaration of war on Germany on September 3, 1939; in June 1940, shortly after assuming the British premiership, he made a personal pledge to fight side by side with the Poles and triumph or perish together with them.[7] But Churchill's government faced a tough predicament in the summer and autumn of 1940: a total absence of continental allies who could take up arms against Hitler, limited military capabilities, frequent and intense German air raids against military and civil targets, and the signs of a defeatist attitude among the elites and the general public.[8] The British leader felt therefore a greater obligation to address these issues than honor diplomatic commitments to the Poles, made

---

5 "Agreement Between the Government of His Majesty the King of the United Kingdom and Northern Ireland and the Government of Poland Respecting the Polish Forces in the United Kingdom," August 5, 1940, PISM, A.XII.1/54, 2–11; and TNA WO 33/2389.
6 Hułas, *Goście czy intruzi?* 88–92; Tusiewicz, *Historia Polski*, 379; Wieczorkiewicz, *Historia polityczna Polski*, 147–149.
7 Ciechanowski, *Defeat in Victory*, 15; Olson, *Last Hope Island*, 61.
8 Bungay, *The Most Dangerous Enemy*, 112; Haslam, *The Spectre of War*, 354–356; Holland, *The War in the West*, 417–418, 434.

under much different geopolitical and military conditions.[9] For Churchill, the US seemed like the natural place to seek urgent aid, but Washington had not yet made the decision to enter the war spreading across Europe.[10] Realizing this, as early as June 1940, the British leader launched diplomatic efforts to win over the hated Communist USSR as an ally against the Third Reich. The fact that since September 1939 the Soviets had occupied Poland's eastern lands (an area known as Kresy Wschodnie in Polish), using draconic repressive measures against local "anti-Soviet elements," did not seem to bother him at all.[11]

Churchill's efforts to achieve rapprochement with the Soviets became common knowledge in November 1940, when the British press published—allegedly at the behest of the Foreign Office—the contents of his private appeal to Stalin. The Soviet leader was urged to renege on the Nazis in favor of a strategic alliance with Britain. In exchange, London promised to recognize the Soviet annexation of East European territories, including the Kresy Wschodnie, made in 1939–1940.[12] "Thus, Churchill made it clear that the fates of the nations of those countries . . . were no more than a bargaining chip in a high-stakes political game, and that the geopolitical interests of the Soviet Union in this region were legitimate and justified." So assessed Pavel Sudoplatov, a prominent Soviet intelligence officer then responsible for secret contacts with other countries.[13]

In December 1940, in an attempt to convince the Kremlin of the seriousness of his intentions, Churchill even went so far as to allow the Soviet military attaché in London to visit a local armor unit—an unprecedented step in the

---

9   Dilks, *Churchill and Company*, 39.
10 Forczyk, *We March against England*, 83–93; Jenkins, *Churchill*, 612–613; Reynolds, *In Command of History*, 199–203.
11 On Churchill's justifying the annexation of the eastern Polish territories for the sake of an accommodation with the USSR as early as the autumn of 1939, and on the reluctance of British officialdom to quarrel with the USSR over Poland at the time, see: Carlton, *Churchill and the Soviet Union*, 70–71; Maisky, *The Maisky Diaries*, 233, 238; Rees, *Behind Closed Doors*, 36–38. The earliest attempt by Churchill, as leader of his country, to reach an agreement with the Russians took place on June 25, 1940, when he sent Stalin a written offer to discuss the prospect of "common resistance to German hegemony." That offer was conveyed by Stafford Cripps, the British ambassador to Moscow. See: Carlton, *Churchill and the Soviet Union*, 77; Reynolds and Pechatnov, *The Kremlin's Letters*, 19. On the Soviet occupation of the eastern Polish territories, see: Wieczorkiewicz, *Historia polityczna Polski*, 176–206.
12 This offer by Churchill to Stalin (which has become down as "Five + Four" in Russian historiography) was formally given by British ambassador Cripps to Vyshinsky, the deputy people's commissar for foreign affairs of the USSR, on October 22, 1940. See: Miner, *Between Churchill and Stalin*, 74–97; Tebinka, *Mocarstwa zachodnie wobec Polski*, 304–305; Falin, *Vtoroi front*, 198. On the publication of the contents of the offer in the British press, and the negative reaction of Moscow to this development, see: Sudoplatov, *Raznye dni tainoi voiny i diplomatii*, 127–128.
13 Ibid.

relationship between the two countries. The Red Army reciprocated by arranging a similar visit for the head of the British defense attaché office in Moscow.[14]

On the other hand, Churchill was in no hurry to cut off longstanding secret contacts between the British intelligence services and the German anti-Nazi opposition. A motley assemblage of (often unrelated) members of aristocratic circles, high-ranking diplomats, political émigrés, and even some officers of the Abwehr, it sympathized with Britain and wished to discuss the terms of a peaceful settlement in the event of Hitler's allegedly imminent fall. However, some members of this group had no intention of changing the regime or renouncing any German territorial acquisition, including Polish territories occupied in 1939. The idea of contacting these Germans was very popular among some government ministers and other members of the British ruling elite even before France fell in June 1940, and Churchill eventually embraced it wholesale. He apparently believed Hitler would be ousted because the German economy had deteriorated badly in the war and hoped to strike a deal with a more reasonable successor. Representatives of the SIS were negotiating the future of Poland with some of these individuals without bothering to involve, or even notify, any Polish officials.[15]

The Polish government-in-exile, based in the city of Angers in western France since the autumn of 1939,[16] followed the backroom negotiations between London and Moscow with concern. Already in early November that year, the Political Intelligence Department of the British Foreign Office warned:

> The Polish Government have been perturbed by the apparent acquiescence on the part of His Majesty's Government in the Russian conquest of Poland. They will not accept the loss of their territory to the east of the so-called Curzon line, nor do they consider this loss to be irremediable.[17]

Sikorski and his people were particularly dismayed by the public statements of Lord Halifax and the British ambassador to Moscow, Sir Stafford Cripps (a former Labour member of the British parliament, known for his far-left views, who advocated the creation of a united anti-fascist front with British Communists). Both declared that the UK was prepared to recognize the Soviet

---

17 Weekly Political Intelligence Summary No. 6, Foreign Office, Political Intelligence Department, November 7, 1939, USHMM, RG-59.006.M-FO371/24054, Scan 00123.

annexation of the eastern Polish territories.¹⁸ The exiled Polish leaders were well aware that their country would have to pay the price of the British-Soviet rapprochement—not only in land, but also in geopolitical status and human lives. They must also have been familiar with the opinion of Polish military intelligence which warned that the desire for such a rapprochement was not a spontaneous outburst on the part of Halifax, Cripps, or other British officials faced with the prospect of a German invasion of their home island, but the product of the longstanding affection of British leftist circles and their representatives in the British political establishment for the "first state of workers and peasants." In this connection, the Dwójka emphasized the willingness of leftist British politicians to seal an alliance with Stalin by trampling all over the Polish national interests.¹⁹

In January 1940, the fear that the British would align with the Soviets led Sikorski to commission Edward Raczyński, the Polish ambassador to London, to do everything within his power to drive a wedge between London and Moscow.²⁰ This fear grew even stronger between March and July of that year, after Polish officials in Paris and London learned of His Majesty's Government's attempts to strengthen economic ties with the USSR, as well as of the fact that Stalin, alarmed by France's defeat, had granted a personal audience to the British ambassador to the Kremlin, for the first time since 1935.²¹ When a year later, following the Nazi invasion of the USSR, Churchill at last achieved a strategic alliance with Moscow and forced Sikorski to fall in line, the Polish leader wrote

---

18 Tebinka, *Mocarstwa zachodnie wobec Polski*, 304–305; Wieczorkiewicz, *Historia polityczna Polski*, 156; see also the diary entry by the Soviet ambassador to London, Ivan Maisky, from October 28, 1939, according to which Sir Horace Wilson, the private secretary of the British prime minister, had assured him in an informal conversation that the possible British negotiations with the German anti-Nazi opposition over the reestablishment of Poland would not cover Western Ukraine or Western Belorussia: *The Maisky Diaries*, 236–237.
19 The Fourth Section of the Second Department of the Polish General Staff, top secret. "An informational and counterintelligence report for the first half of 1941. The attitude of British society to the Polish question." June 13, 1941, PISM, A.XII.1/38, 23.
20 August Zaleski, Foreign Minister of the Polish Government-in-Exile, to Raczyński, the Ambassador to London, secret, January 26, 1940, USHMM, RG-59.036, A-12-1-8_0097-8.
21 Raczyński, the Polish Ambassador to London, to the Polish Foreign Office in Angers, untitled encrypted telegram # 73, March 28, 1940, USHMM, RG-59.036, A-12-53-32_0162; the Polish Chargé D'affaires in Paris to the Polish Foreign Office in Angers, untitled report, secret, April 26, 1940, USHMM, RG-59.036, A-12-1-8_0117-9; Raczyński, the Polish Ambassador to London, to Foreign Minister Zaleski personally, untitled report, top secret, July 8, 1940, USHMM, RG-59.036, A-12-1-8_0137-9. On the British efforts to improve their relations with Moscow in the summer of 1940, see also: Reynolds and Pechatnov, *The Kremlin Letters*, 19–20.

that his worst fears involved "the probable expansion of Soviet influence in Poland, with the consent of Britain."[22]

As for a possible British-German collusion, already in early 1940, before fleeing to Britain, Sikorski and his people feared that London would engage in separate peace talks with Berlin. In their opinion, the British had taken a dislike to Sikorski—they regarded him as "100% Francophile"—and were likely to propose Józef Beck, the former foreign minister of Poland, for prime minister in postwar Warsaw.[23] This was the reason why, in March 1940, the Polish embassy in Dublin was carefully monitoring the contact between the German legation in that city and the Marquess of Tavistock, a British aristocrat and known Nazi sympathizer whom MI5 suspected Hitler would appoint as leader of a pro-German government in London.[24] According to the information the Poles had gathered, the contacts in the Irish capital "were not as insignificant as the press would have it," and the two sides touched on the fate of occupied Poland.[25]

After France was defeated and Polish leadership relocated to the British Isles, the prospect of Britain withdrawing from the war by concluding a peace deal with Berlin seemed even more threatening.[26] For this reason, the Polish diplomatic and secret services, now headquartered in London, focused their efforts on hunting down information about what Churchill, his circle, and Nazi leadership discussed through diplomatic channels. On July 19, 1940, Ambassador Raczyński reported to his superiors about a valuable piece of information he had just received. According to an unnamed but allegedly well-informed American

---

22 Sikorski, an untitled document outlining the views of the Polish leader on the present moment in the war and the involvement of the Polish armed forces in the military operations of the Allies, October 1941, PISM, A.XII.1/107, 13. See also: Rutkowski, *Stanisław Kot*, 213–222.
23 An official memorandum signed by Colonel Jan Kornaus, to Lieutenant Colonel M. for his personal perusal, March 1940, PISM, PRM. 14B, 45.
24 Milmo, "MI5 feared Duke of Bedford was Nazi choice for Britain's leader."
25 The Polish Consul General in Dublin, Wacław Tadeusz Dobrzyński, to the Polish Embassy in London: "The Peace Initiative of Lord Tavistock," secret, March 6, 1940, USHMM, RG-59.036, A-12-1-8_0049-0050. In January 1940, the Marquess of Tavistock made himself trying to elicit peace proposal from German embassy in Dublin—a fact that was leaked to the press—and he continued to do so in February. See: Haslam, *The Spectre of War*, 354.
26 See, for instance, Sikorski's warning, dated October 1941, about the danger of a British decision to withdraw from the war in light of the military defeat and capitulation of the Soviet Union: Sikorski, an untitled document outlining the views of the Polish leader on the present moment in the war and the involvement of the Polish armed forces in the military operations of the Allies, October 1941, PISM, A.XII.1/107, 13. Sikorski's fears seemed especially justified in the summer of 1940, when the expectation spread among the British ruling circles that, if and when the prospect of negotiations with the Germans arose, Churchill could be replaced by a man willing and able to follow this path. See: Haslam, *The Spectre of War*, 356-357.

journalist, the Germans had recently conveyed a peace offer to the British via three separate channels: the Vatican, the head of the Spanish diplomatic service, and the official representative of a neutral country in the British capital (Raczyński suggested that this may have been the Soviet ambassador to London, Ivan Maisky).[27] About a year later, in June 1941, Polish military intelligence informed its leaders about the "traditional sympathy" of certain British elite for the Nazis. The report also pointed out several particularly ardent advocates of a rapprochement with Berlin, such as Churchill's second cousin, Charles Stewart Henry Vane-Tempest-Stewart, Seventh Marquess of Londonderry, and the Governor of the Bank of England, Baron Montagu Collet Norman.[28]

For their part, the British voiced extreme displeasure at the Poles' reluctance to unequivocally and openly side with London in its conflict with Fascist Italy. After September 1939, Rome had allowed fleeing Polish refugees, among them military personnel, to pass through on their way to France; and in the second half of 1940, when Italy joined the war on the side of Germany and Japan, Fascist leadership refrained from declaring war on the Polish government-in-exile. Moreover, Italian diplomats in Spain and Portugal had probed the Polish government's willingness to maintain secret channels of communication with Rome. High-ranking public officials in the Polish Foreign Office advised Sikorski to accept the offer. Resultantly, in August 1940, the government in London sent instructions to Polish diplomatic missions all around the world, letting them know that even though Polish-Italian relationship had deteriorated, the two countries were not in a state of war; Polish diplomats were to act accordingly and avoid stoking tensions in their dealings with the Italians. Some prominent Poles based in Britain like Ignacy Paderewski, chairman of Rada Narodowa (the Polish parliament in exile), openly protested military involvement in the British army's North African campaign.[29] Thus it is hardly surprising that in early 1941, the British intel-

---

27 Raczyński to Polish Foreign Minister Zaleski, an untitled report, top secret, July 19, 1940, USHMM, RG-59.036, A-12-1-8_0143-4. The sources at our disposal indicate that there was at least one attempt by Soviet foreign minister Vyacheslav Molotov, to use Ambassador Maisky's good connections with the British elite to promote dialogue between Berlin and London. See: The German Ambassador to Moscow, Friedrich-Werner Graf von der Schulenburg, to the German Foreign Office, urgent, top secret telegram, October 20, 1939, in Sweet, *Documents on German Foreign Policy 1918–1945*, 8:325.
28 The Fourth Section of the Second Department of the Polish General Staff, top secret, "An informational and counterintelligence report for the first half of 1941. The attitude of British society to the Polish question," June 13, 1941, PISM, A.XII.1/38, 7–8.
29 Hułas, "Wrogowie naszych sojuszników": 205–228; Strzałka, *Między przyjaźnią a wrogością*, 63–76, 186, 241; Sierpowski, *Studia z Historii Włoch XX Wieku*, 360.

ligence agency MI5 issued a warning about "anti-British propaganda" that representatives of the Polish government-in-exile were distributing to soldiers in the Middle East, urging them to refuse to fight against the Italians.[30]

The Kingdom's Most Important Prisoner

Amid the growing divergence between British and Polish national interests, the period from the autumn of 1940 to the summer of 1941 witnessed a marked deterioration in Sikorski's and Churchill's personal relationship. The earliest known piece of evidence of this dramatic process is a harshly worded note from the British prime minister to his Polish counterpart dated November 4, 1940. An unnamed "third party" had informed Churchill that Sikorski had begun to consider the possibility of moving his office to Scotland to be with the Polish troops in the event that Germany invaded the UK.[31] Sikorski replied politely, promising to let Churchill know his decision on moving to Scotland as soon as he made one. However, it took him a full two and a half weeks to respond.[32] Just five months after fleeing occupied France, Sikorski had already felt bold enough to provoke Churchill by concealing his discussions of strategically important moves while on British territory and delaying his replies to Churchill's reprimands. Apparently, this was his way of alerting his hosts to his growing dissatisfaction with Poland's rather miniscule geopolitical role.

In January 1941, the tension between the two leaders climbed to new heights. Churchill quite literally imprisoned Sikorski in the British Isles by denying his request to tour Palestine and inspect the units stationed there. The official reason he gave rings quite hollow:

> It is a great help to me to know that you, as the leader of the largest Allied force in this country and as Prime Minister of our first Ally in this war, are available to give help and guidance at a time when we may at any moment be faced with a heavy attack from the enemy and the Polish Army may be called upon to fight at our side.[33]

---

30 An undated, top secret draft of a memorandum by SOE, titled "Note on the Kot organisation in the Middle East," TNA, HS 4/213.
31 Churchill to Sikorski, November 4, 1940, PISM, A.XII.1/52A, 3.
32 Sikorski to Churchill, November 21, 1940, ibid., 9.
33 Churchill to Sikorski, January 21, 1941, ibid., 20.

In reality, when Churchill wrote these lines, a German invasion no longer seemed like a realistic possibility. Half a year earlier, in July 1940, Hitler and his generals had realized that such an undertaking would have been utterly infeasible with the logistics and technologies available to them.[34] British intelligence learned immediately that the Nazis had given up on crossing the English Channel.[35] Besides, from the very first moment of his premiership, Churchill was certain that such an operation would have been utterly impossible.[36] And yet, he concealed the improbability of this threat from world leaders including Sikorski.

Sikorski reacted to his ban from the Middle East with a polite note thanking Churchill for holding Poland's contribution to the British defense in such high esteem, yet reminded him—rather caustically—that "the Polish soldiers are not yet sufficiently armed and should receive as quickly as possible the promised number of tanks, as well as anti-air and anti-tank guns." He protested his virtual confinement in British territory and reiterated his request to travel outside the United Kingdom—this time to the US[37]—but remained confined despite his pleas. In early March of 1941, Sikorski sent Churchill another request to allow him to visit North America, and asked to meet with Churchill in person.[38] In early 1941, relations between leaders the entire world regarded as brothers-in-arms in the fight against Nazism became so strained that they found it challenging to coordinate foreign policy steps, or even meet face-to-face.

In April 1941, Sikorski was finally able to travel to the US, but two weeks into the month, Churchill refused his request to dispatch four loyal liaison officers to Britain's headquarters in Cairo; Churchill explained, rather condescendingly, that "there are a number of Polish officers in Egypt who could be employed on liaison duties if any increase in the mission is considered necessary."[39] Two months later, Sikorski repeated his demand for "dear Prime Minister" to finally make good on the promise to equip the Polish army.[40]

---

34 Ferris and Mawdsley, "The War in the West": 318; Förster, "Hitlers Entscheidung": 14.
35 Aldrich and Cormac, *The Black Door*, 112.
36 Dilks, *Churchill and Company*, 49.
37 Sikorski to Churchill, January 31, 1941, PISM, A.XII.1/52A, 21–23.
38 Sikorski to Churchill, March 10, 1941, ibid., 24.
39 Churchill to Sikorski, April 15, 1941, ibid., 26-27.
40 Sikorski to Churchill, June 7, 1941, ibid., 30.

The Enemy of My Friend Is My Friend

Sikorski found London's diplomatic maneuvers dangerous, so he attempted to wean Poland from its geopolitical dependence on the UK and limit has own complicated relationship with Churchill. He hoped to cultivate ties with other countries to carry on the struggle for Polish independence if the British should pull out of their agreement. Like Churchill, Sikorski first appealed to Washington for aid, but in late 1940, he was disappointed to learn that Roosevelt was in no hurry to help Poland. After visiting the United States in April 1941, Sikorski became further disillusioned when the American officials seemed indifferent to Poland's woes and unwilling to jeopardize their friendships with the Soviets and the British. The latter, for their part, tried not to anger Moscow's claim to the eastern Polish territory and were forcing Sikorski to do likewise. It became obvious that if Roosevelt were to endorse Sikorski's plan to return the Kresy Wschodnie to Poland, even if only symbolically, Churchill would have responded very negatively.[41]

Therefore, Sikorski's only remaining diplomatic option was working toward a rapprochement with the other European governments-in-exile enjoying British hospitality. The most notable Polish project in this area was the attempt to create a Polish-Czechoslovak confederation to enhance their mutual geopolitical standing in the eyes of the Western powers. This was hoped to improve the Sikorski government's chance of a triumphant return to leadership in liberated, postwar Warsaw. However, it turned out that Czechoslovak president Edvard Beneš was less than thrilled to unite with Poland, since he wanted to stay on Moscow's good side. He did everything he could to drag out Polish-Czech diplomatic negotiations, and as a result, Sikorski and his supporters found themselves in a diplomatic cul-de-sac in the autumn of 1940.[42] Over the past year, they fought bravely against the Nazis, lost their homeland, and had been instrumental to defending of France and Britain while sacrificing the lives and limbs of many thousands of troops. Despite all this, they had failed to secure a firm guarantee that the Western powers would respect Poland's national interests after the war.[43]

---

41 Stańczyk, "Dr Cytowska"; Tebinka, *Mocarstwa zachodnie wobec Polski*, 306, 309; Torkunov, *Istoriia velikoi pobedy*, 605–606; Wieczorkiewicz, *Historia polityczna Polski*, 157–158.
42 Kamiński, *Edvard Beneš kontra gen. Władysław Sikorski*, 45–46; Torkunov, *Istoriia velikoi pobedy*, 608.
43 Ciechanowski, *Defeat in Victory*, 14–24. The fact must be stressed that during the period in question, like Poland, other British allies felt betrayed by Churchill. For example, Australian troops were sacrificed by him twice in 1941 in Greece and Crete, and by early 1942, despite

In this desperate situation, some elements of the Polish elites at home and in exile clamored to reach a settlement with the Germans. These voices grew louder and more insistent with each passing day. At this time, the idea of accommodating Germany did not sound as preposterous to Polish ears as it may sound to us today. For one thing, Polish political tradition—especially among conservatives—dictates a willingness to entertain collaborating with foreign powers to protect the interests of the Polish people. The prototype for this policy formed during what the Poles deemed Germany's "liberal" occupation of their Russia-controlled territories in World War I, when prominent local conservatives became the social and political leaders who built the infrastructure of the independent Polish state to be established in November 1918.[44]

The normality of reorienting Poland's foreign policy toward Nazi Germany was articulated in early 1940 by Władysław Kulski, a veteran of interwar Polish diplomacy, who had been instrumental in creating a Polish-British strategic alliance in the 1930s. On February 5, he wrote to the Polish government in Angers, responding to Paris's and London's refusal to unequivocally endorse Poland's aims: "In March 1939, we were able to guarantee our territorial integrity with the help of the German [foreign] policy."[45] This bitter remark by a prominent Polish diplomat clearly hinted at his belief that even after Poland's military defeat, the country's exiled leadership could still salvage the situation by concluding a strategic alliance with Nazi Germany.

There was yet another reason why many Poles were willing to countenance the possibility of negotiating with the Nazi occupiers. In the prewar period, Poland's ruling conservative elite and its ideological allies in other European countries embraced the idea of reconciliation between Berlin and Warsaw. It resurged already in September 1939, when, after the beginning of the Polish Campaign, the Italian dictator Benito Mussolini called upon the leadership of the Third Reich—in a personal telephone conversation with the German military attaché in Rome, General Enno von Rintelen, through the channels of the Italian Foreign Office, and in the official media—to make a "broad gesture"

---

all their previous pompous promises, the British were ready to abandon Singapore, critically important to Australia's forward defense, to save India from possible Japanese invasion. See: Hughes-Wilson, *Military Intelligence Blunders*, 130. King Peter of Yugoslavia, who cooperated with London against Berlin and, like the Poles, joined the many exiled in Britain, was abandoned in favor of Tito's partisans. See: Aldrich and Cormac, *Spying and the Crown*, 289-290.

44 Kunicki, *Unwanted Collaborators*, 206; Zychowicz, *Opcja niemiecka*, 56.
45 Kulski to the government in Angers, an untitled document, February 5, 1940, USHMM, RG-59.036, A-12-1-8_0099-101. The author of the letter was referring to Warsaw's official rejection of Hitler's offer of a German-Polish strategic alliance. The Polish reply was conveyed to Berlin on March 26, 1939. See: Szeremietiew, *Siła złego*, 443, 448.

toward the Western powers by creating a "shrunken Poland" and thereby preventing the German-Polish conflict from spreading to the rest of Europe.[46] Four months later, in early January 1940, Mussolini advised the Germans once again to "make peace with the brave Poles" and reestablish the Polish state "in some form," a move that would deprive Germany's enemies of any pretext to continue the war.[47]

In October 1939, the Spanish dictator Generalissimo Francisco Franco, shocked by the Soviet annexation of the eastern Polish territories and seeing it as a possible opening salvo of a Communist invasion of Europe, contacted Berlin with the offer to mediate between the Germans and the new Polish leadership. He even floated the possibility of a pan-European settlement with the French and British that could serve as the base for a military-political bloc unified against the Communist threat.[48] A year and a half later, in March 1941, Franco touched on the question of what to do about Poland when he met with the leader of Vichy France, Marshal Philippe Pétain, who had come to visit him in Madrid. Franco suggested that they "recreate Poland in part, and then march with her against the Soviet Union."[49] In December of 1939, at the start of the Winter War between Finland and the USSR, the Finnish foreign minister to Berlin raised the idea of reestablishing a rump Polish state as part of a Europe-wide peace settlement to be achieved without the participation of Communist Russia, and with the explicit purpose of containing it.[50]

---

46 A memorandum signed by Ernst von Weizsäcker, State Secretary at the German Foreign Office, September 23, 1939, in Sweet, *Documents on German Foreign Policy*, 8:125–126.
47 A memorandum signed by Dr. Paul Schmidt, Deputy Director of the News and Press Department of the German Foreign Office, January 11, 1940, in Sweet, ibid., 648; Weitz, *Joachim von Ribbentrop*, 220.
48 Kaczorowski, *Franco i Stalin*, 49–56; the German Ambassador to Spain to the German Foreign Office in Berlin, a telegram from October 1, 1939, in Sweet, ibid., 181–182; a memorandum signed by Ernst von Weizsäcker, State Secretary at the German Foreign Office, October 3, 1939, Sweet, ibid., 203. See also a British intelligence report about Franco's criticism of Britain, which had betrayed Poland, and about the willingness of the Spanish leader to serve as intermediary between the warring sides, to halt the advance of communism into Europe: Weekly Political Intelligence Summary No. 1 (Covering the Period from the Outbreak of War to October 3, 1939), October 3, 1939, USHMM, RG-59.006.M-FO371/24054, Scan 00022.
49 Sokolnicki, *Dziennik Ankarski*, 151. In this regard, it is worth noting that two decades after WWII the French leader, General De Gaulle, still wrote in the draft of his memoirs that in the early 1940s some American forces considered the conservative four of Pétain, Franco, Sikorski, and Goering to be a possible new European leadership that could be used against the Soviets and even against the British. See: Ferro, *Pétain*, 457.
50 A telegram from the German Ambassador to Copenhagen to the German Foreign Office in Berlin; December 19, 1939, in Sweet, *Documents on German Foreign Policy*, 8:557.

In this regard, it is worth stressing that, as of 1940, the Polish government-in-exile still maintained full diplomatic ties with every single country that would soon join the war on the side of Nazi Germany—Japan, Italy, Hungary, Romania, and Finland. Their leaders stuck close to Polish politicians and diplomats.[51] One of the most striking examples of this phenomenon is the extremely warm professional atmosphere that surrounded the Polish ambassador to Fascist Italy, Bolesław Wieniawa-Długoszowski. His connections to the upper echelons of the local regime, stretched as far as Italian foreign minister Count Gian Galeazzo Ciano, allowed him to set up an efficient human smuggling route on Italian soil for Polish refugees, including active military, moving them through Romania and Bulgaria to France.[52] A great number of them joined Sikorski's Polish émigré army and went on to fight the Germans on the frontlines of World War II.

Moreover, in July 1940, the Polish government-in-exile, having just fled to the British Isles, began cultivating diplomatic ties with Vichy France, despite its geopolitical, military, and economic partnerships with the Third Reich. When Ignacy Paderewski, the celebrated Polish composer, became chairman of the Polish parliament in exile in the summer of 1940, he wrote a personal letter to French collaborator in chief Marshal Pétain: "I hasten to express my respect for the one who has now added the title of Father of the Nation to his previous illustrious titles... I greatly esteem your actions in this difficult hour."[53]

Thus, less than a year after Poland's military defeat, its exiled government, despite the allegedly strategic alliance with France and Britain, had thrown its lot in with Nazi Germany's geopolitical fellow travelers. From their point of view, and for much of the general Polish public, Poland's relationship with Berlin had yet to cross the point of no return.

Back in occupied Poland, Władysław Studnicki became the first politician to try to accommodate the Germans in an attempt to forestall the Russian threat

---

51 See on the refusal of the Polish government-in-exile to follow the example of its French and British counterparts, who had cut off diplomatic relations with Italy: Polish Foreign Minister Zaleski to the Polish Ambassadors, secret telegram #172 from Angers; June 11, 1940, USHMM, RG-59.036, A-12-53-34_0059; and on the rupture of Polish-Japanese relations, on the initiative of the Japanese side, in October 1941: the Polish Foreign Office to the Polish Parliament, untitled secret telegram #108 from Tokyo; October 5, 1941, USHMM, RG-59.036, A-12-53-37L_0031.
52 Koper, *Polskie piekiełko*, 59, 201–205; see also a testimony about the involvement of the Italian consulate in Bucharest in the creation of a secret smuggling channel of Polish military personnel from Romania to France in late 1939–early 1940: the testimony of the priest Ant. Kwiatkowski (who arrived on January 1, 1940, after a three-month stay in Romania), January 3, 1940, USHMM, GK_159_228cz2.
53 Ignacy Paderewski to His Excellency Marshal Pétain, Chief of the French State, July 21, 1940, PISM, PRM.32, s. 1–5.

from the east. A prominent political theorist, publicist, and longtime veteran of the Polish conservative party, Studnicki became a famous advocate for a Warsaw-Berlin alliance even before the war.[54] In September 1939, he made the decision to remain in his homeland after its military defeat. Later that year, he told his acquaintances that immediately after the occupation of Kraków he was invited there to meet with some German general, who suggested that he create a pro-German Polish government. At the time, Studnicki claimed he declined the offer and escaped to Warsaw.[55] However, we now know that he acted quite differently. In the autumn of 1939, he wrote in his diary about all the people of every age and stripe who wanted him to start negotiations to establish a Polish National Committee under Germany's aegis.[56] Soon after, he contacted the occupying authorities on his own and proposed building a Polish military force to take part in the coming struggle between the Third Reich and the Soviet Union—a struggle he regarded as inevitable.[57]

This proposal stood a good chance. In November and December of 1939, British intelligence noticed that the citizens of occupied Poland were dissatisfied with the recently established Polish government-in-exile and tolerated the Third Reich much better; they were reasonably appreciative of its "efficiency in constructing roads and bridges and re-establishing railway communications."[58] On December 19, 1939, the Political Intelligence Department of the British Foreign Office reported:

> In Warsaw itself there has been some improvement in living conditions. Food is reported to be plentiful, only sugar and a few other commodities [are] being rationed. The trams are running, and electricity, gas and water supplies are functioning. The population has been inoculated against typhus and typhoid. The Jews, at first confined to ghettos, are now allowed out, but have to wear brassards bearing the shield of David in blue.[59]

---

54 See the new edition of Studnicki's book, written in 1935: Studnicki, *System polityczny Europy a Polska*.
55 Protocol of the interrogation of Jan Brocki, February 7, 1940, USHMM, GK_159_228cz2, 26.
56 Studnicki, *Irrwege in Polen*, 35.
57 See the contents of Studnicki's appeal to the Germans: "A Memorandum Concerning the Rebirth of the Polish army and the Coming German-Soviet War"—an undated document, published in German sometime around February 1940, PISM, PRM. 32, 75–80.
58 Weekly political intelligence summary no. 10, Foreign Office (Political Intelligence Department), December 5, 1939, USHMM, RG-59.006.M-FO371/24054, Scan 00239.
59 Weekly political intelligence summary no. 12, Foreign Office (Political Intelligence Department), December 19, 1939, USHMM, RG-59.006.M-FO371/24054, Scan 00292.

In this encouraging atmosphere, Studnicki went so far as to make a trip to Berlin in February 1940, to present his views to the Nazi leadership. However, the trip ended in failure. Remarkably, the two senior officials to meet him were none other than Nazi propaganda minister Joseph Goebbels and RSHA chief Reinhard Heydrich. For an unknown reason, they assessed Studnicki as "a man of negligible political weight, who was making ludicrous suggestions."[60]

Nevertheless, as early as the summer of 1940, the relationship between Moscow and Berlin became increasingly strained, and Studnicki's idea of a German-Polish military partnership gained a second lease on life. According to rumors spreading through occupied Poland, the Germans were about to reinforce their ranks with ethnically Polish men. Some locals expressed eagerness to "fight side-by-side with the Wehrmacht against the Bolsheviks, in the name of Poland."[61]

Sikorski consistently rejected the idea of collaborating with the Germans. To recap, in June of 1940, about to evacuate to the UK, he declined Pétain's offer of an alliance that would have enabled him to join an armistice agreement with the Third Reich and get Poland out of the war; a month later, he ordered the Polish people to carry on their uncompromising struggle against the German and Soviet occupiers and reject any offers to create a fictional Polish state.[62] On September 1, 1940, the first anniversary of the German invasion of Poland, Sikorski made a public declaration to his people from London: among his compatriots, there never had been, nor ever would be any traitors who would dare consent to creating a new government under German auspices.[63] Nazi collaborators real and imagined would now receive death sentences and other harsh punishments from the underground courts that started operating

---

A corroboration of this British intelligence data has been found in a report by the Polish ambassador to the Hague, based on information obtained in March 1940 from a high-ranking representative of the Dutch Philips firm, who had just returned from Warsaw: W. Babinski, the Polish Ambassador to the Hague, an untitled report from March 27, 1940, USHMM, GK_159_228cz2, 119; and also in the testimonies submitted by Polish refugees from Radom to the Polish émigré counterintelligence, concerning the situation in Warsaw, including the intense night life in the occupied Polish capital: Protocol of the interrogation of Alexander Hodkowski and Stanisław Piotroswki, April 25, 1940, USHMM, GK_159_228cz2, 174.

60 Kochanowski, "Polen in die Wehrmacht?"; Kunicki, *Unwanted Collaborators*, 210–212; Zychowicz, *Opcja niemiecka*, 69–76.
61 Kochanowski, "Polen in die Wehrmacht?"; Kunicki, *Unwanted Collaborators*, 210–212.
62 Kunicki, *Unwanted Collaborators*, 208; Zychowicz, *Opcja niemiecka*, 78–79.
63 Sikorski, "An Order to the Land, Air, and Naval Forces," September 1, 1940, PISM, A.XII.1/11a, s. 90–91.

in occupied Poland in 1940, and their punishments were regularly publicized in the underground Polish press.[64]

Those who advocated for accommodating Hitler's regime, including some high-ranking members of the émigré establishment, harshly criticized Sikorski's decision to a priori exclude a deal with Germany from the Polish wiggle room. In their opinion, this fateful error rendered the government-in-exile incapable of planning for the eventuality of a German-British peace settlement (which still seemed a likely prospect), and using it to reestablish a Polish state in some form. Despite Sikorski's threats, many Poles seemed to embrace the idea of a new government under the Nazis modeled on Vichy France, believing it would keep them safe from mistreatment. One of its most active and vocal adherents was Stanisław Cat-Mackiewicz, conservative journalist, member of the Polish parliament in exile, and the eventual seventh prime minister of the government-in-exile. In June 1940, just before the Franco-German armistice, Cat-Mackiewicz called upon the Sikorski government to cancel its planned evacuation to the British Isles, join the French, and finally put a stop to the senseless (as he saw it) war with Nazi Germany.[65]

Lieutenant Colonel Jan Kowalewski, the chief at the Polish military intelligence station in Lisbon, was similarly convinced that the Poles could not carry on the struggle against Germany after France had fallen. A month after Cat-Mackiewicz tried to convince Sikorski to accede, he and several other Polish émigrés coauthored a special petition to Nazi leadership offering a geopolitical alliance, the creation of a pro-German government in Warsaw, and military cooperation against Moscow.[66] In December, the MI5 reported with some concern that the official press secretary of the Polish embassy in Bucharest—a government official—had expressed the opinion that creating a provisional government in the German-occupied Polish territories was the order of the day.[67]

The debate over the prospect of accommodating the Germans raged on in the Polish expatriate community throughout 1941. It was encouraged by the growing realization that the Poles had been forced to join the Churchill-Stalin strategic alliance now coming to a close,[68] as well as by the ever-intensifying Nazi terror in occupied Poland. Trenchant criticism of Sikorski, who refused to acknowledge

---

64 Kunicki, *Unwanted Collaborators*, 208.
65 Zychowicz, *Opcja niemiecka*, 78–79.
66 Ibid., 81–92.
67 An undated and untitled report by agent A/H.2, late December 1940, TNA, HS 4/213.
68 See on the British pressure applied to Sikorski and his closest associates on several issues, including their opposition to reconciliation with the USSR in Polish émigré circles: Sokolnicki, *Dziennik Ankarski*, 253–254.

the bitter predicament of his people and kept rejecting the possibility of talks with the Germans, now hailed from Polish patriots who had fought valiantly against the Wehrmacht. Among them was Major Jan Józef Ludyga-Laskowski, Józef Piłsudski's erstwhile adjutant. This officer left Poland in September 1939, fought with the Polish troops defending France in the summer of 1940, stayed behind in German-occupied French territory, became renowned as a fearless fighter of the French Resistance, was captured by the Gestapo, stoically endured torture at a concentration camp, and was liberated by American soldiers in the spring of 1945. Ludyga-Laskowski would never be suspected of harboring Nazi sympathies or neglecting the national interests of his homeland, but in June 1941, he said the following to Zbigniew Szubert, deputy head of the Polish diplomatic mission in Vichy-controlled Nice:

> Of all the countries occupied by the Germans, only Poland has no government of its own. The rigidity of the stance adopted by [the Sikorski government] in the current situation reflects an inability to come to terms with the emergent reality. In the present circumstances, with ninety-nine percent [of the Poles] having reconciled themselves to the German victory, we must ultimately recognize the Germans as victors, and it would be absurd for us to ape the behavior of others [on this issue]. A situation in which twenty-five million people lack any political representation is utterly unacceptable. We need individuals who can talk with the Germans and present the essential needs of the Polish people to the occupiers. If a sincere appeal were to be made to the Germans, it would elicit a sincere response from them. Only a government that operates in the territory of its country and alleviates the predicament of the Polish people has a right to exist. [By contrast,] the existence of the Polish government-in-exile is antithetical [to Polish interests].[69]

According to Szubert, Ludyga-Laskowski showed him clippings from Polish émigré newspapers published in the US excoriating Sikorski for his decision to create the Polish armed forces in exile. Without a hint of embarrassment, he bragged of his excellent past relationships with key figures in the Third Reich; as evidence, he showed photographs of himself in their company and a postcard Goebbels allegedly sent him after defeating Poland, reassuring him of his

---

69 Zbigniew Szubert to Stanisław Zabiełło, June 20, 1941, PISM, A.XII.1/66A, 117.

friendship. The inscription on the back of the postcard, which Szubert saw with his own eyes, actually opened with the words "My dear Jan!" Szubert noted that Ludyga-Laskowski spoke of Hitler with deep respect and confided that they had enjoyed a long personal conversation before the war, underscoring his belief that the Führer had a positive attitude toward the Polish people.[70]

The Führer Wishes to Strike a Deal

Did the foreign policy outlook the Poles were now calling "the German option" have a real chance? Could Studnicki, Kowalewski, Ludyga-Laskowski, and other like-minded Poles have realized their aspirations, or was it just a pipe dream born from the desperation of defeated, homeless refugees? Most modern historians both in Poland and outside it are convinced that there were no homegrown quislings in Nazi-occupied Poland—for the simple reason that the Third Reich had no intention of striking a deal with the local elites or giving the Poles any measure of self-government.[71] Rigorous, unbiased scrutiny of the Polish and German primary sources now at our disposal allows us to reconstruct a more complex picture of Polish-German relations in occupied Poland.

As it turns out, Hitler had no clear plan when a week and a half before he invaded Poland, he sent Foreign Minister Joachim von Ribbentrop to Moscow to sign the Treaty of Nonaggression with the Soviet Union. Just before Ribbentrop's world-historic trip to the Soviet capital, Hitler told his senior military officers that he intended to destroy the Polish state and replacement its inhabitants with Germans,[72] but this was, at the time, only a vague aspiration with hazy prospects of success. Later, this fact would be acknowledged even by East German Communist historians, impossible to suspect of sympathetic or exonerative impulses toward the Nazi Führer. One of them, Alwin Ramme, remarked in 1970 that "the objectives of the Polish Campaign were originally open-ended," especially when it came to Poland's central and eastern lands, because an ever-growing number of ever-changing military and diplomatic

---

70 Ibid.
71 See, for instance: Breitman, Goda and Brown, "The Gestapo": 144; Kochanski, *The Eagle Unbowed*, 98; Kunicki, *Unwanted Collaborators*, 204; Młynarczyk, "Pomiędzy współpracą a zdradą": 104–105.
72 See the diary entry by the Chief of the General Staff of the German Army High Command Franz Halder, from August 22, 1939: Halder, *Kriegstagebuch*, 25. And also: The Obersalzberg Speech; August 22, 1939, in Adamthwaite, *The Making of the Second World War*, 219–221; Rossino, *Hitler Strikes Poland*, 227–228.

factions occasioned constant policy shifts that would make such a large undertaking extremely difficult to pull off.[73]

On August 23, 1939 the agreement known to history as the Molotov-Ribbentrop Pact provided ample evidence of just how flexible the Nazis were when it came to defining the objectives of the coming Polish Campaign. Its secret protocol dividing Eastern Europe into German and Soviet spheres of influence states unambiguously that "The question of whether it is in the (signatories') mutual interest to preserve the independent Polish State and what the borders of that state will be ascertained conclusively only in the course of future political development."[74]

Hitler foresaw that this "future political development" would happen in London and Paris. The day after von Ribbentrop triumphantly returned to Warsaw, Edward Raczyński, the Polish ambassador to London, alerted his superiors to a "scandalous meeting" Hitler had arranged with Sir Nevile Henderson, the British ambassador to Berlin, to discuss the future of Poland. After that meeting, British foreign secretary Lord Halifax tried to convince the Poles not to reject Hitler's proposal for resolving German-Polish contradictions out of hand (outraged, Raczyński labeled this move by Halifax "far-reaching defeatism"); while Henderson took a more direct approach by openly supporting Hitler and demanding that the Poles "surrender" at once.[75] Three days later, Raczyński warned his bosses that Hitler's secret envoy was about to arrive in London to hash out plans for Poland.[76] And finally, on August 31, the day before the German invasion, Raczyński's counterpart in Rome, Wieniawa-Długoszowski, reported to Warsaw that, according to his Dutch colleague—who quoted Italian foreign minister Ciano and German ambassador to Italy, Georg von Mackensen—in the event of hostilities, the Germans would occupy only part of Poland and, within a few days of fighting, would submit peace offers to Britain and France.[77]

---

73 Ramme, *Der Sicherheitsdienst der SS*, 141.
74 Felshtinsky, *TSRS-Vokietija 1939*, 62–63; Szeremietiew, *Siła złego*, 487.
75 Raczyński to Polish Foreign Minister Józef Beck, untitled special encrypted telegram No. 2, August 25, 1939, USHMM, RG-59.036, A-12-53-29_0207-8. See also on the meetings between Henderson and Hitler on August 25 and 29, 1939: Raczyński to Polish Foreign Minister Józef Beck, untitled special encrypted telegram No. 3, August 26, 1939, USHMM, RG-59.036, A-12-53-29_0208-10; and also: Adamthwaite, *The Making of the Second World War*, 92; Neville, *Appeasing Hitler*, 162; Rothschild, *Peace for Our Time*, 331.
76 Raczyński to the Polish Foreign Office, untitled telegram No. 182, August 28, 1939, USHMM, RG-59.036, A-12-53-29_00146.
77 Wieniawa-Długoszowski to the Polish Foreign Office, untitled telegram No. 7, August 31, 1939, USHMM, RG-59.036, A-12-53-25_00168.

Furthermore, in the early days of the conflict, when the Polish military still managed to resist a numerically and qualitatively superior enemy, the Nazi leader stated that he was ready to negotiate with the Poles themselves about the *polnische Reststaat* ("Polish rump state"). Such a state would be required to relinquish its western territories, and its exit to the Baltic Sea, as well as to end its strategic partnership with London and Paris; in exchange, the Poles would be permitted to keep their independence under a German protectorate.[78]

At the same time, as early as the morning of September 2, Franz von Papen, the German ambassador to Turkey, tried to reach his Polish counterpart in Ankara, Michał Sokolnicki. Failing to get a reply, he asked his Turkish hosts to help expedite a ceasefire by mediating peace talks with the British. When the Turks asked whether Germany was prepared to withdraw its troops from Polish territories, von Papen answered: "Yes, more or less. We will be able to organize it." The Turkish foreign minister, Şükrü Saracoğlu, who immediately met von Papen in person to discuss the matter, concluded that this was not the ambassador's personal initiative, but a carefully planned attempt by Hitler to strike a last-minute deal with Britain, before the two sides became embroiled in a major war. In Saracoğlu's estimate, Hitler was willing to exchange some already occupied Polish lands for British recognition of German control over Danzig, the port city on the Baltic coast currently known as Gdańsk, and the so-called "Polish Corridor" that connected Danzig to the Reich. Although Saracoğlu hastened to share this information with Sokolnicki, the corresponding entries in the ambassador's diary give the impression that neither he nor anyone else officially representing Warsaw deigned to respond to the German conditions.[79]

The fact of the unexpected German offer to the Poles, conveyed via the Turks, is confirmed by an urgent official notice sent to Berlin by von Papen himself on the night of September 3, 1939. According to him, the Turkish side had been informed of the seriousness of Berlin's intentions regarding (as von Papen put it) "our offer on Poland." Furthermore, the Turks had heard the ambassador's "personal opinion": the Führer would refrain from unleashing all-out war if the "Polish question" was to be resolved.[80]

A decade and a half later, Fritz Hesse—once a public relations officer at the German embassy in London and a representative of the DNB, the official Nazi news service—would write in his memoirs that, on the evening of September

---

78 Kershaw, *Hitler*, 516–517; Longerich, *Hitler*, 1134n10; Zychowicz, *Opcja niemiecka*, 2.
79 Sokolnicki, *Dziennik Ankarski*, 18.
80 Franz von Papen to the German Foreign Office, an extra-urgent telegram, September 2, 1939, in Sweet, *Documents on German Foreign Policy*, 7:523–524.

2, 1939 (i.e., the day when von Papen contacted Sokolnicki and the Turks), von Ribbentrop dispatched him to meet with Sir Horace Wilson, one of the most senior British officials, very close to Prime Minister Neville Chamberlain and an ardent supporter of German-British rapprochement. The Germans asked Wilson to convey a personal offer from the Führer to the British leadership: in exchange for recognizing German control of Danzig and the "Polish Corridor," Hitler would be ready not only to withdraw his troops from the majority of the occupied territories, but also to pay reparations to the Poles for the economic devastation Germany had caused.[81]

Several German historians hoping to fact-check Hesse have searched for surviving German and British documents, but have found only brief reports by both participants in the meeting. As soon as it was over, Wilson informed Chamberlain that Hitler had invited him, Wilson, to Berlin for a "heart-to-heart discussion" of the new situation, but he had already refused the invitation on grounds that Britain was unwilling to negotiate as long as German troops remained in Polish territory. Sir Horace appears to have made no mention of Germany's proposal for troop withdrawal and reparations, so in his interpretation, the appeal delivered by Hesse simply seemed like a banal invitation to yet another round of German-British negotiations, without a simultaneous cessation of hostilities in Poland.[82] As for Hesse himself, on September 3 he sent a telegram marked "To the Führer and the Foreign Minister in person." He did not expound on the contents of the urgent German proposal to the British, but focused instead on Wilson's amiable but negative reaction: negotiations were off the table unless Germany fully restored the status quo before September 1.[83]

Unable to find an original copy of Hitler's proposal to the British from September 2, 1939, German historians concluded that Hesse simply made it up.[84] However, the striking similarity between Hesse's offer to the notice von Papen gave the Turkish foreign minister on that same day leads us to conclude Hesse was telling the truth. It is now clear that the official Nazi representatives in London and Ankara simultaneously conveyed to the British identical conciliatory messages.

---

81 Hesse, *Das Spiel um Deutschland*, 209–212.
82 Brügel, "Eine zerstörte Legende": 386.
83 Ibid., 387; see the original text of Hesse's dispatch to Berlin: The German Embassy in London to the German Foreign Office, telegram No. 558, September 3, 1939, *Documents on German Foreign Policy*, 7:527–528.
84 Brügel, "Eine zerstörte Legende": 385–387; Henke, "Hitler und England Mitte August 1939": 231; Krausnick, "Legenden um Hitlers Außenpolitik": 237–238.

Can we be certain that these diplomats were not just unwitting pawns used to spread disinformation aimed at guaranteeing full freedom of action to the Wehrmacht troops fighting in Poland? The answer to this important question can be found in Soviet intelligence files from the discussed period, eventually published by the Russian Foreign Intelligence Service. German-Slovak diplomatic correspondence dated September 6 and 7, 1939, and intercepted by the Soviets reveals that, on the eve of the German invasion of Poland, Berlin was officially asked to assist the Slovaks in reestablishing control over their territories that had earlier fallen under Polish rule. The Germans replied that, in exchange for Slovak help in the upcoming conflict with Warsaw, they would be ready to look into the question of the Polish territories that had been annexed by Poland during the partition of Czechoslovakia in 1939. As for the territories lost by the Slovaks two decades earlier, Bratislava was told, both before and after September 1, that the time to discuss their fate had not yet come. "Up until the present moment, we have not given any assurances on this question," wrote Ernst von Weizsäcker, secretary of state at the German Foreign Office, to his boss, Joachim von Ribbentrop, on September 7. He went on to clarify: "We would prefer not to bind ourselves with useless promises to a third party *at the very moment when we conclude peace with Poland* [italics mine]."[85] We can very plausibly deduce that a week after Germany invaded Poland and five days after von Papen and Hesse sent out feelers in an unsuccessful bid for peace, Nazi foreign policy chiefs still hoped to reach a settlement with the country that Germany had just attacked.

Meanwhile, the German troops stationed in Poland itself were falling short of Berlin's expectations. The Wehrmacht had an enormous technical advantage over the Polish military, but despite the widely held stereotype (which is largely the product of effective Nazi propaganda), it did not wage a Blitzkrieg ("lightning war") on Poland[86] for the simple reason that Blitzkrieg doctrine did not yet exist, even in theory. German military strategy and operations during the Polish

---

85 A notice from the German Embassy in Bratislava to the German Foreign Office; September 6, 1939, in Sotskov, *Agressiia*, 196–200; a notice by Weizsäcker to the German Foreign Minister; September 7, 1939, ibid., 201–203. See also on the German-Slovak contacts with regard to the Slovak territories annexed by Poland in 1920 and 1939: Chief of the Political Department of the German Foreign Office to the German Embassy in Bratislava, telegram No. 468, August 30, 1939, in Sweet, *Documents on German Foreign Policy*, 7:458–459; a memorandum signed by Weizsäcker, Berlin, August 31, 1939, ibid., 474.

86 Some Polish historians assign part of the blame for the emergence of the "September Blitzkrieg" myth to the postwar Communist leadership of the country and to the Polish government-in-exile. According to them, both of these political camps were thereby trying to besmirch the prewar Polish political and military elite. See, for instance: Wieczorkiewicz, "Wojna polska."

Campaign were not based on any new concept of warfare; rather, the German land forces invading Poland used tactical templates that had come into existence back at the end of World War I.[87] On September 9, simultaneously with the French invasion of western Germany's Saarland region,[88] two fully intact Polish armies—the Poznań and the Pomorze—launched a counteroffensive that soon became the ten-day Battle of the Bzura, Poland's largest and most successful fight in the September campaign of 1939. The Germans suffered massive losses even by the standards of the time, even for an army as large as the Wehrmacht: twelve thousand soldiers and officers were killed, wounded, missing in action, or taken prisoner (more than a thousand a day).[89]

Already on the first day of the Polish counteroffensive, the Nazi DNB news service published a peculiar declaration from Colonel General Walther von Brauchitsch, the commander in chief of the German land forces: there would be no further need for military action on the eastern border of the Reich. Moscow jumped to the conclusion that the Germans were laying the groundwork for a truce;[90] and Berlin hastened to assuage their worries by encouraging the Red Army to invade eastern Poland.[91] However, on September 13, the fourth day of the Battle of the Bzura, when the Poles managed to dislodge some German troops from central Poland and Soviet troops were yet to cross the Polish eastern border, a Berlin radio announcement told the German people that the military would slow its spree of eastern conquest.[92] That same day, Admiral Wilhelm Canaris, the chief of the Abwehr, heard from the Nazi foreign minister von

---

87 Frieser, "The War in the West": 288–293; For a detailed analysis of the Blitzkrieg myth, see: Clark, *Blitzkrieg*.
88 "September 9," *Bulletin of International News, Royal Institute of International Affairs* 16, no. 19 (September 23, 1939), 13. According to William H. Shirer, the French offensive in the West, supposedly designed to relieve the German pressure on Poland, was launched already on the night of September 7-8. Light French forces crossed the frontier on a fifteen-mile front along the Cadenbronn Salient southeast of Saarbruecken where the border bulged southward. On the morning of September 9, they were followed by stronger units from the Fourth and Fifth Armies. The French met little opposition as the German covering forces withdrew toward the Siegfried Line eight miles north of the frontier. To the west, units of the Third Army were thrust forward to occupy a smaller salient, the Wendt Forest, southwest of Saarbruecken. There was no serious fighting, only light skirmishing. For further details, see: Shirer, *The Collapse of the Third Republic*, 496–497.
89 Solarski, "Bitwa nad Bzurą": 41–49; Tusiewicz, "Historia Polski": 363.
90 The German Aambassador to Moscow, Friedrich-Werner Graf von der Schulenburg, to the German Foreign Office, urgent, top secret telegram, September 10, 1939, in Sweet, *Documents on German Foreign Policy*, vol. 8:, 44–45.
91 Ibid.; Ribbentrop to the German Embassy in Moscow, urgent telegram, September 13, 1939, ibid., 56.
92 "September 11," *Bulletin of International News, Royal Institute of International Affairs* 16, no. 19 (September 23, 1939), 13.

Ribbentrop that "in the present situation, the optimal scenario from the Führer's point of view would be the creation of a 'rump Poland,' with a government that would be amenable to a peace deal;"[93] and General Franz Halder, chief of Staff of the German forces High Command, wrote in his diary that, given the Soviets' reluctance to get involved in a fight with Poland, the Führer was now strongly considering more limited territorial claims.[94]

It was against this backdrop that on September 11 Sokolnicki, the Polish ambassador to Ankara, notified his superiors, who had by then moved from Warsaw to Krzemieniec in eastern Poland, that his German counterpart in Turkey had once again brought up the subject of peace. Allegedly, von Papen told the local deputy foreign minister that "there was still hope of an arrangement with the Western powers."[95] Similar moods prevailed during the second week of the Polish Campaign in the political and diplomatic circles of Rome and Budapest. From their contacts in Berlin, including von Ribbentrop, they understood that Hitler planned to occupy Warsaw and then immediately make a peace offer to Britain and France, sticking to his original, quite modest, territorial claims to the Poles. Mussolini even prepared to call for an emergency peace conference, which would decide the fate of Germany's territorial gains in Poland.[96] Undoubtedly, London was well aware: on September 10, Chamberlain wrote in his personal diary that he believed Hitler wished sincerely for peace, and that only in the last days of August had he ruled in favor of "a short war in Poland, and then a settlement."[97]

Summarizing the evidence presented above, we can conclude that during the first two weeks of the German invasion of Poland, local political and military leaders had a real chance to start a dialogue with Berlin—either directly or through intermediaries—and reach an agreement on more or less acceptable terms. Although the Poles would have to concede the western territories and the Baltic coastline, they could have spared the rest of the country from Nazi

---

93 Zychowicz, *Opcja niemiecka*, 21. See also an analogous statement made at the time by Wilhelm Keitel, chief of the German Armed Forces High Command, who told Canaris that Hitler preferred the creation of a "rump Poland," whose government would be amenable to a peace deal: Mueller, *Canaris*, 296.
94 "September 12, 1939," *The Private War Journal of Generaloberst Franz Halder*, 3.
95 Sokolnicki to the Polish Foreign Office in Warsaw, untitled encrypted telegram No. 3, September 11, 1939, USHMM, RG-59.036, A-12-53-26_0117.
96 Wieniawa-Długoszowski, the Polish Ambassador to Rome, to the Polish Foreign Office in Warsaw, untitled telegram No. 13, September 9, 1939, USHMM, RG-59.036, A-12-53-26_0088; Leon Orłowski, the Polish Ambassador to Budapest, to the Polish Foreign Office in Warsaw, untitled encrypted telegram No. 3, September 11, 1939, USHMM, RG-59.036, A-12-53-26_0120.
97 Feiling, *The Life of Neville Chamberlain*, 416–417.

occupation. Moreover, in the face of such a development, the Soviet Union would most likely abandon its claims to Poland's eastern territories: on September 9, just after von Brauchitsch announced that the Germans had achieved their objectives on the Eastern Front, the Soviet commissariat of foreign affairs notified Berlin that in the event of a German-Polish armistice Moscow would not launch "another war."[98]

The Polish leadership fully understood that reaching an agreement with the Nazis would prevent the total destruction of the Polish state, but still refused to consider negotiations. Already by mid-September 1939, Poland's leverage with Berlin had eroded: the Wehrmacht had won at Bzura, neither Britain not France seemed particularly eager to join Polish forces in battle, and the French troops in the Saarland had yet to make any real progress.[99] But all bets were off on September 17, when Soviet forces broke through the eastern border and hamstrung the still fighting Polish army. Empty-handed, its remnants, along with the political leaders of the Second Polish Republic, fled to neighboring countries, mainly Hungary, Romania, and Slovakia.[100]

---

[98] Friedrich-Werner Graf von der Schulenburg to the German Foreign Office, urgent, top secret telegram, September 10, 1939, in Sweet, *Documents on German Foreign Policy*, 8:44–45.

[99] In present-day Polish historiography, one can encounter the opinion that, even as late as the beginning of the third week of the invasion, Poland's military situation was not yet catastrophic, and that the country could have halted the greatly weakened German advance, if only the Western Allies had launched their promised attack on Germany. See: Szeremietiew, *Siła złego*, 465; Wieczorkiewicz, "Wojna polska." If we assume that the Polish political and military leadership in September 1939 shared this assessment, we have a possible explanation for the refusal of official Warsaw to consider the conciliatory signals emanating from the German side. As for the reasons for the French behavior in the Saarland, according to William H. Shirer, who cited contemporary French sources, it was the France's commander in chief, General Maurice Gamelin, who decided to make no more than a gesture. Already by September 12—without any reference to the Polish counteroffensive, which just entered its most active and effective stage—he cancelled his offensive "in the view of the developments in Poland," and about two weeks later announced to his troops that "the hour had come to retreat." Only then were the French prime minister Édouard Daladier and President Albert Lebrun briefed about Gamelin's decision to abandon the Saar and approved it. The approval was due to the growing impression in Paris that the nation refused the war, and that the British were not pulling their full weight in the common struggle and wanted France to fight alone. See: Shirer, *The Collapse of the Third Republic*, 498-502. Also in this context, the statement of French minister of finance Paul Reynaud to the US ambassador in Paris must be mentioned, according to which the clear British object was to see French resources exhausted before there was serious weakening on the part of Great Britain, so that at the end of this war, Great Britain could control the situation absolutely. See: Haslam, *The Spectre of War*, 330.

[100] Kochanski, *The Eagle Unbowed*, 72–75; Lebedeva, "Sentiabr' 1939": 231–249; Slutsch, "Die deutsch-sowjetischen Beziehungen": 99–117; Wieczorkiewicz, *Historia polityczna Polski*, 96 –99.

The Reich's Key Bargaining Chip

The end of the Polish Campaign did not stop Berlin's attempts to negotiate the fate of the Polish territories occupied by the Wehrmacht. The Nazi regime still retained the prospect of granting some autonomy to these territories. Sober minds in the German military command and in von Ribbentrop's office were all too aware that the euphoric propaganda celebrating the Nazi triumph in Poland glossed over the German army's significant logistical problems[101] and concomitant heavy losses (forty-five to fifty thousand wounded or killed in only four weeks!),[102] and for this reason advocated for reaching a settlement as quickly as possible. By giving the Poles semi-independent statehood under a German protectorate, Hitler could forestall a dangerous military clash with the British Empire, put Germany back on good terms with the "family of European nations," and set up a "Polish buffer zone" as a bulwark against the Communist threat from the east.[103]

Even before the fighting officially concluded, Ernst von Weizsäcker, secretary of state at the German Foreign Office, drafted an internal settlement proposal. "The war with Poland is over," it reads in part. "Germany is laying claim to the borders of 1914; the future of the rest of the Polish territories now depends on the willingness of the Western powers to reach a settlement."[104] Von Weizsäcker's high-ranking colleague, the last prewar German ambassador to Warsaw Hans-Adolf von Moltke, opined that the Germans could easily find willing partners among the vanquished Polish political class, especially if they promised to eventually return the Russian-occupied Polish territories. He believed that a pro-German, semi-independent regime in Warsaw would delegitimize the government-in-exile in the eyes of international law, thereby releasing the Western powers from all obligations to Poland and putting a stop to the war.[105] Remarkably, at the same time, Polish diplomats came to the same realization.[106]

---

101 Adamthwaite, *The Making of the Second World War*, 93; Bock, *The War Diary*, 79; Frieser, "The War in the West": 289–290; Kroener, "Der Kampf um den 'Sparstoff' Mensch": 402–417.
102 Davies, *Im Herzen Europas*, 60; Kochanski, *The Eagle Unbowed*, 84.
103 Graml, *Resistance Thinking on Foreign Policy*, 14–17. The idea of a "Polish buffer zone" between Nazi Germany and the Soviet Union played a key role in Hitler's plans until the spring of 1939. See: Wieczorkiewicz, "Wojna polska."
104 A memorandum signed by Ernst von Weizsäcker, September 25, 1939, in Sweet, *Documents on German Foreign Policy 1918–1945*, 8:137.
105 A memorandum signed by von Moltke, September 25, 1939, ibid., 138–139.
106 Polish Ambassador to Budapest Leon Orłowski to an unknown addressee, untitled encrypted telegram No. 10, September 21, 1939, USHMM, RG-59.036, A-12-53-26_0236.

We do not know for certain whether Hitler was aware of this pro-settlement position held by some of his senior diplomats and miliary commanders. However, it can be assumed that such views were expressed to him and approved by him. In late September 1939, he dispatched the well-known Swedish businessman and prewar intermediary Birger Dahlerus to London with instructions to inform the British government that their consent to peace negotiations would help to "preserve something of Poland."[107] At virtually the same time, the German leader told the chief Nazi ideologue Alfred Rosenberg that they must create the "semblance of statehood" in central Poland, and that only several decades later would the Nazi government be able to decide whether additional regions of Poland should be annexed and settled by Germans.[108]

But soon enough, Hitler's plans for Poland ran into a Stalin-shaped hurdle, as evidenced in an urgent September 25 telegram from the German ambassador to Moscow. Stalin had summoned Friedrich-Werner Graf von der Schulenburg to the Kremlin to deliver a message for Hitler: an "independent Polish rump state" had the potential to "create friction between Germany and the Soviet Union," and thus should stay off the table.[109] Since Hitler was still interested in maintaining a strategic partnership with the USSR, he was forced to concede the point. The German-Soviet Boundary and Friendship Treaty, signed on September 28, satisfied Stalin's demand to erase all references to Poland's erstwhile independence. The contract dividing the "former Polish state" featured clearly delineated German and Soviet occupation zones, a "German-Soviet boundary," and a secret supplementary protocol outlined how the countries might cooperate to suppress any resultant "Polish agitation."[110]

After the signing ceremony, von Ribbentrop announced to Stalin and his foreign minister Vyacheslav Molotov that Hitler's decision to subjugate Poland confirmed the sincerity of his commitment to building a durable alliance.[111] In

---

107 The protocol of Hitler's conversation with Dahlerus, in the presence of Hermann Göring, September 26, 1939, in Sweet, *Documents on German Foreign Policy*, 8:140–145.
108 Noakes and Pridham, *Nazism*, 927.
109 The German Ambassador to Moscow to the German Foreign Office, top secret telegram No. 442, September 25, 1939, in Felshtinsky, *TSRS-Vokietija 1939*, 105. According to the US journalist and historian William H. Shirer, already on September 19, during a conversation with von der Schulenburg, Soviet Minister of Foreign Affairs Molotov "hinted that the original inclination entertained by the Soviet Government and Stalin personally to permit the existence of a residual Poland had given away to the inclination to partition Poland along the Pissa-Narew-Vistula-San Line." See: Shirer, *The Collapse of the Third Republic*, 496.
110 "The German-Soviet Boundary and Friendship Treaty," *Pravda*, September 29, 1939, ibid., 107–110.
111 From the recording of Joachim von Ribbentrop's conversations with Joseph Stalin and Vyacheslav Molotov, Moscow, September 28–29, 1939, in Naumov, *1941 god*, 2:587–589.

reality, this was a lie meant to lull the Soviets into complacency while Hitler used his secret diplomatic channels to negotiate a peace agreement with France and Britain. In fact, on the very same day Stalin, Molotov, and Ribbentrop toasted in the Kremlin, Dahlerus once again traveled to England with an important message for the Foreign Office: Hitler was willing to grant the Poles limited independence within a new, smaller territory without its own currency or armed forces.[112] The very next day, General Halder conferred with Hitler, then confided in his diary: "He is ready for peace."[113]

The British met with Dahlerus again a week and a half later, this time at the Hague, and learned that Hitler planned to hold a "peace conference" to discuss the future of the Polish state with the Western powers. Sir Alexander Cadogan, permanent undersecretary at the Foreign Office, attended the meeting, getting the impression that: "If there is no conference, there won't be an independent Polish state, either."[114] Another intermediary, Sven Hedin—famed Swedish explorer, Nazi sympathizer, and a frequent guest in Berlin—issued a statement to the international press in late September: "[If] England makes peace, there will be a small independent Poland. If not, all of Poland will be divided."[115]

On October 1, 1939, conferring in Berlin with Italian foreign minister Galeazzo Ciano, Hitler made a similar reference to a "small Polish state, controlled and not dangerous," which could be created "immediately upon the conclusion of peace." The Nazi leader explained that he preferred to abstain, as far as possible, from governing the Polish territories, given "the woeful state" of their infrastructures.[116] That same day, the Italians, who had declared their neutrality and were trying to arrange an international peace conference for Europe,[117] passed this information straight to the French. The very next day, they informed the German Foreign Office that the French had shown a keen interest in the current terms; an unnamed, high-ranking French official seemed very agreeable to the tripartite conference Hitler had proposed. He thought the French and

---

112 Martin, "Britisch-deutsche Friedenskontakte": 213; see on the meeting of Dahlerus with Göring and Hitler on September 26, 1939, immediately prior to this trip: Fraenkel and Manvell, *Hermann Göring*, 215–216.
113 "September 30, 1939," in *The Private War Journal of Generaloberst Franz Halder*, 19.
114 Martin, "Britisch-deutsche Friedenskontakte": 217.
115 Danielsson, *The Explorer's Roadmap to National-Socialism*, 168.
116 Conversation between the Führer and Count Ciano, held in the presence of the Foreign Minister at the Reich Chancellery on October 1, 1939. Protocol signed by an official of the Chancellery of the German Foreign Office, October 2, 1939, in Sweet, *Documents on German Foreign Policy 1918–1945*, 8:184–194.
117 Muggeridge, *Ciano's Diary*, 136–141; see also: Memorandum No. 535 signed by Weizsäcker, September 2, 1939, in Sweet, *Documents on German Foreign Policy 1918–1945*, 7:509–510.

British governments would not only attend, but eventually come around to the idea of a "symbolic Polish state," since it would let them save face.¹¹⁸

This development hardly came as a surprise to the Germans. Only a month earlier, on the eve of the Polish Campaign, Paris had done everything in its power to make Warsaw accept a compromise with Berlin, even offering to serve as Hitler's intermediary. Ultimately, the French managed to convince the Poles to postpone their declaration of a general military mobilization so they could not mobilize in time to meet the Germans.¹¹⁹ Then, in the first days of the war, France endorsed Italy's proposal of an immediate ceasefire to be followed by a peace conference for parties involved in the conflict. The Italians kept the Germans fully informed of France's evolving stance.¹²⁰

Meanwhile, despite Hitler's efforts to keep Stalin in the dark about his willingness to preserve a token amount of Polish independence, the Soviet leader somehow learned of his German colleague's plan to brazenly violate both the letter and the spirit of the treaty they signed on September 28. On the evening of October 2, the same day Rome told Berlin that Paris was ready to compromise, Stalin confided to Latvian foreign minister Vilhelms Munters that, in his view, "the future treatment of Poland [by the Germans] cannot be predicted . . . A [German] protectorate may be established in [its] western part."¹²¹

If Stalin wanted to signal to the Germans, via the Latvians, that he knew of Hitler's dalliance with Churchill, Hitler failed to take the hint. Encouraged by France's warm reception of their peace initiative, the Germans made two new moves in their diplomatic offensive. On October 6, a day after a brief visit to occupied Warsaw, Hitler proclaimed from the Reichstag, in complete contradiction to his new treaty with Stalin, that he was willing to create a Polish state that would no longer be "a hotbed of anti-German activity."¹²² On

---

118 Memorandum signed by Weizsäcker and the protocol thereto, October 2, 1939, in, ibid., 8:197–198.
119 Adamthwaite, *The Making of the Second World War*, 93; Wieczorkiewicz, "Wojna polska."
120 Rothschild, *Peace for Our Time*, 338–339; see also: Memorandum No. 535 signed by Weizsäcker, September 2, 1939, Sweet, *Documents on German Foreign Policy 1918–1945*, 7:509–510; and also: the commentary of Dr. Paul Schmidt, acting press secretary of the German Foreign Office, according to whom the French initially accepted the settlement framework put forth by Mussolini, but ultimately rejected it under British pressure. Circular letter signed by the Acting Press Secretary of the German Foreign Office, October 12, 1939, in: ibid., 8:274.
121 From the protocol of Stalin and Molotov's conversation with the Latvian delegation, Moscow, October 2, 1939, Naumov, *1941 god*, 2:594–595.
122 Editor's commentary on a telegram from the German Ambassador to Italy to the German Foreign Office, October 6, 1939, in Sweet, *Documents on German Foreign Policy*, 8:227; Noakes and Pridham, *Nazism*, 923.

October 9, Goebbels called a press conference to announce that, in Berlin's view, the new "small Polish state" should not have its own army or make its own foreign policy decisions, but could retain the right to administer its own internal affairs.[123] Remarkably, some British citizens assessed Hitler's offer as both reasonable and sincere, calling to endorse the idea of an international conference that would finally resolve the fundamental disagreements between the European powers.[124]

But Berlin's appeals were in vain. British intelligence and diplomats considered them merely a tactic to buy enough time to plan and carry out more acts of war.[125] Their point of view was shared by many prominent British figures. "Nazi tyranny and aggression are destroying the traditional excellences of European civilization and must be eliminated for the good of mankind," sermonized the archbishop of York on an October 2 radio broadcast. "We should make no terms with Herr Hitler or his Government—not because it is undemocratic, which is Germany's concern and not ours, but because it is utterly untrustworthy."[126]

This mistrust of Berlin's intentions was reinforced by the discovery that Swedish intermediary Birger Dahlerus was financially dependent on the Nazis. The British came to the conclusion that they could no longer regard him as neutral, and had to reassess his statements as disinformation serving Hitler's secret agenda.[127] Another, much stronger confirmation of London's suspicions arrived on October 8, when, at the height of his diplomatic effort to reach an agreement with Britain, the Nazi leader ordered the annexation of Poland's western territories, then home to ten million people.[128] The enraged British responded by sending to Hitler via Dahlerus a list of harsh demands: reestablish the Polish state, destroy the Wehrmacht's offensive weaponry, and hold a referendum on foreign policy.[129] A few days later, the Political Intelligence Department of the

---

123 Zychowicz, *Opcja niemiecka*, 29–30.
124 See, for instance: Beatrice Brown to Foreign Secretary Halifax, October 16, 1939, USHMM, RG-59.006.M-FO371/22949, Scans 00182-3.
125 Stevenson, *A Man Called Intrepid*, 102–103. See also the assessment of the British intelligence community, according to which Hitler's peace offers in the Reichstag on October 6, 1939, were a ruse meant to mask German preparations for a new offensive on the Western Front: Weekly Political Intelligence Summary No. 2, Foreign Office, Political Intelligence Department, October 10, 1939, USHMM, RG-59.006.M-FO371/24054, Scan 00041.
126 Archbishop of York, "The Spirit and Aim of Britain in the War," October 2, 1939, USHMM, RG-59.006.M-FO371/22949, Scans 00238-239.
127 Stevenson, *A Man Called Intrepid*, 102–103.
128 Noakes and Pridham, *Nazism*, 925–926; Tusiewicz, *Historia Polski*, 367.
129 Förster, "Hitlers Entscheidung": 13; Fraenkel and Manvell, *Hermann Göring*, 16; Martin, "Britisch-deutsche Friedenskontakte": 210–214; Self, *Neville Chamberlain*, 400.

Foreign Office reported in one of its publications that this response had been agreed with representatives of the exiled Polish Foreign Office, who had traveled from France to the UK for this purpose.[130]

On October 10, shortly after Dahlerus brought the British ultimatum to Berlin, Goebbels wrote in his diary: "The Führer has no wish for any kind of merger with the Poles. They must be pushed into their shrunken state and be left there in isolation."[131] Four days later, Colonel General Walther von Brauchitsch, commander in chief of the German land forces, addressed his chief of staff, General Franz Halder: "It is our duty to set [ourselves] attainable military goals and use every opportunity to make peace."[132] These two quotes echoed Hitler's own statement made earlier, during his aforementioned meeting with Count Ciano. Thus, they may be taken as evidence that at that time the Nazi leadership did indeed envision the creation of a "shrunken" Polish state as a solution to the "Polish question."

If this is the case, the British cabinet followed the Polish government-in-exile by failing to recognize their chance to "preserve something of Poland." Nowadays, it is no longer possible to know what would have happened if London had made some concessions, or if anything might have dissuaded Hitler from returning to a policy of force. However, numerous, incontrovertible, and mutually reinforcing pieces of evidence confirm that in the early autumn of 1939, the Germans were fully aware that they were unprepared to face the British in conflict and wanted to grant the Poles some measure of independence. Thus, London missed its own brief window of opportunities to change the bitter fate of occupied Poland and avert the catastrophe of the global war that engulfed the European continent.

An Unexpected Short-Term Symbiosis

Within Poland, the German aggressors sowed death, destruction, and terror. Hundreds of tons of aerial bombs and artillery shells hit Warsaw and other Polish cities, inflicting unprecedented damage. Thousands of Polish troops were shot after surrender, and tens of thousands of civilians were killed in their homes or fleeing eastward, away from the front line.[133]

---

130 Weekly Political Intelligence Summary No. 3, Foreign Office, Political Intelligence Department, October 17, 1939, USHMM, RG-59.006.M-FO371/24054, Scan 00068.
131 Reuth, *Joseph Goebbels*, 1326.
132 "October 14, 1939," The Private War Journal of Generaloberst Franz Halder, 30.
133 Kershaw, *Hitler: A Biography*, 518; Rossino, *Hitler Strikes Poland*, 58–120, 227–235; Snyder, *Bloodlands*, 119–122.

Yet in these dire circumstances, some unexpected opportunities for cooperation arose between the occupiers and the occupied. The German military administration, established in the Poland's occupied areas as early as the first week of the war, opposed the brutal behavior of the SS and SD.[134] Almost immediately, it began contacting prominent conservatives among the Polish intelligentsia, considering them as the key to its mission's success. In Kraków, overrun by the Wehrmacht on September 6, the newly appointed head of the military administration, Major General Eugen von Höberth, convened a "city council" of local notables, including the rector of Jagiellonian University and the president of the Polish Academy of Sciences, to help the Germans "normalize the situation in the city." When Warsaw fell on September 28, the Germans allowed Mayor Stefan Starzyński to stay in his post for another month. With the full support of German military governor General Karl Ulrich von Neumann-Neurode, he worked diligently to clean up the damage and restore normality to life on the streets.[135] According to a rumor circulating in the occupied city, Neumann-Neurode even hung a portrait of the late Marshal Piłsudski next to the one of Hitler he was required to display in his office.[136]

In the second half of September 1939, the occupying authorities began actively wooing Polish politicians with offers of collaboration, including the creation of a puppet Polish government. The first to receive such a proposition was Wincenty Witos, a veteran politician and leader of the conservative People's Party. Thanks to his authoritarian leadership style, open Germanophilia, anti-communism, and extensive experience as both a member of the Austro-Hungarian Parliament and as head of one of the interwar cabinets, Witos was apparently regarded as an ideal candidate for Polish collaborator in chief. In the spring of 1939, during his political exile to neighboring Czechoslovakia, Berlin contacted Witos with an offer to lead a pro-German government in Warsaw, but he refused. Shortly after he returned to Poland, the German invasion began, and on September 16, the Gestapo detained him. While Warsaw was still putting up a fight, a high-ranking Nazi official promised to make Witos the leader of all of Poland if he agreed to collaborate with the occupiers, but the proud Witos once again refused, so they

---

[134] Noakes and Pridham, *Nazism*, 938–940; Rossino, *Hitler Strikes Poland*, 109–110, 230; Weitz, *Joachim von Ribbentrop*, 217; Wette, *The Wehrmacht*, 101–102.

[135] Kunicki, *Unwanted Collaborators*, 207; Zychowicz, *Opcja niemiecka*, 37–38; see also on Starzyński's activities during the early period of the German occupation: the Polish ambassador to Bern, Titus Komarnicki, to the Polish government in Angers, an untitled secret telegram, December 7, 1939, USHMM, RG-59.036, A-12-73-2_0062.

[136] Zychowicz, *Opcja niemiecka*, 57.

jailed him indefinitely. Similar overtures to two other members of the People's Party also failed.[137]

Polish far-right politicians like Andrzej Świetlicki and Stanisław Trzeciak received the Nazis far more warmly. These collaborators established the National Radical Organization (NOR), agitating in favor of a joint German-Polish invasion of the USSR and Jewish pogroms. The NOR also made preparations to create a nationalist Polish government to be modeled after the Third Reich. In the end, however, none of the newly minted "Polish Nazis" from the NOR received an offer as generous as the one made to the leaders of the People's Party. Apparently, at this point, when Hitler was still trying to reach a settlement with Britain, a Warsaw copy of the Nazi regime seemed like bad optics to Berlin. Given the fanatical nationalism Świetlicki, Trzeciak, and their colleagues espoused, putting them in charge may have even been dangerous.[138]

The "love affair" between the German military administration and the Polish conservatives and nationalists was to last only about a month. On October 12, Chamberlain rejected the peace proposal Hitler had made six days earlier, calling it purposefully vague, uncertain, and without any concrete suggestions to end the German occupation in Czechoslovakia and Poland.[139] The Nazi Führer responded with an angry declaration that Britain had rejected German's outstretched hand for peace, and so the war would have to continue. That same day, he ordered the creation of a new administrative unit called the General Government (Generalgouvernement or GG) and put it in charge of the approximately one hundred thousand square kilometers and twelve million local citizens squeezed into the territory between the new German and Soviet borders. Control of this new entity would be transferred from the Wehrmacht to a German civil administration as soon as possible.[140]

At present, we do not know the identities or the motivations of the senior Nazi officials who allowed the German military administration in Poland to cultivate the German-Polish symbiosis in governing the occupied territories, and even to foster the seeds of political cooperation with various local politicians and publics figures. According to a highly plausible hypothesis advanced

---

137 Kochanski, *The Eagle Unbowed*, 97; Kunicki. *Unwanted Collaborators*, 206; Zakrzewski, *Wincenty Witos*, 379–415; Zychowicz, *Opcja niemiecka*, 31–32.
138 Kunicki, *Unwanted Collaborators*, 209; Młynarczyk, "Pomiędzy współpracą a zdradą": 106; Zychowicz, *Opcja niemiecka*, 43–49.
139 "British Reply to German Proposals."
140 Gruchmann, "Nationalsozialistische Grossraumordnung": 94; Noakes and Pridham, *Nazism*, 925–927; Tusiewicz, *Historia Polski*, 367.

by Jan Brocki—a former Polish diplomat who remained in his homeland until January 1940, and who then fled to Italy, where he was interrogated by representatives of the government-in-exile—it was a local initiative by the German military command.[141] In this scenario, a small group of high-ranking Wehrmacht officers, who were under the influence of moderate political forces within the Third Reich, and who may even have collaborated with these forces, tried to use the period of Hitler's diplomatic maneuvers to convince Berlin that cooperation with the locals in occupied Poland was both possible and necessary, and that these locals ought to be granted a degree of autonomy. Of course, the initiative for German-Polish rapprochement might have originated within a Nazi elite that wished to lay the groundwork for a puppet Polish government to satisfy the Western powers.

Either way, it would seem that the Polish conservatives who remained in their occupied motherland, Wincenty Witos most of all, had also missed their chance to preserve "something of Poland" during the first weeks of the war and Nazi occupation.

Offers of Friendship amid a Bloody Bacchanal

On October 26, exactly two weeks after Hitler announced his plans for the General Government, political power over the new administrative entity was indeed handed over to a civilian governor general, veteran Nazi politician Hans Frank.[142] Frank's rule was supported by an extensive apparatus of SS and Gestapo forces who soon replaced military officers in management positions. The new regime launched a wave of terror—mass repressions, humiliation, and physical extermination—against the local population, especially the Polish intelligentsia, Jews, and Roma, and by engaging in the ruthless and indiscriminate economic oppression of all the inhabitants of the territories now under Frank's rule. These policies, coupled with the violent expulsion of about a million Polish citizens

---

141 Protocol of the interrogation of Jan Brocki, February 7, 1940, USHMM, GK_159_228cz2, p. 25.
142 According to the Political Intelligence Department of the Foreign Office, the official ceremony of the handover of power to Frank took place in Kraków on November 7, 1939: Weekly Political Intelligence Summary No. 9, Foreign Office, Political Intelligence Department, November 28, 1939, USHMM, RG-59.006.M-FO371/24054, Scan 00207.

from the country's territories annexed to the Reich, resulted in the deaths of forty-five to fifty thousand people by the end of 1939.[143]

Considering this radical change in the nature of the German occupation regime in Poland, it is very surprising to learn that even in late 1939, Berlin was still attempting to negotiate a rump Polish state with London. On October 14—only two days after Hitler's declaration that the war would go on and his decree about the establishment of the GG— the British Foreign Office received, via Dahlerus, a message from the commander in chief of the German Air Force, Reichsmarschall Hermann Göring. One of the seniormost leaders of the Third Reich and a prominent advocate of an alliance with the Second Polish Republic in the prewar period,[144] Göring requested for a secret meeting with British military officials to be held in a neutral country. After failing to receive a response, he continued to send similar messages until early November when, following the abduction of two British intelligence operatives by the SD in Dutch territory[145] (an event that had nothing to do with him), the British decided to cut off all contact with Göring's Swedish intermediary.[146] Likely encouraging this decision were the baseless assertions the Foreign Office's political intelligence unit made on October 24 and 31: the Germans had given up on the idea of a rump Polish state for good and were now doing everything in their power to prevent Polish sovereignty in any form.[147] After the British fired Dahlerus, the Nazis did likewise on November 11. Göring called the Swede personally to inform him of his dismissal. At the same time, Ribbentrop instructed his representatives in Stockholm to notify the former intermediary that the Reich no longer needed his services "because the official

---

143 Gruchmann, *Nationalsozialistische Grossraumordnung*, 93; Rossino, *Hitler Strikes Poland*, 234; Snyder, *Bloodlands*, 122–134; Tusiewicz, *Historia Polski*, 367, 370-73; Williamson, *The Polish Underground*, 16–19.
144 On Göring's desire to conclude a military-political alliance with Poland in the prewar years, see: Wieczorkiewicz, "Wojna polska."
145 Aldrich, *The Black Door*, 86–87; Kessler and Wingate, *Betrayal at Venlo*.
146 Martin, "Britisch-deutsche Friedenskontakte": 210–214; Self, *Neville Chamberlain*, 401.
147 Weekly Political Intelligence Summary No. 4, Foreign Office, Political Intelligence Department, October 24, 1939, USHMM, RG-59.006.M-FO371/24054, Scan 00082; Weekly political intelligence Summary no. 5, Foreign Office, Political Intelligence Department, October 31, 1939, USHMM, RG-59.006.M-FO371/24054, Scan 00105. See also the diary entry by Ivan Maisky, the Soviet ambassador to London, from October 28, 1939, according to which the British leadership was not opposed, in principle, to an accommodation with Berlin, yet it insisted categorically on the "disappearance" of Hitler and his entourage: *The Maisky Diaries*, 236–237.

attitude of the British government has already indicated unequivocal rejection of the German position."[148]

But Dahlerus was not the only diplomatic channel through which Berlin conveyed its proposals on the fate of Poland to London. Another such intermediary was Baron William de Ropp. The scion of a Baltic German aristocratic family, de Ropp moved to the British Isles before World War I, during which he served in the Royal Air Force. In the 1930s, he became a liaison between some key figures in the British and German upper echelons of power, including Prince George, RAF intelligence chief Frederick Winterbotham, and the prominent Nazi ideologue Alfred Rosenberg.[149] In September 1939, de Ropp contacted Nazi leadership to volunteer his services as an intermediary between Berlin and London.[150] Two months later, in November, he informed the British government that the Nazi regime was still prepared to discuss terms for the creation of a rump Poland."[151]

At the same time, on November 17, the official German press reiterated that Nazi leadership still hoped for peace and that, inter alia, it was willing to the creation of a small Polish state that would no longer serve as a platform for hostile Western actions against the Reich. This official announcement did not go unnoticed by the British intelligence community.[152] Several weeks later, the British ambassador to Italy, Sir Percy Loraine, informed his Polish counterpart, Boleslaw Wieniawa-Długoszowski, that according to information he had obtained and passed onto London, Göring was still willing to countenance the idea of reestablishing Polish statehood, albeit in a smaller territory and under German auspices.[153]

However, as stated above, the British government was virtually unanimous in its rejection of all Nazi peace offers—at Poland's expense. The Political Intelligence Department of the Foreign Office noted in its report from December 12 that although the Germans kept dropping hints about their alleged readiness for peace, they seemed to wish only to strengthen their positions before resuming their aggression, and so their offers remained

---

148 The German Foreign Minister to the German Embassy in Sweden, a telegram from November 11, 1939, in Sweet, *Documents on German Foreign Policy 1918–1945*, 8:397–398.
149 Kershaw, *Making Friends with Hitler*, 201.
150 A memorandum signed by Rosenberg, Berlin; September 25, 1939, in Sweet, *Documents on German Foreign Policy*, 8:134.
151 Madajczyk, *Generalna Gubernia w planach hitlerowskich*, 23–24.
152 Weekly political intelligence summary no. 8, Foreign Office, Political Intelligence Department, November 21, 1939, USHMM, RG-59.006.M-FO371/24054, Scan 00178.
153 Wieniawa-Długoszowski to the Polish Foreign Office in Angers, in an untitled secret report, January 5, 1940, USHMM, RG-59.036, A-12-3-2_0012-8.

unpalatable to Britain and France.¹⁵⁴ In parallel, the British press started printing the accumulating reports of Nazi atrocities in occupied Poland and promulgated a view that gained increasing traction both within the leadership and among the British public: "even though these atrocities were initiated by the Nazi elite, their practical realization was made possible through the support of the whole German people."¹⁵⁵ This led to the conclusion that the UK had no choice but to engage in a military confrontation with the monster that had only grown since 1933.¹⁵⁶ Chamberlain, who has gone down in history as the failed peacemaker of the late 1930s, explained in a letter to his sister Ida that the time had come to blunt German morale with "a real hard punch in the stomach."¹⁵⁷

The archival sources at our disposal indicate Berlin's extremely negative reaction to London's stubborn refusal to consider its peace offers. Not a shred of evidence has been found of the failure of a possible Nazi strategic disinformation scheme using the "Polish card" to deceive the West. The sources reflect only genuine frustration and anger at London's "blindness" and its failure to accept the Nazi's real desire for alliance. An internal circular von Ribbentrop disseminated among his underlings on November 18 asserted that "England had slammed the door on any attempt whatsoever at peace mediation" and that "Germany had taken up the challenge flung at her and will now carry on the fight to final victory."¹⁵⁸ Needless to say, this document was not part of some external propaganda campaign.

Meanwhile, at the very end of November, two weeks after the British determined that Germany had given up on the idea of a rump Polish state and severed ties with Dahlerus and de Ropp, London learned that, even after the establishment of the GG, Germany was still looking for potential political partners in occupied Poland. The Political Intelligence Department of the Foreign Office explicitly pointed out this fact in its weekly report from November 21, 1939:

> Outside the western provinces, now officially incorporated in the Reich, the Germans are in a quandary. It is known that *various*

---

154 Weekly Political Intelligence Summary No. 11, Foreign Office, Political Intelligence Department, December 12, 1939, USHMM, RG-59.006.M-FO371/24054, Scan 00256.
155 *Sunday Dispatch*, December 10, 1939; Fromm, *Deutschland in der öffentlichen Kriegszieldiskussion Grossbritanniens*, 46.
156 Held, *Kriegsgefangenschaft in Großbritannien*, 24.
157 Chamberlain to Ida, December 3, 1939, XNC 18/1/1133A.
158 A circular of the German Foreign Office, signed by Foreign Minister Ribbentrop; November 18, 1939, in Sweet, *Documents on German Foreign Policy*, 8:424–425.

Poles [italics mine], though men of very little standing, have been approached by the Germans to form a puppet Government. In every case the offer has been refused. The Germans are now unlikely to persist and will probably be forced to form a purely German Administration. The present administration under Dr. Frank, now established at Cracow, will have no easy task in spite of boastful reports put out by German propaganda.[159]

British intelligence was seemingly ignorant of the fact that, despite Hans Frank's draconian policies, his administration took care to preserve the self-government structures the Poles had established during the brief period of German military administration: Polish bodies like the Red Cross, the lowest courts, and the police continued to operate under strict German control. Moreover, in February 1940, the Principal Protective Council (Rada Główna Opiekuńcza) was established in Kraków, the capital of the GG, led by Prince Janusz Franciszek Radziwiłł, a conservative politician and the scion of two prominent Polish noble families, the Radziwiłłs and the Sapiegas. After being imprisoned by the Soviets, he was released under international pressure and came voluntarily to the GG. Thanks to his connections with German aristocracy, the Nazi occupying authorities treated Radziwiłł leniently, and in December 1939, they apparently offered to put him in charge of a Polish puppet government. He declined the offer. Two months later, he traveled to Berlin, where in an attempt to ease the suffering of his people, he met with his old acquaintance, Hermann Göring.[160] Radziwiłł's council offered various forms of aid to the population of the GG, and many Poles came to regard it as a shadow cabinet representing their interests to the occupiers.[161]

The Polish fascist organization NOR was also allowed to continue its activities in the GG's formative months, remaining under the wing of the Wehrmacht. The Gestapo was able to get its hands on it only in the spring of 1940, after

---

159 Weekly Political Intelligence Summary No. 8, Foreign Office, Political Intelligence Department, November 21, 1939, USHMM, RG-59.006.M-FO371/24054, Scan 00182.
160 Zychowicz, *Opcja niemiecka*, 61–68; general information report No. 42 of the Polish intelligence station in Bucharest, July 18, 1940, USHMM, RG-59.047, KOL-25-10-A_249-50. On the emigration of the Radziwiłł family from the Soviet Union, see: Raczyński, the Polish ambassador to London, to the Polish Foreign Office in Angers, encrypted telegram No. 112, USHMM, RG-59.036, A-12-53-28_0070. See also on the relationship between Radziwiłł and Göring, and on the former's trip to Berlin: Sudoplatov, *Raznye dni*, 111.
161 Kunicki, *Unwanted Collaborators*, 207; a "brief notice" sent by Mr. Falterow to representatives of the government-in-exile via Ms. Elina Zaleska, May 1, 1940, USHMM, RG-59.047, KOL-25-10-A_157-8.

Hitler had explicitly prohibited the German military authorities in Poland from engaging in any contact with local political forces.[162]

Nazi leadership met the project of setting up a pro-German government in Warsaw with renewed urgency in March and April of 1940, on the eve of German invasion of France.[163] This time, they were guided by Hitler's prewar idea of creating a Polish military-political buffer zone between the Reich and the USSR, ahead of the war with the West.[164] Wincenty Witos was released from jail and brought to Berlin for negotiations. By that point, GG infrastructure had been up and running for more than half a year, and an experienced administrator like him could quickly transform it into a full-fledged government. However, for reasons known only to himself, Witos once again rejected the Germans' advances and returned to the GG to serve out his jail sentence.[165]

Berlin simply failed to find any other potential Polish collaborators of comparable stature. Janusz Radziwiłł, as might be recalled, had rejected a similar offer back in December. As for the leaders of the fascist NOR with much less political and administrative clout and far more willingness to capitulate to Nazi demands, they had already been arrested and shot by the Gestapo. Hence, no Polish government emerged in the GG in the spring of 1940, and the buffer zone between the Reich and the USSR remained an unrealized dream—assuming anyone had any intention to build it in the first place. That said, the rumors circulating in Warsaw during this period suggested that Frank and the Gestapo had already set up a "secret government"—an alternative to the Sikorski cabinet—under former Polish minister Bogusław Miedziński, who had quietly returned to occupied Poland.[166] These claims were false. In reality, Miedziński stayed in France until June 1940 and would spend the rest of the war as a refugee in South Africa.[167] Another baseless rumor that Hitler had told Mussolini that he was ready to withdraw from Poland circulated in diplomatic circles in Fascist Rome in the spring of 1940.[168]

---

162 Kochanski, *The Eagle Unbowed*, 97; Młynarczyk, "Pomiędzy współpracą a zdradą": 107; Zychowicz, *Opcja niemiecka*, 53–54.
163 See the assertion of the British historians Noakes and Pridham, according to whom Hitler clung to the idea of a rump Polish state until the late spring of 1940: Noakes and Pridham, *Nazism*, 923.
164 Wieczorkiewicz, "Wojna polska."
165 Kunicki, *Unwanted Collaborators*, 206–207; Zychowicz, *Opcja niemiecka*, 32–33, 38.
166 Ibid., 53; protocol of the interrogation of Maria Ulmanova and Halszka Rupova, March 6, 1940, USHMM, GK_159_228cz2, 117.
167 Jurkowski, "Bogusław Miedziński": 229–230.
168 Wieniawa-Długoszowski to the French Foreign Minister in Angers, an untitled secret report, March 22, 1940, USHMM, RG-59.036, A-12-3-2_0042-4.

In July, after the fall of France, the Nazi regime resumed its efforts to force London to accept a comprehensive settlement of the European conflict.[169] This new round of diplomacy may have been triggered by statements from neutral representatives in London who claimed that a growing number of British politicians wanted to reconcile with Germany.[170] As was already detailed above, on July 19, Polish ambassador to London Raczyński informed his superiors about the most recent German peace initiative, which was conveyed to the British simultaneously through three independent diplomatic channels. That same day, Hitler gave a speech at the Berlin Opera and said he saw no reason to continue the armed conflict against the British.[171]

Despite the immediate negative reaction by British foreign secretary Lord Halifax, Göring once again approached an intermediary. This time, he met with Dr. Albert Plesman, the founder and director of the Dutch airline KLM, to relay detailed instructions on the contents of the new peace offer. Göring assured the Dutchman that "Poland and Czechoslovakia will not be disturbed in their national development" if Germany and the UK were to reconcile.[172] In early August, Plesman arrived in London to deliver Göring's message to the cabinet of the new premier, Winston Churchill. According to US Navy veteran and historian Walter C. Ansel, Plesman's peace mission came to naught, since it "was too late for any talk. The pivotal moment for talk was far gone down the road of history."[173]

A week after the failure of Plesman's mission, in mid-August 1940, Hans Frank addressed high-ranking GG officials in Kraków and solemnly promised that "there will never again be a Polish state!"[174] But at that point, the geopolitical situation in Europe required more ideological and diplomatic nuance than that, and when Hitler started preparations to invade the Soviet Union, German diplomats got to work on potential allies in the fight against the Russians, approaching the Romanians, the Finns,[175] and, naturally enough, the Poles. It

---

169 Noakes and Pridham, *Nazism*, 779.
170 Memorandum signed by the State Secretary of the German Foreign Office, June 19, 1940, in, *Documents on German Foreign Policy*, 9:620; memorandum signed by the State Secretary of the German Foreign Office, June 22, 1940, ibid., 682.
171 Noakes and Pridham, *Nazism*, 786.
172 Ansel, *Hitler Confronts England*, 155.
173 Ibid., 157; see also: Schreiber, Stegemann, and Vogel, *Das deutsche Reich und der Zweite Weltkrieg*, 122–123.
174 Headquarters of the High Command of the Polish Armed Forces in Exile, 5th Dept., quoted from: "Warschauer Zeitung for the period August 4-16, 1940," August 16, 1940, USHMM, RG-59.047, KOL-25-10-A_264.
175 Förster. "Hitlers Entscheidung": 17.

is therefore not surprising that just two days after Frank's pompous declaration, on August 17, the Polish ambassador to Romania, Roger Raczyński (brother of the Polish ambassador to London), updated his superiors that Nazi diplomats and intelligence officers in Bucharest were trying to talk Polish émigré circles in the country, including representatives of the government-in-exile, into making common cause against the Russians.[176]

In all likelihood, the basis for this notification was a meeting between Raczyński's personal assistant, Jerzy Giedroyc, and a special envoy from Berlin, who had arrived in Bucharest to discuss possible terms for a German-Polish peace settlement. This meeting could either be authorized by the ambassador or held on the assistant's personal initiative. Many years later, Giedroyc bragged that he suggested the Nazis reestablish the sovereignty of his homeland, in exchange for an alliance in the face of the Russian threat. As he wrote candidly in his memoirs: "This was my opinion, [but] it was greeted with skepticism [By whom? The German emissary, the authorities in Berlin, Raczyński, or the Polish government-in-exile?], and that was the end of it."[177]

In reality, the Germans continued to approach the Poles. Several weeks later, a Soviet military intelligence agent (code name: Zigmond) informed his handlers in Moscow that the Germans were in touch with "former Polish political figures."[178] In December 1940, NKVD agents reported a rumor circulating in Warsaw that Hitler would replace the GG with a "new Polish government" under his control and rebuild the Polish army to prepare for "war with the USSR and the occupation of Western Belarus and Ukraine." At the head of this new government would be one of the prominent Poles who had stayed behind, like Janusz Radziwiłł or Władysław Studnicki.[179]

The GG-based sources of the Polish government-in-exile reported similar rumors in the second half of 1940, warning their bosses in London that contacts between the Germans and anti-Sikorski political factions had advanced considerably. Allegedly, the sides were in the process of negotiating the creation

---

176 The Polish Ambassador to Bucharest, Roger Raczyński, to the Polish Foreign Office in London, encrypted telegram No. 55, August 16, 1940, PISM, A-27-I/7c.
177 Giedroyc, *Autobiografia na cztery ręce*, 91.
178 "Appendix: for No. 5/11537 from August 24, 1940, the agent "Zigmond." A note by the Information Department of the Intelligence Agency of the General Staff of the Red Army to Fitin, chief of the Fifth Department of the GUGB NKVD of the USSR, with analysis of the intelligence data attached, September 10, 1940, in Naumov, *1941 god*, 1:225.
179 Special report by the GTU NKVD of the USSR, Intelligence and surveillance report on Germany, December 27, 1940, ibid. 464–465.

of a secret government to be led by Radziwiłł and Studnicki, and Hans Frank's underlings were already printing maps of the new Polish state.[180]

The archival research on which this book is based shows that both Soviet and Polish agents were wrong in one important respect. In the second half of 1940, the Germans had indeed resumed their search for a suitable leader of a new Polish puppet government in Warsaw; and this process was not cut short even when yet another peace offer to the British, promising limited Polish independence, remained unanswered.[181] However the candidate favored by Berlin failed to satisfy the basic requirements that the agents had identified: he was not a celebrity on the level of Witos or Radziwiłł, nor he could boast of a dazzling political career, extensive government experience, or an illustrious pedigree. Making matters worse, this would-be quisling did not even live in occupied Poland, but in the UK, the Third Reich's bitterest enemy.

The Loyal Professor's Double Game

Stanisław Kot, a professor at Kraków's Jagiellonian University, had won recognition in the 1920s for his first-rate scholarship on Polish culture in the sixteenth and seventeenth centuries. Beyond these credentials, his most salient virtue was his decades-long, close friendship with Władysław Sikorski, the soon-to-be leader of the Polish government-in-exile. Born in the 1880s, Sikorski and Kot became close during World War I and remained inseparable ever after. In the second half of the 1930s, Kot became a prominent politician in Witos's People's Party, and with Sikorski joined the staunchest opponents of the Sanation

---

180 Williamson, *The Polish Underground*, 44–45; "Colonel Smolenski, chief of the 6th Department of the High Command of the Polish Armed Forces in Exile, to the Supreme Headquarters of the Polish Armed Forces in Exile, to ministers Kot, Zaleski, and others, copy of a report from Warsaw," August 2, 1940, USHMM, RG-59.047, KOL-25-10-A_258; Colonel Smolenski to Kot. Fragment of a report from Lisbon dated August 16, 1940, August 30, 1940, USHMM, RG-59.047, KOL-25-10-A_274; Budapest, August 16, 1940, an unfinished report by the 6th Department of the High Command of the Polish Armed Forces in Exile, without an addressee, USHMM, RG-59.047, KOL-25-10-A_275; Budapest, August 17, 1940, an unfinished report by the 6th Department of the High Command of the Polish Armed Forces in Exile, without an addressee, USHMM, RG-59.047, KOL-25-10-A_276.

181 This offer was conveyed to London via Stockholm, by the SD operative Ludwig Weissauer, who introduced himself to the British as a special envoy from Ribbentrop. See: McKay, *From Information to Intrigue*, 209–211. In this connection, it is worth noting that even during the Nazi invasion of the Soviet Union, in June 1941, the leader of Vichy France Marhsal Pétain still expressed the opinion that the Germans wanted to set up a vassal state in Poland. See: Neiberg, *When France Fell*, 141.

movement lead by Józef Piłsudski. The politicians and military officers who promoted Sanation had comprised the backbone of Piłsudski's authoritarian regime. Using "healing Polish politics from corruption" as their rallying cry, they ruled Poland from the time of Piłsudski's 1926 coup and remained in power after the marshal's death in 1935 until the outbreak of World War II.[182]

After the September campaign—the Poles have referred to it ever since as the September defeat (*klęska wrześniowa*)—Kot went into exile with many of the country's political and scholarly elite. Following after Sikorski, he arrived in France, where he helped create the Polish government-in-exile and became a deputy prime minister. In June 1940, he and the rest of the cabinet relocated to the United Kingdom. Back in 1939, British intelligence analysts had predicted that Kot would "relieve General Sikorski of most of his political activities. . . maintain the liaison with politicians in Poland and will give special attention to the problems of [Polish] Jews and Ukrainians."[183] This is exactly what happened. Despite having no security or intelligence experience, Kot was appointed interior minister. In addition to his civic duties, usual for such officials in other countries, he oversaw political investigations into his compatriots in the UK and abroad, the growing political resistance movement in occupied Poland, and the anti-German operations happening all across Europe.

Thanks to his exceptionally broad powers, coupled with outstanding analytical abilities, an aptitude for intrigue, and a cunning, suspicious, and vindictive character, Kot quickly became the éminence grise of the Sikorski cabinet and enjoyed a reputation for having more power than Sikorski himself. But many Polish émigrés, military and intelligence officials loathed him, referring to him as the "minister of the internecine war," a nickname that suggested his pernicious influence on the expatriate community and the resistance movement within occupied Poland.[184]

In cabinet meetings, public speeches, and private conversations, Kot fully endorsed Sikorski's foreign policy line, including his total ban on secret contact with the Third Reich. It is partly due to his support that generations of Polish

---

182 "Stanisław Kot," an unfinished information report by MI5, November 26, 1943, TNA, KV 2/3429_5, 24–30; brief summary of the contents of a report by the agent Brit from February 1941, June 6, 1944, TNA, KV 2/3429_5, 70; Jacobmeyer, *Heimat und Exil*, 130; Wieczorkiewicz, *Historia Polityczna Polski*, 125.

183 Weekly Political Intelligence Summary No. 11, Foreign Office, Political Intelligence Department, December 12, 1939, USHMM, RG-59.006.M-FO371/24054, Scan 00259.

184 "Stanisław Kot," an unfinished information report by MI5, November 26, 1943, TNA, KV 2/3429_5; Hułas, *Goście czy intruzi?* 88, 155–156; Sokolnicki, *Dziennik Ankarski*, 258; Tazbir, "Stanisław Kot 1885–1975: biografia polityczna," 161–165; Wieczorkiewicz, *Historia Polityczna Polski*, 125.

historians and their foreign counterparts would later be able to assert that "the Polish government-in-exile was united in its desire to prevent any cooperation with the Nazis."[185] However, new archival findings to be detailed in this book indicate that the Polish powerful minister pursued other tactics heretofore unknown: in the second half of 1940 and at the very beginning of 1941, he engaged in secret contacts with two German diplomats, Franz von Papen and Emil Otto Paul von Rintelen. Each held substantive Nazi credentials. Von Papen served in 1932 as German chancellor, then as Hitler's vice chancellor and ambassador to Austria, assisted with the Anschluss of 1938, and became ambassador to Turkey in 1939.[186] Von Rintelen, a Prussian aristocrat and the younger brother of the military attaché in Rome, made a brilliant career in the German Foreign Office, held a senior post at the German embassy in prewar Warsaw, and later joined Ribbentrop's inner circle.[187]

Apparently, this pair was instructed to gauge the readiness of Stanisław Kot (and, possibly, of Sikorski and his entire cabinet) to switch sides and lead a new Polish government under Hitler's auspices. Kot must have seemed an approachable target: like Witos, his boss in the People's Party, he had been a prominent Germanophile in prewar Poland, spoke German, and, according to contemporary rumors, in his youth had worked briefly as an Austro-Hungarian intelligence agent.[188] Those rumors could very well be true: today we know that Habsburg intelligence recruited pro-Austrian Poles living in Europe and in the Russian Empire, and that these agents provided great assistance to Vienna in World War I.[189]

Remarkably, the person whose wide-ranging business activities in Europe and in the Middle East allowed to bring together Nazi senior diplomats and an exiled Polish minister was himself an émigré with Polish citizenship. Even more remarkably, he was a Jew. In his brief and turbulent life, he spelled and pronounced his name in many different ways, but his real name was Samson Mikiciński.

---

185 Kunicki, *Unwanted Collaborators*, 208.
186 Koeves, *Satan In A Top Hat*.
187 Klee, *Das Personenlexikon*, 498.
188 An undated report titled "Mikiciński Samson," JPIA, Archiwum Osobowe, NZ 154, Sygn. 658.
189 Pethö, *Agenten für den Doppeladler*, 63–72.

Part One

A VILE TRAITOR OR A SUPERHERO?

Chapter 1

From Provincial Polish Jew to Chilean Diplomat

Obscure Origins

"He feared nothing and walked the earth with confidence." So sang Adam Aston, a Jewish Pole, in "Thief in Love," among the most popular Polish songs of 1938. Samson Mikiciński must have known these lyrics, and in fact could have used them as a personal motto.

The particulars of his early life are presently unknown: none of Mikiciński's multifarious acquaintances ever laid eyes on any official document that might verify his nationality or place of birth. Only while being interrogated—in Mandatory Palestine, in 1941, in Polish—did he confirm the basic facts of his formative years.

He was born in November 1895 in Boćki,[1] a small town in Bielsk County in northeastern Poland that, in the nineteenth century, had been an important hub of Jewish religious and social life.[2] While the subject of Mikiciński's religion did not arise in his first interrogation, his Jewish origins were plain. Indeed,

---

1 An undated protocol of the interrogation of Samson Mikiciński, HIA, 800/41/0/-/141 Folder 7, Scan 000967.
2 "Boćki—Historia społeczności."

community records from Boćki and other nearby Polish settlements list a number of Jews with surname Mikiciński.[3]

As subjects of the Russian Empire until 1918, most residents of Boćki spoke Russian as well as they did Polish. Mikiciński confessed that he had studied law in Moscow for three and a half years, confirming both his early fluency and his family's comfortable financial situation: at that time, only the wealthy would be able to afford the kind of schools that could prepare their son for law school in Moscow or room and board in one of Russia's most expensive cities. A Jewish community book from Siemiatycze, a town thirty kilometers from Boćki, lists a Mikiciński family as one of the town's most affluent and the source of their wealth as timber sales and estate leasing.[4] Given their proximity, it is quite possible that he was a relation.

The Palestine interrogation protocol reports that World War I interrupted Mikiciński's university studies: he was called to the front as an artilleryman, suggesting he never qualified as a jurist.[5] It leaves out the details mentioned later by an unverifiable source: that, despite his ethnicity, Mikiciński became an officer in the Russian Imperial Army and received the Order of Saint George, the Russian Empire's highest military decoration; that in October 1917, he commanded the artillery battery defending the Winter Palace in revolutionary Petrograd; and that when the Bolsheviks won, he fled to Ukraine and took up with the anarchist Nestor Makhno, later joining General Anton Denikin's White Army as an artillery officer. The same source also claimed that after Denikin's failed advance on Moscow in October 1919, Mikiciński followed the general to the Crimea, but was evacuated to Istanbul shortly thereafter with other Russian refugees.[6]

The protocol makes clear that Mikiciński's interrogator made no real attempt to reconstruct the details of his life before emigration. Later on, we will discuss the likely reason for this apparent blunder.

Renouncing His Roots

Samson Mikiciński was utterly indifferent to his Jewish roots and ancestral religion. In *Opération Haïfa*, Ladislas Michniewicz notes that the family spoke

---

3 Sukenik, *Kehilat Siemiatich*, 135, 290.
4 Ibid., 135.
5 An undated protocol of the interrogation of Samson Mikiciński, HIA, 800/41/0/-/141 Folder 7, Scan 000967.
6 Michniewicz, *Opération Haïfa*, 14–20.

only Russian and Polish, and that Mikiciński stopped thinking of himself as a Jew after three years in Moscow.[7] Quite plausibly, his alleged service in the Tsarist army, and later with Denikin's forces, only increased his alienation from his Jewish roots. He turned from a provincial Jewish boy into an urbanized Muscovite with a secular academic education and became an active participant in the crucial political and military upheavals of the early twentieth century that shook Russia and the whole world.

In later years, this metamorphosis of Mikiciński's identity made it hard for those who encountered him to pinpoint his background. Thus in December of 1940 did the A/H.2, an agent of the Istanbul-based British sabotage and reconnaissance organization SOE, assert confidently—apparently, on the basis of personal observation—that "Mikiciński [was] born in Russia and brought up as a Russian."[8] Similarly, the Intelligence Department of the exiled Polish General Staff (the Dwójka) refused to recognize Mikiciński as a Pole despite being aware that he was not a Russian, either. Hence, the final report about his espionage case, drawn up by employees of the department in April 1941, refers to him as a Żyd (Polish for Jew) who, on account of his place of birth, could not be considered a Polish citizen.[9] This assessment was shared by Michał Sokolnicki, a veteran Polish diplomat who served as ambassador to Turkey during World War II, and who apparently knew Mikiciński in person. In Sokolnicki's commentaries on his own *Ankara Diary*, which came out in 1965, we find the following assertion: "Mikiciński, a White officer of seemingly Russian origin, was actually a Jew from Russia or Lithuania."[10]

The few Polish publications about Mikiciński repeat this claim, and it can yet be encountered in the early twenty-first century.[11] Still, some dissenting voices in the Polish expatriate community never doubted Mikiciński's Polishness, and a detailed postwar report held in the Piłsudski Institute in Brooklyn notes that Mikiciński easily mingled in Polish circles at home and abroad. He was undoubtedly a Polish Jew.[12]

The archival sources at our disposal contain no physical descriptions of Mikiciński. However, various Polish publications throughout the decades have

---

7 Ibid., 41.
8 An untitled and undated report by agent A/H.2, late December 1940, TNA, HS 4/213, 3.
9 A report by ekspozytura "T" (Turkey), "A Brief Summary of the Espionage Case of Samson Mikiciński," April 2, 1941, HIA, 800/41/0/-/141 Folder 7, Scan 000941.
10 Sokolnicki, *Dziennik Ankarski*, 161.
11 See, for instance, footnote 200 in Ciechanowski, *Polsko-Brytyjska współpraca*, 155; Giedroyc, *Autobiografia na cztery ręce*, 101; Wilamowski, *Honor, zdrada, kaźń*, 83.
12 An undated report titled "Mikiciński Samson," JPIA, Archiwum Osobowe, NZ 154, Sygn. 658.

painted a vivid portrait. Colonel Iranek-Osmecki, a former chief of the Polish underground intelligence and counterintelligence service, describes him thusly: "Mikiciński was a tall, broad-shouldered man, with harsh facial features, bulging eyes, and sagging lips. On the whole, he made a repulsive impression."[13]

This description, which gives off an unmistakable whiff of antisemitism, was subsequently repeated in the works of various Polish authors, including historian Olgierd Terlecki.[14] Today we have no way of checking its veracity—not one verifiable photograph of Mikiciński has survived, only the one on the cover of Michniewicz's book, which was printed without comment or attribution. Two decades later, when Polish émigré historian Roman Buczek reproduced this photograph on the cover of his book, he made no comment about the identity of the person it purported to depict, either.

Getting Acquainted with Berlin

According to Michniewicz, Mikiciński stayed briefly in Istanbul before heading to Paris.[15] However, the protocols of Mikiciński's Palestinian interrogations reveal how, in the very early 1920s, our hero—a provincial Jew born about around the beginning of the century who had already studied in Moscow and served in two different Russian armies—found himself in Berlin.

The early 1920s were one of the most difficult periods in Berlin's history. From the bloody clashes and riots of the immediate postwar years (1918–1920) to the subsequent economic crisis and hyperinflation, which peaked in 1923, the city received an influx of immigrants fleeing political persecution in their home countries and seeking to improve their material situations. Among them were hundreds of thousands of Russian refugees driven out by the Red terror and the marvels of Bolshevik economic policy. Like any other large wave of emigration throughout human history, these new arrivals quickly established their own ghetto in Berlin with an active and ramified communal infrastructure that offered various economic and social services; organized political, religious, and cultural events; and published a large number of newspapers, periodicals, and books. In the shadow of these legitimate enterprises flourished a Russian-speaking criminal underworld running protection rackets, sponsoring brothels and gambling

---

13 Iranek-Osmecki, *Wspomnienia oficera*, 187.
14 Terlecki, *Szkice i polemiki*, 279.
15 Michniewicz, *Opération Haïfa*, 41–42.

dens, and maintaining a black market for firearms and counterfeit currency and documents.¹⁶

Mikiciński entered Germany a stateless refugee but managed to obtain a Polish passport (his native Boćki was now part of independent Poland). He quickly became a respectable Berlin businessman, a partner in the local firm of Otto Schmidt und Koch, a manufacturer of water and gas pipes. The company address Mikiciński gave in his Palestinian interrogation (120 Friedrichstrasse, in the borough of Mitte, the city's most upscale area) indicates that this was a lucrative enterprise, but the freshly minted businessman may have invested the family savings he had prudently withdrawn from Russia into the company. There is also a chance that he served as a launderer for dirty money of dubious origin. Be that as it may, very few Russian immigrants at the time could afford an office in the borough of Mitte, let alone rent an apartment like the one Mikiciński rented on 101 Bismarckstrasse, the central avenue of the west Berlin neighborhood of Charlottenburg, the hub of the glitzy entertainment venues of the German capital.¹⁷ He lived there with his wife, Sofia Segal—a fellow Jew and a native of the city of Dvinsk (present-day Daugavpils in Latvia).¹⁸

The Fiasco in Paris and the Return to Poland

The pleasant life of the Mikicińskis in Berlin was cut short as early as 1923, because of the aforementioned economic crisis. That year, many of the Russian immigrants in Germany were getting ready to move a second time, hoping to settle in the more prosperous Western countries. The most popular destinations were France and the United States. Mikiciński, who had been trying his luck on the Berlin black market, made up his mind to leave only two years later, and at the end of 1925 he showed up in the French capital. His wife and little son stayed behind in Charlottenburg for a time, presumably waiting for the necessary French immigration papers to be ready. It seems that in spite of the losses he had suffered in Germany, Mr. Mikiciński's financial situation at the time was far from desperate. Once in Paris, he settled in the Hôtel Majestic, one of the oldest

---

16 Lembke, *Bankier, Fälscher, Historiker. Der Weg des Isaac Lewin durch die Geschichte seiner Zeit*, 50–51, 114, 142; Malzacher, *Berliner Gaunergeschichten*, 13–15; Oltmer, *Prekäre Duldung und aktive Intoleranz*, 34–36; Schlögel, *Stiefmütterchen Berlin*.
17 An undated protocol of the interrogation of Samson Mikiciński, HIA, 800/41/0/-/141 Folder 7, Scans 000967-8.
18 Segal mentioned as Mikiciński's wife in the following source: an undated protocol of the interrogation of Samson Mikiciński, HIA, 800/41/0/-/141 Folder 7, Scans 000967-8.

and most fashionable establishments of its kind in France, and in Europe and a whole. A decade later, the building of the Majestic would be converted into a government office. After the Nazi occupation of France, it would house the headquarters of the German military High Command. To the end of his days, Mikiciński would retain a soft spot for posh hotels.[19]

There is very little information about Mikiciński's first two years on French soil. After the outbreak of World War II, he would return there in a very different capacity and launch into a frenzy of economic activity. For now, according to his own subsequent testimony in Palestine, he "did nothing."[20] The counterintelligence service of the Polish army in exile would later write a report, that, having arrived in Paris, Mikiciński was unable to secure a permanent source of income, got into trouble with the authorities by drawing an uncovered promissory note, and lived at the expense of his mother, Rosa Leviton, who had moved to Brooklyn, New York.[21] As a result, at a certain point Mikiciński

---

19 Ibid.; Hôtel Le Peninsula Paris, http://www.pss-archi.eu/immeubles/FR-75056-29791.html.
20 An undated protocol of the interrogation of Samson Mikiciński, HIA, 800/41/0/-/141 Folder 7, Scans 000967-8.
21 A report by ekspozytura "T," "A Brief Summary of the Espionage Case of Samson Mikiciński," April 2, 1941, HIA, 800/41/0/-/141 Folder 7, Scan 000941. According to the electronic version of the archives of the American Immigration Service, on November 23, 1926, a woman named Rosa Leviton, aged forty-nine, a native of the town of Boćki (the birthplace of Samson Mikiciński), a married housewife, arrived in the USA as an immigrant, aboard the ocean liner *Leviathan*, which had sailed from the French port of Cherbourg. We may assume, with a high degree of probability, that this was Samson Mikiciński's mother, to whom the Polish counterintelligence service was referring. The American data corroborates both the name mentioned by the Poles and their assertion that Ms. Leviton was already living in the USA at the time when her son was still in France. See: US Department of Labor, Immigration Service, List of Manifest of Alien Passengers for the United States, List 13, SS *Leviathan*. Passengers sailing from Cherbourg, France, November 23, 1926, No. on List: 15, https://heritage.statueofliberty.org/passenger-details. As for Ms. Leviton's ability to materially support her son, who had found himself in dire financial straits, the documents found during the present investigation suggest that she did have this ability (at least theoretically). We are led to this conclusion by the fact that, at a certain stage, Rosa Leviton, who lived in Paris with her son, married Evser Leviton, a successful American Jewish businessman of Russian origin and the founder of Leviton, a major electrical appliance company that has survived to the present day. See the aforementioned electronic document from the Ellis Island Foundation database, according to which Rosa Leviton came to the USA to be reunited with her husband and gave the address of the Leviton factory in Brooklyn as her final destination. See also the newspaper notice of Evser Leviton's death (in February 1929), according to which the departed businessman left behind a grieving widow named Rosa: Leviton, Evser, *New York Times*, February 28, 1929, 20; and the naturalization certificate signed by Rosa herself in September 1929, where she indicates her home address, which is identical to the address of the late Leviton, as given in his obituary: //Leviton, Rose; September 17, 1929, No. 3142339, National Archives Identifier: 73176080, https://catalog.archives.gov/search?q=leviton%20rose. In this connection, we should also mention the postwar testimony of Arthur Hermann, the former noncommissioned officer

lost his wife, who left him for a more financially stable German Jew, and his son, Viktor-Vitaly.[22]

Mikiciński would remain unmarried for the rest of his life (about a decade and a half). However, he was able to cope with this personal drama thanks to his indefatigable and adventurous personality.

As early as 1928, he was spotted in Brussels, and a year later he showed up in Warsaw, penniless but brimming with energy and business ideas. In short order, he was hired by a local trading company named Klemik headquartered in Łódź. He became co-owner of the firm rather quickly (according to rumors, the continuing financial support of his mother helped his rise) and devised an original profit-raising strategy: cooperating with the Soviet Union. His new partners on the Soviet side were the trade attaché at the Soviet embassy in Warsaw and the local office of Sovpoltorg, a Soviet-Polish intergovernmental trading company. With their help, Klemik became the official distributor of various Soviet goods in Poland. This mutually profitable partnership lasted several years and ended in 1934 after a sharp decline in Soviet exports of wheat and other foodstuffs brought about by the errors of Stalin's agrarian policy and the resulting catastrophic harvest shortfall in the USSR, as well as by the Great Depression that had gripped the world.[23] That same year, Sovpoltorg ceased its activities, and its Warsaw office was shut down—but not before its official representatives had lodged a complaint against Klemik to the Polish police and sued the company at the local court. The Soviets claimed that the Polish firm had defrauded them of their share of the profits from the sale of the imported goods. Shortly thereafter, Klemik officially filed for bankruptcy.[24]

---

of the Abwehr from Breslau, according to which Samson's mother lived in Chicago. See: CI Consolidated Interrogation Report No. 13, 10 in Mendelsohn, *The Final Solution*. Quite obviously, this was a simple mistake on the part of Hermann, who was a mere driver and errand boy—and illiterate, to boot (see: ibid., 4). This mistake may be attributed to his superficial acquaintance with Mikiciński, and to his lack of access to the latter's personal file in the operational card index of the Abwehr (coupled with the inability to read that file).

22 An undated protocol of the interrogation of Samson Mikiciński, HIA, 800/41/0/-/141 Folder 7, Scans 000967-8; according to British data, Viktor-Vitaly Mikiciński was born in Berlin on September 17, 1920. See: Q 1212, 18.07.41, HIA, 800/41/0/-/141 Folder 7, Scan 001009.

23 See on the decline in the export of foodstuffs from the USSR in the first half of the 1930s: Bakshin and Nazarenko, *Eksport zernovykh*, 105–120.

24 A report by ekspozytura "T," "A Brief Summary of the Espionage Case of Samson Mikiciński," April 2, 1941, HIA, 800/41/0/-/141 Folder 7, Scan 000941; an undated protocol of the interrogation of Samson Mikiciński, HIA, 800/41/0/-/141 Folder 7, Scans 000967-8; the appendix to the undated report titled "Mikiciński Samson," JPIA, Archiwum Osobowe, NZ 154, Sygn. 658; Kapera, "Niemieckie świadectwa": 60.

While the relevant Polish organs looked into Sovpoltorg's complaint, Mikiciński's frequent visits to the Soviet embassy in Warsaw and contact with official Soviet representatives drew the attention of the famous Dwójka. Ever since the reestablishment of Polish independence in 1918, the intelligence and counterintelligence officers of the young republic had been waging an intense, clandestine war against their Soviet counterparts and their constant attempts to infiltrate Polish political, military, and economic structures; set up a secret Communist network on Polish soil; and use the territory of Poland as a springboard for secret invasions of other countries in Europe and beyond. The Polish counterintelligence community saw the Soviet embassy on Poznańska Street in the very center of Warsaw as a hub of espionage whose employees took full advantage of their diplomatic covers as military, cultural, and trade attachés. Hence, Polish citizens who initiated contact with Soviet embassy personnel—especially those who visited the embassy—would come under the intense scrutiny of the Second Department in hopes of thwarting their potential espionage activity or using them in counterintelligence operations.[25]

But when it came to Mikiciński, Polish intelligence operatives were in for a big surprise. He unexpectedly showed up in person to the Blue Palace, the castle of the noble Zamojski family serving as the official headquarters of the Dwójka, and offered his services as a double agent against the Russians. He calmly explained to his host, Captain Stefan Marek, that the complaint Sovpoltorg had lodged against his company was a ploy to force him into spying for the Soviets; Soviet intelligence representatives had allegedly promised him that, should he agree to become their agent in Poland, they would immediately withdraw all the accusations against him. He claimed that, as a Polish citizen and patriot, he had no desire whatsoever to engage in clandestine work on behalf of the USSR; therefore, he had come to the Dwójka office of his own free will to inform the Polish intelligence of the USSR's offer and receive instructions on what to do next. That said, he did not forget to ask for an advance payment for his future work as an agent, citing extreme poverty that had left him without even tram fare.[26]

Captain Marek took his unexpected visitor up on his offer and entered his name as a candidate for recruitment. After giving Mikiciński a little money, he instructed him to agree to cooperate with the Soviet representatives, then

---

25 Ćwięk, *Przeciw Abwehrze*, 78; Machniak, *Polski wywiad i kontrwywiad wojskowy*, 27–43; Pepłoński, *Funkcjonowanie i efekty*, 194–210. See also: Zdanovich, *Pol'skii krest*, 137–325.
26 The appendix to the undated report titled "Mikiciński Samson," JPIA, Archiwum Osobowe, NZ 154, Sygn. 658.

report to the Dwójka about any assignments he received from them. For a time, Mikiciński worked in this capacity for the Polish counterintelligence, but very soon, his paymasters at the Blue Palace realized that the espionage assignments Mikiciński received from the Russians were nonsensical, and hence utterly harmless to Polish security. Having concluded that they were being hoodwinked by the money-hungry businessman, Captain Marek and his colleagues cut all ties with Mikiciński and ceased to take any interest in his activities in the territory of Poland.[27]

Rescuing Jews and Reaching out to the Nazis

Only after World War II would the anonymous writer of the report held at the Brooklyn archive admit that, because of the total rupture of relations between the Dwójka and Mikiciński, the Polish counterintelligence officers knew nothing about the activities of their former candidate for recruitment from 1934 to 1939.[28] Among other things, the Blue Palace never learned how Mikiciński had managed to avoid penal sanctions for the economic crime of which Sovpoltorg had accused him.

Moreover, it was only in early 1941, and only from the statements Mikiciński made during his interrogation in Palestine, that the Dwójka became aware of Mikiciński's business dealings in the tourism field that started shortly after the Nazi Anschluss of Austria, in March 1938. He acquired Poltur, a well-known Polish travel agency (he wouldn't tell his interrogators the source of the money he used to make the acquisition), and became involved in what the British intelligence would later describe as "transactions on the black bourse, false passports, illegal emigration and general business with Jewish refugees."[29] In his interrogations in the spring of 1941, Mikiciński emphasized the fact that he had rescued German and Austrian Jews (probably wealthy ones), enabling them to immigrate to Latin American countries. One such country was Paraguay. Mikiciński mentioned a trip to London to meet with the Paraguayan vice consul

---

27 Ibid. The new data, uncovered during the present investigation, about Samson's relationship with the Polish counterintelligence service in the prewar period disproves the allegation made by the Polish historian Kapera in 2021, according to which this relationship is inaccessible to historical research. See: Kapera, "Niemieckie świadectwa": 60.
28 Ibid.
29 A top secret report titled "The Paluchowicz Case," copy # 1, July 18, 1941, TNA, HS 4/213; according to Ciechanowski, back in 1937 Samson began to work for a Polish travel agency named Argos, and a year later he became the director of Poltur and the holder of 50% of the stock of that company. See: Ciechanowski, *Polsko-Brytyjska współpraca*, 155, n200.

whose name had since "slipped his mind." He also recalled that the contacts between them had been facilitated by Bauer, an Austrian businessman and the former deputy attorney general of Vienna. The sheer number of Polish transit passports Mikiciński brought the Paraguayan representative to stamp with Paraguayan immigration visas—forty in total!—reflects the true scale of our protagonist's "tourism business" under the cover of Poltur.[30] We may assume that his actions saved the lives of dozens, possibly hundreds of Jews from the countries controlled by Hitler.

At about the same time, in the autumn of 1938, Mikiciński took part in an attempt to help the victims of the tragedy that had transpired in the Polish town of Zbąszyń, near the German border. That disaster was the result of a decision by the Nazi authorities to expel all the Polish Jewish citizens living in the Third Reich, a total of seventeen thousand persons. Polish authorities prevented six thousand refugees whose passports had expired—including children and the elderly—from entering the country, instead housing them in a temporary camp set up in Zbąszyń for this purpose, which had de facto become a small concentration camp.[31] With the help of his Polish assistant, Eugeniusz Bielecki, Mikiciński was able to bribe several officials of the Interior Ministry in Warsaw to issue new passports to some of the inmates of the Zbąszyń camp, enabling those fortunate individuals to move to Latin America.[32]

At the same time, in an attempt to find new ways of smuggling Jews out of the Reich and expanding his business, Mikiciński contacted an old acquaintance of his, a fellow shadowy businessman named Feodor Bobajewski. Nicknamed Bobby by his friends, Bobajewski was a native of Russia but had left the country during the civil war and was living in Prague when Mikiciński got in touch with him. Many years later, the Polish historian Roman Buczek would write (albeit without specifying his sources) that Mikiciński and Bobajewski had originally met in Denikin's army.[33] Be that as it may, it was Bobajewski who arranged the first meeting in Prague between Mikiciński and a high-ranking visitor from the Reich, whose last name was Scholz. Bobajewski referred to him respectfully

---

30 An undated protocol of the interrogation of Samson Mikiciński, HIA, 800/41/0/-/141 Folder 7, Scan 000945.

31 Żebrowski, "Obóz przejściowy w Zbąszyniu"; USHMM, RG-11.001M.0001.00001403, Der Reichsführer SS und Chef der Deutschen Polizei im Reichsministerium des Innern, Schnellbrief, Aufenthaltsverbot für Juden polnischer Staatsangehörigkeit, Berlin, den 26. Oktober 1938.

32 A report by ekspozytura "T," "A Brief Summary of the Espionage Case of Samson Mikiciński," April 2, 1941, HIA, 800/41/0/-/141 Folder 7, Scan 000941; an undated protocol of the interrogation of Samson Mikiciński, HIA, 800/41/0/-/141 Folder 7, Scans 000951.

33 Buczek, *Człowiek do złotych interesów*, 9.

as Herr Doktor.[34] The meeting between Mikiciński and Scholz took place at the renowned Hotel Alcron, which used to host such celebrities as Winston Churchill and Charlie Chaplin in the prewar period.

The results of the discussion between the Polish Jewish businessman and the German official were satisfactory to both sides. Hence, as early as April or May of 1939, Mikiciński and Bobajewski paid Scholz a return visit at his regular residence and workplace, the city of Breslau in eastern Germany. After the war, this city would be annexed to Poland and renamed Wrocław. However, at this time, Breslau lay in the territory of the Third Reich and was an important center of the espionage and sabotage campaign waged by the Abwehr against the Second Polish Republic.[35] During this second meeting, Scholz, ever the generous host, introduced Mikiciński and Bobajewski to his two assistants: Hauptmann (captain) Erich Nobis and Arthur.[36] At this point, the two guests realized that Scholz was not just a German official, but an officer of the Wehrmacht. Nobis has still not been conclusively identified, but Arthur was, in all likelihood, Arthur Hermann, Scholz's chauffeur and factotum, who would be arrested and interrogated by American counterintelligence after the war.[37] A year later, the two would play a key role in Mikiciński's activities in the territory of occupied Poland.

---

34 According to Buczek, Scholz's true name was Heinz Habian, and he was an Abwehr officer in the rank of major. See: Buczek, *Człowiek do złotych interesów*, 9. A survey of the Polish and German documentary sources that are accessible to us at present has failed to confirm the existence of an Abwehr officer of that name in the relevant time period. That said, postwar American counterintelligence documents enable us to confidently identify Scholz as Heinz-Heinrich Fabian, chief of the foreign counterintelligence section (III F) of the Abwehr station in Breslau (Abwehrstelle Breslau), who was later transferred to Sofia, the capital of Bulgaria. See: CI Consolidated Interrogation Report No. 13, 3 in Mendelsohn, *The Final Solution*; "Klausnitzer, Alfred" in NARA RG 263, NN3-263-02-008, Box 66, Folder 4, 3, https://catalog.archives.gov/id/139357331. According to the Polish historian Grzegorz Bębnik, Fabian was born in 1900 and died shortly before the end of the war, aged forty-four. In the late 1930s, he served in the branch of his organization attached to the Headquarters of the 8th Military District of the Wehrmacht in Breslau. In 1937, he was promoted to the rank of captain, and was made a major three years later. See: Bębnik, *Sokoły kapitana Ebbinghausa*, 489. According to Zdzisław Kapera, the Polish intelligence organs failed to identify Scholz-Fabian because of his mastery of spycraft, which enabled him to keep his identity secret. See: Kapera, "Niemieckie świadectwa": 62.
35 Ćwięk, *Przeciw Abwehrze*, 45, 54–55, 60–61, 120.
36 A report by ekspozytura "T," "A Brief Summary of the Espionage Case of Samson Mikiciński," April 2, 1941, HIA, 800/41/0/-/141 Folder 7, Scan 000941; an undated protocol of the interrogation of Samson Mikiciński, HIA, 800/41/0/-/141 Folder 7, Scans 000951.
37 Zdzisław Kapera claims that the true name of Captain Erich Nobis was Ernst Nobis (1901–1963). A person of that name is mentioned in various German documents as an Austrian officer who, following the Anschluss of 1938, became a captain in the Wehrmacht; he subsequently fought in the territory of the Soviet Union, where he was awarded the Iron Cross for his service. At the same time, Kapera admits that he has not found the name of Ernst

In 1941, summing up the Mikiciński affair, the Polish military counterintelligence service would identify Scholz, Nobis, and Arthur as a trio of Abwehr employees. Its final verdict: during his first trip to Breslau, Mikiciński accepted the Nazis' offer to become their secret agent in Poland.[38] Arthur Hermann expressed a similar view—in his postwar interrogation by the Americans, he gave some very terse information on Mikiciński, full of inaccuracies and blatant errors, claiming that Mikiciński had been one of Scholz's most valuable agents.[39] This assertion is not supported by any of the German documents at our disposal, nor by any of the oral or written testimonies Mikiciński gave in his Palestinian interrogation or elsewhere. It will be analyzed in detail below, and we will present clear evidence exonerating Mikiciński of the charge of being a German spy. But for now, let us look at some alternative explanations of what went down between Mikiciński and Scholz in Breslau in the spring of 1939.

The most likely possibility is that the Abwehr bigshot from Breslau, like many of his colleagues and fellow Nazi functionaries, decided to use his official position for monetary gain, profiting from the emigration of German and Austrian Jews out of the Reich. To this end, he got in touch with the Jewish businessman, who had been successful in this field, and who therefore seemed like a very promising partner for money-making, not intelligence-gathering purposes. Such partnerships between businesspeople and intelligence operatives were very common in those days, and they are far from rare even today. In cases like these, the business side acts as the handler of the intelligence operative, and not the other way round.

Nobis in the prewar lists of employees of the Breslau branch of the Abwehr (Ast Breslau). See: Kapera, "Niemieckie świadectwa": 61. The identification of "Arthur" as Arthur Hermann was made possible thanks to the protocol of his interrogation by the Americans in January 1946, where he described his work at the Breslau branch of the Abwehr and his contacts with Scholz-Fabian and Mikiciński. His American interrogators characterized him as a "a typical peasant, illiterate but extremely shrewd," and stressed the fact that the information given by him, although deemed reliable, was "limited to personalities and incidents." See: CI Consolidated Interrogation Report No. 13, 4 in Mendelsohn, *The Final Solution*.

38 A report by ekspozytura "T," "A Brief Summary of the Espionage Case of Samson Mikiciński," April 2, 1941, HIA, 800/41/0/-/141 Folder 7, Scan 000941.

39 CI Consolidated Interrogation Report No. 13, 10. In addition to his assertion that Samson had been recruited by the Abwehr, Arthur Hermann also made the following claims in his aforementioned interrogation by the Americans: that, on the eve of the war, Samson was on the staff of the Chilean embassy in Warsaw; that, after the military defeat of Poland in September 1939, he smuggled 70-80 million złotys, which he had received from the Polish government-in-exile, into the occupied country; that he smuggled twelve prominent Polish Jews from Warsaw into Turkey; and, finally, that his mother lived in the US city of Chicago. As we will show later, all these assertions were inaccurate, not to say erroneous.

Another possible explanation of the events in Breslau that should not be dismissed out of hand is that Scholz was carrying out an assignment from his boss, Admiral Canaris. The latter, known to have been hostile to Hitler's regime, had tried even before the invasion of Poland to establish a secret dialogue with the Western governments; these efforts included aiding Jews. With this aim in mind, Canaris would orchestrate the escape of the Lubavitcher Rebbe, Yosef Yitzchak Schneersohn, from occupied Warsaw less than a year later in late 1939.[40] Even Polish historian Zdzisław Kapera, who believed Arthur Hermann's claim that Mikiciński had been recruited by the Germans (even though Kapera deemed the former's testimony inaccurate, and possibly intended to impress the Americans), ultimately concluded that it was Canaris, playing his geopolitical card, who stood behind the relationship between Scholz and his Polish Jewish confidant.[41]

After the end of the war, certain elements of the Polish diaspora in the West, including former military intelligence officers, would claim that Mikiciński's connections with the Abwehr began not in the spring of 1939, but much earlier. Mikiciński was allegedly recruited by the Germans back in the early 1920s, when he lived with his family in Berlin; in exchange for his services as a spy, he was granted full freedom of action in his international financial machinations.[42] This claim—like most other assertions on the subject of Mikiciński, derived from rumors circulating among the Polish émigrés—suffers from a fatal weakness: it is not corroborated by any of the Polish, German, or British intelligence documents that are accessible to us today.

In the Frock Coat of a Diplomat

Regardless of the real reason behind the new partnership between Mikiciński and Scholz, the former behaved quite oddly upon returning from Breslau. He sold his shares in the prospering Poltur travel agency that had netted him a monthly income of up to three thousand złotys (equivalent to six hundred US dollars, or half of the annual income of the average American), then decided to

---

40 Rigg, *Rescued from the Reich*. See also the article by the Polish historian Andrzej Brzeziecki, about the alleged involvement of Canaris in the evacuation of the spouses of Polish émigré leaders to the West via Berlin, with the goal of facilitating behind-the-scenes peace talks with Britain; Brzeziecki says nothing about any role played by Samson Mikiciński in this process: Brzeziecki, "Zagadka Wilhelma Canarisa."
41 Kapera, "Niemieckie świadectwa": 69, 74-75.
42 Lisiewicz, *W imieniu Polski podziemnej*.

lay low until early August 1939, when an even more inexplicable event occurred. Héctor Briones Luco, the Chilean chargé d'affaires in Istanbul, unexpectedly showed up in Warsaw while the city was gearing up for a possible war. The sole purpose of his trip was to deliver an authentic diplomatic passport of his country to Mikiciński, who was languishing in idleness. At that time, there was no permanent Chilean diplomatic representative in the Polish capital. Hence, with Luco's help, our protagonist—a Jewish native of Boćki, a former Russian law student and artillery officer, a failed Polish counterintelligence agent, and a recently prosperous local businessman and partner of the German Abwehr—became the only Chilean diplomat in the territory of Poland.[43]

None of the documents or other sources at our disposal offer any explanation for Luco's actions. The counterintelligence operatives of the Polish General Staff would later claim that the Chilean was working for the Nazis, who wished to safeguard their new super-agent during the coming German-Polish military clash by granting him the status of a foreign diplomat. As evidence of this hypothesis, they would cite the close ties between Berlin and faraway Santiago.[44] Modern historians have indeed confirmed the existence of a special German-Chilean relationship, both on the eve of World War II and after its outbreak. Remarkably, it turns out that the Nazis allowed Chilean diplomats to operate even in those German-occupied cities from which all other official foreign representatives

---

43 A report by ekspozytura "T," "A Brief Summary of the Espionage Case of Samson Mikiciński," April 2, 1941, HIA, 800/41/0/-/141 Folder 7, Scan 000941; Polish historians claim that, at the time described here, Luco served as the Chilean *chargé d'affaires* in Brussels. See footnote 200 in Ciechanowski, *Polsko-Brytyjska współpraca*, 155; Rutkowski, *Stanisław Kot*, 144. However, an examination of the Turkish sources makes it clear that, as of 1939, Luco had been serving as the chargé d'affaires in Istanbul for nine years. See: Cikar, *Türkischer Biographischer Index*, 211. In 2021, the Polish scholar Zdzisław Kapera wrote that Mikiciński had allegedly received a Chilean diplomatic passport after beginning work at the secretariat of the Chilean legation in Warsaw; he did not bring up Luco's name in this context. See: Kapera, "Niemieckie świadectwa": 60-61, 69. We must stress that this hypothesis is in complete contradiction to the archival evidence at our disposal. It may have originated from the testimony given by Samson himself in one of his Palestinian interrogations, according to which he had received the Chilean diplomatic passport "from the ambassador," by whom he meant Briones Luco. In this connection, we should cite the explanation given by ekspozytura "T" (Turkey) of the Dwójka, according to which "there was no [Chilean] embassy [in Warsaw], no secretariat, and no questions [in need of resolution]; there was only Briones, the brother of Ambassador Briones from Rome, who showed up in Warsaw four weeks before the outbreak of war and took up residence at the Hotel European. The sole purpose of [this] Chilean embassy was issuing a diplomatic passport to Samson Mikiciński in mid-August 1939." See: Major Binkowski, "A Brief Summary of the Espionage Case of Samson Mikiciński," April 2, 1941, HIA, 800/41/0/-/141 Folder 7, Scan 000942.

44 Ibid., Scan 000941.

had been expelled.⁴⁵ Furthermore, according to the Chilean sources that are accessible to us at present, Luco, a veteran of the Chilean Foreign Office, had served as consul general in Hamburg in the early 1930s and had even published a brochure on German-Chilean relations; his elder brother, Ramon Briones Luco, was appointed the Chilean ambassador to Fascist Rome in 1939.⁴⁶ Thus, the Polish counterintelligence service had reasonable grounds to suspect the hand of Germany in Mikiciński's acquisition of the Chilean passport.

However, as in the case of his dealings with Scholz, Mikiciński's relationship with the Chilean may have had a different explanation that had nothing to do with espionage. According to the protocol of Mikiciński's interrogations in Palestine on March 15, 1941, this relationship was purely commercial in nature. In exchange for giving diplomatic cover to the frenetic activities of the businessman from Boćki on the European continent and allowing him to use diplomatic mail, the Chilean chargé d'affaires regularly demanded and received thousands of dollars, either in cash or in transfers to a private account in the New York branch of the National City Bank.⁴⁷ This statement is corroborated by the contents of a letter mailed in November 1940 from Istanbul to London by the former Polish ambassador to Bucharest, Roger Raczyński, which indicated that Mikiciński had drawn Luco "into various financial speculations in the territory of Romania."⁴⁸

Thus, it is quite possible that Mikiciński's new diplomatic status was not a gift bestowed upon him by some non-existent handlers in the German military intelligence, but rather an acquisition, bought at a very steep price, to protect himself and his business interests throughout Europe, which was hurtling toward the abyss of a new war. This assessment seems to have been shared by the abovementioned Polish ambassador to Turkey, Michał Sokolnicki. His *Ankara Diary* tells us that, even prior to meeting Luco, Mikiciński had done a stint as the (equally advantageous) honorary Peruvian consul.⁴⁹ Unfortunately, we have no other evidence to confirm this episode in his turbulent life.

---

45 Breitman, *Intelligence and the Holocaust*, 24–25.
46 Ramón Briones Luco, AGH, Lista de representantes [cit. 2009-08-15], disponible en: http://163.247.50.16 >; AGH, Ministerio de RR.EE. de Chile. Oficios intercambiados con las Misiones y Consulados de Chile en Europa, Egipto y Australia, De: 18-01-1943 A: 10-12—1943, N° 2101 Letra, http://163.247.50.16 >.
47 A protocol of the interrogation of Samson Mikiciński, March 15, 1941, HIA, 800/41/0/-/141 Folder 7, Scan 000966.
48 Ambassador R. Raczyński to the Polish Foreign Minister in London. On the temporary cessation of Polish-Romanian relations, secret telegram, November 30, 1940, PISM, PRM.32, 32.
49 Sokolnicki, *Dziennik Ankarski*, 161.

Mikiciński did not reveal this wondrous transformation into a foreign diplomat to anyone,[50] and the Polish security services never learned of it on their own. For one thing, as stated above, they had stopped taking any interest in the fate of their former source back in 1934, having dismissed him as unreliable. And secondly, in August 1939, they had bigger things to worry about. On the twenty-third of that last month of peace, Berlin and Moscow unexpectedly signed a nonaggression pact, which de facto gave the Germans free rein ahead of their planned military invasion of Poland on September 1. In the final few days leading up to this tragic event, the Polish intelligence and counterintelligence services devoted all their attention to trying to puzzle out the true intentions of their western and eastern neighbors. As a result, the newly minted Chilean diplomat in the Polish capital was left alone, free to act as he saw fit.

---

50 Protocol of the interrogation of Samson Mikiciński, March 6, 1941, HIA, 800/41/0/-/141 Folder 7, Scan 000963.

Chapter 2

The Miracle Worker of Occupied Warsaw

The Escape from Hell as a Pleasure Trip

The first shots of the German-Polish military conflict that would enter history as the opening salvo of World War II were fired on the Westerplatte peninsula near the port city of Danzig (Gdańsk). For a whole week, the small Polish garrison of the fortress on this tiny strip of land heroically repelled the assault of thousands of enemy soldiers, who were supported by sea and air power. By September 7, 1939, when the surviving defenders of Westerplatte finally laid down their arms, the German invasion force, numbering about two million soldiers and officers and more than four thousand airplanes and tanks, had managed to penetrate deep into Polish territory, approaching Warsaw.[1]

By that time, Mikiciński was already very far from the front lines. Almost two years later, in the summer of 1941, the British intelligence service would claim that he left the territory of Poland only after the end of the military campaign, and that he arrived in Paris, via Berlin and Brussels, together with his new boss, Hector Briones Luco.[2] Ambassador Sokolnicki partly corroborated the British version, writing in his *Ankara Diary* that Samson and Luco had fled from Warsaw

---

1 Tusiewicz, *Historia Polski*, 360–363.
2 A top secret report titled "The Paluchowicz Case," copy # 1, July 18, 1941, TNA, HS 4/213.

to Bucharest together.³ By contrast, Jerzy Giedroyc, a Polish journalist and diplomat who hated Mikiciński, and whom we will meet again later, asserted in his memoirs that "the Russian Jew who became the Honorary Chilean Consul in Warsaw... reemerged in Istanbul following the outbreak of war."⁴

However, our protagonist gave a very different account of his activities in September 1939 to his interrogators in Palestine. By his own admission, as early as September 5, when the weakness of the Polish defenses had become apparent and the German bombing raids on Warsaw intensified, he drove out of the city in his car, heading toward the Polish-Lithuanian border. He was accompanied on this trip by two young ladies: Irena Szarska-Potocka, ex-wife of Count Jaroslaw Potocki, Polish fashion queen of 1932, and popular cabaret dancer; and her friend, Krystyna Ostrowska-Koch, the ex-wife of the French Baron Koch and a French citizen. The border posts on the Polish side were deserted. Thousands of Polish refugees, both civilians and soldiers of the defeated army, were storming the Lithuanian checkpoints, hoping to escape the horrors of the Nazi occupation. Many of them were forced to turn back, and some even lost their lives in the chaos that prevailed in the border zone.

Mikiciński and his companions were seemingly untouched by any of this. Thanks to Mikiciński's Chilean passport, which listed Irena as his wife, the three were able to pass unscathed through that seething mass of humanity, and, once safely on Lithuanian soil, they drove on to Kaunas, and thence to the Latvian capital of Rīga. There, the fortunate refugees left their car behind and boarded a flight to Stockholm, where they hitched a car ride to Copenhagen. There, they boarded a second flight, this time to Amsterdam. They then took a train from the Dutch capital to Brussels before setting out on the final leg of their journey, which turned out to be another car ride. In the end, only a few days after leaving the burning Poland behind, they drove into carefree Paris. Later, the Polish military counterintelligence officers would describe this dizzying odyssey as a pleasure trip while admitting that they were at a loss as to how Mikiciński had managed to afford the passage to France for himself and the two young women.⁵

---

3   Sokolnicki, *Dziennik Ankarski*, 161.
4   Giedroyc, *Autobiografia na cztery ręce*, 101.
5   A report by ekspozytura "T," "A Brief Summary of the Espionage Case of Samson Mikiciński," April 2, 1941, HIA, 800/41/0/-/141 Folder 7, Scan 000941; protocol of the interrogation of Samson Mikiciński; March 6, 1941, HIA, 800/41/0/-/141 Folder 7, Scan 000963; an undated protocol of the interrogation of Samson Mikiciński, HIA, 800/41/0/-/141 Folder 7, Scan 000967; a report by the Dwójka titled "Mikiciński—information," June 1941, HIA, 800/41/0/-/141 Folder 7, Scan 001006.

On this question, we may reasonably assume that, thanks to his successful prewar career and the timely sale of his shares in Poltur for the sum of almost fifty thousand dollars, Mikiciński was then in possession of considerable funds, at least some of which had been deposited in Western banks. Thus, paying for a Warsaw-Berlin trip for three persons out of his own pocket was not a problem. However, as stated above, the Polish secret service had ceased to keep tabs on Mikiciński long before the outbreak of war, so its officers knew nothing about his financial situation at the time.

Major Tadeusz Nowiński, a veteran of the Polish military intelligence, would testify after the end of the war—citing a source known only to him—that during the trip, as Mikiciński was passing through the Netherlands, he allegedly got in touch with the local station of the Abwehr to get instructions pertaining to his job as a German spy.[6] By way of comment, we must reiterate that all such accusations against Mikiciński have one crippling flaw: they cannot be corroborated by any of the documents at our disposal.

The Great Comeback in France

When he arrived in the French capital, Mikiciński learned that immediately after the outbreak of war, his ex-wife's new husband had been detained by the local authorities but was able to ransom or bribe his way to freedom, then took his family to Britain. Mikiciński, who had not seen his son for eight years, immediately flew to London to meet Viktor-Vitaly. He spent three days in the British capital, staying at the luxurious Savoy Hotel (a choice of accommodation that reflects both his abiding fondness for posh hotels and his continuing financial wellbeing).[7] It is quite possible that he then lived on his prewar savings and on the profits from the very successful sale of Poltur. However, a widespread view among Polish historians, which is probably based on rumors circulating among the Polish diaspora, holds that, from the very beginning of his second sojourn in Paris, Mikiciński became involved in currency speculations that allegedly earned him tens of thousands of dollars.[8]

Regardless of its origins, Mikiciński's fortune immediately made him a welcome guest in the homes of the Parisian elite. There, he liked to present

---

6   Lisiewicz, *W imieniu Polski podziemnej*.
7   Undated protocols of the interrogations of Samson Mikiciński, spring 1941, HIA, 800/41/0/-/141 Folder 7, Scans 000945 and 000967.
8   Szczepański, "Błyskotliwy agent czy zdrajca?"

himself as either a former officer of some army or as a theater or movie actor. He adopted a Frenchified form of his true name, Sanson de Mikiciński. In an attempt to enhance his social standing and expand his business network, he may also have paid for the upscale lodgings of Irena and Krystyna, the women who had accompanied him from Warsaw, and encouraged the two young ladies to socialize with suitors from the local upper classes and the foreign diplomatic corps.[9] Possibly, it was this calculated use of feminine charms that quickly enabled Mikiciński to have Luco installed as the official Chilean chargé d'affaires of the Polish government-in-exile, which was then based in France. Mikiciński, a master of backstage intrigue, became Luco's private secretary and office manager—and even more crucially, the permanent liaison between the Chilean diplomat and the Polish Foreign Office in exile. These appointments took place in early October 1939, mere weeks after our protagonist's flight from Warsaw.[10]

About a month later, in the first days of November, Mikiciński acted in his new diplomatic capacity to meet in Paris with Count Morsztyn, head of the Protocol Department of the Polish Foreign Office. The latter, upon learning that his interlocutor was not just a solicitous representative of a faraway, exotic country, but a Polish citizen with extensive connections in Europe and in occupied Poland, immediately introduced his new acquaintance to Prince Sapieha, the office manager of General Kazimierz Sosnkowski. A renowned military officer, aristocrat, and intellectual, Sosnkowski was one of the founders of the Polish army, the former representative of Poland to the League of Nations, and a relative of the late Marshal Piłsudski—and was regarded as the leader of the anti-Sikorski camp consisting of supporters of the former Sanation regime. He enjoyed such popularity among the Polish military and civilian émigrés—and among those still living in Poland—that Sikorski decided to let him join his cabinet as a minister without portfolio, and he even appointed him chairman of the Committee of Ministers for Homeland Affairs (Komitet Ministrów dla Spraw Kraju). As part of his new duties, Sosnkowski was responsible for fostering ties with the recently established Union of Armed Struggle (Związek Walki Zbrojnej), a clandestine Polish combat organization and the predecessor of the more famous Home Army.[11]

Upon meeting, Mikiciński and Sapieha immediately recalled their prewar contacts as businessmen. The Prince was happy to reconnect with his erstwhile

---

9 A report by the Dwójka titled "Mikiciński—information," June 1941, HIA, 800/41/0/-/141 Folder 7, Scan 001006; Strumph-Wojtkiewicz, *Piąta kolumna w Paryżu*, 102, 116.
10 See the same report by the Dwójka titled "Mikiciński—information."
11 Hułas, *Goście czy intruzi?*, 73–74, 78–79; Wieczorkiewicz, *Historia polityczna Polski*, 121, 123.

acquaintance, who had since become a foreign diplomat, and was now offering his services as a defender of the Polish national interests (such generous offers were not at all self-evident in those days). Hence, he hastily granted Mikiciński an audience with his boss, Sosnkowski, and Sikorski himself. Mikiciński assured the two Polish grandees that, as a citizen of Poland, he deemed it his duty to aid his suffering homeland. He informed them of his upcoming trip to occupied Warsaw—allegedly in order to liquidate the abandoned Chilean legation in the city—and offered to serve as a courier, delivering money and secret messages to Sosnkowski and Sikorski's contacts in the Polish capital.[12]

According to Polish and British intelligence sources, the meeting between Mikiciński and Sikorski lasted no more than a quarter-hour. And yet, its outcome was nothing short of fantastic: Sikorski asked a person whom he had never seen before, who had undergone no background check for possible connections with the enemy, to contact numerous individuals in occupied Poland—including the prime minister's wife and daughter, who had stayed behind in the defeated country living under assumed names. General Sosnkowski likewise asked Mikiciński to convey a calming message to his wife, who had also remained in Warsaw. The relevant functionaries of the new Polish government were immediately instructed from above to assist Mikiciński's mission in every possible way. One of them, Colonel Henryk Bagiński from Sikorski's chancellery, gave Mikiciński a large sum in cash, blank international passports, and secret messages to various persons in Poland.[13]

What was the reason the exiled Polish leaders had such amazing trust in Mikiciński? This question would later puzzle British intelligence officers. The best explanation they could come up with was the severe mental stress suffered by Sikorski and Sosnkowski as a result of the military, political, and personal tragedy the two had experienced in September 1939. According to the British, it was this extreme psychological state that forced the Polish prime minister and

---

12 An undated message titled "Mikiciński Samson," JPIA, Archiwum Osobowe, NZ 154, Sygn. 658; a report by ekspozytura "T" titled "A Brief Summary of the Espionage Case of Samson Mikiciński," April 2, 1941, HIA, 800/41/0/-/141 Folder 7, Scans 000942-3; the undated protocol of an interrogation of Samson Mikiciński, spring 1941, ibid., Scan 000952; a top secret report titled "The Paluchowicz Case," copy # 1; July 18, 1941, TNA, HS 4/213.

13 The undated protocol of an interrogation of Samson Mikiciński, spring 1941, HIA, 800/41/0/-/141 Folder 7, Scan 000952; protocol of the interrogation of Samson Mikiciński; March 15, 1941, ibid., Scan 000966; a report by ekspozytura "T" titled "A Brief Summary of the Espionage Case of Samson Mikiciński," April 2, 1941, ibid., Scans 000942-3; "The Case of P.," a synopsis of D.S.(E) P2446; March 24, 1941, TNA, HS 4/213; a top secret report titled "The Paluchowicz Case," copy # 1; July 18, 1941, ibid.

his charismatic cabinet member to grasp at every straw in a desperate attempt to rescue their wives and daughters from the clutches of the Nazi occupiers.[14]

Nowadays, we know for certain that in early 1940, the Polish government-in-exile had information about "mass arrests of [Polish] women, especially officers' wives, who were to be deported into the Reich as agricultural laborers or sent to the Western Front to pleasure German soldiers."[15] This may serve as an indirect confirmation of the British claim about the despair that gripped the senior Polish officials, driving them into the arms of an international swindler. We may assume that by late 1939, when they met Mikiciński, Sikorski and his entourage were aware of the terrible fate that awaited their female relatives in the occupied homeland, and they were therefore prepared to put their trust in any character, no matter how shady, who held out the promise of miraculous deliverance for their kin.

However, we may also posit some alternative explanations for Mikiciński's transformation into the trusted courier of the Polish leadership. Here, we may take advantage of certain facts that were unknown to the British intelligence agencies at the time. These facts have to do both with the highly complex relations among Polish exiles, and with the intentions and actions of the German side. As present-day historians know, and as this book will expound in great detail in connection with the Mikiciński affair, the earliest channels of communication between the Polish émigré elite and occupied Poland, open as early as the autumn of 1939, were controlled by the proponents of the Sanation—the masters of prewar Poland and bitter opponents of the Sikorski government. Hence, it seems quite logical that Sikorski and his men, aiming to establish personal control over the nascent resistance movement in their occupied homeland, were happy to seize on the unexpected opportunity Mikiciński provided to communicate directly with their supporters and family members who had stayed behind.

There is yet another possible reason for their amazingly warm reception: Mikiciński may have given them a personal, secret message from a high-ranking German official. A likely candidate for this role was Admiral Canaris, chief of the Abwehr. As stated above, in 1939, Canaris made several tentative overtures to the West to discuss the possible removal of Hitler from power. In this connection, he was quite capable of extending personal security guarantees to

---

14 "The Case of P.," a synopsis of D.S.(E) P2446, March 24, 1941, TNA, HS 4/213.
15 "Protocol of the interrogation of Ms. Helena Lisova, who left Warsaw on February 15, 1940," an undated document, USHMM, GK_159_228cz2, 35; "[Interrogation protocol] of P.H.R., who left Warsaw on February 15, 1940," an undated document, ibid., 40.

relatives of the fugitive Polish leaders who had remained in Poland. In support of this version, we may cite the story of the rescue of the Polish countess Halina Szymańska, who traveled to Switzerland with the assistance of the Abwehr, and who later served as an intermediary between that body and the British intelligence service;[16] and the similar story of the wife of a high-ranking Polish officer, who, with Mikiciński's help, was brought to London from Poland via Berlin, and whom Canaris received in person in the German capital. This story, too, will be told later on.

The Office on Frascati Street

Mikiciński's business activities as a Chilean diplomat outside France stood in marked contrast to the ostentatious, even flamboyant pose that he struck in Parisian high society. The professional side of his life was concealed behind an impenetrable and meticulously planned layer of secrecy, which would have been the envy of many contemporary intelligence services. Thanks to these measures, not a single soul in Paris—except for Luco, Mikiciński's direct superior—knew the exact dates of his first trip to occupied Warsaw.

Much later, British intelligence would assume that this journey must have taken place sometime in late November or early December of 1939 (about a month after Mikiciński's abovementioned audience with Sikorski, and three and a half after his flight from Poland). In a confidential report published in July 1941, a nameless analyst of the British SOE asserted that it was Mikiciński who had convinced Luco to visit Warsaw in order to check up on the abandoned Chilean legation in the city, and that the initially reluctant Chilean eventually relented and empowered his "secretary and office manager" to "make sure that their trip was safe."[17] The British document does not specify whether Luco was aware of the secret assignments Sikorski and Sosnkowski gave Mikiciński, or of the Polish-Jewish businessman's German connections. However, given the businesslike nature of the relationship between Mikiciński and Luco, we may assume with a high degree of probability that some of the money received by the former from Colonel Bagiński was spent to convince the latter of the extreme necessity of the trip.

From Paris to Warsaw, the travelers passed through the German cities of Aachen and Berlin. Upon arriving in the capital of the Reich, Mikiciński and

---

16 Jeffery, *MI6*, 380–382, 511–512; Orbach, *The Plots Against Hitler*, 145–146.
17 A top secret report titled "The Paluchowicz Case," copy # 1; July 18, 1941, TNA, HS 4/213.

Luco stayed at the upscale Hotel Eden, whose famous bar had been the prewar haunt of numerous celebrities including Erich Maria Remarque and Marlene Dietrich. Mikiciński immediately sent a telegram to Feodor Bobajewski, his friend and former partner from Prague, and Bobajewski hurried to Berlin to link up with the Abwehr officer Erich Nobis. Together, the two went to meet the visitors at Hotel Eden. It was Nobis who supplied the trio of Mikiciński, Luco, and Bobajewski with the necessary documents guaranteeing freedom of movement in Reich territory. This done, the unusual company of four—a Chilean, a Jew, a Russian, and a German—traveled to Breslau, to rendezvous with Nobis's high-ranking colleague, Scholz. Mikiciński explained to Luco that this was merely a formal visit to an influential German official, who would give them permission to travel on to Warsaw (naturally, in exchange for money). Scholz received Mikiciński and Luco cordially, putting a personal chauffeur named Arthur at their disposal whom Mikiciński knew from his prewar visit to Breslau. This time, Arthur had to accompany the two diplomats to the occupied Polish capital, doing everything in his power to help them accomplish their goals. The Abwehr man did as he was told, taking Mikiciński and Luco to Łódź, and thence to Warsaw, in a private car. Once there, he took care of all the needs of the two men.[18]

In the conquered Polish capital, Mikiciński and the Chilean saw the grim reality of the war: streets pockmarked with bomb craters and artillery blasts, a population stunned and traumatized by the unexpected disaster, and the ubiquitous signs of the presence of the new German civil administration, which was swiftly and brutally bringing the Polish territory to heel. Mikiciński, who planned to spend only a few days in the city, wasted no time bemoaning the loss of the prewar paradise now gone forever. Apart from checking up on the condition of the Chilean legation (the official reason for his visit), he had two crucial tasks: finding and renting an office space for future work in the territory of the General Government and establishing contact with the families of Sikorski and Sosnkowski.

He accomplished the first task very quickly renting an office on 2 Frascati Street, an elegant, four-story house on a tranquil street in the very center of Warsaw, right across from the former government quarter. It would serve as Mikiciński's base of operations for the next six months, until May 1940. Looking

---

18 Ibid.; protocol of the interrogation of Samson Mikiciński, March 6, 1941, HIA, 800/41/0/-/141 Folder 7, Scan 000963; protocol of the interrogation of Samson Mikiciński, March 15, 1941, ibid., Scan 000966; undated protocol of the interrogation of Samson Mikiciński, spring 1941, ibid., Scan 000967.

through the large office window at the Nazi flags festooning the facade of the orphaned presidential chancellery, he took care of the business of the Chilean legation and the Polish government-in-exile, as well as of his own private affairs. Initially, he hired only two local women to work at the new office. One of these, Anna "Nyusya" Alexandrova, was an old acquaintance of his from the Russian period of his life. They were soon joined by Feodor "Bobby" Bobajewski, who had moved from Prague to Warsaw for this purpose, and by Bobajewski's friend and partner in shady business, the Ukrainian expatriate Leonid Volokhov. The latter found lodgings on Poznańska Street that used to house the prewar Soviet embassy and began procuring German exit visas for the individuals whom Mikiciński had to extricate from the General Government. Volokhov turned out to be so good at this job that Mikiciński suspected him of being a Gestapo agent. However, it soon turned out that both Mikiciński and the resourceful Ukrainian were operating under the auspices of the Nazi military intelligence.[19]

Thus, in late 1939, on a small quiet street in the very heart of Warsaw, right under the noses of Governor-General Frank's men and the German security agencies, there emerged an unusual enterprise whose very existence contradicts everything we know about the reality of the Nazi occupation of Poland. There were at least four Russian-speaking employees (including Mikiciński) on staff, and it engaged in the illegal smuggling of people out of the General Government, under the aegis and with the assistance of the Abwehr.

As for getting in touch with the families of Sikorski and Sosnkowski, Mikiciński had no particular trouble with this part of his assignment, either. On one of the days of his brief sojourn in Warsaw, he simply showed up at Pani Pfeifferova's boardinghouse, where Sikorski's frightened wife and daughter were hiding under aliases. Another lodger there was Dr. Karol Bader, a former employee of the Polish Foreign Office and an old friend and political associate of Stanisław Kot. The unexpected guest brought news from General Sikorski, along with a

---

19 An undated protocol of the interrogation of Samson Mikiciński, spring 1941, ibid., Scan 000953; an undated and untitled report by agent A/H.2, late December 1940, TNA, HS 4/213. A list of Abwehr agents compiled by the American counterintelligence service in 1946 includes data on a certain Alexander Volokhov (the compilers of the list were not certain whether *Alexander* was his true first name). According to this document, he was a Russian émigré from the city of Gomel in Belarus, born in 1892; he spoke Russian, Polish, and German (with a Russian accent); he lived in Prague with his wife and their child; he was recruited by the Prague branch of the Abwehr under the codename Parsifal, and subsequently also worked in Bulgaria and Turkey; he oversaw a network of Polish agents who supplied information related to Russia. In all likelihood, this is the same Volokhov who was mentioned by Mikiciński in his Palestinian interrogations. See his description, as given by the Americans: CI Consolidated Interrogation Report No. 13, in Mendelsohn, *The Final Solution*, 47.

large sum of money and a promise to have all three smuggled to France in the near future. Jadwiga Sosnkowska, the wife of General Sosnkowski, received a similar visit. At that time, in late 1939, she was employed as an ordinary nurse at the surgery unit of the famous Ujazdowski military hospital built in 1818 upon the orders of Prince Konstantin Romanov.[20] An anonymous report preserved at the Polish archive in Brooklyn summarizes this brilliant move by Mikiciński: "Unsurprisingly, he appeared to them like an angel sent from heaven."[21]

On their return trip from Warsaw to Paris, Mikiciński and his Chilean boss made another brief stopover in Breslau. Yet again, Scholz cordially received them, then inquired about the success of their mission in Poland and ensured their safe passage to Berlin. Traveling via the Nazi capital, Mikiciński and Luco reached the Belgian border, and were soon back in France.[22]

The Road to Freedom through the Enemy Lair

The success of the first trip of Chilean diplomat Mikiciński to the General Government made a huge impression on the exiled Polish leaders. They now regarded Mikiciński as a veritable godsend and hoped to use him not only to smuggle their loved ones from occupied Poland to France, but establish a permanent connection with the steadily growing Polish resistance movement at home. The unprecedented honor the Polish émigré elite showered upon the native of Boćki shocked Captain Stefan Marek, his former handler from the Polish military counterintelligence. Likewise forced into exile, Marek would testify that, one day in late 1939 or early 1940, while staying at the lobby of the Parisian Hotel Regina, now the headquarters of the Polish military High Command in exile, he came face to face with Mikiciński, who had just emerged from a luxury car that had stopped at the central hotel entrance. Immaculately dressed, exuding health and self-confidence, he was waiting graciously for Sikorski's head of office, who was running down the grand hotel staircase toward him. Noticing Marek, Mikiciński approached him and asked in a markedly patronizing tone: "How's it going, Mr. Captain?" Failing to elicit a response, he added: "Hold your head up high, and everything will be fine!" and hurried away,

---

20 A top secret report titled "The Paluchowicz Case," copy # 1, July 18, 1941, in ibid.; an undated report titled "Mikiciński Samson," JPIA, Archiwum Osobowe, NZ 154, Sygn. 658.
21 Ibid.
22 Ibid.; a top secret report titled "The Paluchowicz Case," copy # 1; July 18, 1941, TNA, HS 4/213.

leaving the stunned veteran of the Dwójka to watch his receding back melt into the gloom of the hotel corridors.[23]

In January 1940, a mere month after his triumphant return from Warsaw, Mikiciński made another trip there, this time without Luco. Once again, he traveled from Berlin to Breslau in the company of the Abwehr officer Erich Nobis, then proceeded to Warsaw.[24] The stopover in Breslau was used for another meeting with Scholz, who wished to have a more casual conversation with his Parisian guest and so held a tête-à-tête (or, as the Poles say, a "rozmowa w cztery oczy") with him.

In the spring of 1941, Mikiciński would admit to his Polish interrogator (whose own testimony is problematic, as we shall see later on) that from the end of 1939 to April 1940, he made four visits to Warsaw; these trips were independent (he was unaccompanied by his Chilean superior), and each time he met with the Abwehr bigshot in Breslau on his way there and back. Thus, Mikiciński and Scholz saw each other eight times in total. In some cases, the German would show up at the hotel where Mikiciński was staying, but more often, he would instruct one of his underlings, Arthur or Fritz, to drive him to the apartment used for covert meetings.[25]

From his interactions with Scholz, Mikiciński gradually deduced that the latter was a senior intelligence officer of the Eighth Army, deployed in Breslau, and that he specialized in gathering information on the Balkan region. During their conversations, Scholz took an interest in the general situation in France and Belgium, the foreign policy of both countries, the mood of the local population, the state of the Polish government-in-exile, the internecine struggle among the various factions of the Polish émigré community, and the Polish armed forces that had just been established in France. Mikiciński would claim in his interrogations that all the information he gave Scholz on these subjects had been taken exclusively from open sources, and that the German never once asked about the details of his interlocutor's activities and contacts in the territory of the General Government. Only during Mikiciński's third or fourth trip to occupied Poland—in the spring of 1940—did Scholz briefly mention the possibility of having the Abwehr sponsoring Mikiciński's travels in Europe, but did not expound on the subject.[26] In the event, this was to be their last discussion on the

---

23 An undated report titled "Mikiciński Samson," JPIA, Archiwum Osobowe, NZ 154, Sygn. 658.
24 A top secret report titled "The Paluchowicz Case," copy # 1; July 18, 1941, TNA, HS 4/213.
25 An undated protocol of the interrogation of Samson Mikiciński, spring 1941, HIA, 800/41/0/-/141 Folder 7, Scan 000968.
26 Ibid.

topic because, as stated above, his trips to the General Government (and, ergo, his visits to Breslau) came to an end in April 1940.

Later on, it will be shown in detail how Polish and the British counter-intelligence services interpreted Mikiciński's relationship with Scholz as one of the strongest pieces of evidence of his involvement in espionage for the Third Reich. However, as in the case of the prewar contacts between Mikiciński and Scholz, the categorical certainty of this judgment may well have been wrong. It is true that the Nazi military intelligence operative used these meetings with Mikiciński to sound out the situation in France and Belgium and learn about the Polish expatriates in those countries. Yet, as Mikiciński would point out later, we must not forget that his interlocutor was primarily interested in gathering intelligence on the Balkan region, and not on the Poles or the Western countries. Thus, it is quite possible that the questions he asked Mikiciński were a manifestation of his personal curiosity. But there is yet another possibility: by asking these questions, Scholz may have been trying to secure an alibi in case someone in the Reich—for example, Himmler's men—wondered as to the purpose of his contacts with a Polish Jew who used a Chilean diplomatic cover. Finally, as stated above, Scholz may have been driven by simple greed; Mikiciński stated in his interrogation that, from the end of 1939 to April 1940, he had been paying Scholz's underlings for their services,[27] and they might well have given a cut of their profits to Herr Doktor from Breslau.

Indeed, personal testimony from Poles who lived through the occupation indicates that the period of late 1939 through early 1940 saw a flowering of corruption. Many Nazi functionaries, including Wehrmacht and Gestapo officers, eagerly took bribes for solving sundry problems, even if their solutions required them to violate the laws of the Reich and the General Government. Unsurprisingly, sharp-tongued locals and even some occupiers began to claim that the German abbreviation for Generalgouvernement, GG, actually stood for *Gangstergau* [gangster region].[28]

In April 1940, one of the eyewitnesses to this stunning phenomenon reported to agents of the Polish government-in-exile about the existence in the GG of a ramified network of local entrepreneurs, tightly connected to high-ranking occupation officials, who for three thousand złotys would issue almost anyone a prewar Polish foreign passport and an entry visa to any foreign

---

27 An undated protocol of the interrogation of Samson Mikiciński, spring 1941, HIA, 800/41/0/-/141 Folder 7, Scan 000950.
28 See: CI Consolidated Interrogation Report No. 13, 9 in Mendelsohn, *The Final Solution*.

state; for an additional 150 złotys, they would procure an exit permit from the German occupying authorities to leave Polish territory. Although these sums were quite hefty at the time, they were not astronomical enough to dissuade a substantial clientele from purchasing documents and leaving the occupied territory—traveling through neighboring Romania, Hungary, Slovakia, and sometimes even Nazi Germany—to settle in the West, the Middle East, and South America.[29]

Again, a high-raking Abwehr officer from Breslau like Scholz may have very well been acting under the orders of his boss, Canaris. In the summer of 1941, British intelligence officers wrote a summary report of their investigation into Mikiciński's activities in Palestine that indicates its subject admitted to fully informing Scholz of his smuggling activities.[30] Nevertheless, the Nazis made no attempt to put an end to these operations, nor did the German occupying authorities arrest nor persecute Bobajewski, Volokhov, Alexandrova, nor Mikiciński himself.

Moreover, any assertion that the relationship between Scholz and Mikiciński served the intelligence-gathering goals of the Abwehr is refuted by a simple fact of which Mikiciński's investigators in Palestine were well aware: in violation of all the written and unwritten operational rules of every intelligence agency under the sun, then as today, agent Mikiciński made no secret of his dealings with Scholz. Au contraire, during his stay in Paris, he eagerly informed various individuals that his amazing successes in occupied Poland were made possible by the support of a German bigwig. As for the beginning of their acquaintance, Mikiciński invariably claimed that he had gotten to know the German during World War I, when the latter was in Russian captivity. Later, in Palestine, he

---

29 "A report by I. Chapski and J. Chapski, who left Warsaw on April 11, 1940, and traveled via Berlin, Wrocław, Vienna, and Budapest," an undated document, USHMM, RG-59.047, KOL-25-10-A_151–152; the Polish Foreign Office in Angers to the Polish embassies in London, Washington, Tokyo, Paris, Rio de Janeiro, Buenos Aires, and Ottawa. A message from a trustworthy source, "A few remarks on the political and economic situation of Polish society in late December 1939," January 25, 1940, ibid., RG-59.036, A-12-73-A2_0057; the testimony of Maria Maisnerova, who traveled from Poland to Hungary via the territory of the Reich, about the bribes paid to various German officials, including Gestapo officers: an untitled document; February 5, 1940, ibid., GK_159_228cz2, 14; the testimony of Jan Brocki, according to which in late 1939 the Jews of Będzin and Kraków were paying a "regular salary" to the local Gestapo officers, thereby improving their living conditions: protocol of the interrogation of Jan Brocki, February 7, 1940, ibid., 29; reports of corruption in the ranks of the security services of the GG can also be found in messages sent by the Polish underground to London in 1942. See: "Dispatches from the homeland," an untitled document with no addressee, March 21, 1943, ibid., RG-59.036, A-12-73-5_0013. See on the same subject: Noakes and Pridham, *Nazism*, 994.
30 A top secret report titled "The Paluchowicz Case," copy # 1, July 18, 1941, TNA, HS 4/213.

would admit that this was pure invention on his part, and that he had actually met Scholz for the first time only in late 1938.[31] However, even this admission (assuming that it was actually made) does not negate the fact that he did not regard his relationship with Scholz as some terrible secret he had to keep under wraps at all costs.

Be that as it may, during each of his trips, after arriving in Breslau from Paris and talking to Scholz, Mikiciński would invariably proceed to occupied Warsaw in a car driven by Arthur, the Abwehr chauffeur.

The second such visit, which took place in January 1940, was dedicated to rescuing Sikorski's wife and daughter. Both women were in Paris by the end of that month. Unfortunately, most of the details of this amazing operation are still shrouded in the mists of history, and all we know at present is the fugitives' stunning route through Berlin and Brussels. In March 1940, they were followed by Ms. Jadwiga Sosnkowska—who, like Irena Szarska-Potocka before her, was listed in Mikiciński's diplomatic passport as the Chilean's lawful wife. And, like Helena and Zofia Sikorski, she used the capital of the Third Reich as a stopover on her way to France.[32] In her postwar memoirs, Jadwiga chose to gloss over the Berlin stage of her voyage to freedom, writing instead that she and Mikiciński had traveled straight from Breslau to Aachen near the Belgian border. However, her reticence did not prevent her from informing her readers that her Jewish rescuer had managed to smuggle a suitcase crammed with jewelry from Poland into France in an unmistakably antisemitic passage.[33]

These two evacuations of the relatives of exiled Polish leaders from Nazi-occupied territory were among the most daring and successful covert operations of World War II, and they won Mikiciński deserved acclaim in Polish émigré circles in France. For his exploits, he received one of the most prestigious awards of the Polish state (a story that will be told in detail later on). However,

---

31 An undated protocol of the interrogation of Samson Mikiciński, spring 1941, HIA, 800/41/0/-/141 Folder 7, Scan 000954.

32 An undated protocol of the interrogation of Samson Mikiciński, spring 1941, ibid., Scan 000972; an extract from an undated interrogation of Mikiciński, TNA, HS 4/213; a top secret report titled "The Paluchowicz Case," copy # 1, July 18, 1941, ibid.; an undated report titled "Mikiciński Samson," JPIA, Archiwum Osobowe, NZ 154, Sygn. 658; Rutkowski, *Stanisław Kot*, 145–146. We should point out that, in Polish historiography, credit for the rescue of Sikorski's wife and daughter from occupied Poland is given not to Mikiciński, but to various other figures. See, for instance: Strachanowski, "Guwernantka Zubczewska, czyli ucieczka generałowej." See also on the rescue of Ms. Sosnkowska by Mikiciński: Giedroyc, *Autobiografia na cztery ręce*, 102.

33 Koper, *Polskie piekiełko*, 127; Kowalski and Sosnkowska, *W kręgu mitów i rzeczywistości*, 75–80.

these rescues were only the opening salvo in a series of similar operations carried out by the Polish-Russian Jew on German-controlled soil under a Chilean diplomatic cover; some twenty persons followed a similar route from the General Government to France, including the wives of Colonel Henryk Bagiński, a representative of Sikorski's staff in constant touch with Mikiciński, and Colonel Alexander Kendzior, the chief of that staff.[34]

Most of the rescued people from Mikiciński's list appear to have been Poles. At present, we know of only one Jew who was rescued by Mikiciński.[35] This was Karol Eiger, a wealthy industrialist from Łódź, the Jewish brother-in-law of the Pole Zygmunt Graliński, the deputy foreign minister in Sikorski's cabinet. Karol's sister Dorota (also known as Dora), who had fled to France with her husband, asked Mikiciński to rescue her brother from a concentration camp in occupied Poland, and he agreed to help. Sometime later, Eiger was released from his place of imprisonment by Arthur the Abwehr chauffeur and delivered to Breslau in a private car. From there, the lucky former camp inmate and Mikiciński, accompanied by Abwehr officer Nobis, set out for Berlin, where they immediately boarded a flight to Bucharest. Later, Mikiciński would boast to his acquaintances that he secured Eiger's release by appealing directly to Heinrich Himmler, chief of the SS and the Gestapo. However, he would recant this claim during his interrogation in Palestine, referring to it as a fabrication meant to impress his gullible interlocutors.[36] In any case, the evacuation of Karol Eiger appears in retrospect to be a highly unusual event, especially in light of what we know about the futile attempts of the Dutch Philips company (an influential conglomerate) to rescue the specialists of its Polish factory arrested

---

34 An undated protocol of the interrogation of Samson Mikiciński, spring 1941, HIA, 800/41/0/-/141 Folder 7, Scan 000972; an extract from an undated interrogation of Mikiciński, TNA, HS 4/213; a top secret report titled "The Paluchowicz Case," copy # 1, July 18, 1941, ibid.; an undated report titled "Mikiciński Samson," JPIA, Archiwum Osobowe, NZ 154, Sygn. 658.

35 In his postwar interrogation by the Americans, the former Abwehr chauffeur Arthur Hermann asserted that Mikiciński had rescued twelve prominent Jews from occupied Poland. See: CI Consolidated Interrogation Report No. 13, 10 in Mendelsohn, *The Final Solution*. This assertion, like all of Hermann's other claims on the subject of Samson, is not corroborated by the archival sources available to us at present.

36 An undated protocol of the interrogation of Samson Mikiciński, spring 1941, HIA, 800/41/0/-/141 Folder 7, Scan 000974. The protocol makes it clear that Mikiciński was not well-acquainted with Ms. Gralińska, since he referred to her as "the wife of Karol Eiger, the daughter of a Polish deputy minister," whereas in reality she was the wife of Zygmunt Graliński and the sister of Karol. See on Graliński's relatives: "Graliński Zygmunt Stanisław Cyprian 1897–1940" in the section "Sources and Bibliography."

and imprisoned by the German occupying authorities.[37] Karol Eiger's name will come up later.

The last person able to escape from the GG with Mikiciński's assistance was Bronisława Gano, the wife of the chief of the Polish military intelligence. She left Warsaw only in the spring of 1941, after the fall of France and the arrest of Mikiciński. She headed straight to London. Her husband, Colonel Stanisław Gano, who seems to have been aware of Mikiciński's relationship with the Germans[38] (as stated above, Mikiciński made no secret of this relationship), had asked Mikiciński to rescue her in the spring of 1940. Mikiciński paid a visit to Ms. Gano in Warsaw, probably during his last trip to the city. To prove that he was not an agent provocateur of the Gestapo, he showed her a photograph of her husband (or, according to another version, a photograph of herself), on which Stanisław Gano had written, in his own hand, a private nickname known only to the two of them.[39] This photograph was subsequently found during the search of Mikiciński's apartment in Istanbul following his arrest. The author of the report from the Brooklyn archive claims that, given Mikiciński's absence, Bronisława's trip to the British capital was facilitated directly by the Abwehr, and that her route took her to Berlin where she was the honored guest of Admiral Canaris.[40] Present-day Polish historiography adds that, according to the postwar reports of the spies of Communist Poland in London, Bronisława Gano was delivered to the German-Swiss border by Abwehr agents, who proceeded to hand her over to their Polish counterparts/adversaries.[41] This story ties well with the theory outlined above, according to which the Mikiciński-Scholz relationship was not a German intelligence-gathering operation, but a way for Canaris, and possibly for other opponents of the Nazi regime inside Germany, to advance their secret dialogue with Paris, and later with London.

---

37 The Polish Ambassador to the Hague, W. Babiński, to Angers, an untitled secret report, March 27, 1940, USHMM, GK_159_228cz2, 119.
38 Koreś, "Tajemnice generała Gano": 49.
39 An undated report titled "Mikiciński Samson," JPIA, Archiwum Osobowe, NZ 154, Sygn. 658; Buczek, *Człowiek do złotych interesów*, 183.
40 An undated report titled "Mikiciński Samson," JPIA, Archiwum Osobowe, NZ 154, Sygn. 658.
41 Koreś, "Tajemnice generała Gano": 48. Polish historian Andrzej Brzeziecki adds that, in Berlin, Ms. Gano stayed at a luxury apartment that was guarded by the Abwehr, and that, after receiving the necessary travel documents (probably through the mediation of Canaris), she headed, via Switzerland and Portugal, to Britain. See: Brzeziecki, "Zagadka Wilhelma Canarisa."

Gestapo Officers Thrown into the Street

Mikiciński would claim that he refused offers of remuneration for rescuing people from Poland.[42] His major source of income in the territory of the GG was delivering funds from Sikorski's government to its supporters in the occupied homeland. Back in September 1939, the Polish authorities had managed to pull off a daring operation that merits a separate book, smuggling all the gold reserves of the rapidly disintegrating state—eighty tons in total—to France via, Romania, Turkey, Syria, and Lebanon and depositing them in the French Central Bank for safekeeping.[43] Thanks to this precaution, between November 1939 and April 1940 the Polish government-in-exile was able to give Mikiciński about ten million złotys, which he then safely transported into the GG and distributed among Sikorski's loyalists.[44] The Germans had quite arbitrarily pegged the Polish currency to the reichsmark, with a fixed exchange rate of one to two. Hence, the overall sum brought by Mikiciński into occupied Poland amounted to about five million reichsmark, or some two million US dollars—a king's ransom in those days.[45]

Based on prior agreement with Sikorski's representatives, Mikiciński was entitled to a commission fee of 10% of this money—that is, a million złotys, or five hundred thousand reichsmarks.[46] Even if we were to calculate this fee based on the exchange rate of the Warsaw black market in the spring of 1940, where one reichsmark was worth three złotys,[47] we would still come up with a sum of more than three hundred thousand reichsmarks. By way of comparison, the official annual salary of the German Führer at the time was a mere thirty

---

42 An undated protocol of the interrogation of Samson Mikiciński, spring 1941, HIA, 800/41/0/-/141 Folder 7, Scan 000974.
43 Koper, *Polskie piekiełko*, 102–107; Rojek, "Wojenne losy polskiego złota"; Szustakowski, "Jak uratowano skarb narodu": 2–3; Sokolnicki, *Dziennik Ankarski*, 27–38.
44 An undated protocol of the interrogation of Samson Mikiciński, spring 1941, HIA, 800/41/0/-/141 Folder 7, Scan 000974. Arthur Hermann, the former noncommissioned officer of the Abwehr from Breslau, told his postwar American interrogators that Mikiciński had smuggled 70–80 million złotys into occupied Poland. See: CI Consolidated Interrogation Report No. 13, 10 in Mendelsohn, *The Final Solution*. Obviously, this was a baseless exaggeration, or even a wholesale fabrication, on the part of Hermann—who, as shown above, did not have accurate information about Samson, and made numerous erroneous assertions on the subject of the latter.
45 Calculated with: http://www.historicalstatistics.org/Currencyconverter.html.
46 An undated protocol of the interrogation of Samson Mikiciński, spring 1941, HIA, 800/41/0/-/141 Folder 7, Scan 000974.
47 First Secretary of the Polish embassy in Bern, Stefan Ryniewicz, to the Headquarters of the Polish Ministry of Information and Documentation, Paris, "A report by Swiss citizen D. B., who left Warsaw on March 8," May 20, 1940, USHMM, GK_159_228cz2, 26.

thousand reichsmarks.⁴⁸ Thus, Mikiciński, who had been no pauper even before the beginning of his relationship with the Polish government-in-exile, now became a very wealthy man (certainly, by the standards of the GG) thanks to this very relationship. Already after his presumed date of death, in the spring of 1942, the exiled Polish Ministry of Justice would learn that fabulous sums of money were left in his bank accounts in Switzerland, Belgium, and the USA. To give only one example, an account of his in some New York bank was found to contain approximately two hundred thousand USD, which was equivalent to about one hundred annual salaries of the average American at the time.⁴⁹

Hence, we should not be surprised at the fact that, in early 1940, as he ran his business from the office on Frascati Street, Mikiciński was not afraid to clash with the Gestapo, nor that he emerged victorious. The author of the report from the Brooklyn archive cites the testimony of an anonymous Polish expatriate. The latter told Mikiciński that while fleeing from Warsaw on the eve of the capitulation in September 1939, he had concealed three kilograms of platinum in his apartment. Now, having heard of Mikiciński's amazing exploits in occupied Poland, he was asking him for help in retrieving this treasure, and he promised to give Mikiciński a third of the platinum for his troubles. The author of the report goes on to write that, to the amazement of that expatriate, Mikiciński agreed to the deal without hesitation. "But I must warn you that there are Gestapo officers living in the apartment," said the stunned petitioner. "So what?!" answered the unflappable Mikiciński. "We will throw them out and take the platinum!"

A little later, the émigré did indeed receive the promised two kilograms of platinum from the resourceful Mikiciński, who had pocketed the other third of the treasure, as agreed.⁵⁰

Compared to such heroics and the smuggling of large sums of money across the borders of the GG, Mikiciński's services as a political courier between Sikorski's chancellery and the growing Polish underground turned out to be a mere sideshow and a relatively easy job. In his Palestinian interrogations, he stated that on each of his trips from Paris to occupied Warsaw, he would take along propaganda materials of the Polish government-in-exile; then, upon his return, he would bring back fresh issues of illegal Polish publications, personal letters, and verbal messages from the leaders of the underground to the exiled

---

48 Kellerhoff, "Hitler's Milliarden."
49 Mieczysław Sędzielowski, Head of the Consular Referat (Department) of the Polish Foreign Ministry, an untitled top secret memorandum; April 14, 1942, HIA, 800/42/0/-/312, Box 1, Folder 1, Skan 000651.
50 An undated report titled "Mikiciński Samson," JPIA, Archiwum Osobowe, NZ 154, Sygn. 658.

leaders.⁵¹ Once, when he was chided for bringing letters from the GG without formal authorization, he explained that as soon as he had set foot in Warsaw, he was subjected to a veritable assault by local residents begging him to deliver letters to Sikorski; he could not find it in his heart to refuse them.⁵²

The Birth of the Wondrous Union of the "Tiger" and the "Fox"

Mikiciński's daring and wildly successful actions in the territory of the General Government made him the darling of the Polish émigré community in France. Ms. Sikorski worshipped him, publicly naming him as her rescuer.⁵³ Hence, she may have been the one to introduce Mikiciński to Stanisław Kot, the best friend and closest associate of her husband. However, Kot would later claim that Sosnkowski had introduced him to Mikiciński.⁵⁴ This assertion looks rather strange, since the professor and the general had been at bitter odds from the inception of the government-in-exile, fighting for control over channels of communication with occupied Poland. Therefore, it seems implausible that Sosnkowski could have handed one of his best secret couriers (and possibly the very best of them, as of that moment) over to Kot. Be that as it may, Mikiciński and Kot first met sometime in early February 1940, shortly after Mikiciński's return from his second trip to the GG.⁵⁵ The bewitched professor, who immediately recognized the vast potential of a partnership, offered Mikiciński a strategic alliance.

Some two months prior to that, Kot had been appointed minister of the interior of the government-in-exile. Thanks to the appointment, coupled with his longstanding close friendship with Sikorski, Kot became the official Polish deputy prime minister, serving as acting prime minister during Sikorski's trips outside France.⁵⁶ At the time of his meeting with Mikiciński, Kot's major preoccupation was creating a permanent and stable link with his occupied homeland, bypassing the channels of communication that had been opened by the

---

51 An undated protocol of the interrogation of Samson Mikiciński, spring 1941, HIA, 800/41/0/-/141 Folder 7, Scan 000972.
52 Rutkowski, *Stanisław Kot*, 148.
53 An undated report titled "Mikiciński Samson," JPIA, Archiwum Osobowe, NZ 154, Sygn. 658.
54 Koper, *Polskie piekiełko*, 129; Rutkowski, *Stanisław Kot*, 145.
55 "The case of P.," a summary of D.S.(E) P2446, March 24, 1941, TNA, HS 4/213.
56 Rutkowski, *Stanisław Kot*, 126.

supporters of the Sanation—his and Sikorski's political adversaries.⁵⁷ The future of the exiled government was at stake: Sikorski and his followers aimed to establish firm political and military control over the Polish underground, regarding this as a prerequisite for their return to postwar Warsaw as the legitimate rulers of a reborn Poland.⁵⁸

The British counterintelligence service, MI5, was well aware of these aspirations. According to an anonymous MI5 report from November 1943, "[He] is . . . out all for himself with a burning desire to return to Poland as an active Cabinet Minister. All his activities, official as well as private, are concentrated on achieving this aim."⁵⁹ Furthermore, British counterintelligence noted that even before June 1940, when he was still in France, Kot had allegedly surrounded himself with a network of aides, advisers, secret agents, and personal emissaries in an attempt to shore up his power. MI5 described some of these individuals as "doubtful characters," singling out "a number of Polish Jews, reported to be members of the [masonic] Grand Orient Lodge . . . who exerted strong influence both on Kot and on Sikorski."⁶⁰ Michał Sokolnicki, the Polish ambassador to Ankara and one of Kot's bitterest enemies, referred to them as Kot's "Mafioso friends."⁶¹

One of Kot's personal emissaries who struck such fear into the hearts of MI5 was a man named Jan Romuald Kozielewski, better known today by his nom de guerre, Jan Karski. He was to be the first person who informed the world about the tragedy that had befallen Polish Jewry following the Nazi occupation of the country. Like Mikiciński, he came from Warsaw to Angers in early 1940 and made the acquaintance of the new minister of the interior in Sikorski's cabinet. It was Kot who received Kozielewski-Karski's first report about the persecution of Polish Jews by the Nazis (as part of a more general report about the situation in occupied Poland), and it was he who supervised its editing for publication.⁶² Given the extreme antipathy of the British intelligence community toward the

---

57 In late 1939—early 1940, General Sosnkowski, who was already in Paris and regarded as the leader of the Sanation camp, had three channels of communication with occupied Poland: through the Polish consulates in Budapest and Bucharest, and via the Polish military attaché office in Stockholm. See: Jacobmeyer, *Heimat und Exil*, 57.
58 Paszkiewicz, "Komitet dla Spraw Kraju": 160.
59 An unsigned summary of Stanisław Kot's personal file, titled "Stanisław Kot," November 26, 1943, TNA, KV 2/3429_5, 24.
60 Ibid., 25.
61 Sokolnicki, *Dziennik Ankarski*, 258.
62 See the full version of this report by Kozielewski-Karski: Friedrich, *Die Verfolgung und Ermordung*, Dok. 90, 233–241. See also the first report by Kozielewski-Karski about the fate of Polish Jewry, and the response of Polish minister Kot to this report: Zimmerman, *The Polish Underground and the Jews*, 73–75.

professor and his coterie of "suspicious types," it is hardly surprising that the information brought by Kozielewski-Karski failed to make any impression on the Western leaders.

Remarkably, Karski failed to find anything demonic about the interior minister. In the postwar memoirs of the famous Polish underground courier, he describes Kot as a "short, gray-haired man, quiet, precise in his habits and movements, and inclined to be pedantic in speech," and also as an "intelligent, well-informed, and shrewd" person, with a considerable ability to understand people.[63] On the eve of Jan's return to occupied Warsaw, the minister handed him a list of key figures in the Polish underground whom he was to meet, adding: "Traditionally, I should compel you to swear that you will not betray us. But if you are wicked enough to turn traitor, you are wicked enough to break an oath. So let us simply shake hands. Good luck, Karski!"[64]

We do not know whether Mikiciński, too, was exempted by Kot from the customary oath of loyalty to the government-in-exile. If we are to believe the British intelligence reports, the professor was much more interested in bringing Mikiciński's activities in the GG under his control, and in preventing him from cooperating with the pro-Sanation camp led by General Sosnkowski (whose wife, Jadwiga, Mikiciński had just spirited out of Warsaw). For this reason, the interior minister (and deputy prime minister of the Polish government-in-exile) demanded that Mikiciński report to him, and to him alone, about his activities in Poland. He also made Mikiciński promise that not a single złoty given to him by the exiled government would fall into the hands of Sikorski's enemies. In exchange, Kot pledged to give Mikiciński his full patronage, which would shield him from possible attempts by the Polish military counterintelligence, with its pro-Sanation sympathies, to disrupt the connections between Mikiciński and Sikorski's retinue and interfere with his activities in the occupied homeland.[65] For the purposes of future secret communication with the minister, Mikiciński received the operational codename Lis (fox in Polish).[66] Nowadays, it is impossible to determine whether Mikiciński chose the name, or whether it was issued by Kot, who used the alias Tigris (Tiger) for his clandestine contacts with the

---

63 Quoted from the Israeli edition of Kozielewski-Karski's memoirs: Karski, *Story of a Secret State*, 143.
64 Ibid., 148–149.
65 An undated report titled "Mikiciński Samson," JPIA, Archiwum Osobowe, NZ 154, Sygn. 658; "the case of P.," a summary of D.S.(E) P2446, March 24, 1941, TNA, HS 4/213; a top secret report titled "The Paluchowicz Case," copy #1, July 18, 1941, ibid.
66 "Code names used by the Skupień, Kaczmarek, and Vogel intelligence stations," an undated document, USHMM, RG-59.047, KOL-25-13_3. See also: Dubicki, *Konspiracja Polska w Rumunii*, 234.

network of spies and saboteurs subordinated to his ministry.[67] Either way, it must be admitted that the new nickname aptly described Mikiciński's character and methods.

In accordance with this agreement, Kot fully coordinated Mikiciński's three subsequent trips to the GG in the spring of 1940 for what Kot's opponents would later dub a "dangerous liaison."[68] Mikiciński thus became one of his new patron's most important contact agents in occupied Poland.[69] He was a crucial asset for the "network of aides, advisers, secret agents, and personal emissaries" giving MI5 such a headache. Thanks to him, the network now stood a much better chance of accomplishing its operational goals.

A year later, during his interrogation in Palestine, Mikiciński would claim that he kept Kot in the dark on the subject of his relationship with his second patron, the high-ranking Abwehr officer from Breslau.[70] In all likelihood, this was a lie. It is inconceivable that the "intelligent, well-informed, and shrewd" Kot, with his ability to understand people, could have shown no interest in the real reason for the stunning successes of his new Jewish agent in German-occupied territory, and he must have received some explanations on this score from the latter. And, indeed, Mikiciński's opponents in the intelligence community and diplomatic corps of the Polish government-in-exile, followed by certain Polish historians, would assert after the end of the war that as soon as he got to know Mikiciński, Kot demanded that the latter give him the secret of his phenomenal success. He was allegedly satisfied with his protégé's explanation—namely, that he was being assisted (in exchange for generous bribes) by a German military intelligence officer from Breslau, an old acquaintance of his from Denikin's army.[71]

"I Have Done Something for Poland"

Kot's desire to encourage Mikiciński to continue their partnership and to shield his new agent from possible persecution by the Polish military counterintelligence may have been the reason for the decision by the exiled cabinet, on May 3, 1940, to confer the highest Polish order, Polonia Restituta, upon Mikiciński.

---

67 Ibid.
68 Sokolnicki, *Dziennik Ankarski*, 161.
69 "The case of P.," a summary of D.S.(E) P2446, March 24, 1941, TNA, HS 4/213.
70 An undated protocol of the interrogation of Samson Mikiciński, spring 1941, HIA, 800/41/0/-/141 Folder 7, Scans 000954-5.
71 Iranek-Osmecki, "Afera Mikicińskiego": 198; Kurcyusz, *Na przedpolu Jałty*, 44; Rutkowski, *Stanisław Kot*, 146.

This award, which translates "restored Poland," had been established in 1921, and it is still being awarded to Polish and foreign citizens for exceptional services (both civilian and military) to the Polish state.[72] According to the British SOE, the decision to award the order to Mikiciński was publicized in the Polish émigré press on the same day it was taken.[73] Echoes of this event reached even Palestine. The Office of the British Military Censor in Tel Aviv covered it in a special report, which was sent to the local department of His Majesty's Military Counterintelligence Service.[74]

Naturally, Mikiciński was unaware of the keen interest of the British in the minutiae of his eventful biography. Therefore, during his Palestinian interrogation in the spring of 1941, he tried to bolster the case against his being a German spy by alluding to the fact that he was the recipient of the most prestigious Polish award, which had been bestowed upon him for covert operations carried out in enemy territory. "Apparently, I have done something for Poland," he threw in the face of his British interrogator.[75] As we would later see, this desperate act failed to impress his jailers and did nothing to avert his bitter end. Moreover, Mikiciński's status as a recipient of Polonia Restituta did not prevent him from becoming the anti-hero of several Polish publications on the subject of World War II. Some anonymous hand even struck his name from the full list of recipients of that coveted decoration.[76]

---

72 Order Odrodzenia Polski.
73 A top secret report titled "The Paluchowicz Case," copy #1, July 18, 1941, TNA, HS 4/213.
74 An undated excerpt from a report by the British Military Censor in Tel Aviv, TNA, HS 4/213.
75 A quote from an undated protocol of the interrogation of Samson Mikiciński, TNA, HS 4/213.
76 Puchalski and Wojciechowski, *Ordery i odznaczenia polskie*.

Chapter 3

The Top Player of Fascist Bucharest

The Polish War on Romanian Soil

On September 17, 1939, as the Red Army was moving into eastern Poland, the leaders of that beleaguered country were already on its southeastern outskirts in the small town of Kuty, within hailing distance of neighboring Romania. The growing threat of capture by the Russians sent the high-ranking fugitives scampering across the border without delay; they intended to ask the Romanians for temporary asylum and seek their permission to pass through their territory to France, as by that time, the French had already agreed in principle to host them should the need arise. As they stepped across the Polish-Romanian border into exile, the ministers and generals were accompanied by a flood of refugees both military and civilian. Historians would later calculate that in those September days, some fifty thousand Polish subjects, including approximately twenty-three thousand soldiers and officers, passed through the border post in Kuty and entered Romania.[1]

Despite the anti-democratic nature of his regime, Romanian monarch Carol II favored a strategic alliance with the Western powers and had maintained friendly relations with neighboring Poland in the prewar period. Accordingly,

---

1 Kania, "Kolejny świadek wrześniowego dramatu na Kresach": 133.

he gave a warm reception to the unexpected guests from the north, supplying the Polish refugees with ample food, private lodgings, and an excellent exchange rate on Polish złotys. At the same time, the Polish national gold reserves—which, as noted above, would later be used to finance the activities of the anti-German Polish underground—were headed for France on a special freight train through Romanian territory to Constanţa, the country's largest port.[2]

In very short order, the Germans learned of the benevolence that Romanian authorities had shown toward the defeated Poles, and of the pledge the official Bucharest gave to assist with the relocation of the fugitive Polish government, the remnants of its army, and its gold reserves to the West. As Berlin saw it, this was a flagrant violation of the neutrality declared by the Romanians on September 6. Hence, the Nazi authorities began a campaign of official and unofficial pressure on Carol II and his entourage. Its major objectives were the extradition to Germany of key Polish figures—the president, the prime minister, the foreign minister, and the commander in chief—and the internment of the Polish military personnel in Romanian territory. In these circumstances, on September 18, Romanian prime minister Armand Călinescu, who was considered a friend of Poland, was forced to order the detention of the high-ranking Polish politicians, soldiers, and officers under his jurisdiction. Overnight, the president of the vanquished Polish Republic, its premier, government ministers, and military top brass were deprived of their freedom of movement and scattered among different Romanian provinces, effectively unable to communicate with each other. Only three days later, on September 21, Călinescu was assassinated by a group of fanatics from the local fascist movement, the so-called Iron Guard, sponsored by Berlin. The new premier, Constantin Argetoianu, immediately adopted a pro-German course while taking a much harsher line toward the Polish refugees.[3]

Paradoxically, the new anti-Polish orientation of the Romanian regime, adopted to placate Berlin, worked out to the benefit of the official Paris. The French leaders were pleased by the unexpected opportunity to avoid an in-person meeting with prewar Polish colleagues whom they had deemed too

---

2 Dubicki, *Dzieje polskiej placówki dyplomatycznej w Bukareszcie*, 115–16; Dubicki, *Polscy uchodźcy w Rumunii*, 11; Kochanski, *The Eagle Unbowed*, 238; Koper, *Polskie piekiełko*, 44, 48–49, 59, 102–107; Koskodan, *No Greater Ally*, 42–43; Patterson, *Between Hitler and Stalin*, 187; Tusiewicz, *Historia Polski*, 365; Wieczorkiewicz, *Historia Polityczna Polski*, 99.

3 Carol II, *Însemnări zilnice*, 261–263; Chivulescu, *Armand Călinescu*, 300–301; Dubicki, *Dzieje polskiej placówki*, 123; Jacobmeyer, *Heimat und Exil*, 21; Kochanski, *The Eagle Unbowed*, 90-91; Koper, *Polskie piekiełko*, 48–49, 135–36; Koskodan, *No Greater Ally*, 43; Ţiu, "Terrorism as Political Tool": 61–69.

independent, and from whom they had essentially withheld promised military assistance. Instead, the government of Édouard Daladier preferred to set up an alternative Polish government on French soil, one far less independent and hence far more accommodating. Its designated leader, General Władysław Sikorski, was a Francophile and an implacable foe of the leaders of the Sanation camp now bogged down in Romania. It seems that by banking on Sikorski, the French primarily sought to promote their own security interests: their General Staff wished to lay its hands on the thousands of draft-age Poles then living in France, and the French military was interested in the refugee Polish military officers starting to trickle into the Third Republic. Already on September 19, by arrangement with the French, the Polish ambassador to Paris launched an official campaign recruiting Polish citizens into the Polish armed forces now being reestablished in the territory of France.[4] Sikorski, who had enjoyed great popularity as a general and politician in prewar Poland, was expected to grant this new formation the status of a regular Polish army subordinated to the legitimate Polish government. Officially, it was at the command of this government, rather than at the behest of the French, that the Poles were supposed to carry on the struggle for the liberation of their homeland on French soil, fighting side by side with their French allies.[5]

Sikorski, who had already arrived in Paris on September 24, was promptly recognized as the official Polish political and military leader and began to organize a large-scale evacuation of Polish soldiers and officers from Romania, Hungary, and Slovakia to France, via Yugoslavia, Italy, and Turkey. Many Romanian civilian officials and military and police officers facilitated the Polish exodus, very often in exchange for money.[6] However, quite a few of the former soldiers of the Second Polish Republic who had found themselves on Romanian soil in the autumn of 1939 were denied the opportunity to travel on to France.

The Polish military attaché in Bucharest, Colonel Tadeusz Zakrzewski, who had rushed to swear allegiance to the new commander in chief and endorse

---

4   The British Ambassador to France, Sir Eric Phipps, Paris, "Formation in France of Polish, Czecho-Slovak and Austrian Units," September 22, 1939, USHMM, RG-59.006.M-FO371/22949, Scans 00107-9; Szeremietiew, *Siła złego*, 488.
5   Weekly Political Intelligence Summary No. 1 (Covering the Period from the Outbreak of War to October 3, 1939), October 3, 1939, USHMM, RG-59.006.M-FO371/24054, Scan 00022; Szeremietiew, "1939."
6   The autobiography of Lupian Edward Marian, October 1, 1941, HIA, A.XII.1/82, 15–16. See on Sikorski's appointment to the post of commander in chief of the Polish Armed Forces in Exile, November 7, 1939: Weekly Political Intelligence Summary No. 8, Foreign Office (Political Intelligence Department), November 21, 1939, USHMM, RG-59.006.M-FO371/24054, Scan 00178.

his unofficial representative in Romania,⁷ rigorously vetted all candidates for evacuation. His goal was to screen out all the supporters of the former Sanation government and, more broadly, any real or imagined opponents of the new Polish leader and the exiled cabinet he was setting up. All those Zakrzewski classified as politically unreliable were firmly refused permission to relocate to France. The Polish ambassador to Romania, Roger Raczyński (one of the first Polish officials to openly come out in support of Sikorski in September 1939), behaved similarly. His new duties included screening fugitive Polish politicians seeking admission to France for political reliability. From Raczyński's point of view, the major criterion for a refugee's inclusion on the list of evacuees was his or her potential usefulness to Sikorski.⁸ As the analysts of the Political Intelligence Department of the British Foreign Office remarked in their summary from October 10, 1939, "General Sikorski . . . has been badly treated by Polish Governments for some years past, and is not likely to forget the fact."⁹

Over the subsequent months, as the new leader openly declared his desire to "break radically" with the prewar regime,¹⁰ the Polish diaspora became split into two warring camps: Sikorski's supporters and opponents. Romania, whose territory still hosted the majority of Polish refugees, was a flashpoint of this internecine struggle. An eyewitness to those events would later recall that "the thick network of secret and open agents, cast by Prof. Kot over the Polish community in Romania through the allocation of funds and jobs, monitored the opponents of the new government, eavesdropped on their conversations, interrogated and denounced them."¹¹ Ambassador Raczyński and his predecessor at the Polish embassy in Bucharest, Mirosław Arciszewski (a veteran diplomat appointed by Sikorski to the post of Special Representative for Polish Refugee Affairs in Romania), petitioned local officials and foreign diplomats to ban former Polish statesmen from leaving the country and prevent them from communicating with their supporters in Poland and elsewhere. To this end, Arciszewski (whose enmity toward the Sanation camp was, according to the

---

7   This unofficial representative of Sikorski in Romania was no other than Professor Kot, who went to Paris only in early November 1939. See: Rutkowski, *Stanisław Kot*, 126.
8   Dubicki, *Dzieje polskiej placówki*, 119–122; Kochanski, *The Eagle Unbowed*, 91; Koper, *Polskie piekiełko*, 58–70; Miszewski, "Polska polityka zagraniczna": 152–153; Patterson, *Between Hitler and Stalin*, 187–190; Rutkowski, *Stanisław Kot*, 122; Tusiewicz, *Historia Polski*, 379; Wieczorkiewicz, *Historia Polityczna Polski*, 112–120.
9   Weekly Political Intelligence Summary No. 2, Foreign Office (Political Intelligence Department), October 10, 1939, USHMM, RG-59.006.M-FO371/24054, Scans 00044-5.
10 Zimmerman, *The Polish Underground and the Jews*, 73.
11 Pobóg-Malinowski, *Na rumuńskim rozdrożu*, 51.

report from the Brooklyn archive, rooted in a longstanding personal feud with the former foreign minister, Józef Beck[12]) drew on all his connections in the upper echelons of the Romanian regime.[13]

At the same time, the anti-Sikorski camp in Bucharest managed to embed an agent of their own in Ambassador Raczyński's office. This was the above-mentioned Jerzy Giedroyc, a well-known journalist and activist in prewar Poland with conservative, pro-German views considered to be an associate of the aforementioned Władysław Studnicki, the veteran Polish conservative.[14] Giedroyc was hired as Raczyński's private secretary back in September 1939 and quickly became a key figure in pro-Sanation circles in Bucharest. His opponents went so far as to regard him as the chief ideologue of the local Piłsudchiks (the followers of Marshal Piłsudski). According to the information now available, he filled his confederates in on Raczyński's activities while working on Raczyński's loyalties in an attempt to turn him against Sikorski and his representatives in Romania.[15] Responsible for encrypted radio communications between the embassy and the headquarters of the Polish Foreign Office (initially based in Angers, later in London), Giedroyc edited out the messages that Kot's people were trying to send their patron and Sikorski through Raczyński.[16]

Furthermore, in the first half of 1940, the Polish military intelligence station in Bucharest, or ekspozytura, was still comprised of veterans of the prewar Dwójka. As loyalists of the Sanation regime, they hurried to swear allegiance to the pro-Sosnkowski Union of Armed Struggle, newly established in Poland, and threw their weight behind Sikorski's political opponents. They had at their disposal several clandestine groups of former Polish diplomats and military and intelligence officers who had fled to Romania, and who maintained ties with the supporters of the Sanation in neighboring Hungary. With their aid, the ekspozytura tried to hamstring Sikorski's nascent army, hindering the evacuation of the interned Polish soldiers and officers from Romania to France.

---

12 An undated report titled "Mikiciński Samson," JPIA, Archiwum Osobowe, NZ 154, Sygn. 658.
13 Dubicki, *Dzieje polskiej placówki*, 123–126; see also on Arciszewski's close ties with the Romanian regime: an official memorandum signed by Colonel Jan Kornaus, for the private use of Lieutenant Colonel M., an undated document, March 1940, PISM, PRM. 14B, 36.
14 Zychowicz, *Opcja niemiecka*, 120.
15 An official memorandum signed by Colonel Jan Kornaus, for the private use of Lieutenant Colonel M., an undated document, March 1940, PISM, PRM. 14B, 35–36; Alexandrowicz, Kurcyusz, Kuźniarz, and others to Sikorski, November 20, 1940, PISM, PRM. 50, 16-16/reverse side; Dubicki, *Dzieje polskiej placówki*, 120.
16 Dubicki and Rastworowski, *Sanatorzy kontra Sikorszczycy*, 141.

They also established channels of communication with their occupied homeland, especially with the Piłsudchiks who had stayed behind.[17]

The struggle between Sikorski's loyalists and the proponents of the Sanation in Bucharest greatly intensified in late 1939 and early 1940, when the two warring camps set up permanent channels of secret communication between the new seat of Polish power in Angers and the territory of Poland, which was now divided between Germany and the USSR. Dozens of undercover couriers were tasked with creating an invisible, indissoluble link between the French offices of Sikorski and Sosnkowski and the growing Polish underground. They were supposed to wrest control over the political, economic, and military activities of the Polish resistance, and to supply their bosses in France with information about the occupied country to be used for the internal political struggle in the Polish diaspora and the needs of Polish diplomacy. Both antagonists believed that success in this risky venture held the key to their postwar political triumph.

General Sosnkowski made first move. As mentioned above, Sikorski had been forced to let him join his new cabinet, and even appointed him chairman of the Committee of Ministers for Homeland Affairs. In late 1939, Sosnkowski's confidants started setting up two secret bases of communication with Poland at the embassies at Bucharest and Budapest. Known respectively as Bolek and Romek and staffed by Sanation loyalists from the Polish military, the two bases began sending couriers into Polish territory without delay. Colonel Stanisław Rostworowski led Bolek. Acting under the official diplomatic cover of the Polish vice consul, he had built covert networks in the Soviet-annexed Lwów and Białystok regions and established control over the Council of Seven, or K-7, a clandestine Polish organization active in Romania whom he dispatched to carry out covert operations in Soviet territory.[18]

Professor Stanisław Kot, whom Sikorski had just appointed interior minister, hit back against Sosnkowski's loyalists by setting up two bases of his own at the Polish embassies in Budapest and Bucharest. In the spring of 1940, Edmund Fietz-Fietowicz, who used the aliases Educhowski and Piast, led Kot's Hungarian base. A veteran of Wincenty Witos's People's Party and an implacable ideological foe of Sosnkowski and the other leaders of the Sanation, Fietz-Fietowicz

---

17 Adamczyk, "Piłsudczycy na emigracji": 100; Iranek-Osmecki, *Wspomnienia Oficera*, 185; see also: an official memorandum signed by Colonel Jan Kornaus, for the private use of Lieutenant Colonel M., an undated document, March 1940, PISM, PRM. 14B, 42–44; a report by Mr. [name illegible], May 11, 1940, USHMM, RG-59.047, KOL-25-45A_175–178.

18 Jacobmeyer, *Heimat und Exil*, 57, 59–60; see also the profile of Rostworowski: an official memorandum signed by Colonel Jan Kornaus, for the private use of Lieutenant Colonel M., an undated document, March 1940, PISM, PRM. 14B, 41.

hastened to join Sikorski's camp and Kot's circle, the so-called Kotowcy. Remarkable managerial skills, the backing of the interior minister, and generous funding quickly enabled Fietz-Fietowicz to turn the Budapest base of political communication into Sikorski's and Kot's key channel of communication with occupied Poland. Educhowski masterfully controlled the ramified network of covert couriers smuggling secret messages and funds in and out of Poland while evacuating Polish politicians and military officers deemed useful to his political camp into France. At the same time, he competed ruthlessly with Sosnkowski's Romek base: according to later testimonies by the general's men, he would intercept the couriers they dispatched into Poland and convert them to his side. With this operational accomplishment, Fietz-Fietowicz managed in one fell swoop to greatly limit the scope of action of the Piłsudchiks in the territory of the GG. The latter would admit in the first half of 1940 that the government-in-exile (read: Stanisław Kot) had been able to reduce significantly the influence of the Sanation camp on the emerging structures of the Polish resistance.[19]

By contrast, attempts to establish a Polish base of political communication in Bucharest were far less successful. Initially, Kot delegated this task to two men utterly unfit for the job: Professor Adam Wetulani and Dr. Karol Alexandrowicz, his former junior colleagues from Kraków University, both of whom specialized in the history of Polish law and opposed the Sanation regime. In September 1939, the two escaped to Romania, where they joined the Kotowcy and worked on behalf of their colleague and mentor to strengthen Sikorski's grip on the Polish refugees. Alexandrowicz was even officially appointed a representative in Romania of the special commission Sikorski established to investigate the causes and circumstances of the September defeat. In his new capacity, he did practically nothing, apart from compiling reports about real and imagined supporters of the Sanation in Romania he then sent to Angers.[20] His partner, Wetulani, did no better at his job.

At that time, Bucharest hosted two other loyal representatives of the Polish government-in-exile: the aforementioned military attaché, Colonel Zakrzewski, and Ambassador Raczyński. However, neither was formally subordinate to the interior minister and could not lend their services to the base. Even unofficial

---

19 Dubicki, *Konspiracja Polska w Rumunii*, 222; Hułas, *Goście czy intruzi?*, 223; Jacobmeyer, *Heimat und Exil*, 130–132; Rutkowski, *Stanisław Kot*, 130, 143–144, 186.

20 According to the Polish ambassador Sokolnicki, the sole purpose of this commission, whose representative in Romania was Alexandrowicz, was monitoring the supporters of the Sanation. See: *Sokolnicki, Dziennik Ankarski*, 137; see also on the activities of Alexandrowicz in Romania: Armitage and Pitts, *Alexandrowicz*, 6–7; Dubicki and Rastworowski, *Sanatorzy kontra Sikorszczycy*, 56, 81, 84, 101; Rutkowski, *Stanisław Kot*, 121, 124, 142.

service was out of the question, since the two were unreliable: Zakrzewski was ill-tempered and prone to insubordination, which made him virtually uncontrollable from France,[21] whereas Raczyński was increasingly falling under the sway of his secretary, the fanatical Piłsudchik Giedroyc, leading Kot and his entourage to trust him less and less. In this challenging situation, Kot sent his new ally to Bucharest to create an effective channel of communication with occupied Poland. This ally was the miracle worker Samson Mikiciński.[22]

No More Trips to the General Government

A foreign visitor to Bucharest today will see islands of modern buildings lost in the endless sea of the blandly oppressive and ponderously clumsy architectural legacy of the Communist era. Only occasionally, in the central thoroughfares, will they stumble upon the last traces of the Bucharest of yore: the magnificent capital of Romania that enjoyed a brief flowering in the interlude between the two World Wars. In the 1930s, Bucharest was one of the largest metropolises of continental Europe. Its ultra-modern center, planned and built under the strong influence of French urbanism, earned it the nickname Little Paris. Its population, which had reached one million by 1939, presented a colorful panoply: the local aristocrats, businesspeople, military officers, and civilian officials, many of whom had become fluent in French and adopted West European ways wholesale, lived side by side with large numbers of migrant workers from the impoverished Romanian countryside, and with the foreign refugees, mostly from Russia and Greece, who had flocked to Romania to escape the political, social, and economic upheavals wracking their home countries.[23]

The exact date of Samson Mikiciński's arrival in the city is unknown. Upon interrogation in Palestine in early 1941, he would initially claim to have realized, during his fifth visit to Poland in April 1940, that he would no longer be able to keep up the charade with the Abwehr, feeding Scholz useless scraps of non-confidential information; therefore, he supposedly decided to wind down his activities in Warsaw and set up an alternative base of operations

---

21 See the profile of Zakrzewski: an official memorandum signed by Colonel Jan Kornaus, for the private use of Lieutenant Colonel M., an undated document, March 1940, PISM, PRM. 14B, 38–39.
22 An undated report titled "Mikiciński Samson," JPIA, Archiwum Osobowe, NZ 154, Sygn. 658; Rutkowski, *Stanisław Kot*, 144.
23 Nicoară, *Istoria și tradițiile minorităților din România*, 34–38; Lampe, "Interwar Bucharest": 267–290.

in the Romanian capital.[24] However, Polish military counterintelligence knew that as early as March 1940, Mikiciński had smuggled money for the Polish government-in-exile and private individuals into occupied Poland via Bucharest.[25] Mikiciński's interrogators might have disclosed this, since he subsequently changed his account: he now claimed that he started planning to relocate from Warsaw to Bucharest in February 1940 and flew from Berlin to Romania for multi-day trips on his third and fourth visits to Poland.[26]

On April 11, just after Mikiciński returned to Bucharest from his fourth voyage to the GG, he informed Kot that the German police had unexpectedly raided the Chilean legation in Warsaw. Another of Kot's sources in occupied Poland fully corroborated this report.[27] Hence, it is quite possible that Mikiciński's decision to relocate to Little Paris was not motivated by concerns over his continuing ability to keep up the charade with Scholz. Rather, it seems much more likely that by early 1940, Mikiciński realized the growing influence of Hans Frank and the Gestapo in the GG—at the expense of the Wehrmacht and the Abwehr—had put him in danger. It is for this reason that Mikiciński decided to cease his activities on the Paris-Berlin-Breslau-Warsaw axis; the Nazi raid on his premises in April was the last straw, proving once and for all that his fears were grounded. Immediately afterward, he left occupied Warsaw for good, preferring the relative safety of the Romanian capital.

The anonymous author of the report from the Brooklyn archive, fairly conversant with the details of Mikiciński's life during this period, asserts that on his first visit to Bucharest, Mikiciński showed up unannounced at the Polish embassy on 23 Alexandru Alley. Using the secret password Kot had given him, he entered the building and immediately confronted the embassy treasurer to demand a large sum of money in Polish złotys—allegedly, to be given to the Polish underground. The Polish diplomats, stunned by the highly unusual demand and by the imperious manner of their unbidden guest, hurried to contact their superiors in Angers for clarifications and instructions. Only then did they learn that their visitor was, indeed, Kot's special representative and that they had to give him the required sum.[28]

---

24 An undated protocol of the interrogation of Samson Mikiciński, spring 1941, HIA, 800/41/0/-/141 Folder 7, Scans 000954-5.
25 A report by the Dwójka titled "Mikiciński—information," June 1941, HIA, 800/41/0/-/141 Folder 7, Scans 001006-7.
26 An undated protocol of the interrogation of Samson Mikiciński, spring 1941, HIA, 800/41/0/-/141 Folder 7, Scan 000968.
27 Rutkowski, *Stanisław Kot*, 146–147.
28 An undated report titled "Mikiciński Samson," JPIA, Archiwum Osobowe, NZ 154, Sygn. 658.

A subsequent report drawn from the Office of the British Military Censor in Tel Aviv provides some interesting information about the recipients of these funds: a Polish document or letter they examined had indicated that Mikiciński was in Bucharest on behalf of the Polish government-in-exile and with the sworn assistance of the local Polish embassy, with the primary goal of rendering material assistance to the Polish academics who had stayed behind.[29] This conclusion is borne out by Mikiciński's private correspondence with Kot[30] indicating that the money he had smuggled into Poland had been divided between the management of the Jagiellonian University in Kraków and Janusz Radziwiłł's Principal Protective Council.[31] It is quite possible that Mikiciński was responsible for supplying Radziwiłł's organization with the funds it needed to start giving humanitarian aid to Poles suffering under the Nazi jackboot.

One of the major beneficiaries of the funds, Władysław Szafer—a globally renowned botanist and the former rector of the Jagiellonian University—would later recall that Mikiciński showed up in Kraków in February 1940 and handed him the enormous sum of 1,140,000 złotys, money that all but ensured the survival of the professor, his university colleagues, and their students.[32]

Mikiciński made no secret of his ties with the Polish government-in-exile; au contraire, he blabbed to all and sundry in Bucharest that he was acting in the interests of Sikorski and his followers.[33] It seems that this was no idle tongue-wagging, let alone reckless braggadocio, but in all likelihood, a carefully calculated ploy to gain useful connections among the local elites and officialdom. A new Romanian premier, Gheorghe Tătărescu, took power in November 1939 and sought to correct his country's foreign policy course by rekindling warm relations with the Western powers. In the eight months while Tătărescu held office, Polish diplomats and envoys enjoyed an elevated status,[34] and Mikiciński must have taken advantage of this to hasten his entrenchment in Bucharest.

---

29 An undated extract from an untitled report by the Office of the British Military Censor in Tel Aviv, TNA, HS 4/213.
30 Quite plausibly, this correspondence between *Lis* and *Tigris* was facilitated by Tomasz Kuźniarz, a former employee of the Polish National Bank who then served as treasurer of the Polish embassy in Bucharest and enjoyed the trust of Minister Kot (he had a separate channel of encrypted communication with Angers). See on the relationship between Kuźniarz and Kot: a report by the British censors about an article published in the *Dziennik Polski* newspaper, which was based in Detroit (USA), under the title "Mr. Kuźniarz, the Consul at the Polish Embassy in Washington, DC, is Accused of Being a Troublemaker and Informer," September 4, 1943, TNA, KV 2/3429_5, 34–35; and also: footnote 125 in Ciechanowski, *Polsko-Brytyjska współpraca*, 136.
31 Rutkowski, *Stanisław Kot*, 148.
32 Szafer, *Wspomnienia przyrodnika*, 253.
33 An undated and untitled report by agent A/H.2, late December 1940, TNA, HS 4/213.
34 Dubicki, *Dzieje polskiej placówki*, 127.

Indeed, according to the report from the Brooklyn archive, Mikiciński succeeded in striking deep roots in the operational environment of that city. While carrying out the government-in-exile's orders, especially Kot's, he advanced his own business interests: his network of Bucharest representatives sought out potential customers to offer their services in occupied Poland, like transferring money to relatives in exchange for a 15% commission. The report also says that Mikiciński would meet the most lucrative clients in person and try to impress them by telling them about his excellent relationships with the Germans, including Kraft, the economic advisor to the German embassy. According to the report, Kraft was a Nazi intelligence operative working under diplomatic cover. Sometimes, when Mikiciński was trying to impress his clients, he would point at some nearby German and say in a confidential tone, "He is a Gestapo agent assigned to guard me!"[35]

But Mikiciński's work with private customers failed to satisfy his ambitions. Using special agents in the Nazi-occupied Polish territory and the commission fees he received from the Polish government-in-exile, he bought foreign currency and valuables in the GG and then smuggled them out for selling at great profit.[36] During one of his interrogations in Palestine, he also indicated that, while in Bucharest, he would lend money at interest, sometimes to employees of the local Polish embassy.[37]

The Polish Rival and His Bulgarian Connections

Mikiciński's new enterprise was just getting into gear when he learned of another man in Bucharest who specialized in smuggling money across the borders of Romania and the GG. This was Viktor Kutten, most probably an ethnic Austrian or Jew, a native of Vienna, a Polish citizen, the former owner of a Polish cement consortium, and a very wealthy man. After fleeing to Bucharest in September 1939, he had quickly established business relations with Jerzy Kurcyusz (code names Ali, Azis, and Novina), chief of the operational intelligence network of the exiled Polish Interior Ministry and a confidant of Kot. In early 1940, Kurcyusz worked in Rome; he later moved to Athens and ended up in Istanbul.[38] Under

---

35 An undated report titled "Mikiciński Samson," JPIA, Archiwum Osobowe, NZ 154, Sygn. 658.
36 Ibid.; Iranek-Osmecki, "Afera Mikicińskiego": 188–189.
37 An undated protocol of the interrogation of Samson Mikiciński, spring 1941, HIA, 800/41/0/-/141 Folder 7, Scan 000947.
38 A top secret report titled "The Kutten Affair," copy # 1; July 18, 1941, TNA, HS 4/213; Derbyshire—Shillito (F.2 b/c), June 8, 1943, TNA, KV 2/3429_5, 56; according to

his patronage, and in cooperation with a fellow Polish refugee named Bronisław Stefanowski-Syrokomla (once a prominent journalist), Kutten began to smuggle money and secret messages to the underground Polish structures subordinated to Sikorski and Kot.[39]

The Polish military counterintelligence reported to the top echelon of the émigré government, including Sikorski, that Kutten did not travel to the GG with the money and the letters, but used the services of three intermediaries—the Bulgarian diplomats Trayanov, Tsokov, and Ikonomov—who were in contact with Stefanowski-Syrokomla throughout. In the opinion of the analysts, these Bulgarians were no altruists since they skimmed off a certain percentage of every sum they transported across the Bucharest-Warsaw line. The analysts went on to assert that, by means of bribes and other corruption mechanisms, Kutten had established an excellent working relationship with the Romanian officials, who apparently preferred to turn a blind eye to his smuggling operations. In the summer of 1940, they even helped him organize the evacuation of a group of Polish refugees to Brazil.[40]

British counterintelligence was even more knowledgeable about the fugitive Polish businessman. According to their data, Kutten's activities were not limited to Bucharest: the Bulgarian capital of Sofia was also part of his sphere of business interests. There, he received assistance from the local Polish ambassador Adam Tarnowski, yet another of Kot's protégés. Thus, Tarnowski gave Kutten access to diplomatic mail channels shielded from prying eyes, enabling him to keep in regular touch with their common patron in Angers, and with the patron's agents in Istanbul.[41] This web of operatives, cast by the new Polish interior minister over southeastern Europe and the Middle East with stunning speed

---

Ciechanowski, the official post held by Kurcyusz in Istanbul was that of chief of the "Department of General and Political Communication between the Government and the Homeland" (*Kierownik placówki łączności ogólnej i politycznej rządu z krajem*). See on this, plus some other details about Kutten: footnote 85 in Ciechanowski, *Polsko-Brytyjska współpraca*, 126.

39 A report by the Dwójka titled "Mikiciński—information," June 1941, HIA, 800/41/0/-/141 Folder 7, Scan 000999; according to modern Polish historiography, Kutten was also involved in the trade of currency and valuables that were smuggled out of the GG. See footnote 156 in Ciechanowski, *Polsko-Brytyjska współpraca*, 144.

40 A report by the Dwójka titled "Mikiciński—information," June 1941, HIA, 800/41/0/-/141 Folder 7, Scan 001007; modern Polish historiography has endorsed the claim about the allegedly criminal underpinnings of the partnership between Kutten and the Bulgarian diplomats. See footnote 156 in Ciechanowski, *Polsko-Brytyjska współpraca*, 144.

41 An undated, top secret draft of a memorandum by SOE, titled "Note on the Kot organisation in the Middle East," TNA, HS 4/213; a top secret report titled "The Kutten Affair," copy #1, July 18, 1941, ibid.

and efficiency, was interpreted by the British officials (and by those of their Polish counterparts who were not affiliated with Kot) as a weapon in the hands of Nazi espionage. It was feared that the true goal of these agents was to help their handlers in Berlin uncover and destroy the fledgling Polish underground. This suspicion may have been strengthened by a confession Mikiciński allegedly made in one of his interrogations in Palestine asserting "the Bulgarian channel, which connected Kutten to the occupied homeland, was under tight German control."[42] The Polish Foreign Ministry clung to this view until the end of World War II and maintained that by the time of his escape from Poland to Romania in the autumn of 1939, Kutten was already an agent of both the Gestapo and the Abwehr, and he was trying to get in touch with the Polish military intelligence station in Bucharest at the behest of his Nazi handlers.[43]

Nowadays, we can assert confidently that everything Polish and British diplomats and counterintelligence operatives wrote about Kutten's activities from the autumn of 1939 give only a limited picture, and a very distorted one at that. This may have been a deliberate falsification through which General Sosnkowski's followers, including officers of the Dwójka, tried to hamstring their rivals in the Kotowcy by presenting them as pro-Nazi to Sikorski and the British. In reality, the dominant partner in the Kutten-Tarnowski duo was not Kutten but Tarnowski, a high placed Polish diplomat from Sofia and one of the star players of the Polish Foreign Ministry in the 1930s and 1940s. Following disagreements with the prewar foreign minister Józef Beck, Tarnowski was "exiled" to the Bulgarian capital, where he established exceptionally cordial relations with the local elites. In September 1939, Tarnowski openly endorsed Sikorski's new government and joined the relief efforts for the Polish refugees. He also worked on developing channels of communication between Angers and occupied Poland. His key ally in this arduous undertaking was his Bulgarian friend and colleague, Krum Tsokov, a Polonophile who had served as economic advisor at the Bulgarian embassy in Warsaw in 1936–1939. Tsokov returned to his homeland immediately after the German invasion of Poland. Shortly thereafter, he received a new appointment to the Bulgarian embassy in Berlin and, loathing the Nazis, initially tried to refuse to work in the capital of the Third Reich. However, Tarnowski managed to convince him to agree to the posting

---

42 An undated protocol of the interrogation of Samson Mikiciński, spring 1941, HIA, 800/41/0/-/141 Folder 7, Scan 000972.
43 The Headquarters of the Polish Foreign Office in London to Szczerbiński, the Polish Consul in Jerusalem, concerning the release of Kutten, Stefanowski, and Kąsinowski, May 24, 1945, HIA, 800/42/0/-/325 Folder 2, Scan 000297.

so as to be able to aid secretly the development of the Polish anti-Nazi underground from Berlin.[44]

The small, close-knit group set up by Tsokov to aid the Poles consisted only of him and two other persons. The first of these was Krum's close friend and former secretary, Dimitar Ikonomov, who shortly thereafter returned to Nazi-occupied Warsaw as an economic advisor and stayed there until March 1941. Tsokov's second partner in the clandestine struggle was Petar Trayanov, the former Bulgarian ambassador to the Second Polish Republic. A little later, another Bulgarian citizen joined the trio: Trifon Pukhlev, a young clerk from the consular department of the Bulgarian embassy to the General Government. For security reasons, their Polish friend and handler Tarnowski designated them in his secret operational correspondence as Group B (Bulgaria).[45]

As early as October 1939, Tsokov traveled from Berlin to Warsaw, allegedly to check up on the Bulgarian embassy in the ruined city. In reality, he was to establish ties with the Polish underground on Tarnowski's behalf. His mission was a success, and he would make many additional trips from Berlin to Warsaw. In his official capacity as a diplomat, Tsokov met repeatedly with representatives of the German occupying authorities (including Governor General Hans Frank) while also serving as a secret courier for the Poles, smuggling money and letters from Tarnowski into the occupied territory. Ikonomov and Pukhlev would distribute these items among the Polish clandestine fighters. Trayanov, as a secret Polish courier, shuttled along the Sofia-Bucharest-Budapest triangle. Apparently, it was he who contacted Kutten and Stefanowski-Syrokomla, who were working in Bucharest.[46]

In the last months of 1939, Group B transported a total of about three thousand letters and secret messages and as many as 3,500,000 złotys along the routes between Berlin, Sofia, Bucharest, and Warsaw. Dimitar Ikonomov supplied many residents of the occupied Polish capital with official documents identifying them as local employees of the Bulgarian embassy, thereby saving these Poles from deportation to forced labor in the Reich and incarceration in Nazi concentration camps. Trifon Pukhlev issued Bulgarian transit visas to hundreds of Polish refugees (Jews, Polish army officers, and prominent Polish scientists, including former colleagues of Kot's from Kraków University), enabling them to travel through Bulgarian territory to Hungary, Romania, and the Balkan

---

44 Chimiak, "Adam Tarnowski—nasz poseł w Sofii," 227–251; Sendek, "Południowcy w polskiej konspiracji;" Tsokov, "Moja droga do Polski," 168–206.
45 Ibid.; Klisurova, "B'lgari spasiavat Polski evrei."
46 Ibid.

countries, then onto the West or Palestine. On many occasions, Polish refugees staying on Romanian soil received similar Bulgarian visas from members of the Bulgarian group (probably via Trayanov, Kutten, and Stefanowski-Syrokomla).[47]

The Bulgarian friends of Ambassador Tarnowski scored another amazing success: passing detailed and reliable information about the situation in the German-occupied Polish territories (including accounts of the occupiers' crimes) to the West. Krum Tsokov made contact with Edward Stanisław Fikus, a photographer who worked for one of the first Polish underground newspapers and captured tragic events in occupied Warsaw: public executions in the streets, the destruction of the symbols of Polish independence and culture, and the persecution of the local Jews. In late 1939, Fikus secretly gave Tsokov 120 of his photographs accompanied by explanatory notes and the exact dates on which they had been taken. Tsokov then smuggled them in three batches, via Berlin, to the Polish ambassador in Sofia. After being delivered to the exiled Polish government in Angers, these images were widely circulated in the Western press as vivid illustrations of Nazi barbarity, and in March 1940, they came out in a brochure titled *Les atrocités allemandes en Pologne* (Nazi crimes in Poland). In May 1945, Fikus's photographs were handed over for permanent storage to the Polish Institute and Sikorski Museum newly opened in London. To this day, they are a testament to the heroism of the photographer and the members of Group B who worked with him, the first to let the world see the true face of the German New Order in Poland.[48]

The activities of Group B came to a sudden end in June 1940, when the Hungarian police arrested Krum Tsokov at the behest of the German authorities. The brave Bulgarian diplomat was handed over to the Nazis, who tried him for "intentionally sabotaging the German efforts to build the General Government" and sentenced him to five years of imprisonment in the Mokotów Prison in Warsaw. This was a dreadful place, used by the Nazis throughout the occupation period to incarcerate prominent Polish social and military leaders, as well as underground activists. Many of the inmates died or were killed within its walls. Fortunately, Tsokov managed to survive, and after the end of the war he published his memoirs about the war years and his own clandestine anti-Nazi activities. At the time of Tsokov's arrest in Hungary, Trifon Pukhlev, too, was forced to cease his work on behalf of the Poles. Under German pressure, he was recalled from Warsaw to Sofia and accused of violating the local law on the issuing of visas. In the early twenty-first century, authorities in Bulgaria finally recognized and

---

47 Ibid.
48 Ibid.; "Edward Stanisław Fikus": 25–33; Vallentin, *Les atrocités*.

commemorated the heroic deeds of Tsokov, Trayanov, Ikonomov, and Pukhlev. Bulgarian state television aired a documentary film describing the activities of Group B called *Through Sofia to Freedom*, the Bulgarian government installed a special memorial plaque on the façade of the Bulgarian embassy in Warsaw, and the recently built Museum of the History of Polish Jews in that city received copies of the original Bulgarian documents testifying to the contribution of the group to the rescue of Polish Jews during the Holocaust.[49]

Needless to say, in 1940, none of this was known to the Polish and British counterintelligence operatives, who suspected Group B—and Kutten, who was in touch with them—of collaborating with the Nazis. As will be shown later on, these suspicions would affect not only the lives of Kutten and his partners in Bucharest, but play a particularly tragic role in Mikiciński's fate: the British would use the treason Kutten and his Bulgarians ostensibly committed as a pretext for the overblown charges of espionage against him, and as a justification for his liquidation in Palestine.

The End of the Fragile Partnership

The anonymous author of the report from the Polish archives in Brooklyn and the British intelligence analysts who compiled Kutten's profile both agree that when Mikiciński and Kutten learned of each other's existence in early 1940, enmity flared up between the two men. Each knew that he was dealing with a very successful and hence dangerous rival in the struggle for access to the secret flows of capital that connected the Polish émigré circles with the underground fighters and private individuals who had stayed behind.[50] As shown above, the illegal transfer of money into occupied Poland was a lucrative business thanks to the hefty commission fees its brokers demanded. Naturally, neither party to this conflict was willing to share profits with the other. In this connection, the eyewitness from Brooklyn adds that the German intelligence community immediately realized that the clash between its two valuable agents posed a grave threat to its operational interests. Therefore, already in the spring of 1940, the Germans forced Mikiciński and Kutten to reconcile. Their meeting in

---

49 Klisurova, "B'lgari spasiavat Polski evrei;" "Posolstvo na Republika B'lgariia v'v Varshava," December 12, 2018.
50 An undated report titled "Mikiciński Samson," JPIA, Archiwum Osobowe, NZ 154, Sygn. 658; a top secret report titled "The Kutten Affair," copy #1, July 18, 1941, TNA, HS 4/213.

Bucharest was allegedly attended by Mikiciński's old acquaintance, the Abwehr officer Erich Nobis, who had flown in from Berlin for that purpose.[51]

The British, for their part, failed to mention any German involvement in the reconciliation of the two erstwhile rivals. According to the data of MI5, the two men made the decision to bury the hatchet on their own, and their agreement pertained largely to their private projects like smuggling money into occupied Poland regardless of the interests of the government-in-exile.[52] Polish military intelligence concurred with their British colleagues, pointing out that Kutten made an offer of reconciliation, even partnership, to Mikiciński on his own initiative. According to Dwójka headquarters, Kutten had been initially suspicious of Mikiciński's German connections, believing that they were Nazi intelligence instruments. However, he was soon convinced that these dealings were not harmful to Polish interests and could even be used to advance his own business goals.[53] Mikiciński would state in one of his Palestinian interrogations that only after reaching an agreement with his new partner did he let him in on the secret of his business partnership with Nobis and Scholz.[54] British intelligence endorsed this account. In stark contrast to the Brooklyn reporter's assertion about the alleged involvement of the Abwehr in Mikiciński's and Kutten's reconciliation, the British analysts determined that it was Mikiciński who had introduced Kutten to Nobis after Nobis's official transfer to Bucharest in the spring of 1940, and went so far as to warn Kutten that this useful German was a Nazi intelligence officer.[55]

The cooperation between Kot's two Bucharest-based confidants culminated in May 1940, when Kutten asked Mikiciński to help him smuggle approximately two million złotys—about a million reichsmarks, an enormous sum by the standards of the time—to Warsaw.[56] At the same time, Kutten did not hesitate to contact the Germans directly, behind his new partner's back. The most blatant example of Kutten's uncomradely behavior was the request he gave Nobis

---

51 An undated report titled "Mikiciński Samson," ibid.
52 A top secret report titled "The Kutten Affair," copy # 1, July 18, 1941, TNA, HS 4/213.
53 A report by the Dwójka titled "Mikiciński—information," June 1941, HIA, 800/41/0/-/141 Folder 7, Scan 001008; chief of the Dwójka, Colonel Mitkiewicz-Żółtek, to General Sikorski, an untitled report, January 20, 1941, HIA, 800/41/0/-/141 Folder 7, Scan 001022.
54 An undated protocol of the interrogation of Samson Mikiciński, spring 1941, HIA, 800/41/0/-/141 Folder 7, Scan 000954.
55 A top secret report titled "The Kutten Affair," copy #1, July 18, 1941, TNA, HS 4/213; a top secret report titled "The Paluchowicz Affair," copy #1, July 18, 1941, TNA, HS 4/213.
56 A report by the Dwójka titled "Mikiciński—information," June 1941, HIA, 800/41/0/-/141 Folder 7, Scan 001008; chief of the Dwójka, Colonel Mitkiewicz-Żółtek, to General Sikorski, an untitled report, January 20, 1941, HIA, 800/41/0/-/141 Folder 7, Scan 001022.

sometime in the summer of 1940, when Mikiciński was not in Bucharest, to assist him in sending a precious shipment to Poland. On that occasion, the cargo consisted of twenty-two suitcases and parcels (or, according to another version, ten satchels) with letters, a large sum of money, and jewelry. Those responsible for sending it were the Polish government-in-exile, Kot, and probably Kutten as well; the intended recipients were underground fighters and private individuals in the occupied homeland. The author of the Brooklyn report claims that Nazi military intelligence ordered Nobis to assent to this request; the British counterintelligence, for its part, adds that four independent witnesses observed Kutten pass this cargo on to Nobis at the international airport in Bucharest. The crucial fact about this story is that the precious cargo never reached its destination. Upon returning from Warsaw to Bucharest, the Abwehr officer told a stunned Kutten that his baggage had been confiscated by the Gestapo in the GG, and that he had barely avoided detention. Analyzing the consequences of this failure, the British assumed that "the would-be recipients of the confiscated cargo must have been identified by the Germans, and later punished."[57]

That was the end of the short-lived alliance of Mikiciński and Kutten. The latter immediately demanded that his partner, whom he had just tried to swindle, reimburse him for the major financial loss. In all likelihood, this claim was rooted in the fact that it was Mikiciński who had introduced Kutten to Nobis, effectively vouching for the reliability of the German officer. Mikiciński, for his part, imposed strict conditions on a settlement, effectively precluding the possibility of resolution of the financial and personal conflict between the parties.[58] About six months later, while being interrogated in Palestine, Mikiciński was still trying to harm his former rival/partner, accusing him of criminal negligence, at the very least. According to Mikiciński, Kutten was well aware of Nobis's affiliation with the Nazi military intelligence and made a fatal error when he contacted the German behind Mikiciński's back and gave him access to the confidential correspondence between the Sikorski government and the Polish underground.[59]

---

57 An undated report titled "Mikiciński Samson," JPIA, Archiwum Osobowe, NZ 154, Sygn. 658; an undated protocol of the interrogation of Samson Mikiciński, spring 1941, HIA, 800/41/0/-/141 Folder 7, Scan 000972; a top secret report titled "The Kutten Affair," copy #1, July 18, 1941, TNA, HS 4/213.
58 An undated report titled "Mikiciński Samson," JPIA, ibid.
59 An undated protocol of the interrogation of Samson Mikiciński, spring 1941, HIA, 800/41/0/-/141 Folder 7, Scan 000972.

The Move to Turkey

Even before the conflict with Kutten flared because of his dealings with Nobis, on May 14 (the very day Wehrmacht troops crossed the French border and steamrolled their way into the country), Mikiciński left the French capital. As with his departure from Warsaw eight months earlier, he traveled comfortably in a private car. Passing through Genoa, he reached Rome, where he boarded an airliner to Bucharest, and thence to Istanbul.[60]

Over the next two months, in the lulls between trips to the Romanian capital, Mikiciński devoted his time to setting up a new base of operations in the city on the Bosporus. (It was during one of his stays there that Kutten had his secret meeting with Erich Nobis at the Bucharest airport.) Mikiciński's preparations for relocating to Turkey were done by early August 1940, and the Turkish Foreign Office received an official request from the local Chilean legation to register him as the secretary and chief clerk of Mr. Héctor Briones Luco, the chargé d'affaires of the Republic of Chile.

In an office in the modern Ayaspaşa district, between Taksim Square and the Bosporus, Luco and Mikiciński worked as the only Chilean diplomats in Turkey at the time. Luco was still receiving thousands of dollars from Mikiciński, while the latter was enjoying all the privileges of a foreign diplomat. Even more importantly, Mikiciński had unrestricted access to Chilean diplomatic mail, which he used for Kot's assignments and his own business, which now included smuggling money, precious jewelry, and other assets belonging to those he rescued from occupied Poland and the refugee camps in Romania. According to Mikiciński, the commission fees for such transactions did not exceed 5% of their nominal value, and in some cases, he offered his services free of charge. The owners of the money and property could receive their possessions on the spot or in Palestine.[61]

The British intelligence agency SOE, active in Turkey, determined that after Mikiciński moved to Istanbul, his business there continued to prosper. In fact, he became even richer thanks to commission fees and through illegally trading Polish currency in the Balkans and the Middle East, including Iran.[62] In October

---

60 An undated protocol of the interrogation of Samson Mikiciński, spring 1941, HIA, 800/41/0/-/141 Folder 7, Scan 000968; a top secret report titled "The Paluchowicz Affair," copy #1, July 18, 1941, TNA, HS 4/213.
61 A protocol of the interrogation of Samson Mikiciński; March 15, 1941, HIA, 800/41/0/-/141 Folder 7, Scan 000966; a report by the Dwójka titled "Mikiciński—information," June 1941, HIA, 800/41/0/-/141 Folder 7, Scan 001008.
62 A top secret report titled "The Paluchowicz Affair," copy #1, July 18, 1941, TNA, HS 4/213.

and November of 1940, Polish diplomats in Ankara reported to their leadership in London that Mikiciński, now settled in Istanbul, was transferring money and valuables in cooperation with Bulgarian diplomats.[63] In all likelihood, these diplomats were the members of the Tsokov-Ikonomov group Kutten had bequeathed to Mikiciński.

The Polish Desk at the Chilean Embassy

The permanent relocation of Mikiciński's base of operations to Turkey did not put an immediate stop to his activities in Romania; au contraire, these activities reached their apogee in the autumn of 1940. At that time, Romania was going through one of the most dramatic upheavals in its history. Having lost all its strategic allies on the European continent because of the string of German victories and the evacuation of the British from France, it was forced to concede extensive territories with large Romanian populations to its neighbors, Hungary and Bulgaria, which were backed by Berlin. King Carol II, who could not handle this diplomatic crisis and the subsequent wave of popular unrest, hurriedly appointed a new government under General Ion Antonescu and his deputy, Horia Sima, the commander of the fascist Legionary Movement (also known as the Iron Guard). In early September, the King was forced to abdicate in favor of his son, who was crowned as King Michael I. Immediately after its establishment, the Antonescu-Sima cabinet concluded a strategic alliance with Berlin and agreed to the stationing of German troops on Romanian soil. Just two months later, Bucharest officially joined the Berlin-Rome-Tokyo Axis. Against this backdrop, the Romanian military and special forces, now subordinate to Antonescu and the fascist Legionaries, launched a wave of political terror that included persecuting Romanian Jews and looting their property.[64]

This ever-expanding vortex of violence quickly sucked in foreign refugees who had sought asylum in Romania and the official representatives of the countries fighting against Nazi Germany. New Romanian foreign minister Mihail Sturdza (scion of an old Moldavian aristocratic family and an active member

---

63 Rutkowski, *Stanisław Kot*, 149.
64 An unfinished secret telegram titled "The political mood in Romania and the condition of the Poles [there] after the departure of the embassy of the Polish Republic from Bucharest," November 22, 1940, PISM, PRM.32, 60–66; a secret telegram from Istanbul, signed by Ambassador Raczyński, to the Polish Foreign Minister in London, titled "On the temporary cessation of Polish-Romanian relations," November 30, 1940, ibid., 24–32; Kershaw, *Hitler*, 584.

of the Iron Guard) ordered these representatives to leave the country at once. The Polish diplomats—still tending to the needs of thousands of compatriots scattered all over Romania with virtually no legal protections—tried to sabotage the implementation of this order and delay their departure, aiming to stay at least as long as their British counterparts. To hurry them up, the local security forces occupied two buildings in Bucharest that housed the trade and financial departments of the Polish embassy and the local station of the Dwójka. This operation involved arresting employees of these Polish institutions and confiscating property, documentation, and large sums of money.[65]

As a result, on November 4, 1940, the Polish ambassador to Romania, Roger Raczyński, along with most of his staff (including the Polish military and intelligence officers who had been working under the cover of the embassy) left Bucharest for Istanbul.[66] The only Polish diplomats left in the Romanian capital were Raczyński's secretary, the Sanation activist Jerzy Giedroyc, and several of his colleagues from the diplomatic corps. They now had to establish a Polish desk at the Chilean embassy.[67] The details of the Polish-Chilean-Romanian contacts that enabled the establishment of this desk are still shrouded in the mists of history, and their success seems surprising, given what we know about the Chilean Foreign Office in Santiago in those days: its chiefs showed no interest in the Polish problem, and its temporary chargé d'affaires in Romania, the Chilean businessman Miguel A. Rivera (who had been appointed to this post purely by chance after the expulsion of the ambassador), was completely ignorant of the internal situation in Romania and the complex geopolitical context, and content to keep a low profile, refraining from any meaningful involvement in events.[68]

The only thing we currently know for certain is that the decision to establish a Polish desk in Bucharest was made in late October 1940. In exchange for taking the rump Polish diplomatic representation in Romania under their wing, the Chileans demanded to take control of the picturesque Polish embassy building on Alexandru Alley in the city center. Their demand was granted, and the desk

---

65 Ambassador Raczyński to the Polish Foreign Minister in London, "On our protests and appeals prior to the temporary cessation of Polish-Romanian relations," November 22, 1940, PISM, PRM.32, 6–23.
66 See on the arrival of the embassy staff in Istanbul, on November 7, 1940: Sokolnicki, *Dziennik Ankarski*, 153.
67 An unfinished secret telegram titled "The political mood in Romania and the condition of the Poles [there] after the departure of the Embassy of the Polish Republic from Bucharest," November 22, 1940, PISM, PRM.32, 64–66.
68 See the profile of Rivera: a secret telegram from Istanbul, signed by Ambassador Raczyński, to the Polish Foreign Minister in London, titled "On the temporary cessation of Polish-Romanian relations," November 30, 1940, PISM, PRM.32, 31–32.

was to operate in this very building. According to the pledge the Poles gave the Chileans, the desk's primary purpose would be the provision of consular services to the Polish citizens stranded in Romania. In reality, from the earliest days of its existence, it unofficially helped former soldiers and officers of the Polish army, as well as Jewish refugees from occupied Poland, to travel to Palestine via Turkey.[69]

Needless to say, Sikorski and Kot were not pleased with the fact that the desk would be working for pro-Sanation agents. Kot's representatives in Istanbul had learned that Giedroyc and his aides had begun to liquidate the outposts of the Polish government-in-exile in the countries bordering occupied Poland.[70] As a result, Mikiciński, who was already safely ensconced in Turkey, had to rush back to Bucharest. His mission there was not just to frustrate Giedroyc's plan, but to oust the pro-Sanation diplomat and his colleagues from Romania. Thus, the war between the Sikorski-Kot faction and its opponents on Romanian soil reached the final, decisive phase. It quickly became apparent that Mikiciński's rivals had no hope of victory. Drawing on his extensive connections in the Romanian establishment and on his close ties with Chilean diplomats, he quickly launched a "smear campaign against Giedroyc" (as subsequently described by the Sanation supporters themselves and by the Polish historians who took their side).[71] Already on November 19—two weeks after the closure of the Polish embassy in Bucharest—the pro-Sanation Polish consul in Istanbul, Tadeusz Kunicki, complained to his bosses in London:

> Mikiciński, by having himself appointed desk chief at the Chilean embassy in Bucharest, has officially become an employee of the Polish Desk at that same embassy. He has appointed his loyalist, the Warsaw lawyer Zygmunt Blenau (a weak-willed man with suspected ties to the Germans), as chief of this desk. He has done all this as part of an arrangement with the ambassador, without the knowledge or consent of the government in Santiago.[72]

The author of the report from the Brooklyn archive adds that back in early November, immediately after Polish embassy personnel departed Bucharest,

---

69 Ibid., 29–30; Dubicki, *Dzieje polskiej placówki*, 133–36, 166, 197.
70 Dubicki, *Konspiracja Polska w Rumunii*, 232.
71 An undated and untitled report by Agent A/H.2, late December 1940, TNA, HS 4/213; Dubicki, *Dzieje polskiej placówki*, 136.
72 An encrypted telegram by Kunicki to the Polish Foreign Office in London, November 19, 1940, HIA, 800/41/0/-/141 Folder 7, Scan 000108.

Mikiciński arrived in the vacant building on Alexandru Alley, occupied the ambassador's office and, with the help of the lawyer Blenau, began to implement his plans, including exercising control over the Polish desk. In this new capacity, he continued to facilitate Polish immigration to Turkey and Palestine, accepting money and valuables at the Polish desk and sending them along to his customers' final destinations through Chilean diplomatic mail.[73] The tone of the Brooklyn report reflects an extreme antipathy, and Roger Raczyński, the former Polish ambassador in Bucharest, held similar sentiments. Having drifted away from the Sikorski-Kot camp even before his move to Turkey, Raczyński came under the powerful influence of the pro-Sanation camp. And now, from his new seat in Istanbul, he did everything in his power to harm Mikiciński. A complaint he sent to his superiors in London indicated that Jerzy Giedroyc and his colleagues who had stayed in Romania to manage the Polish desk were unable to carry out their jobs because of various hindrances (like the disconnection of the phones in their offices) allegedly put in their way by Romanian authorities.[74] Although Mikiciński is not mentioned by name in this document, there was an unmistakable hint that he had influenced these acts of obstruction.

Kunicki, the Brooklyn reporter, Raczyński, and all other contemporaries critical of Mikiciński forgot (or, more plausibly, deliberately suppressed) the fact that despite his wealth of useful connections in the Romanian establishment, his activities in Romania in late 1940 involved great personal risk. The officials of the Foreign Office in Bucharest were well aware that he was not a real Chilean but a Polish Jew who had obtained a Chilean diplomatic passport. For this reason, they refused to officially recognize him as a diplomat, and he had to make do with the status of a mere employee of the Chilean embassy. Therefore, Mikiciński lacked diplomatic immunity and could be attacked by the Romanian security organs at any moment. On at least two occasions, he came within a hair's breadth of such an attack when he had his luggage thoroughly searched after disembarking in the port of Constanța.[75]

Mikiciński may have regarded such incidents as the byproduct of Giedroyc's plots against him. Be that as it may, the fight between the two men for control over the local Polish desk ended on December 2, 1940, when the exiled Polish

---

73 An undated report titled "Mikiciński Samson," JPIA, Archiwum Osobowe, NZ 154, Sygn. 658.
74 An unfinished secret telegram titled "The political mood in Romania and the condition of the Poles [there] after the departure of the Embassy of the Polish Republic from Bucharest," November 22, 1940, PISM, PRM.32, 64–65.
75 Ibid., 64–65; a secret telegram from Istanbul, signed by Ambassador Raczyński, to the Polish Foreign Minister in London, titled "On the temporary cessation of Polish-Romanian relations," November 30, 1940, ibid., 32; Buczek, *Człowiek do złotych interesów*, 142.

government in London, at Mikiciński's urging, officially dismissed Giedroyc from the post of desk chief. The Romanians learned of this at once (presumably with a little help) and demanded that Giedroyc leave their country within a week. Giedroyc managed to delay his departure from Romania for another two months but spent this time as a semi-legal resident, risking his liberty and even his life. His ambitious plans against the Sikorski government came to naught. In reports to his confederates in London, Giedroyc attributed his failures to a collusion between "Mik" (probably Mikiciński) and the officials of the Romanian Foreign Office. He also accused his rival of callous disregard for the plight of the refugees left in Romania, and of using the Polish desk almost exclusively for "smuggling money and Romanian Jews who had obtained Polish passports." To make his accusations more credible, Giedroyc cited an anonymous source in the Romanian Foreign Office, who claimed that Mikiciński's actions under the auspices of the Polish desk were "the most outrageous financial fraud in the history of the Romanian State." Giedroyc summed up his accusations: "Mikiciński possesses that mixture of broad-mindedness and daring that is typical of great conmen," and added bitterly: "Through a cruel twist of fate, this sinister character has been exalted by the government-in-exile as the savior of our homeland!"[76]

These reports from the humiliated Giedroyc, now forced into semi-legality, made a deep impression on Roger Raczyński, his friend and former boss. On December 21, Raczyński sent a report of his own from Istanbul to London, offering a scathing criticism of Mikiciński's behavior in Bucharest: although Mikiciński claimed to be acting on the explicit instructions of the government-in-exile, he used the Polish desk for his own ends, making no effort to coordinate his actions with Polish diplomats and appointing "his own man" as chief. Raczyński demanded that his colleagues in London investigate which Polish higher-ups were covering for Mikiciński's shady business in Romania, determine the actual instructions London had sent him, and find out whether the Chilean government knew what kind of man had set up shop in their embassy in Bucharest.[77]

And yet, all the complaints and demands of Giedroyc and Raczyński were in vain. Polish foreign minister August Zaleski was well-informed of the interests Mikiciński actually represented and decided not to meddle in his affairs, to say nothing of his patron's in London. Héctor Briones Luco likewise refused to

---

76 Dubicki, *Konspiracja Polska w Rumunii*, 365. According to Giedroyc's memoirs, he left Bucharest as early as November 1940, with the help of British embassy employees who were likewise leaving Romania. See: Giedroyc, *Autobiografia na cztery ręce*, 102–103.

77 An untitled encrypted telegram from Ambassador Raczyński to the Polish Foreign Office in London; December 21, 1940, HIA, 800/41/0/-/141 Folder 7, Scan 000103.

respond to Raczyński's denunciation of Mikiciński's behavior in the Romanian capital.[78] As a result, in late 1940 to early 1941, Mikiciński continued to divide his time and activities between Istanbul and fascist Bucharest, and this game on two boards lasted right up to his abduction from Turkey to Palestine in mid-January 1941. Curiously, despite Raczyński's allegation that his agency was in no way coordinating with Mikiciński, a document preserved in the Sikorski Archives in London indicates that, as of late December 1940, the Chilean embassy in Bucharest (the desk that Mikiciński controlled) was still supplying the Polish Foreign Office with valuable information about the plight of refugees in Romania.[79]

The sudden, reluctant termination of Mikiciński's activities on Turkish soil (a subject that will be covered in detail later on) also marked the end of the Polish desk at the Chilean embassy in Bucharest. Jerzy Kurcyusz—the chief of the operational intelligence network of the Polish Interior Ministry and Kot's confidant—was supposed to replace Mikiciński in Romania in February 1941, even receiving a genuine Chilean diplomatic passport. However, the news of Mikiciński's disappearance threw a wrench into this plan, and Kurcyusz was forced to stay in Istanbul for a few more years.[80] Besides, the Poles' ability to pay the Chileans for hosting the desk in their Bucharest embassy was gone for good by that point: back in November 1940, the premises of the former Polish embassy, which had been promised to the Chileans, were occupied by the Romanian fascist militia and subsequently handed over to the Germans.[81] Presumably, in the brief interlude between the loss of the embassy building and his abduction, Mikiciński (with Luco's assistance) may have reached an agreement with the Chileans on the question of payment for their hosting services. However, any such agreement was rendered moot in mid-January 1941, and the responsibility for taking care of the Polish citizens in Romania passed over to the Swiss embassy.[82]

---

78 A secret telegram from Istanbul, signed by Ambassador Raczyński, to the Polish Foreign Minister in London, titled "On the temporary cessation of Polish-Romanian relations," November 30, 1940, PISM, PRM.32, 32.
79 The Polish Foreign Office to Antoni Baliński, Secretary of the Polish Embassy in London; December 24, 1940, PISM, A.XII.1/66A, 34.
80 An undated, top secret draft of a memorandum by SOE, titled "Note on the Kot organisation in the Middle East," TNA, HS 4/213; an undated report titled "Mikiciński Samson," JPIA, Archiwum Osobowe, NZ 154, Sygn. 658; according to Ciechanowski, Kurcyusz was to replace Mikiciński in his official capacity as employee of the Chilean embassy in Bucharest. See footnote 85 in Ciechanowski, *Polsko-Brytyjska współpraca*, 126.
81 Dubicki, *Dzieje polskiej placówki*, 136.
82 Ibid.

Seven months later, the former curator of the Polish desk, amateur Chilean diplomat Miguel A. Rivera, completed his mission in Romania and returned home. The Polish ambassador to Ankara, Michał Sokolnicki, made no effort to hide his contempt for the man in a later report: "An utterly unremarkable man, who obviously belonged to the same criminal circle as the previous ambassador, and who showed no concern for the Polish people or their interests."[83] And yet immediately after leaving Europe and setting foot on Latin American soil, this "utterly unremarkable man" suddenly called a press conference in Montevideo, the capital of Uruguay. There, he told his stunned audience and the whole world about the tragedy that had befallen Romanian Jewry under the rule of General Antonescu and showed photographs that gave vivid proof of his words.[84] Since Mikiciński was the only Jew who had closely interacted with Rivera in the year prior to the press conference, we may assume that it was he who had passed this information on to the Chilean with instructions to publicize it.

---

83 Sokolnicki, *Dziennik Ankarski*, 172, 184.
84 "Documents and Photos of Jewish Pogroms in Rumania."

Chapter 4

A Base of Operations and Secret Negotiations on the Banks of the Bosporus

In the Backyard of the World War

Visitors to the Hall of Martyrs at the Military Museum in Istanbul are bound to notice a large stone plaque with a laconic, multilingual inscription: "Peace at home, peace in the world." This slogan was first proclaimed in 1931 by Mustafa Kemal Atatürk, the founder of the Republic of Turkey and its first president, and immediately adopted as the core tenet of the new Turkish state's foreign policy. The product of the Turks' severe collective trauma at the end of World War I and the dissolution of their centuries-old Ottoman Empire, this principle exhorted Turkish statesmen and diplomats to cultivate happiness and prosperity in their homeland by tirelessly working for the cause of collective peace and security throughout the world. In practice, this mindset led Turkish leadership to uphold strict diplomatic and military neutrality in a world that was hurtling precipitously into the abyss of a new global conflict.[1]

After the death of Atatürk in 1938, his successor and former confederate, General İsmet İnönü, continued to adhere to the principle of "Peace at home, peace in the world" while skillfully playing a very dangerous game: charting a course between the Western powers and Nazi Germany. Following the

---

1 Hassel and MacRae, *Alliance of Enemies*, 93; Isci, *Russophobic Neutrality*, 1–2.

Italian occupation of Albania in April 1939 and the unexpected signing of the Soviet-German nonaggression pact several months later, Ankara, fearful of the prospect of triple German-Italian-Soviet aggression, pivoted in the direction of Paris and London. A British-French-Turkish treaty was signed shortly thereafter that gave the Turks access to credits to purchase Western arms while also requiring them to "co-operate effectively" with France and the UK if the belligerent behavior of a certain "European power"—this was a reference to Fascist Italy—were to provoke a large-scale military conflict in the Mediterranean Basin. However, the fall of France in the summer of 1940 radically altered the balance of power in Europe, including its Mediterranean periphery. Therefore, despite its prior obligations and British pressure to carry them out, Turkey used the full weight of its diplomacy to stay out of the international military conflict rapidly gathering steam. To this end, Ankara was even prepared to flirt with the Nazi regime. The pro-Axis tendency in Turkish foreign policy culminated in the summer of 1941. In those months, following the successes of the Wehrmacht in the Balkans and the USSR, the fire of the new European conflagration approached the borders of the assiduously neutral Turkish Republic, while the rapprochement between Moscow and London raised the prospect of an Allied military campaign against Turkey—like the one taking place in neighboring Iran at the time. In this situation, the British were smart enough to realize the strategic value of the declared Turkish policy of neutrality, coupled with tacit cooperation between London and Ankara, and they tried to reinforce it, exerting both covert and overt pressure on President İnönü's cabinet.[2]

One of the instruments of this pressure was the longstanding Turkish-British cooperation in the areas of intelligence gathering and national security. On the British side, this cooperation involved virtually all of His Majesty's special services; on the Turkish side, it included the police, the security service, and the military intelligence. This secret dialogue was greatly facilitated by the presence of a large number of British "knights of cloak and dagger" in Southern Europe and the Eastern Mediterranean. Another, equally significant factor was the Turkish desire to use the police forces and counterintelligence organs of a major Western power to neutralize the threat posed by the flood of legal and illegal refugees from war-torn Europe that had swept over the country. Many of these unfortunates remained in Turkey for a long time, and their communities were a fertile soil for foreign spy agencies and criminal syndicates both local and international. Apart from the British, Nazi and Soviet special services also

---

2   Isci, ibid., 8–9, 162–64; Tamkin, *Britain, Turkey and the Soviet Union*, 19–51; Zürcher, *Turkey*, 212–13.

took advantage of this peculiarity of the Turkish operational environment. The Germans—mostly Abwehr officers, but also some members of the Reich Security Main Office subordinate to the SS—were busy recruiting agents and proxies among the Turkish officialdom, foreign diplomats and businessmen, and groups of refugees. Their most notable accomplishment in this field was the enlistment of a local ethnic Albanian who worked as the valet of the British ambassador in Ankara who gave his Nazi handlers access to his boss's confidential correspondence.[3]

Soviet intelligence operatives likewise reaped considerable success. According to the memoirs of Pavel Sudoplatov, the Soviet agent Sultanov kept in touch with the advisor of the Polish embassy in Ankara, and in 1940, this source gave him valuable intel about the Polish government's plans to destabilize the Soviet South Caucasus, acting via Turkey.[4]

Against this backdrop, it would seem quite natural that the multicultural and multilingual city on the Bosporus enjoyed the unofficial status of one of the capitals of global espionage. Its squares and narrow, winding lanes; its innumerable inns, hotels, restaurants, and gambling dens were crawling with local and foreign agents who were rubbing shoulders with criminals—hired killers, smugglers, counterfeiters, pimps, local black marketeers, and so on. All of them were willing and able to change their personal data, national identity, clientele, and patrons at the drop of a hat. For the right price, they would assassinate any individual, forge any document or banknote, and procure and sell any bit of information, no matter how confidential and well-guarded.[5] Samson Mikiciński, who was known to friends and enemies alike as Solomon, Lis, and Mik—a Chilean diplomat, a special envoy of the Polish foreign minister, a gifted entrepreneur, and an equally gifted smuggler of people, money, and valuables across the borders of wartime Europe—found this milieu very congenial to his work for the good of Poland and for the cultivation of his own ever-growing business.

---

3 Hassel and MacRae, *Alliance of Enemies*, 93–94; Kahn, *Hitler's Spies*, 340–346; Seydi, "The Intelligence War in Turkey": 75–85; West, *Double Cross in Cairo*, 73–122.
4 Sudoplatov, *Raznye dni*, 296. The true identity of the Soviet agent Sultanov mentioned by Sudoplatov remains unclear. According to another Soviet intelligence veteran, a famous defector to the West Georges Agabekov, in the late 1920s there was a Soviet agent in Turkey and Iraq nicknamed Sultanov, but he was fired by his handlers due to his inefficiency. No evidence exists about possible connection between these two "Sultanovs." See: Agabekov, *Sekretnyi terror*, 237, 291.
5 Hassel and MacRae, *Alliance of Enemies*, 94–95.

An Open and Cynical Struggle

In late July–early August 1940, as Mikiciński was busy finishing his relocation from Romania to Turkey, a new round of the political battle between Stanisław Kot and the pro-Sanation camp led by General Kazimierz Sosnkowski was playing out in London and Warsaw. Kot and his supporters in the Polish government-in-exile decided that the time had finally come to wrest control over the growing, clandestine Polish resistance movement from the esteemed general. Sosnkowski's position as chairman of the Committee of Ministers for Homeland Affairs and his influence on the Union of Armed Struggle (ZWZ)—the key organization of the Polish underground and the forerunner of the Home Army, established even before the birth of the government-in-exile and consisting of many of those who supported the prewar Polish regime—had firmly convinced his political opponents in London that he was using his status to usurp power, not only over all the military units of the Polish resistance, but also over its numerous political factions. Some Polish parties opposing the Sanation camp, Sosnkowski in particular, continued to operate in secret under the German occupation, and their leaders flooded Sikorski, Kot, and other prominent members of the government-in-exile with a steady stream of complaints. They alleged that the ZWZ was literally forcing them to subordinate themselves to the general, only letting them communicate with London through him, and subjecting their messages to strict censorship in accordance with his political interests. All this led the complainers to conclude that Sosnkowski and company were trying to isolate the Sikorski government from the suffering and struggling Polish people, thereby paving the way for a future seizure of power in the liberated homeland to inaugurate a military dictatorship similar to the colonel's regime that had dominated prewar Poland.[6]

At a session of the Committee of Ministers for Homeland Affairs held on August 2, Interior Minister Kot responded to the stream of complaints by firing a broadside at General Sosnkowski and his protégés in the leadership of the ZWZ that demanded they cease and desist from further attempts to usurp the authority of the legitimate government in all matters related to organizing and controlling the Polish national resistance.[7] Sikorski officially endorsed this demand, and for the next few months worked on setting up a clandestine representation of his cabinet in occupied Warsaw. Finally, in December of that year, after lengthy hesitations in Britain and in the occupied homeland, the head

---

6 Paszkiewicz, "Komitet dla Spraw Kraju": 163–167.
7 Ibid.

of this representation was selected and given the all-clear to travel to Poland in secret. He was required to maintain a direct channel of bilateral communication between Sikorski and his cabinet and the political underground in the country. He also had to exercise political control over the whole infrastructure of the ZWZ.[8]

Needless to say, this step, which signified the victory of the Kot-led anti-Sanation camp, was not to the liking of the Sosnkowski faction. Thus, the standoff between the two focal points of the Polish resistance movement in London and Warsaw dragged on into the next year, 1941. Several weeks before the arrival of the government representative in Warsaw, Sikorski was forced to remind Sosnkowski of the need to put an end to the interventions of the ZWZ commanders in political affairs. He altered the text of the pledge recited by fresh recruits joining the Union: henceforth, instead of swearing to unconditionally obey the orders of the leaders of the ZWZ, the new fighters of the Polish national underground had to pledge their loyalty to the head of the government-in-exile and to the persons appointed by him to lead the resistance on the occupied Polish soil.[9]

This new clash between Kot's faction and the Piłsudchiks led to a marked intensification of the conflict between their supporters beyond occupied Poland and the UK. In the period from the summer to early October 1940, when the Polish embassy in Bucharest closed, Turkey became a new flashpoint for this confrontation, which soon spread out across the Middle East. The Piłsudchiks's side of the barricades included such luminaries of the Polish diaspora as the consul in Istanbul, Tadeusz Kunicki, who had previously served in Budapest and was one of the most ardent local supporters of the Sanation; the aforementioned ambassador to Ankara, Sokolnicki; and Sokolnicki's colleague, Roger Raczyński, the former ambassador to Bucharest. Raczyński had endorsed the Sikorski government at first, but grew disillusioned and fell out with Kot's representatives in the Romanian capital. By the time of his arrival in Turkey in November 1940, he maintained open ties to the opponents of the new Polish regime. He and Sokolnicki were constantly in touch with Jerzy Giedroyc, the animating spirit of the Piłsudchiks in Bucharest. Even after Mikiciński fired him from the Polish desk at the Chilean embassy, Giedroyc remained in the Romanian capital, serving as liaison between Raczyński, Sokolnicki, and the famous Józef Beck, the prewar Polish foreign minister who had gotten stuck in Romania partly because of the intrigues of the Sikorski government. At this

---

8 Zimmerman, *The Polish Underground and the Jews*, 50–69.
9 Ibid.

time, many of the Piłsudchiks (and their opponents) believed that Beck was still capable of challenging Sikorski for the title of the Polish leader-in-exile and was trying to break free from his Romanian captivity in order to move to the West and stake his claim.[10]

Those who opposed the Kunicki-Raczyński-Sokolnicki trio included Jerzy Kurcyusz, Kot's confidant and a senior member of his operational intelligence network, permanently stationed in Istanbul; Mirosław Arciszewski, the special representative of the government-in-exile for Polish refugee affairs in Romania; Karol Bader, the Polish consul general in Beirut whom Mikiciński had rescued from occupied Warsaw; and finally, the chief of Kot's base of communication in Romania, Władysław Kański, who had moved to Istanbul with his staff, but soon relocated to Palestine to establish a new operational center in Jerusalem under the official cover of the Polish consul's deputy. According to Kot's plan, Kański's center in Jerusalem consisted of six employees and was tasked with exposing and thwarting activities hostile to Polish interests (meaning the interests of the Sikorski government in general, Kot in particular) among Polish citizens, civilian and military, residing in the Holy Land. Furthermore, the center was required to monitor Jewish organizations, both local and American ones, insofar as they touched on Polish interests, and also to assist the representation of the Polish Interior Ministry in Istanbul in ferrying those arriving from the occupied homeland to the British Isles and other parts of the world.[11] In addition, Kański assumed responsibility over the Polish propaganda apparatus in the Middle East.[12]

The prominent Kotowcy who had stayed in Turkey incessantly accused Kunicki, Sokolnicki, Raczyński, and their aides of purposefully sabotaging the government-in-exile in the Turkish Republic and the Middle East. As the Kotowcy saw it, this sabotage primarily took the form of constant denunciations to the local security organs, occasionally resulting in the Turks canceling the

---

10 Alexandrowicz, Kurcyusz, Kuźniarz, and others to Sikorski, November 20, 1940, PISM, PRM. 50, 16–16/reverse side; Dubicki and Rostworowski, *Sanatorzy kontra Sykorszczycy*, 118, 140–142.
11 "A draft version of the statute on setting up a branch of the Interior Ministry in Jerusalem," an undated and unsigned document, with no addressee indicated, the first half of 1941, USHMM, RG-59.047, KOL-25-25A_225-30; see also: Dubicki, "Sprawozdanie ppłk. dypl. Stanisława Orłowskiego": 369, footnote 10. Jerzy Giedroyc claims in his memoirs that he was friends with Kański, who quarreled with Kot. However, this assertion contradicts what we know today about Giedroyc's relationship with Kot and with the Sanation cam See: Giedroyc, *Autobiografia na cztery ręce*, 104.
12 Józef Grabowski and Piotr Rysiewicz. On countering the harmful propaganda of the Sanation, top secret, May 19, 1942, USHMM, RG-59.047, KOL-25-25A_236–239.

long-term and short-term visas of the representatives of the government-in-exile, thereby denying them the right to stay on Turkish soil. Furthermore, it was alleged that the Piłsudchiks were intercepting Kurcyusz's and Mikiciński's correspondence with officials in London, including Kot.[13] Kurcyusz went so far as to claim that the end goal of their provocations was to hurt Kot, his associates, and the whole of the Polish government-in-exile while ensuring that the Bucharest base that Giedroyc ran on behalf of the Sanation camp could maintain communications with occupied Poland.[14]

For his part, Stanisław Kot made every effort to weaken his rivals in the Middle East—especially in Turkey and Palestine, which he regarded as the key Polish footholds in the region. Back in the first half of 1940, the interior minister had attempted to remove Michał Sokolnicki from the post of ambassador to Ankara. Sokolnicki learned in mid-June—on the eve of the fall of France—that Kot was trying to talk Sikorski into sending General Sosnkowski from Angers to the faraway Turkish capital to stay for an indefinite period of time serving as the Polish ambassador. "This is a cunning ploy aimed at driving a wedge between me and my best friend, thereby neutralizing us both," Sokolnicki wrote in his diary.[15]

In the postwar edition of his *Ankara Diary*, the veteran diplomat either did not know or did not wish to reveal a crucial fact his political allies in Polish military counterintelligence and their British counterparts had learned in late 1940 or early 1941: in their attempts to curb the threat posed by the Piłsudchiks, Kot and his followers were willing to engage in direct dialogue with the Nazi enemy. Without naming their source of information (they may have been tipped off by the Polish Dwójka), the authors of a special British intelligence report asserted that Kot's proteges Kurcyusz and Kański had met with representatives of the Nazi regime in Romania and Turkey and, back in the 1930s, had both belonged to a notorious Polish ultra-nationalist party suspected of taking Nazi money.[16] The document plainly tried to convince its readers that Kot maintained a secret channel of communication with Berlin through his pro-Nazi associates.

When it came to Mirosław Arciszewski—the abovementioned high-ranking official of the Polish Foreign Office who had joined Sikorski and been dispatched to Romania to assist the Polish refugees there—the Dwójka, Ambassador

---

13 Alexandrowicz, Kurcyusz, Kuźniarz, and others to Sikorski, November 20, 1940, PISM, PRM. 50, s. 16-16/reverse side.
14 Dubicki and Rostworowski, *Sanatorzy kontra Sykorszczycy*, 142, 233–234.
15 Sokolnicki, *Dziennik Ankarski*, 90.
16 An undated, top secret draft of a memorandum by SOE, titled "Note on the Kot organisation in the Middle East," TNA, HS 4/213.

Raczyński, and the British were unanimous in their assessment that he had a very close relationship with the fascist, Romanian Iron Guard and that, even before his departure from Bucharest in November 1940, he had been in touch with two Nazi emissaries. Allegedly, these were Mikiciński's friend, the Abwehr officer Erich Nobis, and the German diplomat von Rintelen. According to the British, at least one of the two—namely, Nobis—had discussed the prospect of setting up a pro-German puppet government in Warsaw with Arciszewski.[17] As for the second Nazi, we can assume with a high degree of confidence that he was Emil von Rintelen, a senior official at Ribbentrop's office. In all likelihood, von Rintelen and Arciszewski had become professional acquaintances before the war. The British were apparently convinced that Hitler had sanctioned their wartime contact and referred to von Rintelen in their report as "a German agent and a personal emissary of Hitler."[18] August Zaleski, the Polish foreign minister in the Sikorski government, learned of these connections after the fact and instructed Raczyński to meet with Arciszewski to clarify, as Zaleski put it, "the details of the negotiations with the Germans."[19]

We do not know whether the clarification meeting demanded by Zaleski ever took place. All we can deduce from the documentary sources at our disposal is that Mirosław Arciszewski, an official in the government-in-exile and Kot's confidant, did not sever his contacts with the Nazis even after he relocated to Istanbul in late 1940. For this reason, Polish counterintelligence operatives in Romania and Turkey referred to him disdainfully as a Germanophile and a "friend of von Papen, the German Ambassador to Ankara" when writing to their British counterparts.[20] Von Papen, a high-ranking Nazi diplomat, former chancellor of Germany, and vice chancellor under Hitler, had become acquainted with the minutiae of Turkish domestic and foreign policy in World War I while serving as a German General Staff officer in the Ottoman capital of Istanbul and at the German garrison in Palestine. The American diplomats who came into contact with von Papen in Ankara described him as a sophisticated and pleasant person with extensive connections to the Turkish elite and foreign diplomats, one who was always ready to discuss urgent geopolitical issues and ardently

---

17 A top secret report titled "The Kutten Affair," copy #1, July 18, 1941, ibid.
18 An undated, top secret draft of a memorandum by SOE, titled "Note on the Kot organisation in the Middle East," TNA, HS 4/213.
19 Langenfeld, "Final Summary of the Kutten Affair," September 25, 1940, HIA, 800/41/0/-/141 Folder 7, Scan 001041. See also the laconic reference to Arciszewski's contacts with the Nazis in Giedroyc's book of memoirs: Giedroyc, *Autobiografia na cztery ręce*, 91.
20 "Cooperation with the Polish security service," December 15, 1941, TNA, KV 2/517_5, 30.

defend the positions of the official Berlin.²¹ Although we do not know the exact contents of his discussions with his "friend" Arciszewski, we cannot discount the possibility that they continued the dialogue von Rintelen had started back in Bucharest.

British counterintelligence was incensed to learn that the meetings between Kot's men and the Germans—among them at least one Nazi intelligence officer—had taken place without its knowledge. Even more outrageous to His Majesty's operatives was the fact that Kot and his men had carried out their day-to-day communications through British diplomatic mail and over British radio stations in the Middle East—channels of communication the British had graciously opened to the Poles after official, personal requests from Kot and Sikorski! Such behavior from the "Polish ally," the British complained, made it impossible for their intelligence apparatus to monitor the Polish-German contacts; hence, there was no way to discount the possibility of these "double-dealing" Poles having gone over to the enemy and betrayed sensitive information, thereby endangering both the British themselves and the anti-Nazi fighters in occupied Poland.²²

Remarkably, however, none of Kot's supporters in the Middle East—Kurcyusz, Kański, Arciszewski, and others—regarded themselves as despicable spies serving the interests of their national enemy; rather, they saw themselves as Polish patriots carrying out a vital mission on behalf of their occupied homeland. Apparently, it is for this reason that Kurcyusz was greatly troubled about the possibility that his opponents from the pro-Sanation camp would try to paint him as a "German spy."²³ He and the other Kotowcy, for their part, claimed that it was the Piłsudchiks who engaged in an illicit dialogue with the Nazis, discussing the creation of a puppet government in Warsaw. In all likelihood, this referenced the aforementioned meeting in Bucharest between Jerzy Giedroyc and an unnamed special envoy from Berlin, the reality of which Giedroyc would acknowledge many years later in his memoirs.²⁴ A letter of complaint about the "insidious behavior" of the Piłsudchiks, signed by Kurcyusz and his confederates in Istanbul, landed on Sikorski's table in late November 1940—the very moment Mirosław Arciszewski was allegedly in contact with von Papen. Its authors wished to convince the supreme Polish leader that the adherents of the former government had not renounced the traditional Sanation view of Polish

---

21 Hassel and MacRae, *Alliance of Enemies*, 94–95.
22 An undated, top secret draft of a memorandum by SOE, titled "Note on the Kot organisation in the Middle East," TNA, HS 4/213.
23 Dubicki and Rostworowski, *Sanatorzy kontra Sykorszczycy*, 142, 233–234.
24 Ibid.

national interests prioritizing the struggle against Russia over the fight against Germany; for this reason, the Piłsudchiks were now highly critical of Sikorski's alliance with Churchill, believing that it would be of no use in liberating the eastern Polish lands from the Bolshevik yoke, and were secretly negotiating the future eastern border of Poland with Nazi representatives. While the letter did not name any specific Sanation activists who had met with the Germans and did not expound on the contents of these meetings, it did denounce the behavior of the enemies of the government-in-exile as "an open and cynical struggle for power in the Polish state to come."[25]

Another, no less remarkable fact is that, for all the trenchant criticism British and Polish counterintelligence operatives leveled at the Kotowcy who contacted the Nazis, none of the individuals who had met with von Papen, von Rintelen, or Nobis were ever punished in any way by the Polish government-in-exile, or even by the relevant organs in London. Mirosław Arciszewski—the prime suspect whose extensive contacts with the Nazi enemy were amply documented in British evidence—completed his mission in the Middle East in 1941, whereupon he traveled to London unhindered; there, he received a prestigious appointment to serve as the chief of the political department of the Polish foreign service.[26] Władysław Kański—who, as stated above, had moved from Bucharest to Jerusalem—was active in Mandatory Palestine as an official emissary of the Polish government and Kot's personal representative; he was also given freedom of movement throughout the Middle East thanks to his status as a high-ranking member of the Polish National Party (Stronnictwo Narodowe).[27] And, finally, Jerzy Kurcyusz—Kot's right-hand man in the Middle East—went on to represent the Polish Interior Ministry in Turkey until 1944 while maintaining responsibility for a crucial channel of secret communication with the occupied homeland.[28]

In a later chapter, we will try to get to the bottom of the mystery of the British's persistent silence in the face of clear and abundant evidence that the second most senior member of the exiled Polish government (who, moreover, permanently resided in Britain in those years) was openly flirting with the archenemy in Berlin. When it came to what Mikiciński did in Turkey, the British punished only him for maintaining secret channels between the fugitive Polish elite and the Nazis, and he paid with his life.

---

25 Alexandrowicz, Kurcyusz, Kuźniarz, and others to Sikorski, November 20, 1940, PISM, PRM. 50, 16–16/reverse side.
26 "Cooperation with the Polish security service," December 15, 1941, TNA, KV 2/517_5, 30.
27 Sikorski, "Wyznajemy zasady narodowe polskie i uniwersalne katolickie": 15.
28 Terlecki, "'Za sprawę ojczyzny...'"

Among Criminals and Nazi Spies

In the summer of 1940, as Mikiciński was becoming established on Turkish soil, he needed to make a concerted effort to build working relations with the right locals. According to A/H.2 (an agent of the British SOE in Istanbul, who was in all likelihood an officer of the Polish Dwójka), by the end of that year Mikiciński already had firm ties with a large and exceptionally dangerous international criminal gang that had set up shop in the city on the Bosporus. Its members were allegedly circulating counterfeit British banknotes printed in Nazi Germany and smuggled into the Middle East. However, this was a mere sideline to their very lucrative primary business: the production and sale of fake official documents. The gang's leader, a person named Ludwig Buchwald, passed himself off as the Bolivian consul—apparently through the use of high-quality, counterfeit diplomatic documents. However, its most dangerous member was a refugee from Berlin named Alfred Janssen, who used the aliases Alfred Heim and Ali. According to tales circulating in Istanbul and beyond, this man could fake any document in the world.[29]

British historian Nigel West agrees that the Buchwald gang stood out significantly among the criminal groups active in Istanbul in early 1940. According to him, they were a motley band of refugees from Germany and Austria, most of them German-speaking Jews who had initially settled in Italy, where they did a brisk trade in passports, transit documents, and visas; after Rome entered the war on the side of the Third Reich in June 1940, they moved to the non-belligerent Turkey. West has determined that Janssen and several of his partners in the illegal enterprise were arrested by the Turks and the British in the course of 1941 and were subsequently held at the Mia Mia isolation camp in Lebanon, which would become one of the most well-known Palestinian refugee camps in the Middle East after 1948.[30] Agent A/H.2 reported to his British handlers that Mikiciński had a very close relationship with Buchwald, supplying the criminal boss with authentic blank Polish passports that Mikiciński had retrieved from the abandoned Polish embassy in Bucharest. The British agent also claimed that the Turkish police was closely monitoring their criminal partnership, but at the request of A/H.2, it refrained from taking measures against them, fearing that Mikiciński might go underground or leave Turkey altogether.[31]

---

29 An undated and untitled report by agent A/H.2, late December 1940, TNA, HS 4/213.
30 West, *Double Cross in Cairo*, 125–130.
31 An undated and untitled report by agent A/H.2, late December 1940, TNA, HS 4/213.

The protocol of one of Mikiciński's Palestinian interrogations, along with the report on his case by ekspozytura T (the Ankara station of the Polish military intelligence), indicate that, alongside his dealings with the German criminal mastermind, he continued to be in touch with Nazi intelligence organs. In July 1940, the Abwehr officer Erich Nobis—who, as might be recalled, had accompanied Mikiciński on his trips from Berlin to Breslau, and had assisted him in smuggling money and messages from the Polish government-in-exile into occupied Poland—sent a telegram to Mikiciński summoning him to an urgent meeting at the Sofia International Airport. He accepted the invitation at once, flying out to Bulgaria.[32] The above documents do not explain the reason for this urgency, and they remain silent on the contents of the meeting. Quite possibly, the subject did not arise during Mikiciński's interrogations in Palestine. However, the timing of Nobis's telegram and the aforementioned incident with Kutten's money, allegedly confiscated from Nobis by Gestapo officers in occupied Poland, leads us to assume that the meeting in Sofia was purely "businesslike," and had nothing to do with espionage.

Some four months later, in November 1940, Leonid Volokhov, Mikiciński's former business partner from occupied Warsaw, showed up in Istanbul with no advance warning. The unexpected visitor admitted that he had been sent by Herr Scholz, the high-ranking Abwehr officer from Breslau and Mikiciński's old acquaintance. Scholz wished to know the reason for Mikiciński's sudden disappearance and suggested that their partnership be renewed, or even expanded. This time, Volokhov was to be made an official employee of the Chilean embassy in Ankara, and he would use this diplomatic cover to conduct an intelligence-gathering operation against Soviet targets in Turkey. Volokhov questioned his interlocutor in detail about his contacts in the Soviet diplomatic corps and even promised to reward him for his cooperation by extending German protection to his international financial operations. Mikiciński would later claim to have immediately suspected Volokhov and his German handlers of intending to work in Turkey not only against the Russians, but against the British as well. He gave a non-committed answer and made a counteroffer of putting his guest in touch with local representatives of the British Secret Intelligence Service. In a simultaneous move apparently unrelated to the Abwehr's offer, Mikiciński introduced Volokhov to Buchwald, who later took advantage of the Ukrainian's connections to rescue a certain Pole from a concentration camp.

---

32 A report by ekspozytura T (Turkey), "A Brief Summary of the Espionage Case of Samson Mikiciński," April 2, 1941, HIA, 800/41/0/-/141 Folder 7, Scan 000944; a protocol of the interrogation of Mikiciński, March 13, 1941, HIA, 800/41/0/-/141 Folder 7, Scan 000964.

During one of his subsequent trips from Istanbul to Bucharest, Volokhov paid Mikiciński another unexpected visit and passed along a second German offer of patronage in exchange for services rendered. Mikiciński confessed under interrogation that he once again avoided giving a definite answer, and until his arrest in January 1941, he never saw Scholz's Ukrainian emissary again.[33]

Acting at the Behest of the Polish Government

Mikiciński's involvement in the bitter struggle for control over the future Poland between the political factions of Kot and Sosnkowski continued and even deepened on Turkish soil. This time, the Kotowcy wished to take advantage of the business connections made by their patron's Chilean friend, with his customary speed and efficiency, in Istanbul and Ankara. These new contacts were prominent members of the German communities of the two cities, including official representatives of the Third Reich. Unfortunately, at present, we have only a few sketchy reports about the aid Mikiciński rendered to Jerzy Kurcyusz, now head of the Polish Interior Ministry's station in Turkey and the unofficial leader of the Kot faction in the country. However, even this scant data makes it clear that this aid included the creation of a channel of secret communication with senior representatives of the Nazi regime. One particularly remarkable piece of evidence in this connection is a message sent by ekspozytura T of the Polish Dwójka to its London headquarters on January 25, 1941:

> Mikiciński has recently been *holding negotiations here* [italics mine] with the participation of von Papen and Kot's emissary, Kurcyusz. . . Have you been notified of this? Can they be stopped? Answer at once, because the British are planning to do something about it, fearing that Poland is aiming to negotiate with the Germans.[34]

---

33 A report by ekspozytura T (Turkey), "A Brief Summary of the Espionage Case of Samson Mikiciński," April 2, 1941, HIA, 800/41/0/-/141 Folder 7, Scan 000944; an undated protocol of the interrogation of Mikiciński, spring 1941, ibid., Scan 000948; an undated protocol of the interrogation of Mikiciński, spring 1941, ibid., Scan 000949; a protocol of the interrogation of Mikiciński, March 15, 1941, ibid., Scan 000965; an undated protocol of the interrogation of Mikiciński, spring 1941, ibid., Scan 000971.

34 "Mikiciński—information," a radio report by the chief of the Dwójka ekspozytura in Turkey, forwarded via the chief of the West Department of the Dwójka, Major Jan Żychoń, to the chiefs of the Dwójka, January 25, 1941, HIA, 800/41/0/-/141 Folder 7, Scan 001018.

This message indicates that its author (or authors) was/were convinced that the Kot faction, in the person of its most prominent Turkish representative, engaged in so-called negotiations with the high-ranking Nazi diplomat Franz von Papen. It is also quite obvious that the ekspozytura firmly believed that Mikiciński had a key role in these secret Polish-German contacts. Furthermore, the Polish operatives had no doubt that the British authorities knew of these negotiations and feared they were being conducted on Poland's behalf and not for a group of private individuals; therefore, the British intended to take some measures that could prove harmful to the Polish government-in-exile.

Clear confirmation of the Dwójka's belief in the existence of Polish-German contacts on Turkish soil can be found in a lengthy report drawn up by the British SOE in 1941 under the title, "Note on the Kot organisation in the Middle East." This document alleges that the Polish counterintelligence had intercepted messages from Kot to Kurcyusz and Mikiciński with instructions to establish ties with German and Soviet representatives in Turkey.[35] Samson himself, in his first interrogations in Palestine, would claim that his Polish higher-ups in London had no inkling of his contacts with the Germans. Later, however, he broke down and admitted that, after relocating from Romania to Turkey, Kot had instructed him to get in touch with the Germans and the Russians on his behalf. For some reason, the British neglected to specify the purpose of the minister's act, but we may reasonably assume that it was part of the same "attempt to engage in dialogue" with the Nazis that has been mentioned by ekspozytura T. Under interrogation, Mikiciński would confirm that he helped establish a secret contact with the Germans, yet he categorically denied any contacts with Soviet representatives.[36]

Even more weighty evidence of Mikiciński's clear role in establishing secret contacts between Kot (and possibly the Polish government-in-exile as a whole) and the Nazi elite in late 1940 through early 1941 comes from Jerzy Kurcyusz's highly emotional reaction to Mikiciński's arrest by Polish military counterintelligence working for the pro-Sanation camp:

> The time and place for this move have been deliberately chosen so as to cause *the maximum damage to Polish interests and to the*

---

35 An undated, top secret draft of a memorandum by SOE, titled "Note on the Kot organisation in the Middle East," TNA, HS 4/213.
36 Ibid.; MX in a message to M, Cairo; June 1, 1941, ibid.

> *activities sanctioned by the Polish government* [italics mine], to whose execution Mikiciński was indispensable.[37]

At present, we know absolutely nothing about the contents of these contacts between Mikiciński, Kurcyusz, and von Papen. In fact, the parties may have deliberately chosen not to leave any documentation, given the extremely sensitive nature of the situation. However, even without knowing any details, we can safely assert that at this particular juncture—a year after the establishment of the General Government in occupied Poland, and on the eve of 1941, a year that would transform the European military conflict into a new world war—the Jew from the godforsaken shtetl of Boćki, who had now become an international businessman and diplomat, found himself in a pivotal position that allowed him to affect the fate of all humanity. Thanks to his business acumen, extensive connections, and talent for mediation, he gave his Polish patron (or patrons, if we are to believe Kurcyusz) a real chance to radically alter the behavioral strategy of the Polish national leadership. The Polish-British military-political alliance, which had turned out to be counterproductive for the Poles, could have been scrapped in favor of a Polish-German one.

Obviously, history took a different course. We can now only guess at the potential consequences of an agreement between Kurcyusz, his colleague Arciszewski, and their patron with the Nazi von Papen. At the very least, such a geopolitical development would have made it much harder for the UK to pursue its war against Germany and persuade the USA to join this war. After all, by the end of 1940, the Nazis had clearly given up on their planned landing in the British Isles, so the UK could no longer claim to the Americans that they were in existential danger. Still, one can speculate about—and I must stress that this is sheer speculation—a scenario in which the Polish government-in-exile, either in whole or in part, returns to their homeland and is given full or partial authority over the General Government; then, in the summer of 1941, it goes so far as to join the international, German-led coalition that invades the Soviet Union. We must not forget that, in the period described here, many Poles—both politicians and ordinary people, both in the homeland and in exile—openly supported just such a geopolitical scenario.

Could a Polish-German collusion have alleviated the lot of the three million Jewish victims of the Holocaust in Poland, as some Polish historians assert today? This is unclear. Still, it must be admitted that Poland's official decision to

---

37 An extract from a secret report by the Polish Interior Ministry representation in Istanbul; August 26, 1941, PISM, PRM. 50, 10.

quit the war against Germany in early 1941 and the possible restraining influence of such a development on the policy of London and Washington vis-à-vis Berlin would have deprived Hitler of some of the official pretexts for his decision to exterminate the Jews of Poland and Europe. In particular, the Nazis would no longer have had any reason to kill Jews as a means of revenge against the British and Americans for their uncompromising war on Germany.[38]

Be that as it may, the above scenario is purely hypothetical. Mikiciński's arrest in Istanbul and subsequent transfer to Palestine for further investigation put an immediate and permanent end to Jerzy Kurcyusz and Stanisław Kot's contacts with Franz von Papen—and, through him, the leadership of the Third Reich.

---

38 See on Hitler's desire to take revenge on the UK and the US, for their decision to wage war against Germany, as one of the official pretexts for launching the Holocaust: Aharonson, *Hitler, ba'alot ha-brit ve-ha-yehudim*, 93; Snyder, *Bloodlands*, 214; Simms and Laderman, *Hitler's American Gamble*, 54-55.

Chapter 5

Suspicions, Preparations for Neutralization, and an Abduction in Istanbul

The Beginning of the Great Hunt

As the reader may recall, the Polish counterintelligence service, which operated under the auspices of the Dwójka, let Mikiciński drop off its radar after 1934. At that time, the aces of Polish counterespionage had unanimously concluded that he was an ordinary small-time crook trying to make easy money by telling tall tales about recruitment offers from Soviet intelligence operatives. In September 1939, amid the chaos of military defeat and its hasty flight from the occupied homeland, the Polish counterintelligence community lost its operational archives and much of its experienced staff. Therefore, the organization's new headquarters, reestablished in Paris in late 1939, was hamstrung initially by an almost total lack of information about the mass of Polish refugees flooding into France, one of whom was Mikiciński. The initial suspicions against him surfaced early on—in late 1939 and early 1940—when reports about his travels through Europe, including Nazi Germany and occupied Poland, began to pile up on the desks of the Polish counterintelligence officers who had found a temporary home in France. However, at this stage, they assumed he might be connected to the Soviets. The key argument in favor of this explanation of Mikiciński's miraculous abilities were his ties to a prominent Russian émigré businessman living in France, André (Andrei)

Golovannikov, who owned a private bank that had suspicious financial dealings with the Soviet Union.[1]

Since the early 1920s, France had been one of the major targets of the intelligence organs of the young Soviet state and a very convenient platform for conducting Soviet espionage operations against third countries like Germany, the UK, and Spain. The local state security apparatus was well aware of this and engaged in a constant hunt for Soviet spies often covered extensively in the French press.[2] In such an atmosphere, it was quite reasonable for the Poles to suspect Mikiciński of being a Soviet agent, all the more so since he was quite open about the Russian period of his biography and his knowledge of the Russian language. Polish military counterintelligence's suspicions strengthened after Mikiciński's accidental encounter with his former handler, Captain Stefan Marek, in the lobby of the Parisian Hotel Regina. The surprised officer hurried to inform the Dwójka about the former small-time crook from Warsaw who had undergone such a stunning transformation, making sure to bring up Mikiciński's past contacts with the Soviets.[3]

However, several months later, as they analyzed the outcome of Mikiciński's successful trips to occupied Poland, Dwójka counterintelligence officers changed their mind, deciding he was, in all likelihood, being sponsored by the Nazis. At the time, Samson himself assured his close acquaintances and some high-ranking Polish officers (and these assurances immediately reached the ears of the "Dwójka") that his amazing exploits in the occupied homeland were due to a large number of generous bribes he had given to various German officials. In the view of the Polish counterintelligence, such bribery could explain some of his accomplishments, but not all of them; in order to travel to Poland through Belgium and Germany or through Hungary and Romania, he would have had to lavishly bribe a whole army of Nazi officials in disparate areas, a virtually impossible feat for one individual. Therefore, the analysts concluded that Mikiciński was probably operating under the auspices of the Gestapo with a cover story as a lucky smuggler. (In the Polish underground argot, such agents were nicknamed Morka—"sea breeze.")[4]

---

1   A report by the Dwójka titled "Mikiciński—information," March 13, 1941, HIA, 800/41/0/-/141 Folder 7, Scan 000999; a report by the Dwójka titled "Mikiciński—information," June 1941, ibid., Scans 001006 and 001007.
2   Andrew and Mitrokhin, *The Mitrokhin Archive*, 98–100; Volodarsky, *Stalin's Agent*, 50-59, 84, 121, 123–124, 240–241.
3   An undated report titled "Mikiciński Samson," JPIA, Archiwum Osobowe, NZ 154, Sygn. 658.
4   "Code names used by intelligence stations—Skupień, Kaczmarek, Vogel," an undated document, USHMM, RG-59.047, KOL-25-13_4.

That said, in late 1939 and early 1940, the Dwójka still lacked firm proof of Mikiciński's treachery and was therefore unable to arrest him.[5] Instead, it asked its French colleagues from Sûreté nationale to intervene. In February or March 1940, the French detained Mikiciński at the French-Belgian border as he was returning from one of his trips to Poland and tried to interrogate him about the details of his travels through the Reich and his activities in occupied Poland. However, the detainee refused to be cowed, and even behaved provocatively. After telling the French officers that he was acting under the mandate of the Polish government, an ally of France, he angrily demanded that the Polish Interior Minister Kot be notified of his detention. The French agreed to contact the professor, who reacted with lightning speed, ordering the Dwójka to clear his protégé of all suspicion and asking French counterintelligence to release him at once. The humiliated Dwójka had no choice but to obey, and the French security apparatus, which had no evidence against Mikiciński, hurriedly let him go, allowing him to travel on to Angers to meet with Minister Kot.[6]

Colonel Kazimierz Iranek-Osmecki, whom we have met before, was then serving as deputy chief of the Dwójka ekspozytura in Bucharest and about to become the founder and first head of the Intelligence and Information Department at the Parisian headquarters of the Union of Armed Struggle. He claimed in his postwar memoirs that already in late November or early December 1939, two Dwójka officers had shown up at Sosnkowski's office and tried to convince the general to sever his ties with Mikiciński, whom they claimed was a former agent of theirs exposed as a "double dealer" (double agent). Iranek-Osmecki goes on to write that upon hearing this sensational news, the general approached Sikorski and shared it with him. Together, the two decided to end their dealings with the Mikiciński at once and instructed the commanders of the Polish underground to do likewise. According to Iranek-Osmecki, this account was based on a report written in early 1941 by General Sosnkowski to Władysław Raczkiewicz, the Polish president in exile.[7]

In his biography of Stanisław Kot, the Polish historian Tadeusz Rutkowski, quite correctly points out that the testimony by Iranek-Osmecki, which he

---

5 The Second Department of the Polish General Staff in Exile, "A profile of Mikiciński," January 15, 1941, HIA, 800/41/0/-/141 Folder 7, Scan 000101.
6 An undated report titled "Mikiciński Samson," JPIA, Archiwum Osobowe, NZ 154, Sygn. 658. According to a report about this incident drawn up by the Polish Foreign Office in Exile, Mikiciński's detention by the French took place in late April 1940. See: Kapera. *Niemieckie świadectwa*, 72.
7 Iranek-Osmecki, *Wspomnienia oficera*, s. 188; see also: Kapera, *Niemieckie świadectwa*, 72. According to Kapera, the two officers who paid a visit to Sosnkowski and accused Mikiciński of being a German collaborator were Majors Tadeusz Nowiński and Tadeusz Szumowski.

ascribed to General Sosnkowski, contradicts the fact that both Sosnkowski and Sikorski remained in touch with Mikiciński after December 1939, going so far as to entrust him with the lives of their loved ones.[8]

We must also point out another crucial flaw of Iranek-Osmecki's memoiristic account of the Mikiciński affair. According to testimony at the Brooklyn Polish archives, the Dwójka never denounced Mikiciński as a double agent before the war and doubted that the ties he maintained with Soviet diplomats had anything to do with espionage.[9] Hence, the two visitors to Sosnkowski's office—assuming their visit actually took place—could not possibly have claimed that the new special government courier to occupied Poland had a long and proven track record of dealing with the Nazi enemy, and might therefore pose a threat to the fledgling resistance movement in the homeland.

Moreover, at the time the two Dwójka officers and General Sosnkowski had their candid talk—again, possibly a figment of the aging Iranek-Osmecki's imagination—the newly minted internal security system of the ZWZ had not yet heard of Mikiciński and knew nothing about his activities in occupied Poland. Therefore, its operatives could not possibly have provided the Dwójka or Sosnkowski with any information that might have caused him to cancel Samson's mission as a courier. According to Iranek-Osmecki, such information would begin to filter in only in early 1940, thanks to the Polish underground's regular monitoring of Mikiciński's activities in Warsaw and Kraków. The ZWZ sent its first report on the subject to Sosnkowski in February. According to its authors, upon arriving in occupied Warsaw, the new special courier disbursed large sums of money to a few clandestine organizations and several dozen individuals; he made no attempt to hide his ties with the Abwehr and the Gestapo, socialized with officers of both of these Nazi services in local restaurants, and even openly visited the headquarters of Himmler's organization on Jana Szucha Avenue. The report goes on to say that this behavior on his part caused certain members of the underground to shun him and refuse to take his money; a few of these individuals went so far as to change their addresses.[10]

---

8 Rutkowski, *Stanisław Kot*, 145.
9 An undated report titled "Mikiciński Samson," JPIA, Archiwum Osobowe, NZ 154, Sygn. 658.
10 Iranek-Osmecki, *Wspomnienia oficera*, 193–194; Rutkowski, *Stanisław Kot*, 146–147. Ladislas Michniewicz and Jerzy Kurcyusz—with Zdzisław Kapera following their lead—deem it likely that, apart from Scholz and his men, Mikiciński's activities in occupied Poland were supervised by another Abwehr officer, whose last name is variously given as *Werner*, *Weber*, or *Wieser*. See: Kapera, *Niemieckie świadectwa*, 62-63; Kurcyusz, *Na przedpolu Jałty*, 44; Michniewicz, *Opération Haïfa*, 27.

Regarding the institutional identity of Mikiciński's alleged Nazi handlers, the ZWZ assured its Parisian bosses that they belonged to the German military intelligence. They had arrived at this conclusion on the basis of their careful scrutiny of his movements through occupied Poland. He was observed repeatedly in the company of Abwehr officers from Breslau, and the ZWZ recorded his meetings in Warsaw with Erich Nobis, another representative of Canaris's agency. In light of this, the security officers of the Polish underground concluded that Mikiciński's visits to Poland were part of a Nazi scheme aimed at exposing the infrastructure of the Polish resistance and its channels of communication with the government-in-exile. According to the ZWZ, the strongest piece of evidence in favor of this interpretation was... Mikiciński's activity as a rescuer of Polish Jews. The clandestine counterintelligence officers authoritatively concluded (albeit without trying to gauge the precise number of rescued persons) that Mikiciński's ability to smuggle Jews out of the occupied country was the result of the highly valuable information he supplied to the Germans. And what about the fact that none of the Polish citizens who had come into contact with Mikiciński were arrested or punished in any way? According to the report, the explanation for this was simple: the crafty Abwehr had decided to refrain from harsh measures for the time being, so as not to endanger its extremely valuable agent.[11]

The Object of Surveillance from the Ambassador Hotel

At the very moment when the counterintelligence aces of the Polish underground were busy drawing up their denunciatory report painting Mikiciński as a German spy, their colleagues from the Bucharest ekspozytura of the Dwójka got the chance to observe him up close. Upon being notified by London that Samson would soon arrive as a special emissary from Minister Kot tasked with bringing a large sum of money into the occupied homeland, the chief of General Sosnkowski's Romanian base of communication, Colonel Stanisław Rostworowski, instructed the deputy chief of the ekspozytura, Iranek-Osmecki, to look thoroughly into the question of ensuring the safety of the financial operation and of its recipients on the Polish side. Iranek-Osmecki decided that to successfully carry out this assignment, he would have to meet the expected courier (Mikiciński) in person and have an extended discussion with him. To this end, he asked the treasurer of the Polish embassy in Bucharest to notify him

---

11 Ibid.

as soon as Mikiciński showed up at the embassy to receive the money intended for Poland.[12]

In the meantime, as Iranek-Osmecki tells it, the ekspozytura received an unexpected visit from Captain Ernest Carlton, an officer of the British MI6 stationed in Bucharest who maintained a constant working relationship with his Polish colleagues and was well-versed in the affairs of the Polish citizens who had found themselves stranded on Romanian soil. Carlton informed the future memoirist that his organization (the British foreign intelligence service) had learned from its representatives in Paris about the imminent arrival in the Romanian capital of a Chilean consul named Mikiciński who had been given some important official assignment by the Polish government-in-exile. The captain warned his host: "Although this man enjoys the full confidence of the Polish authorities, he has a very sinister reputation in our counterintelligence community, which suspects him of contacts with the Germans, among other things."[13] This is apparently the earliest indication that the British were aware of Mikiciński's existence and keeping tabs on his activities; they even took the initiative in warning their Polish counterparts of the risks the Polish leaders incurred by availing themselves of his services. This was obviously a crucial point in the whole Mikiciński affair. After all, at this stage, in February 1940, the evidence of Mikiciński's contact with the Germans gathered by the Polish underground had yet to be received and checked by the Parisian headquarters of the Dwójka and the Polish military counterintelligence. Hence, if we are to believe Iranek-Osmecki's version of events, British intelligence operatives were the first to open the eyes of their Polish colleagues to the fact that Samson was collaborating with the Germans—not with the Russians, as the Polish operatives used to think. (This incidentally refutes Iranek-Osmecki's own assertion cited above to the effect that, back in late 1939, the Dwójka had already warned Sosnkowski about Mikiciński's collusion with the Germans.)

Today, we can no longer know why MI6 decided to deliver its warning to the Poles in Bucharest rather than those in Paris. London may have assumed that the Bucharest ekspozytura of the Dwójka, staffed by pro-Sanation officers, would be more amenable than its Parisian leadership to helping neutralize Kot's dangerous personal emissary. However, it is unclear why the British began to regard Mikiciński as a threat in early 1940. His personal file in the British archives says nothing about the alleged danger he posed. Alternatively, the February meeting between Carlton and Polish intelligence may never have taken place, and the

---

12 Iranek-Osmecki, *Wspomnienia oficera*, 186.
13 Ibid.

same may be true of the aforementioned earlier warning the Dwójka delivered to Sosnkowski. Is it possible that Iranek-Osmecki's account of the meeting with the British captain was a later fabrication designed to retroactively justify the behavior of the Polish colonel and his colleagues in the Mikiciński affair?

Either way, shortly after Carlton's (real or imagined) visit to the Bucharest ekspozytura, Mikiciński made his expected appearance at the Polish embassy on Alexandru Alley, where Iranek-Osmecki and Rostworowski met him. To their own surprise, they found his explanation of the method of smuggling the government funds into occupied Poland quite reasonable. He made them privy to a "big secret" long known to all his acquaintances in France, Germany, and Poland, but somehow a surprise to the Dwójka operatives in Bucharest: he had a Chilean diplomatic passport! Germans respected his diplomatic status and allowed him to carry money and letters in his baggage.

Thanks to this "stunning" revelation, Kot's special emissary was able to leave the embassy with the required sum of money and continue his journey into the occupied homeland. However, Iranek-Osmecki and his fellow military intelligence officers knew that Mikiciński's operations in Poland raised many questions that remained unanswered. They found it quite puzzling that the Nazi occupiers, who had expelled most official foreign representatives from Poland, now turned a blind eye to the frequent and hectic visits of a minor diplomat from a Latin American country. And why were the Germans willing to overlook the Jewishness of this Chilean, letting him enter at will even as they mercilessly persecuted local Jews?

The most reasonable explanation, as the ekspozytura officers saw it, was that the Germans were using Mikiciński's services—with his knowledge, or without it—to achieve some obscure end. To test this hypothesis, Rostworowski and Iranek-Osmecki decided at once to subject the worrisome emissary to constant surveillance for as long as he remained in Romanian territory. However, since they lacked the necessary manpower for such an operation, the Polish officers concluded that their best course of action was to request help from the Romanian counterintelligence service, the Siguranța, which was on good professional terms with the Dwójka, both on the eve of the war and during its first year.[14]

As stated above, that period saw a brief renaissance in the relationship between the Romanian regime, the Western powers, and their Polish ally. For this reason, the leaders of the Siguranța looked favorably upon the plea for help from the Poles. The surveillance teams of the Romanian counterintelligence service,

---

14 Ibid., 187.

instructed to watch over Mikiciński's every step, learned very quickly that he was staying at the modern, upscale Ambassador Hotel in the heart of Bucharest, and that his daily schedule was filled with business meetings. Apart from Polish compatriots who sought his help to make money transfers to their relatives in occupied Poland, his list of visitors also included Captain Erich Nobis, who had made a special trip from Berlin, and several Bulgarian diplomats, presumably members of the abovementioned clandestine network run by Adam Tarnowski, the Polish ambassador to Sofia. The Romanians went so far as to secretly enter Mikiciński's room at the ambassador to take a surreptitious look at his personal belongings and learn where he was keeping the money he received at the Polish embassy. However, this operation did not yield any sensational discoveries, and the money was not found in the hotel safe; hence, the place where he kept it has remained a mystery.[15]

However, the Romanians and their Polish partners did make an unexpected breakthrough by closely watching Mikiciński's behavior on the day of his departure from Bucharest. As it turned out, he boarded a flight to Berlin at the Bucharest international airport and was accompanied by none other than Erich Nobis, the Abwehr officer. Nobis presented a German diplomatic passport and the credentials of a special courier of the German Foreign Office to the Romanian customs officers, and for this reason his luggage was not inspected. Furthermore, the Siguranța observers reported that the German had been holding several sealed bags. From their description, Rostworowski and Iranek-Osmecki realized that these were the money bags Mikiciński had received at the Polish embassy, ultimately intended for the Polish underground. This was a shocking discovery for both Polish operatives. Was the German officer aware of the contents of the bags? Had Mikiciński recruited him in exchange for money? Or was their relationship part of a Nazi scheme aimed at enabling Mikiciński to infiltrate the Polish underground? According to Iranek-Osmecki, these questions kept nagging him on that day.[16]

A Partner in the Crosshairs

No sooner had Mikiciński left Romania for the capital of the Third Reich than the Bucharest ekspozytura, deeply shaken by its discoveries, concentrated its intelligence-gathering efforts on his new business partner, Viktor Kutten. As

---

15 Ibid., 187–188.
16 Ibid.

might be recalled, Polish military counterintelligence was convinced that the emergence of the Mikiciński-Kutten tandem in early 1940 had been deliberately engineered by Erich Nobis, who had allegedly made a special trip from Berlin to Bucharest for this purpose. And a few short months later, Rostworowski and Iranek-Osmecki already suspected that Kutten, like Mikiciński, allowed Nobis free access to the sensitive political and military information that flowed between the resistance in occupied Poland and the government-in-exile in France, and that he was even trying to help the Abwehr officer get in touch with the Bucharest ekspozytura in order to spy on it.[17]

Because of these suspicions, Polish operatives decided to place Kutten under constant surveillance. This task was delegated to an anonymous ekspozytura agent who was able to insinuate himself into the social circle of the fugitive Polish businessman in the Romanian capital. Shortly thereafter, the agent fingered the popular Polish journalist Bronisław Stefanowski-Syrokomla as the closest associate of the object of surveillance.[18] From other sources we learn that Bronisław, an affiliate of Arciszewski and other prominent supporters of the new Polish government, also had a constant direct contact with the Paris office of the Dwójka. The exact nature of this relationship is unclear, but it is known that in April 1940 Stefanowski-Syrokomla tried to assure the Polish spy agency that Mikiciński was totally reliable. He achieved the opposite result: the Dwójka and its military counterintelligence branch grew even more certain in their suspicions of Kutten and his coterie, which now grew to include Stefanowski-Syrokomla himself.[19] As a result, on April 29, 1940, the exiled Polish Ministry of Justice, based in Angers, launched an official investigation on charges of high treason against Viktor Kutten, Bronisław Stefanowski-Syrokomla, and another person named Stanisław Kąsinowski.[20]

The hasty relocation of the Sikorski government from France to the United Kingdom in the summer of 1940 led to a hiatus in the exchange of encrypted telegrams between the head office of the Dwójka and the Bucharest ekspozytura. When this channel of communication finally reopened in August that year, Iranek-Osmecki's superiors, now based in London, learned from his reports

---

17 A report by the Dwójka titled "Mikiciński—information," June 1941, HIA, 800/41/0/-/141 Folder 7, Scan 001007.
18 Ibid., Scan 001008; an untitled report by the chief of the Second Department of the Polish Armed Forces in Exile, Colonel Mitkiewicz, to Supreme Commander Sikorski, January 20, 1941, HIA, 800/41/0/-/141 Folder 7, Scan 001022.
19 Ibid.
20 Justice Minister Bronisław Kuśnierz to War Minister Kukiel, April 24, 1945, HIA, 800/42/0/-/325 Folder 2, Scan 000315.

that, in the meantime, the suspicions against Viktor Kutten and his associates had only grown stronger. On August 22, the leadership of the Dwójka was notified that Kutten and several other suspects had left Romania for Palestine, allegedly on business, and that the Bucharest ekspozytura had dispatched one of its agents, Second Lieutenant Edward Szarkiewicz, to follow them to the Holy Land. Szarkiewicz took along the incriminating material against Kutten and Co. gathered by the ekspozytura. He was to hand this material over to the British Mandatory authorities to convince them of the need to immediately arrest the suspects and investigate their possible espionage activities on behalf of Nazi Germany. The text of the message received in London makes it clear that the officers of the Bucharest ekspozytura made the decision to contact the British on their own, and that they saw fit to inform their London-based superiors of this development only retroactively, in a very terse form. Exactly one week later, London received another code cable from Bucharest stating that the mission of Second Lieutenant Szarkiewicz to Palestine had been a success. The local British authorities had allegedly received all the information necessary for the successful management of what the Polish operatives now officially referred to as the "Kutten Affair."[21]

"A Little, Cunning Jew"

Edward Szarkiewicz's personal file, administered for many years by MI5, was classified as exceptionally sensitive ("Y File").[22] Access to such files was restricted to a limited group of people within MI5 itself, and documents could be taken out of their home department, for operational and other needs, only in the most extreme cases, in a special, sealed envelope. Edward's colleagues in the British security and intelligence community called him "the Little Man" and "Our Little Friend," alluding to his stature (five feet and four inches, or 162 cm), short by British standards.[23] His commander in the Polish military intelligence described

---

21 Langenfeld, Summary of the Kutten Affair, September 25, 1940, ibid., 800/41/0/-/141 Folder 7, Scan 001041; an untitled report by the chief of the Second Department of the Polish Armed Forces in Exile, Colonel Mitkiewicz, to Supreme Commander Sikorski, January 20, 1941, ibid., Scan 001022; a report by the "Dwójka" titled "Mikiciński—information," June 1941, ibid., Scan 001008.
22 See the title page of Edward Szarkiewicz's personal file, TNA, KV 2/517_1, 2.
23 An undated, filled request form for permission to leave the United Kingdom, April 1943, TNA, KV 2/517_7, 21–22; Unknown (signature unclear) to Brigadier Roberts, August 2, 1945, ibid., KV 2/518_1, 22; Brigadier Roberts to Colonel Butler from the Department of Foreign Citizens, August 14, 1945, ibid., 21.

him as a "little bastard," albeit one gifted with the ability to tackle tangled cases of espionage,[24] whereas his opponents from Stanisław Kot's camp nicknamed him "sprytny a podły Żydek" ("a cunning and nasty Jew"), claiming that it was only through a tragic twist of fate that the Polish Dwójka and the British secret service had come to unconditionally trust this man, regard him as a true Polish intelligence operative, and give him full freedom of action.[25]

According to Polish and British sources, he was born on April 1, 1900, in the town of Wybranówka (present-day Vybranivka in Lviv Oblast, Ukraine). His parents were Aron and Ida Szapiro, and his birth name was Mojżesz (Moses). In the early twentieth century, Wybranówka was ruled by the Austro-Hungarian Empire and had about a thousand inhabitants, three hundred of whom were Jews. At the age of twenty-six, having qualified as an economist at an institution of higher education in Lwów (present-day Lviv), then part of independent Poland, the young Mojżesz became a full-time businessman and a reserve officer in the Polish army. He had many gifts, including an exceptional aptitude for languages: in the course of his relatively short life, he would master Polish, Ukrainian, Russian, German, and English, and became conversant in Romanian, Bulgarian, French, Italian, and even Arabic.[26] Did he also speak Yiddish? He probably did—but, as a blue-eyed, blond-haired man,[27] he concealed this knowledge, and his Jewish origins in general. In fact, he converted to Catholicism. According to one account, his conversion took place in the 1920s during his studies in Lwów, but other sources indicate he converted after the outbreak of World War II, while a refugee in Romania.[28] Having turned his back on Judaism, Mojżesz Szapiro adopted the Polish-sounding name Edward Szarkiewicz; later, on forms and questionnaires (including those of the British secret service), he invariably described himself as a hereditary or ethnic Pole.[29]

As the MI5 data testify, the young Szarkiewicz had managed to join Marshal Piłsudski's inner circle and became his personal advisor on economic crimes.

---

24 An undated, top secret draft of a memorandum by SOE, titled "Note on the Kot organisation in the Middle East," TNA, HS 4/213.
25 An extract from a secret report by the Polish Interior Ministry representation in Istanbul, August 26, 1941, PISM, PRM. 50, 10.
26 Registration details in A. O. E. R./Egypt, March 8, 1944, TNA, KV 2/517_2, 1; an undated report titled "Mikiciński Samson," JPIA, Archiwum Osobowe, NZ 154, Sygn. 658. According to some modern Polish sources, Szarkiewicz was born in 1904, but this is most likely an error. See: Ciechanowski, *Polsko-Brytyjska współpraca*, 117–118.
27 Buczek, *Człowiek do złotych interesów*, 185.
28 Iranek-Osmecki. *Postscriptum II*, 542.
29 See, for instance: registration details in A. O. E. R./Egypt, March 8, 1944, TNA, KV 2/517_2, 1.

After Piłsudski's death in 1935, Szarkiewicz stayed loyal to the ruling Sanation camp, and when World War II broke out, he joined the opposition against Sikorski.[30] Some modern Polish historians whose ideologies align with the Sanation describe Szarkiewicz as a true Polish patriot and a devoted Piłsudchik who "regularly informed the Marshal of various actions by his co-religionists, which might prove harmful to the Polish economy." The same sources identify him as an advocate for Polish Jews within the Piłsudski cabinet and an arms dealer to Franco on behalf of the Polish army during the Spanish Civil War.[31] Historians critical of the Sanation deny Szarkiewicz's alleged patriotism, insisting he was out for his own interests. One adherent of this view, Jakub Szczepański, writes that Szarkiewicz was personally involved in illegally shipping Polish weapons to the Francoists and that the Dwójka suspected him of being a German agent, a suspicion proven by the Polish court martial in London in 1943.[32] However, this account is not supported by any of the documentary sources available to us, and other Polish authors assert that in the 1930s, Szarkiewicz was a British agent—and possibly a Soviet one, too.[33]

Szarkiewicz informed British counterintelligence in August 1941 that the German invasion of Poland had caught him in Warsaw. He fled to neighboring Romania, and in early 1940 moved on to Paris,[34] apparently having passed the political reliability test administered by the representatives of the new Polish government in Bucharest. Regarding the timing of his recruitment by the Polish military intelligence, he gave two different versions, both of which have been preserved in the British sources. According to the first account (from 1941), he joined the staff of the Dwójka headquarters shortly after his arrival in Paris, in February 1940;[35] according to the second, which may be found in a statement he forwarded to Sir David Petrie, director general of MI5, on July 26, 1945, his career in the counterintelligence community began as far back as November 1939, when, a simple refugee, he miraculously turned overnight into a full-fledged

---

30 Captain F. Derbyshire to Major S. Alley from Section 2 of the Department of Foreign Citizens (E2), December 5, 1942, TNA, KV 2/517_4, 13.
31 Cynk, *Rewelacje Szarkiewicza*, 53–56; Koper. *Polskie piekiełko*, 132; Iranek-Osmecki. *Postscriptum II*, 540, 542.
32 Szczepański, *Błyskotliwy agent czy zdrajca?*
33 Gulbicki, *Tropem zabójcy generała*; see also footnote 57 in the collection of documents compiled by the Polish historian Jan Stanisław Ciechanowski, which alleges that, even before the war, Szarkiewicz was suspected of collaborating with the British and the German intelligence organs: Ciechanowski, *Polsko-Brytyjska współpraca*, 118.
34 Room 055 of the War Office [the secret address for MI5 during WWII] to Sir David Petrie, G.L. 1657/41, August 13, 1941, TNA, KV 2/517_6, 26.
35 Ibid.

employee of the Bucharest station of the Dwójka—ekspozytura R—thereby becoming a subordinate of our old acquaintance Colonel Iranek-Osmecki.[36]

Be that as it may, in late February 1940, just after he arrived in France, Szarkiewicz was, indeed, already a member of the fugitive Polish General Staff, and had even managed to request and obtain a visa enabling him to officially visit the United Kingdom. Furthermore, his visa request had been handled by none other than Lieutenant Colonel Colin Gubbins, chief of staff to the military mission to the Polish army in France and future founder and leader of SOE.[37] In the same month, Szarkiewicz, despite his lack of experience in intelligence work, was somehow appointed supervisor of the counterintelligence operations of the Dwójka throughout the Balkan region. In this new capacity, he became closely involved in the Mikiciński affair, which was rapidly gathering steam. According to the anonymous author of the postwar report from the Polish archives in Brooklyn, "he followed this affair from the very first moment."[38]

About three months later, with the Nazi invasion of France in full swing, Szarkiewicz was dispatched to Bucharest. His duties there involved foiling the activities of enemy spies, both against official Polish targets in Romania and against the secret channels of communication between the Polish government-in-exile and the occupied homeland that passed through Romanian territory.[39]

We might ask how a person like Szarkiewicz—who knew nothing of the art of intelligence and counterintelligence—was hired by the Dwójka chiefs (who did not bother to examine his knowledge or experience, nor check him for possible ties with the enemy) and promoted to a senior position almost overnight. To explain this puzzle, modern Polish historiography invokes the special relationship between Szarkiewicz and the Polish general Izydor Modelski (whom we shall discuss in detail later on) that had started in late 1939. However, these historians fail to elucidate the circumstances of the acquaintance between those two very different men or the details of their lengthy partnership.[40]

---

36 Szarkiewicz to Sir David Petrie, July 26, 1945, TNA, KV 2/518_1, 24–25.
37 Gubbins to the head of the Passport Control Department, February 21, 1940, TNA, KV 2/517_6, 31; a passport control officer, Paris, February 27, 1940, TNA, KV 2/517_6, 30.
38 An undated message titled "Mikiciński Samson," JPIA, Archiwum Osobowe, NZ 154, Sygn. 658.
39 Room 055 to Sir David Petrie, G.L. 1657/41, August 13, 1941, TNA, KV 2/517_6, 26; Szarkiewicz to Petrie, July 26, 1945, TNA, KV 2/518_1, 24–25; see also footnote 57 in the collection of documents compiled by the Polish historian Jan Stanisław Ciechanowski, which asserts that Szarkiewicz was dispatched to Romania from the UK: Ciechanowski, *Polsko-Brytyjska współpraca*, 118. This assertion contradicts the materials gathered during the present study.
40 See ibid., note 57

The results of this study point to a different explanation, and we can assert with a great deal of confidence that the real reason for Szarkiewicz's meteoric rise in the early stages of his career was more prosaic. It can be found in a harshly worded letter Dwójka leader Colonel Miniewski sent General Sosnkowski in November 1944 complaining about the weakness of military counterintelligence. According to him, from the start of World War II, this service was unpopular among the Polish officer corps: its diminutive size made it very hard for them to get promoted in rank and position, and once they were in, it was equally hard for them to get transferred to a different branch, since the other branches held an equally low opinion of those forever searching for the "enemy within." For this reason, summarized Miniewski, the military counterintelligence was constantly "starving" for qualified officers and was forced to make do with random and unqualified personnel whose ineptness only hampered the unit's work.[41]

At present, we know very little about the brief period the "counterintelligence ace" Szarkiewicz served in the Romanian capital. There are some indications that in the summer of 1940, he began to serve as a liaison officer between ekspozytura R and the British MI6, and that this position put him in constant touch with a certain Major McLaren.[42] The full name of this British officer is unknown. He may have been Moray McLaren, a Polish-speaking Scottish journalist who authored a book about prewar Poland and who, following the outbreak of war, was called up to serve in His Majesty's forces. In early 1942, McLaren was appointed chief of the Polish section of the Political Warfare Executive, a special military information and propaganda unit that operated during the war under the auspices of the British Foreign Office. McLaren's immediate superior at the time was his friend Bruce Lockhart, a British diplomat with former ties to MI6 who had become famous for being accused by the Soviets of mastering a failed plot to assassinate the first Soviet leader Vladimir Lenin.[43]

McLaren may have been the one who officially recruited Szarkiewicz into the British intelligence organs: later in 1944, summing up his service on behalf of the British Crown (a subject that will be taken up in detail later on), Szarkiewicz would assert that this service began in June 1940 at the very moment he arrived in Bucharest and got in touch with McLaren.[44] Hints about the

---

41 Colonel Miniewski to General Sosnkowski, "Conclusion regarding the process of promotion of officers of the Counterintelligence Department in the Ministry of National Defense," November 22, 1944, PISM, A.XII.1/82, 82–83.
42 An undated message titled "Mikiciński Samson," JPIA, Archiwum Osobowe, NZ 154, Sygn. 658.
43 Bines, *The Polish Country Section*, 292; Lockhart, *The Diaries*, 135.
44 Roberts to Sir David Petrie, August 28, 1944, TNA, KV 2/518_2, 35.

intelligence-gathering nature of that service may be found in the secret reports on the subject from Brigadier Raymund John Maunsell, head of British Security Intelligence Middle East (SIME) in Cairo, and from Captain Derbyshire from the MI5 headquarters in London. Both men regarded Szarkiewicz as "more pro-British as any Pole," who was, moreover, "always most co-operative about all Polish matters."[45] Another noteworthy fact is that an undated report by MI5 (probably written in 1941) identifies Szarkiewicz by the code name ESS13, while another report by the same body, published in July 1941 and dealing with Mikiciński's abduction from Istanbul, states explicitly that a plot involved "ESS13, a Polish agent."[46] This evidence seems to confirm the supposition that at an early stage in his career as a counterintelligence officer in the Polish army in exile, the British recruited Szarkiewicz as a secret agent and assigned him a secret code to protect him from exposure. If this penetration into the military establishment of the Polish ally actually took place, it fit the modus operandi of the British intelligence community in those days: at virtually the same time, a highly valuable source of information was acquired in the chancellery of the commander of de Gaulle's forces in the Levant.[47]

As stated above, Szarkiewicz's period of service in Romania came to an end in late August 1940, when he was sent by ekspozytura R to Palestine in order to orchestrate, in cooperation with the Mandatory authorities, the arrest of Viktor Kutten and his associates, and eventually to lay his hands on Mikiciński. Immediately upon arriving in Haifa, Edward got in touch with the Criminal Investigation Department (CID) of the Mandatory Police and began to collaborate actively with its renowned chief, Arthur Giles, in a sphere both sides diplomatically referred to as "intelligence work in the interests of mutual security."[48] Apparently, the CID was overjoyed at the prospect of this new partnership with the Polish military counterintelligence—at that time, the Mandatory police authorities, in addition to their traditional role in suppressing anti-British activities among the local Jews and Arabs, also had to devote considerable resources to combating German and Italian espionage and sabotage efforts.[49] Meanwhile, Szarkiewicz closely collaborated with Colonel Prosser from the Immigration

---

45 Maunsell to Sir David Petrie, a secret personal letter, July 24, 1942, TNA, KV 2/517_4, 20; Captain F. Derbyshire to Major S. Alley from E2, December 5, 1942, TNA, KV 2/517_4, 13.
46 An undated, top secret draft of a memorandum by SOE, titled "Note on the Kot organisation in the Middle East," TNA, HS 4/213; a top secret report titled "The Paluchowicz Case," copy No. 1, July 18, 1941, TNA, HS 4/213.
47 Jeffery, *MI6*, 434–435.
48 Szarkiewicz to Sir David Petrie, July 26, 1945, TNA, KV 2/518_1, 24–25.
49 Charuvi, *Ha-boleshet chokeret*, 151–152.

Department of the British Mandatory authorities in an attempt to screen the Polish-speaking refugees arriving in the country from war-torn Europe. Both Jewish and non-Jewish, they were so abundant that in many of the larger cities, Polish was heard as commonly as Hebrew, Arabic, and English.

Very soon, however, the British partners in Palestine came to know all the virtues and vices of their new friend. An undated draft version of a report on "the Kot organisation in the Middle East," probably written in 1941, claims that he "is a most unpleasant type, but has twenty-eight years [of] experience of counter-espionage, and everyone seems agreed that he has a flair for this work."[50] The assertion that Szarkiewicz has had almost thirty years of experience in counterintelligence work seems very odd, since, as already mentioned, he entered the world of cloak-and-dagger operations no earlier than 1940 (at the age of forty). This error on the part of the British may have stemmed from Szarkiewicz's poor health (he suffered from a chronic heart condition that made him appear much older than his years) and from his penchant for embellishing his past. For example, besides pretending to be an ethnic Pole, he presented himself to the British as "a personal friend of Minister Kot" and stated that he was acting against the Kotowcy in the Middle East solely out of the desire to protect the professor from "making a fool of himself."[51] The absurdity of this claim was so obvious that one of the MI5 analysts rejected it with a judicious remark: "I doubt myself if his motives are quite so simple."[52]

The Odd Inmates of the Latrun Prison Camp

One of the most significant outcomes of the successful alliance between Szarkiewicz and the Mandatory police was the quick arrest of Viktor Kutten, Bronisław Stefanowski-Syrokomla, and Stanisław Kąsinowski. The British apprehended all three as early as September 26, 1940, just two weeks after their arrival in the Holy Land. The arrest was hastened by the fact that, for some reason (possibly on the basis of "incriminating information" provided by Szarkiewicz), the British suspected them of being involved in an ambitious criminal scheme aimed at circulating counterfeit British banknotes manufactured in Nazi

---

50 An undated, top secret draft of a memorandum by SOE, titled "Note on the Kot organisation in the Middle East," TNA, HS 4/213.
51 Ibid.
52 Ibid.

Germany throughout the Middle East.[53] British Mandatory authorities arrested two other Polish subjects, Andrzej Łebkowski and Marian Hemar (Hescheles), who had arrived in Haifa from Europe on the same (or nearly the same) day as Kutten and his partners, and were suspected of involvement in the Kutten affair.[54] In Hemar's case, this was an egregious error: a Jew and the cousin of Stanisław Lem, who would later become a globally renowned science fiction author, he had been one of prewar Poland's leading writers and poets, winning acclaim as a playwright, translator, and journalist. Obviously, such a person could not have been connected to the Nazi espionage apparatus, and his arrest led to a wave of protest among the Polish émigré elite. Six months later, in March 1941, the British relented and released him.[55]

All the Poles arrested in the Kutten affair were held in pre-trial detention at a prison camp in Latrun, opened officially by Mandatory authorities only a few months earlier. Its first inmates were Italian prisoners of war who had served in North Africa, but they were soon joined by German POWs, Arab and Jewish opponents of British rule in Palestine, and locals and foreigners with suspected ties to the enemy.[56] Kutten, Stefanowski-Syrokomla, Kąsinowski, Łebkowski, and Hemar belonged to this last category. They would periodically be taken out of the camp under police escort to Jerusalem fifteen kilometers away, where with British permission, they were subjected to intense questioning by representatives of the Dwójka, including Szarkiewicz, and by members of a special commission of the Polish Ministry of Justice targeting the activities of the Kutten group in Romania who studied the official Polish documents pertaining to those activities.[57] In the end, the charges made no mention of their alleged attempt to undermine the British economy by circulating counterfeit banknotes—the matter was never mentioned again—and instead focused on their

---

53 The 2nd Department of the Supreme Command Headquarters, an undated extract of information about Alexander Grabarsky, circa mid-1941, HIA, 800/41/0/-/141 Folder 7, Scan 001003. According to the Polish historian Jan Ciechanowski, the arrest of Kutten and his confederates in Palestine took place on September 17, immediately after they had disembarked in Haifa. See footnote 156 in Ciechanowski, *Polsko-Brytyjska współpraca*, 144.
54 Major Zichoń to the leadership of the 2nd Department of the Supreme Command Headquarters, October 3, 1940, HIA, 800/41/0/-/141 Folder 7, Scan 001032.
55 Buczek, *Człowiek do złotych interesów*, 109—111, 116; footnote 170 in: Ciechanowski, *Polsko-Brytyjska współpraca*, 147.
56 Misgav, *Mahanot ha-ma'atsar be-Latrun*, 158–185.
57 Major Zichoń to the leadership of the 2nd Department of the Supreme Command Headquarters, October 3, 1940, HIA, 800/41/0/-/141 Folder 7, Scan 001032; the Polish Foreign Office in London to the 2nd Department of the Supreme Command, October 8, 1940, HIA, 800/41/0/-/141 Folder 7, Scan 001024; Justice Minister Bronisław Kuśnierz to War Minister Kukiel, April 24, 1945, HIA, 800/42/0/-/325 Folder 2, Scan 000315.

imaginary collusion with two Nazi spy agencies, the Abwehr and the Gestapo. It was asserted that the Germans had tried to use the operational network Kutten had established in Romania to gain access to the secret channel of communication between the Polish government-in-exile and the underground in occupied Poland, and also to get directly in touch with the official Polish representatives in Bucharest.[58]

Another charge leveled against Viktor Kutten involved his "extensive connections with the Romanian ruling elite," which ostensibly made him a very attractive target for enemy spies.[59] The absurdity of this accusation must have been apparent to his contemporaries. Many Poles working in Romania at the time had such connections, including representatives from the Sanation camp like Jerzy Giedroyc, who was in very close touch with Antonescu's and Sima's underlings; and therefore the very existence of such ties could not be taken as automatic proof of treason. Secondly, the Germans had no need of a fugitive Polish merchant to strengthen their hold on the Romanian leadership, since it was already sufficiently receptive.

The first Polish official to realize that the Kutten affair was essentially a fabrication was General Stanisław Kopański, commander of the Carpathian Riflemen Brigade. This combat unit of the Polish army in exile had been established in the Syrian city of Homs in April 1940 and was made up of Polish soldiers and officers who had arrived from Romania and Hungary. After the fall of France and the decision of the French authorities in Damascus to pledge loyalty to the new Vichy Regime, the brigade crossed the border into Palestine to join the British forces.[60] In a telegram sent to Sikorski in early October 1940, Kopański asserted that the Kutten affair—which was, at bottom, a "trivial matter"—had become the object of an "exceptionally intense investigation" since "the British have gone overboard, as they themselves now admit." The telegram also mentioned one other crucial detail: "Szarkiewicz has strictly prohibited to divulge any details of the affair to the British."[61]

From this, we may deduce that shortly after arresting Kutten, his two associates, and two other Polish citizens who had nothing to do with him on charges of involvement in a Nazi sabotage operation, Szarkiewicz assumed full control

---

58 Justice Minister Bronisław Kuśnierz to War Minister Kukiel, April 24, 1945, HIA, 800/42/0/-/325 Folder 2, Scan 000316.
59 A report by the "Dwójka" titled "Mikiciński—information," March 13, 1941, HIA, 800/41/0/-/141 Folder 7, Scan 000999.
60 Brio, Pol'skie muzy, 55–59; Wieczorkiewicz, Historia polityczna Polski, 137, 141.
61 Major Zichoń to the leadership of the 2nd Department of the Supreme Command Headquarters, October 3, 1940, HIA, 800/41/0/-/141 Folder 7, Scan 001032.

over the investigation and, for some obscure reason, decided not to give his British partners full access to the arrest testimonies. Did he intentionally try to mislead the Mandatory police about the nature of the Kutten affair in an attempt to secure their cooperation in putting a stop to Mikiciński? We will probably never know, nor are we likely to find out why the Dwójka headquarters in London was informed of Kutten's arrest on October 8, two weeks after the fact. And why was this news delivered not by Second Lieutenant Szarkiewicz, but the London headquarters of the Polish Foreign Office, which had received it from the Polish consulate in Jerusalem?[62] We might interpret Szarkiewicz's behavior as an attempt to secure for himself, if only for a short time, full freedom of action not only from the British, but his superiors in London.

In response to the report from the Polish consulate in Jerusalem on the arrest of Kutten and his men, Polish officials in the UK and in Continental Europe unconnected to the pro-Sanation camp, categorically denied the charges against the arrestees. As early as October 9, Stanisław Stroński, vice premier and minister of information and documentation in the Sikorski cabinet (who used to be a professor at Kraków University and an ardent opponent of the Sanation regime), sent an urgent message to his colleague, Minister Kot, and to Dwójka chief Colonel Mitkiewicz-Żółtek, where he asserted that, in his view, the arrests in Palestine might have been driven by "impure motives." He wrote: "I am not personally acquainted with Kutten, but I do know Stefanowski-Syrokomla as an outstanding person." "We must make sure that this arrest is not the result of an internecine struggle among the Polish officialdom, as has happened repeatedly in the past,"[63] he added.

Similar reactions came from Władysław Kański—then still chief of the Bucharest base of communication with the homeland—and from the ambassador to Sofia, Adam Tarnowski (who, as might be recalled, had used the services of the network of Bulgarian diplomats to aid people in occupied Poland). Both men tried to intercede on behalf of the arrestees with the British, but to no avail.[64] Tarnowski did not relent, and on January 13, 1941, sent a personal appeal to Sikorski asking him to review, as soon as possible, the decision to arrest

---

62 The Polish Foreign Office in London to the 2nd Department of the Supreme Command, October 8, 1940, HIA, 800/41/0/-/141 Folder 7, Scan 001024.
63 Stroński to Kot and Mitkiewicz-Żółtek, October 9, 1940, HIA, 800/41/0/-/141 Folder 7, Scan 001011.
64 An undated, top secret draft of a memorandum by SOE, titled "Note on the Kot organisation in the Middle East," TNA, HS 4/213; a top secret report titled "The Kutten Affair," copy No. 1, July 18, 1941, TNA, HS 4/213.

Kutten and his men. "In my opinion, the charges of espionage against them are baseless," he wrote to the Polish national leader in exile.⁶⁵

And yet, all the attempts to help the Polish inmates of the Latrun camp were in vain. On November 29, 1940, the aforementioned General Kopański, then the highest-ranking Polish military officer in Palestine, informed the London headquarters of the Dwójka that he had no objection to the Kutten group's upcoming trial . Six days later, Leon Mitkiewicz-Żółtek officially empowered the chief of the second intelligence department of the Carpathian Riflemen Brigade to begin preparations for a trial on the basis of the incriminating investigation protocols Szarkiewicz had delivered.⁶⁶ It was assumed that the court martial of the brigade would try Kutten, Stefanowski-Syrokomla, and Kąsinowski. However, at the very last moment, the trial was postponed indefinitely. The reason was exceedingly prosaic, even though it somehow caught all the trial organizers by surprise: the Polish court marital in Palestine lacked the statutory power to try Polish civilians. We do not know who recalled this inconvenient fact. More importantly, this pesky legal hurdle could not be overcome with fake military papers: to the chagrin of their persecutors, the men were past the legal age of conscription. They could not be handed over for trial to the British authorities, either, since the British lacked the authority to try Polish subjects in the territory of Mandatory Palestine.

Being unable to untangle this thorny legal knot, the Polish and British captors of Kutten, Stefanowski-Syrokomla, and Kąsinowski simply chose to put them in "cold storage" at the Latrun camp for four long years, right up to the end of World War II.⁶⁷

The Last Stage in the Struggle for the Fate of "Lis"

Despite their inability to put Viktor Kutten and his partners in crime in the dock, the Sanation proponents still clung to the hope of using him to justify their accusations against Samson Mikiciński and fully neutralize him. An SOE agent in Turkey called A/H.2, apparently associated with the Piłsudchiks and possibly a member, reported to his British handlers in December 1940 that

---

65 Tarnowski to Sikorski and Stroński, January 13, 1941, HIA, 800/41/0/-/141 Folder 7, Scan 001037.
66 Chief of the "Dwójka," Colonel Mitkiewicz-Żółtek, to General Sikorski, an untitled report; January 20, 1941, HIA, 800/41/0/-/141 Folder 7, Scan 001023.
67 Captain Czechowicz, chief of the "Security Chancellery" of the Polish Armed Forces, "The Affair of Kutten and His Partners," May 1942, HIA, 800/41/0/-/141 Folder 7, Scan 000996.

Kutten and Stefanowski-Syrokomla were complicit in Mikiciński's crimes, and that, for this reason, local British and Polish authorities had arrested them in Palestine, charged them with high treason, and sent them to Cairo for further investigation.[68] This report contained not a word of truth. As stated above, after their quarrel in the summer of 1940, Kutten and Mikiciński had stopped cooperating in the smuggling of government money into occupied Poland and the rendering of financial services to individual Polish refugees. Furthermore, the arrestees were never presented with official charges or transported to Cairo; rather, they continued to languish in Latrun.

The British agent went on to give a litany of accusations against Mikiciński without bothering to substantiate any of them. Samson had allegedly disclosed to his Nazi handlers the identities of hundreds of Polish underground activists, many of whom were subsequently caught and killed by the occupiers; he smuggled the family members of prominent Poles to France solely in order to clear himself of suspicions of collaboration with the Germans; he turned the official Chilean representation in Bucharest into a hotbed of Nazi espionage on Romanian soil; finally, he supplied the Germans with blank Polish passports that he had looted from the abandoned Polish embassy in the Romanian capital.[69]

Meanwhile, Szarkiewicz continued to provide his British contacts with a steady drip of compromising information that ought to be examined very critically. Almost a year and a half later, in February 1942, while being interrogated by MI5 representatives in London about the details of his involvement in the Kutten and Mikiciński affairs, he would summarize this information by declaring that Minister Kot "used the services of some highly suspicious types, who were determined to have taken money from the Germans."[70] That was a blatant lie, since the investigation of the activities of Mikiciński and Kutten—including Szarkiewicz's interrogation of the two men by in Palestine—failed to uncover a shred of evidence of Nazi financing and had not resulted in charges, not to mention the fact that both the accused were quite wealthy, even by modern standards.

At this point, we should make a brief detour to try to get to the bottom of the motives of Mikiciński's opponents, whose activities were turning into a savage witch hunt. Quite plausibly, Szarkiewicz's attempts to hype up the Mikiciński and Kutten affairs were driven by personal ambition, a desire for rapid promotion in the Polish (and, with a bit of luck, the British) counterintelligence community. Just as plausibly, the key operatives of the pro-Sanation camp—Giedroyc,

---

68 An undated and untitled report by agent A/H.2, late December 1940, TNA, HS 4/213.
69 Ibid.
70 A top secret memorandum titled "E. Szarkiewicz," February 6, 1942, TNA, KV 2/517_4, 5.

Iranek-Osmecki, Raczyński, Kunicki, and others—saw Mikiciński as a dangerous rival because of both his influence on the shape of the future Polish government (especially in light of his contacts with von Papen) and his prominence in the highly lucrative field of transferring money and valuables into occupied Poland and out of it.

That said, we must not overlook two additional motives that may have fueled the persecution of the "Chilean diplomat" from Boćki. The first of these was the ordinary antisemitism that infected many segments of the exiled Polish state apparatus, including its security and intelligence organs. The most blatant manifestation of this anti-Jewish prejudice in this period was an interview an anonymous Polish officer gave the *Catholic Herald*, a British periodical that served as the mouthpiece of the supporters of Irish nationalism and the opponents of rapprochement with Communist Russia. The officer's musings, published under the heading "Why Do Our Polish Guests Believe in the Existence of a Jewish Problem?" and presented as an "objective account" of the prewar relationship between Polish Jewry and the Polish people, included the following grave statement:

> [Three] and a half million Polish Jews, who before the war made up about ten percent of the entire population of Poland and the absolute majority in the middle class of Polish society, do not identify with their country of residence, do not speak its language for the most part, and support it only when its interests coincide with their own, as in the case of the present struggle against the Germans.[71]

The second likely motive of Mikiciński's persecutors was the spy mania that had gripped the Polish resistance movement in the occupied homeland and the Polish expatriate circles in the UK and elsewhere. The widespread belief that the downfall of the Second Polish Republic had been engineered by the machinations of the Nazi and Bolshevik spies now busy undermining the true Polish patriots greatly exacerbated the paranoia of Poles at home and abroad. As a result, suspicious persons often lost their jobs—and, in some cases, their lives. We may recall the story of Krystyna Skarbek-Granville, a half-Jewish Polish agent of the British SOE. Like Mikiciński, she became famous thanks to her amazing ability to repeatedly enter occupied Poland and leave alive and

---

71 Ignacy Schwarzbart, query, June 25, 1941, PISM, A.XII.1/66A, s. 91–92; an undated Polish translation of the interview from the *Catholic Herald*, PISM, A.XII.1/66A, 93–94.

unharmed. The Polish underground and the Dwójka suspected her of being a German spy and nearly killed her.[72]

The Polish security apparatus, both in Poland and in exile, was particularly suspicious of stories of liberation from Nazi camps and of flight from the occupied homeland. These suspicions infected even the official Polish organs abroad in Britain and the Middle East. Apparently, this was the reason why in 1947, the representatives of Delek—the intelligence section of the Jewish underground National Military Organization (the Irgun) in Palestine—were reluctant to believe the tale of a Polish Jew who had escaped from a Nazi camp and managed to reach his historical homeland via some obscure route. "His story is hard to credit," wrote the clandestine Jewish counterintelligence operatives in their report, making the remarkable conclusion: "We cannot exclude the possibility that he has been sent here by the Russians."[73]

By the autumn of 1940, Mikiciński high-placed friends in London were well aware of the massive smear campaign targeting not only him, but Stanisław Kot, and possibly even Sikorski. "They are shooting at you, but trying to hit me," Kot said in one of his meetings with Mikiciński in France, according to British intelligence data.[74]

Mikiciński's friends spoke openly in his defense. In early November, a representative of the Polish Foreign Office headquarters contacted the deputy chief of the Dwójka, Lieutenant Colonel Stanisław Gano (whose wife, as might be recalled, had been rescued from Warsaw via Berlin with Mikiciński's assistance) with a request to respond to the constant stream of denunciations flowing out of the Polish embassy in Istanbul. Gano, a veteran of Polish political infighting who would rise to the top position in his organization the following year, prudently refrained from giving a clear answer, only stating that, in his opinion, Mikiciński could not have become so successful in occupied Poland without rendering some services to the Germans (possibly even unintentionally). When the diplomat asked directly whether Mikiciński should be given further assignments on behalf of the government-in-exile, Gano gave another evasive reply, asserting that one had to be extremely cautious when working with him and careful to avoid giving the impression he enjoyed the exceptional confidence of the Polish government.[75]

---

72 Koper, *Polskie piekiełko*, 416–421.
73 The archives of the *Irgun* (Arhion Etzel—hence: AE). An undated report, 1947, file No. Kaf-4-31/1/9, 21, paragraph No. 32.
74 "The P. Affair," a synopsis of D.S.(E) P2446, March 24, 1941, TNA, HS 4/213.
75 Rutkowski, *Stanisław Kot*, 148–149, footnote 153.

In reality, this senior officer of the Dwójka (who, incidentally, used to be quite willing to meet Mikiciński in person[76] and had even appealed to him to help rescue his wife) admitted that his organization had no idea if Mikiciński was actually a Nazi spy. Gano did so in a manner typical of all the intelligence agencies in the world when forced to assess a situation without being in command of the relevant facts. In response, Kot and Sikorski did what most politicians do in cases when their intelligence organs refrain from giving clear answers: they simply ignored the lieutenant colonel's vague warning about Mikiciński. For this reason, on November 3, 1940, the London leadership of the Polish Foreign Office officially informed the Polish consul in Istanbul, Tadeusz Kunicki—an ardent Piłsudchik and one of Mikiciński's major enemies—that the Interior Ministry and its headquarters (read: Kot and Sikorski) objected to the idea of removing Mikiciński from his post. (This probably referred to his activities in Turkey and Romania on behalf of Polish refugees and his efforts to maintain contact with the occupied homeland). They demanded to see concrete evidence of this man's criminal activities at once, stating that no such evidence had been presented to them yet.[77]

Kunicki refused to "give up without a fight," and on November 19 he informed his superiors in London by telegram: "Since our military officers are fully convinced of Mikiciński's role as a Gestapo agent, we are bound to view him with deep distrust, which completely paralyzes our work with the 'Polish Desk' at the Chilean embassy in Bucharest." His complaint ended with a request to ask the authorities in Santiago to remove Mikiciński from the Romanian capital at once. According to a comment scribbled on Kunicki's telegram by some anonymous official on November 25, Stanisław Gano delivered the request to have Mikiciński removed from Bucharest to Minister Kot in person, but Kot categorically rejected the idea of involving the Chilean authorities in this matter.[78] Nine days later, Kunicki informed the Polish Foreign Office—this time, too, in very vague terms—that the British intelligence officers in Turkey and their Turkish counterparts believed that Mikiciński was a German agent.[79] This may have been a deliberate hoax, or possibly an indirect result of the Turks'

---

76 See about one such meeting in London in May 1940: an untitled report by the chief of the Second Department of the Polish Armed Forces in Exile, Colonel Mitkiewicz, to Supreme Commander Sikorski, January 20, 1941, HIA, 800/41/0/-/141 Folder 7, Scan 001022.
77 The Headquarters of the Polish Foreign Office in London to the Polish Consul in Istanbul, November 3, 1940, HIA, 800/41/0/-/141 Folder 7, Scan 000106.
78 An encrypted telegram by Kunicki to the Polish Foreign Office Headquarters in London; November 19, 1940, HIA, 800/41/0/-/141 Folder 7, Scan 000108.
79 An encrypted telegram by Kunicki to the Polish Foreign Office Headquarters in London; November 28, 1940, HIA, 800/41/0/-/141 Folder 7, Scan 000105.

constant surveillance of German ambassador von Papen,[80] as they could have easily recorded his meetings with Mikiciński without knowing the latter was acting at the behest of a key figure in the Polish government.

Be that as it may, about a month later, on December 21, Polish ambassador Roger Raczyński, who had escaped from Bucharest and found a temporary home in Ankara, sent a similar message to Foreign Minister Zaleski in London detailing the British suspicions about Mikiciński. According to the ambassador, the British counterintelligence community was convinced that he was working for the Gestapo (an assertion with no factual basis, and possibly an outright fabrication originating with Raczyński or his confederates). For this reason, His Majesty's diplomats allegedly refused to work with the Chilean embassy in Bucharest. In light of the above, the complainer asked his bosses for an investigation into Samson's sponsorship (a rather odd request, since Iranek-Osmecki and other Polish officials in Romania had long been aware that Mikiciński enjoyed the patronage of Stanisław Kot), what instructions Samson received from London, and whether the government in Santiago knew what kind of "diplomat" was working at their Bucharest embassy. Raczyński summed up, "Without such an investigation, a huge scandal may erupt, and it would be really disastrous for us, even before Mikiciński is removed for good."[81]

However, as with the telegrams of Consul Kunicki, Raczyński's letter failed to have the effect desired by the writer and by his fellow Sanation supporters. Probably for this reason, in December 1940, the abovementioned British agent A/H.2 stationed in Turkey wrote with unconcealed despair that his government continued to blindly trust Mikiciński despite the many warnings about his connections with German espionage coming from official Polish representatives in Bucharest and Ankara and Polish military intelligence.[82] An echo of that complaint is discernible in the anonymous author's assertions in the document held at the Brooklyn archive:

> Even having been pushed up against the wall by the evidence of Mikiciński's espionage, Kot stubbornly insisted that the latter could not possibly do us any harm, even if he did collaborate with the Germans.[83]

---

80 See on the surveillance of von Papen: Isci, *Russophobic Neutrality*, 68 n197.
81 An encrypted telegram by Ambassador Raczyński to the Polish Foreign Office Headquarters in London, December 21, 1940, HIA, 800/41/0/-/141 Folder 7, Scan 000103.
82 An undated and untitled report by agent A/H.2, late December 1940, TNA, HS 4/213.
83 An undated message titled "Mikiciński Samson," JPIA, Archiwum Osobowe, NZ 154, Sygn. 658.

In January 1941, the Polish government-in-exile reiterated its firm stance on this issue to its representatives in Turkey. According to a telegram from London received by the Polish embassy in Ankara on January 14, Minister Kot had personally ascertained that, at present, the British authorities had no incriminating information against Mikiciński. Therefore, Ambassador Raczyński and Consul Kunicki were to stop obstructing his activities in Bucharest.[84]

At first blush, this message seems to indicate that only a few days prior to Mikiciński's abduction in Istanbul, the British had officially acknowledged that they harbored no suspicions against him nor had any intention to hinder his activities in Southeastern Europe and the Middle East. However, it could have been a deception to lull Mikiciński's Polish patrons into complacency as the British prepared to abduct him. Maybe Kot himself had fabricated the telegram in an attempt to make it easier for his protégé to leave Turkey, which had become a veritable death trap.

On January 15, the day after the arrival of that telegram and the eve of Mikiciński's planned abduction, Dwójka chief colonel Mitkiewicz-Żółłtek finally admitted the Polish military intelligence and counterintelligence community's failure to prove that the man was a spy. The official summary of this affair signed by Mitkiewicz-Żółłtek openly stated that despite their long-standing suspicions of Mikiciński's alleged ties with the Gestapo and over a year of close surveillance, intelligence officers had failed to uncover a single piece of firm evidence of his collusion with the Germans, let alone of any damage he might have done to the Polish national interests. Moreover, the authors of this document were forced to acknowledge that none of the Polish underground activists whose existence and whereabouts became known to Mikiciński during his visits to occupied Poland had come to any harm from the German occupiers. "Apparently, he does not tell them everything he knows, especially on Polish affairs," concluded the document.[85]

The only compromising fact against Mikiciński that the report managed to dredge up was. . . his connection with Viktor Kutten—"the one whose trial is currently under way in Palestine."[86] As might be recalled, no trial convened over the Kutten affair, and key figures in the Polish government-in-exile cast the collaboration charges into doubt. Thus, not even this piece of evidence

---

84 An encrypted telegram by the Polish Foreign Office to the Polish Embassy in Ankara, January 14, 1941, HIA, 800/41/0/-/141 Folder 7, Scan 000100.
85 The Second Department of the Polish General Staff in Exile, "A Profile of Mikiciński," January 15, 1941, HIA, 800/41/0/-/141 Folder 7, Scan 000101.
86 Ibid.

could substantiate the grave accusations Kot's political opponents spread against Mikiciński.

A Belated Alibi from the Gestapo Files

One fact clearly unknown to the Dwójka operatives at the time—and one subsequently overlooked by Polish and foreign historians—was that the Nazi intelligence community was just as afraid of Mikiciński as the Polish and British were and had characterized him as "a person suspected of espionage, who is to be monitored."

This fact can be gleaned from Mikiciński's personal card, which was opened by the Frankfurt Gestapo in September 1940.[87] This card—a single, small, yellowed page—is stored in the digital database of the Claims Conference, a US-based Jewish organization that helps Holocaust survivors with the restitution of property that belonged to them prior to World War II and their negotiations for material compensation from the German government. Unfortunately, the information in the card is very scant, and it does not explain why the Frankfurt branch of the Nazi secret police took an interest in Mikiciński, nor how the card landed in the Claims Conference archives after the war. Similar cards may have been opened by other Gestapo branches throughout Nazi Germany following instructions from the Berlin headquarters, but the Frankfurt card is the only one to have survived World War II.

From the laconic description of Mikiciński as a "Chilean diplomat staying in Istanbul," we learn that for some obscure reason, the Nazi counterintelligence officers had not become acquainted with the suspect during his earlier trips through German territory into occupied Poland and learned of his existence only in the late summer or early autumn of 1940 when, because of his contacts with von Papen in Turkey, he appeared on the radar of the security officer of the German embassy in Ankara. Such amazing blindness on the part of Hitler's secret service may be attributed to the Abwehr, who likely took pains to prevent the German border control from recording Mikiciński's movements through the Reich and keep the Gestapo in the dark about his existence. Their concern for his welfare probably stemmed from his key role in rescuing family members of the exiled Polish leadership from occupied Poland, acts possibly sanctioned by Admiral Canaris to strengthen his secret ties with the West.

---

87 Samson Mikicinski, Kanzleichef der Chilenischen Gesandtschaft, Ankara, Kartei Gestapo Frankfurt, 23 September 1940, S 693/4.1.1962, 0.1/1.2.3.1/ ITC Digital Collection, YVA.

In any case, this amazing finding from the Claims Conference archives finally puts to rest the Dwójka's allegations that Mikiciński collaborated with the Gestapo, and it refutes all the oral and written accusations of Nazi collaboration actively circulated by his enemies during his lifetime, and by the historians who took these calumnies at face value after his death.

The Failure of the Game of Prevention

Mikiciński became aware of British and Polish counterintelligence's suspicions roughly two months before his arrest when in late October or early November of 1940, Karol Alexandrowicz, Stanisław Kot's confidant in Bucharest, debriefed him in a private meeting. (Briefly imprisoned by the Legionaries, Alexandrowicz had left for Istanbul, where he continued to wage his struggle against the Sanation camp.) At the meeting's outset, Alexandrowicz asked Mikiciński about the details of his contact with the Germans and told his interlocutor (apparently at Kot's behest) that Kutten, then already under arrest in Palestine, had given incriminating information against him to the Dwójka and the British.[88] About a month later, at the very end of the year, Kot's representatives in the Middle East sent Mikiciński several warnings to the effect that the British believed him to be a German agent. One such warning signed by Zdzisław Szczerbiński, secretary of the Polish embassy in Ankara, was found among Mikiciński's personal effects after his abduction.[89]

In those same days, probably not coincidentally, the Turkish security apparatus launched an extensive crackdown on foreign citizens suspected of being international swindlers—and even more unpleasantly, of intentionally circulating counterfeit British and American currency. The Turks managed to nab some seventy suspects, most of them Jewish refugees from Europe and some Mikiciński's men, among them a certain Stanisław Schwarzstein. The author of the Brooklyn report described him as a "merchant from Warsaw, and Mikiciński's private secretary in Istanbul;"[90] according to Ambassador

---

88 An undated protocol of the interrogation of Samson Mikiciński, spring 1941, HIA, 800/41/0/-/141 Folder 7, Scan 000947.
89 An undated message titled "Mikiciński Samson," JPIA, Archiwum Osobowe, NZ 154, Sygn. 658; see also a personal message from Kurcyusz to Kot, reminding the latter that Lis ought to be exceptionally careful: Kurcyusz to Kot, Istanbul, December 16, 1940, USHMM, RG-59.047, KOL-25-45A_252-3.
90 An undated message titled "Mikiciński Samson," JPIA, Archiwum Osobowe, NZ 154, Sygn. 658.

Sokolnicki, he was a "Jew from Łódź, a Polish citizen, the secretary of the Chilean embassy, and Mikiciński's right-hand man, who was implicated in the use of the Chilean diplomatic mail to send counterfeit British pounds produced by the German government."[91] Polish historian Roman Buczek wrote (without naming his sources, unfortunately) that Schwarzstein had been Mikiciński's business partner before the war and had even assisted in his abovementioned flight from the Polish capital in September 1939.[92] Shortly after the crackdown, the Turkish authorities released most of the suspects. Yet, as the officers of ekspozytura T (the Ankara station of the Polish military intelligence) learned from an unnamed source in the local political police, some of Mikiciński's associates remained under arrest and had allegedly given incriminating evidence against their patron.[93]

In light of the fact that an identical accusation of circulating counterfeit British money had served as the formal (and soon forgotten) pretext for arresting Viktor Kutten and his partners, we may assume with a great deal of confidence that Schwarzstein's arrest was, in reality, a ploy by Mikiciński's British, Polish, and Turkish hunters to lure him into a trap. And the brouhaha in the press that accompanied the crackdown on the "international swindlers" was just a smokescreen intended to mask the true objectives of this counterintelligence operation and lull Mikiciński's vigilance.

The quarry of this hunt, not yet arrested or questioned by the Turks, showed a great deal of interest in the counterfeit banknotes affair and made every possible effort to have Stanisław Schwarzstein released.[94] Ambassador Sokolnicki noted acidly in his diary that "Mikiciński has asked Rychlewicz [the Polish consul general in Ankara] to help our fellow citizen."[95] At this stage, Samson was probably fully aware of the gravity of his predicament and had decided to preempt the blow about to fall on him. With the help of a Jewish acquaintance named Rosen, an agent of MI6 in Turkey, he personally contacted the Istanbul branch of the British spy agency to offer his services as an informant.[96] According to the report from Brooklyn cited repeatedly above, the British, like their Polish counterparts in the early 1930s, considered this offer but ultimately rejected it. Allegedly, the

---

91 Sokolnicki. *Dziennik Ankarski*, s. 162.
92 Buczek, *Człowiek do złotych interesów*, 12–13.
93 A report by the "Dwójka" titled "Mikiciński—information," June 1941, HIA, 800/41/0/-/141 Folder 7, Scan 001008.
94 An undated message titled "Mikiciński Samson," JPIA, Archiwum Osobowe, NZ 154, Sygn. 658.
95 Sokolnicki, *Dziennik Ankarski*, 162.
96 A protocol of Mikiciński's interrogation, March 15, 1941, HIA, 800/41/0/-/141 Folder 7, Scan 000965.

reason for this rejection was the information from the Turkish security organs, according to which Mikiciński's men had indeed been involved in circulating counterfeit British currency.[97]

A secret SOE report on the Mikiciński affair from July 1941 gave a totally different account of Mikiciński's failed attempt to contact the British foreign intelligence service. According to this document, the Istanbul branch of MI6 responded favorably to his request and even began the process of recruiting him as a double agent in order to use him to lure Abwehr officers Nobis and Scholz to Turkey. However, the SOE analyst goes on to write, Kot warned his protégé that the British were communicating with him solely in order to keep tabs on him.[98]

Another British document, this one dedicated to the "Kot organisation in the Middle East," reads that Dr. Karol Bader, the Polish consul in Beirut, delivered Mikiciński's warning from the Polish minister of the interior.[99] As might be recalled, about a year earlier, Mikiciński had found Bader in Pani Pfeifferova's boarding house in Warsaw hiding with Sikorski's wife and daughter. Apparently, he was subsequently smuggled by the "Chilean diplomat" to the West and was now trying to repay the debt to his rescuer by aiding the latter's attempts to extricate himself from the trap set by the British secret service. As a result, the SOE report sums up, the British canceled the planned operation to use Samson as bait to catch his alleged Abwehr handlers.[100] This cancellation put paid to any hopes he may have had of convincing the British of his trustworthiness, and his position in Turkey became more precarious than ever.

Stanisław Kot was well aware of this. According to the author of the Brooklyn report, the Polish minister had become greatly worried about Mikiciński's fate and urgently tried to have him evacuated to territories beyond Britain's reach using the services of Szczerbiński, the secretary of the Polish embassy in Ankara.[101] Kot's worries likely grew when, on January 2, 1941, after a long and bitter struggle, he was finally able to snatch the key post of chairman of the Committee of Ministers for Homeland Affairs from his sworn enemy, General Sosnkowski.[102] One did not have to be a genius to see that the enraged Piłsudchiks would now do their best to hamstring the activities of the Kotowcy

---

97 An undated message titled "Mikiciński Samson," JPIA, Archiwum Osobowe, NZ 154, Sygn. 658.
98 A top secret report titled "The Paluchowicz Case," copy No. 1, July 18, 1941, TNA, HS 4/213.
99 An undated, top secret draft of a memorandum by SOE, titled "Note on the Kot organisation in the Middle East," TNA, HS 4/213.
100 A top secret report titled "The Paluchowicz Case," copy # 1; July 18, 1941, TNA, HS 4/213.
101 An undated message titled "Mikiciński Samson," JPIA, Archiwum Osobowe, NZ 154, Sygn. 658.
102 Paszkiewicz, *Komitet dla Spraw Kraju*, 167–171; Rutkowski, *Stanisław Kot*, 200–201.

in Europe and the Middle East. Mikiciński, a key player in these activities, whose "removal for good" had been mentioned by Ambassador Raczyński back on November 21, was a very likely target for this revenge.

Thus, it is possible that the order Kot had given Raczyński and Kunicki on January 14, 1941, not to prevent Mikiciński from leaving Istanbul for Bucharest, was actually an attempt to get him out of danger at the last possible moment. Moreover, the minister secured a promise from Dwójka leadership in London to drop all suspicions against Samson and inform the British of this decision. Overjoyed, he sent to Mikiciński an urgent message about this success, but it failed to reach the addressee in time.[103]

The Most Sensitive Undertaking

The attack on Mikiciński about which Kot had been so afraid was in the works for five months, starting in September 1940. While Szarkiewicz was busy investigating Kutten and his friends, he found ample time to plot Mikiciński's arrest in Istanbul. In early autumn, he contacted Commander W. Wolfson, chief of the Istanbul branch of the British naval intelligence. Wolfson, who acted under the guise of deputy naval attaché at the British embassy in Ankara, was a key figure in the intelligence, counterintelligence, and propaganda operations carried out by his government in Turkish territory. Later, in 1941–1942, he would play a prominent role in the operations of MI9, a British special service tasked with evacuating British soldiers and officers stranded in the Balkans, which had been overrun by the Germans and Italians.[104] Szarkiewicz, according to his own testimony from 1945, discussed with Wolfson "matters of counterintelligence" and "specific files of the naval intelligence."[105]

We can quite plausibly assume that these nebulous terms referred to the Mikiciński affair, and that it was Wolfson, an expert in the field of maritime traffic along the western Turkish coast with close ties with local navigators, who first came up with the idea of abducting Mikiciński in Istanbul and spiriting him out of Turkey by sea. Initially, the plotters intended to use a large seagoing vessel with a Greek name, *Agios Nikolaos*, which may have reflected its origins in one of

---

103 A telegram from the Istanbul branch of SOE to the London Headquarters of the organization, January 18, 1941, TNA, HS 4/213.
104 Berridge, *British Diplomacy in Turkey*, 181.
105 Szarkiewicz to Sir David Petrie, July 26, 1945, TNA, HS 4/213.

the eponymous port cities on the islands of Cyprus or Crete. However, for some reason, they ultimately settled on a small trading craft.[106]

The abduction plan was fleshed out during the autumn of 1940. Mikiciński would be brought by sea to Palestine, where the anti-Sikorski, pro-Sanation camp had great freedom of action and enjoyed the sympathy and support of both local Polish military officers and émigrés and the British Mandatory authorities. Responsibility for the actual abduction was given to the Cairo-based counterintelligence department[107] of SIME (Security Intelligence Middle East), which had been established a year earlier under MI5. The local Turkish branches of SIME, SOE, and MI6 were to carry out the abduction;[108] a certain Polish officer attached to SIME—in all likelihood, Szarkiewicz—was to assist the operation; and the Turkish counterparts' involvement would become auxiliary. None doubted that Mikiciński constituted a "grave public threat" that had to be removed from Turkey as soon as possible.[109]

The commanders of this undertaking considered it "the most sensitive." This exceptional sensitivity stemmed not only from the justified fear of information being leaked to Minister Kot's circle or to the Germans—but also, even more importantly, from the desire to keep the involvement of the Turkish side in the abduction under wraps. If the collusion between Ankara and London in the field of counterintelligence were to come to light, Turkey might decide to significantly reduce its cooperation and possibly even cancel it altogether—a serious blow to British interests in the region. For this reason, the information relating to the abduction was subjected to the strictest security rules, including a rigid compartmentalization between the intelligence and counterintelligence bodies involved. Thus, those who received correspondence on the subject of the vessel chosen to transport Mikiciński were required to destroy all the relevant papers immediately after reading them;[110] and representatives of the Cairo branch of SOE who wished to order Mikiciński's personal file from SIME were denied permission to borrow it (such permission would usually be granted in other, less sensitive cases) and were required to visit the headquarters of the Security Intelligence in Cairo in person to read the relevant documents on-site.[111]

---

106 D/H.2 in a telegram to D/H.1, Istanbul, December 26, 1940, TNA, HS 4/213.
107 In the original: G.S.I. (b).
108 An undated, top secret draft of a memorandum by SOE, titled "Note on the Kot organisation in the Middle East," TNA, HS 4/213; a top secret report titled "The Kutten Affair," copy No. 1, July 18, 1941, TNA, HS 4/213.
109 A top secret report titled "The Paluchowicz Case," copy No. 1, July 18, 1941, TNA, HS 4/213.
110 D/H.2 in a telegram to D/H.1, Istanbul, December 26, 1940, TNA, HS 4/213.
111 A top secret report titled "The Kutten Affair," copy No. 1, July 18, 1941, TNA, HS 4/213.

In retrospect, we can see clearly that these seemingly paranoid secrecy measures turned out to be effective. Not a scrap of information about the planned abduction leaked. Therefore, despite heightened suspicions and a full awareness of the danger he was in, Mikiciński and his friends and patrons in the Middle East and London were caught unprepared.

"The Turks Have Given an Outstanding Performance!"

The countdown to the implementation of the Mikiciński abduction scheme began in the first days of 1941. According to the anonymous Brooklyn report, Mikiciński, still trying to get his associate Schwarzstein released from police custody, contacted a certain Turkish police officer via an unknown intermediary with a request for help in exchange for generous remuneration. The officer, for his part, replied that such sensitive decisions could be taken only by his superior. Undeterred, Mikiciński asked to meet this superior in person.[112] If, as postulated above, this was all part of the trap laid by the British, the Turks, and Szarkiewicz, then Mikiciński's behavior could mean only one thing: the victim was swallowing the bait dangled by the hunters. The Brooklyn document goes on to say that Mikiciński's Turkish contact initially refused to introduce him to his boss but shortly thereafter showed up in Mikiciński's office bringing the good news that his boss had deigned to meet. In all likelihood, this, too, was part of the ruse enacted by the secret services to allay the target's suspicions.[113]

On January 8, the two men met for a confidential discussion at a private apartment in Istanbul whose exact address has been lost to the mists of history. In accordance with the traditional rules of Turkish hospitality, the assistant (or assistants) of the "high-ranking police officer" served coffee. Anyone who has ever been to Turkey knows the Turkish custom of pouring coffee from a small pot known as a *cezve*, but there was no cezve at this particular meeting. Instead, the coffee was served in espresso cups mounted in glass holders—a very important detail. Mikiciński's cup had been laced with a powerful sedative intended to render him helpless. However, to the immense surprise and disappointment of the conspirators, the drug had no effect on him. According to the Brooklyn report, "Mikiciński, a robust man of exceptional physical strength, showed no

---

[112] An undated message titled "Mikiciński Samson," JPIA, Archiwum Osobowe, NZ 154, Sygn. 658.
[113] Ibid.

signs of drowsiness." Unprepared for this possibility, under some pretext his hosts cut the meeting short and postponed it to a later date.

As unbelievable as it might seem, Mikiciński apparently failed to realize that he had miraculously escaped a trap—and so, in a week's time, late in the evening of January 15, he showed up at the same place to resume the discussion. Once again, the honored guest was served black Turkish coffee in a cup; once again— miracle of miracles!—the drug did not affect him, even though he had received a triple dose. This time, however, the plotters were far better prepared to carry out their intent. Seeing that Mikiciński was stubbornly refusing to fall asleep, they simply fell upon him and immobilized him. "As a result," the Brooklyn report sums up, "on the night of January 15–16 Mikiciński was bundled into an unidentified airplane and flown from Istanbul to Egypt, and possibly further on to Sudan, where the investigation of his case began."[114]

This foregoing account of Mikiciński's abduction, written by a nameless Polish author, may seem implausible because of its excessive dramatism. Russian history buffs may be reminded of the assassination of Grigorii Rasputin, a mystic who in the early twentieth century had befriended the Russian imperial family and was accused by his critics of having a destructive influence on Russian domestic and foreign policies. As is well known, Rasputin was lured by his enemies into the Yusupov palace in Saint Petersburg and served poisoned cakes. When the poison failed to take effect, the conspirators shot him. This story has been told in detail in numerous Russian and Western books, including the biography of Rasputin by the American historian Elizabeth Judas, which became a bestseller immediately upon publication in the US in 1942.[115] Hence, we may reasonably assume that the author of the Brooklyn report borrowed certain elements of the popular narrative of Rasputin's death for his description of Mikiciński's abduction in Istanbul, suggesting a parallel.

Be that as it may, it must be admitted that the British accounts of the abduction available to us at present largely bear out the story told by the anonymous Pole. The British, too, mention the two meetings at the safe house in Istanbul and the triple dose of sedative.[116] They also saw fit to mention the important contribution of their Turkish counterparts to the success of the operation. "The Turks have given an outstanding performance!" wrote a high-ranking British officer in Cairo to a colleague in London. This colleague is referred to as M.

---

114 Ibid.
115 Judas, *Rasputin*, 163–164.
116 A top secret report titled "The Paluchowicz Case," copy No. 1, July 18, 1941, TNA, HS 4/213.

in the text of the letter. From this, we may deduce that he was probably Major General Stewart Menzies, director general of MI6.[117]

Moreover, the British reporters fleshed out the account with several key details omitted (either purposefully or innocently) by the author of the Brooklyn report. The most important of these is the active involvement in the operation of the Polish agent ESS13—who, as we have conjectured above, may have well been Edward Szarkiewicz. An SOE report from July 1941 states that during the abduction operation, he was assigned to the counterintelligence department of SIME in Cairo and the officers of SO.2, an operational department of SOE active in Turkey. According to this source, it was not some random Turkish police officer but the agent ESS13 who lured Mikiciński to the meeting at the safe house in Istanbul, and it was he who "pacified" the awake and alert captive. If we believe the British report, this process was very rough indeed: the conspirators had to hit him on the head, then put him to sleep with a rag soaked in chloroform. The next stage of the operation is described in the British document as an "interagency muddle." Contrary to what was claimed in the anonymous Brooklyn report and several other Polish documents,[118] Samson was not flown out of Turkey straight away, but kept there for a while as his captors debated what was to be done with him. Only sometime later did they decide to transport him by air (not by sea, as originally planned) to Palestine, where he would be brought before a Polish court.[119]

Remarkably, the author(s) of this British report do(es) not mention the fact that, in mid-January 1941, when the British and the Poles made the decision to bring Mikiciński to Palestine (allegedly in order to put him on trial), both parties were well aware after the fiasco with Kutten and his comrades that they had no right to try a Polish civilian in Mandatory Palestine. Thus, it is quite possible that the British, and the Polish agent assisting them were prepared to discreetly eliminate Mikiciński after the end of the investigation. From another British document, we learn that the British Security Intelligence Middle East in Cairo in charge of the operation was very pleased with its outcome. The above-mentioned high-ranking SIME officer went so far as to assure his anonymous correspondent in London that, in his opinion, it was his organization's greatest success since the outbreak of World War II.[120]

---

117 MX in a letter to M, Cairo, June 1, 1941, TNA, HS 4/213.
118 Buczek, *Człowiek do złotych interesów*, 149–150; Iranek-Osmecki, *Wspomnienia oficera*, 196–197; Michniewicz, *Opération Haïfa*, 183.
119 A top secret report titled "The Paluchowicz Case," copy No. 1, July 18, 1941, TNA, HS 4/213.
120 MX in a letter to M, Cairo, June 1, 1941, TNA, HS 4/213.

Hints in the Ambassador's Diary

Dr. Jan Ciechanowski, one of the leading experts on the wartime Polish intelligence community, describes the important role played by Sikorski's Foreign Office in giving diplomatic cover to the Dwójka's covert missions. The example he gives of the close cooperation between the two agencies dates to 1941, when the Polish embassies in Madrid and Lisbon helped Major Zdzisław Żurawski organize the flight of King Carol II and his Jewish mistress, Magda (Elena) Lupescu, from fascist Spain to neighboring Portugal. Notwithstanding his official diplomatic status, Spanish security authorities arrested Żurawski. Upon learning of the arrest, the Polish diplomats posted in Madrid drew on their connections with Spanish leadership, hired a lawyer for their compatriot, secured his transfer to a jail in Portugal, and had him released quickly.[121]

A careful reading of Michał Sokolnicki's *Ankara Diary* mentioned repeatedly above reveals possible hints of the diarist's intention to play a similar role in Mikiciński's abduction. He may have been expected to give Szarkiewicz diplomatic cover in case something in Istanbul went off-plan. The first such hint is Sokolnicki's surprisingly detailed knowledge of Mikiciński's fate. As it turns out, while the Turkish criminal police and the local and international mass media were wondering what had befallen him, the diarist already knew for certain that Mikiciński had not merely "vanished." "Last night, Mikiciński was arrested in Istanbul," he wrote, adding, "His arrest was supposed to take place . . . shortly before the New Year, but he managed to slip away and remain at large, holed up in the Park Hotel."[122] This postscript clearly proves that Michał Sokolnicki—one of the most prominent members of the pro-Sanation camp in the Middle East and a bitter enemy of Stanisław Kot—had been made privy to the plan to eliminate Mikiciński despite the exceptional secrecy surrounding the preparations for his abduction in Istanbul. Thus, it is quite plausible that, at a certain point, the honorable ambassador was included in the tiny circle of operatives who planned and carried out the abduction. His role, as stated above, may have been extending diplomatic protection to the only Polish member of the team, Second Lieutenant Edward Szarkiewicz.

Another curious detail in the *Ankara Diary* suggests that Sokolnicki's involvement in Mikiciński's abduction was an apparent attempt on the part of the diarist to obfuscate its timing and his own whereabouts before, during, and after the event. The sentence "Last night, Mikiciński was arrested in Istanbul"

---

121 Ciechanowski, *Polski wywiad wojskowy w Portugalii*, 251.
122 Sokolnicki, *Dziennik Ankarski*, 161–162.

is preceded by an entry marked "Ankara, no date given," indicating that the day after Mikiciński's abduction, Sokolnicki was in Turkish capital when he received the news and wrote about it in his diary; since we know for certain from other sources that the abduction took place on the night of January 15-16, we can quite plausibly deduce that on January 16, 1941, Sokolnicki was busy with his official duties in Ankara, and it was there he first learned of Mikiciński's arrest. However, amazingly enough, the diary entry that follows is dated January 14, two days before the actual abduction! The dateline of this strange entry was Yeniköy, an upscale Istanbul suburb on the European shores of the Bosporus.[123] It turns out that in the days before the British and Szarkiewicz's joint action, Sokolnicki had moved from Ankara and was now very close to the site where the abduction was to take place.

From subsequent entries in the *Ankara Diary*, we learn that the diarist remained in Yeniköy until the evening of January 20 (almost a week), and that, from January 17 on, he regularly inquired about the results of the ongoing search for Mikiciński from those he came into contact with: the Polish consul general in Ankara, Wojciech Rychlewicz; the chief of the Istanbul criminal police; and even the Chilean chargé d'affaires in Istanbul, Hector Briones Luco.[124] Sokolnicki's behavior may have been part of the aforementioned diplomatic cover, and his departure on January 20 coincides with the end of the multi-day interagency muddle that followed Mikiciński's abduction and lasted until he was spirited away to Palestine. When the plane carrying Szarkiewicz and Mikiciński finally took off from Turkish soil, the cover became unnecessary, and the senior diplomat who had been responsible for providing it was free to leave the picturesque Yeniköy and resume his regular duties in Ankara.

Why did Sokolnicki, putting pen to paper twenty years after the fact, feel the need to falsify the date of Mikiciński's abduction and leave the reader with the impression that he was still in the Turkish capital the next day? Was the author of the *Ankara Diary* trying to create an alibi in hopes obscuring the true date of the abduction? Did he think the glaring contradiction between his account and the historical record would never come to light? Impossible to say. Another mystery: Why did Sokolnicki make no attempt to expunge all the references to Mikiciński from his diary prior to publication even though nothing prevented him from doing so? One possible explanation is that he was driven by a longstanding desire to tarnish the image and legacy of Stanisław Kot and his associates. Many of Sokolnicki's confederates and the Polish historians who

---

123 Ibid, 162–164.
124 Ibid.

took their side did likewise, and this historiographical tradition has remained with us to this day.

A Noble Flight

On January 25, 1941, the British authorities in Palestine and Trans-Jordan issued Edward Szarkiewicz an official pass with a note: "Will be regarded as a member of H. M. Forces."[125] We can assume with a great deal of confidence that this coincided with Szarkiewicz's arrival with his precious captive. Thus, before being bundled onto the plane that would take him to Palestine, Mikiciński had been held in an unknown location in Turkey for about one week. This conclusion matches the assumption made above, according to which the diplomatic cover Sokolnicki extended to Szarkiewicz lasted until January 20.

As it turned out, the shield of secrecy surrounding the operation that had worked so well in Turkey cracked as soon as it moved to Palestine. News of Mikiciński's arrival spread like wildfire among the Polish expatriates there and soon reached the ears of Kot's representatives in Turkey. "We do not know exactly how they managed to smuggle him from Turkey to Palestine without drawing anyone's attention," the Istanbul branch of the Polish Interior Ministry would later claim.[126]

This riddle remained unsolved for decades. After the war, veterans of the Polish intelligence community would claim Mikiciński arrived in Palestine on a British airplane provided by MI6 and piloted by "some young British aristocrat."[127] However, they were ignorant as to the type of this aircraft, the exact location of its takeoff, and—most crucially—the pilot's identity. Only fifty years after these events did Polish historian Roman Buczek—who as stated above did not bother to cite any sources—discover that the plane carrying Mikiciński to Palestine was piloted by the British aristocrat Lord Forbes, who allegedly arrived in Turkey in a light aircraft a few days before the designated abduction date, joined up with Szarkiewicz, and then met Mikiciński at Çulu Airport near Istanbul after a Turkish intelligence officer had delivered him there in a private car, bound hand and foot.[128]

---

125 Room 055 to Sir David Petrie, G.L. 1657/41, August 13, 1941, TNA, KV 2/517_6, 26.
126 A secret extract from a report by the Polish Interior Ministry representation in Istanbul, August 26, 1941, PISM, PRM. 50, 10.
127 Iranek-Osmecki, *Wspomnienia oficera*, 196–197, 553; Michniewicz, *Opération Haïfa*, 183.
128 Buczek, *Człowiek do złotych interesów*, 147, 149–150.

British sources flesh out Buczek's terse account with a wealth of important detail and offer an alternative account of Mikiciński's forced departure from Turkey. First of all, Lord Forbes's full name was Arthur Patrick Hastings Forbes, the Ninth Earl of Granard, scion of an old Irish aristocratic family which traces its origins to the seventeenth century. Sir Arthur was born in April 1915 (making him only twenty-five years old at the time of Mikiciński's abduction) and served in the Royal Air Force from the outbreak of World War II. According to the memoirs of intelligence officer and diplomat Sir David Hunt, in the autumn of 1940, the young Forbes, "a bright and tenacious officer" with the rank of wing commander (lieutenant colonel), had already served as intelligence chief at the headquarters of the British Expeditionary Force in Greece, and before that, as an air attaché in Bucharest—a post that was probably cover for intelligence work.[129]

Possibly, Forbes first met Szarkiewicz in Bucharest. We know for certain that their association did not end with their arrival in Palestine. Documents found in the Kew Archives indicate that in April 1941, Szarkiewicz was in close contact with Forbes, who had just been evacuated to Egypt from German-occupied Greece;[130] and that after the end of the war in Europe, in July 1945, Szarkiewicz asked Forbes to help him become a naturalized British citizen. He even claimed in a letter to the director general of MI5 that he, Szarkiewicz, was a good acquaintance of His Lordship, who could vouch for him.[131]

And there are further discoveries connected with the name of the Ninth Earl of Granard. According to an obituary from 1992, the first decoration he received during World War II was the British Air Force Cross, awarded for outstanding achievements not related to the combat activities of the RAF.[132] A perusal of the list of recipients of this decoration shows that, on February 21, 1941, Arthur Forbes, an officer of No. 204 Squadron RAF, was indeed awarded the Air Force Cross with the permission of His Royal Majesty.[133] As for the duties of this particular squadron, it consisted of seaplanes, both light patrol craft and heavy bombers, and after September 1939, it carried out combat missions in the Atlantic Ocean. However, some of its Saro London flying boats—six-person workhorses with an operational range of up to twelve hundred kilometers—were transferred to the Mediterranean theater and distributed among the British naval bases in the area.[134]

---

129 Sir David KCMG OBE Hunt, *A Don at War*, 26–27, 32.
130 Major Alley, memo, September 9, 1941, TNA, KV 2/517_6, 21.
131 Szarkiewicz to Sir David Petrie, July 26, 1945, TNA, KV 2/518_1, 24–25.
132 Sir Arthur Forbes, Earl of Granard, 77. See the section "Sources and Bibliography."
133 *Flight*, March 6, 1941, 197; "Air Ministry, 21st February 1941."
134 Halley, *The Squadrons of the Royal Air Force*, 264; Israel, *Flugboote des zweiten Weltkrieges*, 86–87.

By collating all these details, we can see a picture of Mikiciński's abduction different from the one in Buczek's book. According to David Hunt, Forbes was an avid pilot who continued his flying practice while serving in Greece.[135] Is it possible that he flew to Istanbul from Athens on a light Saro London seaplane? Did he then use this flying boat to transport his top secret cargo to Palestine? Did he take off not from an ordinary airport (as Buczek would have it) but from the sea? Was the small seagoing vessel that Szarkiewicz and Wolfson originally envisioned ultimately replaced with a small, amphibious aircraft that could take off from any point near the Turkish Mediterranean coast? From a practical point of view, this was an almost perfect solution that eliminated the need to smuggle the abductee through a Turkish airport where he might be discovered or possibly even liberated by local security personnel unaware of the operation.

As for the decoration bestowed upon Forbes, the official date of the award in late February 1941 suggests that almost certainly the young airman received the Air Force Cross for his role in Mikiciński's abduction, which had taken place only a month previously. The high prestige of the award is probably an indication of the great importance London attached to the success of the covert flying mission from Turkey to Palestine. At this point, we must emphasize that this was a step taken by official British organs against a man trying to advance the strategic interests of the Polish government-in-exile—then (supposedly) the closest ally of the UK in its war against Germany. From this, we can conclude that behind the facade of the common struggle against the Nazis, far from the prying eyes of the British, Polish, and worldwide public, the governments of Churchill and Sikorski engaged in a secret, persistent, and occasionally brutal struggle. At stake was the future of the war rapidly gathering steam and the Polish political regime. Only six months later, the British would strong-arm Sikorski into a reconciliation with Stalin (to the chagrin of multitudes of Poles, including some high-ranking émigrés), and were doing their utmost to prevent a similar reconciliation between Hitler and the Poles.

The archival sources at our disposal are silent on the exact route of Mikiciński's flight from Turkey to Palestine, and on the abductee's behavior aboard the plane. Therefore, we have no choice but to rely on the (rather dubious) testimonies of Iranek-Osmecki and Buczek. According to both men, the weather conditions on the day of the flight were poor, forcing Forbes to make a detour to Cyprus, where he made a brief stop for refueling; only then did he set out for the Holy Land. As Iranek-Osmecki tells it, Mikiciński came back to his senses during the lengthy flight and tried to turn the situation to his advantage. He struck up a

---

135 Sir David. KCMG OBE Hunt, *A Don at War*, 26–27, 32.

conversation with Szarkiewicz and offered him a fat bribe in exchange for his freedom. When Szarkiewicz refused, Mikiciński allegedly tried to overpower him, so he had no choice but to immobilize him with a pistol blow to the head.[136] This Hollywood-style account does not explain how Mikiciński managed to free himself from the ropes that bound him, nor how he might had convinced the pilot to divert the plane. Hence, Iranek-Osmecki's testimony should be regarded not as an objective account of historical events, but as a product of the overactive imagination of an aging veteran of the Polish intelligence and counterintelligence community—who was, moreover, an inveterate Piłsudchik and Mikiciński's sworn enemy. This impression is strengthened by Buczek's account, which has Mikiciński bound and motionless on the plane's floor under Szarkiewicz's watchful eye.[137]

---

136 Iranek-Osmecki, *Wspomnienia oficera*, 196–197.
137 Buczek, *Człowiek do złotych interesów*, 150.

Chapter 6

Publicity, Investigation, and a Mysterious Death in the Sands of Haifa

A Worldwide Sensation

If Mikiciński's abductors hoped the public would not notice his disappearance, they made a grave miscalculation: this mysterious occurrence drew the immediate attention of local and foreign journalists working in Istanbul. In this period described, the city was positively swarming with such individuals offering their services to global press outlets, news agencies, and intelligence operatives hoping to acquire valuable information about the European war. The Turkish censors may have tried, at least for a time, to discourage media coverage of Mikiciński's fate: the first reports about him did not appear until January 22, 1941, six days after the abduction. The Turkish morning daily *Vatan*, which represented the views of the local democratic, pro-Western circles, was the first to run a lengthy announcement of his disappearance with the headline "What Happened to Samson Mikiciński?" The article's author emphasized Mikiciński's role as an international dealer in passports and transit visas, offering several possible explanations for his disappearance that included revenge by his Polish compatriots, criminal entanglements, and even an ill-fated love affair.[1]

---

1 "Samson Mikiciński Ne Oldu?," 1, 5.

Newspapers in English-speaking countries followed suit, showing considerable interest in the mysterious (as they unanimously described it) Mikiciński affair. Ambassador Sokolnicki confided to his *Ankara Diary* that, three days after Mikiciński's arrest, he ran into a correspondent of the London *Times* daily in Istanbul who proceeded to subject him to an intense interrogation about, as the journalist put it, the "extremely murky Mikiciński affair."[2] The American press claimed that the Turkish criminal police were pursuing several lines of investigation, but the most plausible explanation for the disappearance was politically motivated murder. The missing person was described as a former Russian military officer and a consul at the Chilean legation in Istanbul who had been assisting the scores of Polish refugees stranded in Romania, and who made frequent trips to Bucharest to this end. He was allegedly seen for the last time in the evening of January 15 in the company of a Romanian refugee named Menielescu, a former advisor to the deposed Romanian king, Carol II.[3]

Crafty American journalists had obviously obtained this last detail from a Turkish official closely involved in the investigation. It sheds a new light on Mikiciński's connections to the Romanian regime. "Menielescu" is in all likelihood a misspelling of the last name of Mihail Manoilescu, one of the top Romanian economists in the prewar period, a prominent pro-fascist and anti-semitic politician, and a member of the inner circle of the deposed king. Until September 1940, Manoilescu, who was of an age with Mikiciński, had served as the Romanian foreign minister and earned a reputation as a Germanophile. According to rumors circulating in Bucharest at the end of that year, he was expected to join the fascist government of Ion Antonescu and Horia Sima any day now and regain control of his former ministry.[4] He probably came into contact with Mikiciński in 1940 as a result of the latter's extensive activities in the Romanian capital. This relationship can be seen as yet another example of Mikiciński's uncanny ability to gain access to the prominent European politicians he was interested in meeting. It is also an example of the ties that existed between the Kotowcy (and possibly Sikorski himself) and the Axis powers, the enemies of Britain.

At the same time, it seems plausible that Mikiciński's abductors (most probably the British, but possibly the Poles, too) exploited at least some of the foreign

---

2 Sokolnicki, *Dziennik Ankarski*, 164.
3 "Chilean Chancellor Sought in Istanbul," *Wilmington Morning Star* (Wilmington, NC), January 22, 1941, 1.
4 "The Political Mood in Romania and the Situation of the Poles after the Departure of the Embassy of the Polish Republic from Bucharest," an unfinished secret telegram, Istanbul, November 22, 1940, PISM, PRM.32, 60.

media outlets active in Turkey at the time to spread misinformation about the operation. *Le Journal d'Orient*, a French-language daily based in Istanbul and close to Zionist circles in Europe and the Middle East, cited "knowledgeable Turkish sources" when reporting that Mikiciński had not been murdered or abducted but had staged his own disappearance in order to avoid an attempt on his life, or possibly even to leave the country in secret.[5]

A similar claim with some surprising additional details appeared in the *Ostdeutscher Beobachter*, a German-language daily published in the Polish areas annexed by Nazi Germany. According to this version, whose sources are obscure, Mikiciński vanished shortly after the arrest in Tel Aviv of a certain Pole who was found to be in possession of a pack of counterfeit British banknotes. The arrestee allegedly testified that he had received this money from Mikiciński personally. The British passed this information to their Turkish colleagues, but the latter were unable to keep it under wraps, and it was quickly leaked to the Chilean chargé d'affaires, Hector Briones Luco, who hastened to warn Mikiciński of this development and help his partner escape abroad before he could be arrested.[6]

In retrospect, knowing what we do today about the real circumstances of the affair, we can clearly see these reports for the lies they were. As noted above, the story about the counterfeit British money was apparently concocted by the British, Polish, and Turkish counterintelligence operatives as part of their efforts to capture Mikiciński. We can assume, with a great deal of confidence, that by spreading these insinuations, they hoped to deceive Samson's (imaginary) Nazi handlers and his friends among the Kotowcy about his real fate. In this way, the abductors tried to buy time to transport their victim to Palestine and begin to investigate him there without interference.

Much more puzzling are the motives of the Soviet press, which echoed the claim that Mikiciński had been circulating counterfeit British currency in the Middle East and even added some details mentioned nowhere else about the role of Luco in Mikiciński's arrest. According to a "dispatch from Istanbul" published in Moscow, a certain "official representative of a South American country" was at the head of a whole "network of counterfeiters;" when his criminal activities came to light, he hurried to save his own skin by handing over his secretary, also involved in the enterprise, to Polish authorities. Ambassador Sokolnicki wrote

---

5   Iranek-Osmecki, *Wspomnienia oficera*, 196.
6   A Polish translation of the article "The Mikiciński Affair," from the *Ostdeutscher Beobachter*, February 13, 1941, The branch of the Polish military intelligence in Lisbon, March 17, 1941, HIA, 800/41/0/-/141 Folder 7, Scan 001012.

in the *Ankara Diary* that this Soviet report had given Luco a nasty fright.[7] Could this be the very effect that the Soviet organs were aiming for? Quite possibly, the relevant people in Moscow were aware of Mikiciński's role as an intermediary and were sending Luco a warning to discourage communications between Kot and von Papen, but this matter cannot be settled without access to Soviet foreign intelligence archives.

The Mysterious Inmate P.

As the journalists in Turkey and abroad were trying to puzzle out what had really happened to our protagonist, he landed in Palestine and was immediately taken to a British-run penitentiary. According to the Dwójka veteran Ladislas Michniewicz, it was located in Jerusalem,[8] whereas Roman Buczek asserts that it was a "British prison camp near Haifa," most probably referring to the famous camp in the Haifa suburb of Atlit.[9]

However, a report by SOE from July 18, 1941 leaves no room for doubt: it says that Mikiciński had "languished in the Citadel for nearly six months."[10] The Citadel was a common name for the old citadel in the city of Acre (also known as Akko and Akka) near the Mediterranean coastline. Built almost three hundred years ago, it became a prison at the end of Ottoman rule, and under the British Mandate (1918–1948), it was regarded as the largest establishment of its kind in Palestine. In early 1941, it housed fighters of the Jewish underground, participants in the Arab Revolt of 1936–1939, illegal immigrants and refugees from Europe and the Middle East, and ordinary criminals—some six hundred inmates in total. From time to time, the British jailers would subject them to summary execution.[11] In 1947, the Acre citadel became famous all over the world thanks to the daring prison break staged by the Irgun, when Jewish

---

7 Sokolnicki ascribed this report to the Soviet *Pravda* daily. See: Sokolnicki, *Dziennik Ankarski*, 168. However, the examination of the issues of *Pravda* from the relevant time period, during the writing of this book, could not trace any reports on this subject. From this, it may be concluded that the Polish diplomat made a mistake regarding the name of the Soviet newspaper or magazine that had run the story about the "Mikiciński Affair."
8 Michniewicz, *Opération Haïfa*, 192.
9 Buczek, *Człowiek do złotych interesów*, 150. This assertion was later echoed by the Polish historian Jan Stanisław Ciechanowski. See footnote 200 in the collection of documents compiled by him: Ciechanowski, *Polsko-Brytyjska współpraca*, 155.
10 A top secret report titled "The Paluchowicz Case," copy no. 1, July 18, 1941, TNA, HS 4/213.
11 Kaspi, "Batei ha-soar": 148–150.

underground fighters brought down the southern wall of the ancient structure with explosives and liberate many of their imprisoned fellows.[12]

The conditions in which the inmates were held under both Turkish and British rule were downright appalling. In the rainy winter months (and the winter of 1940–1941 in Palestine was exceptionally rainy and cold),[13] water would seep freely through the age-old, crumbling prison walls, pooling on the stone floors of the cells. Those cells were not equipped with bunks, and the prisoners, forced to sleep on the floor, developed chronic ailments.[14] Mikiciński, who arrived there in early 1941, was treated no differently from the others. According to Michniewicz, he was held "in a waterlogged cell, which was kept constantly lit."[15]

Because of the exceptional secrecy surrounding the Mikiciński affair, official British documents refrained from spelling out the real name of the new inmate of the Acre prison. Instead, they used the pseudonym Paluchowicz. Why this particular name was chosen remains a mystery. It is a relatively rare Polish surname, and also the name of several obscure Polish hamlets. The archival sources at our disposal make no mention of any connection between Mikiciński and any of these localities. Quite possibly, they picked the name totally at random. Some of the British officials involved in this operation felt the need to be even more circumspect in their correspondence. In those cases, the Paluchowicz affair became the P. affair, while Mikiciński was Mr. P. or X. These arbitrary designations remained in use for many months, indicating that the British continued to treat the matter as highly sensitive for a fairly long time.[16]

As might be recalled, Szarkiewicz was acting in Palestine as a special emissary of the Bucharest ekspozytura. He kept the local Palestinian station of his own service (called Nova in operational correspondence)[17] completely in the dark about the progress of his investigation into the P. affair. Dwójka headquarters had a hard enough time keeping in regular contact with representatives in Jerusalem and Tel Aviv: Colonel Mitkiewicz-Żółłtek, chief of Polish military intelligence, admitted to Sikorski that his investigation into Viktor Kutten lacked courier service to Palestine and relied on fragmentary radio messages for

---

12 Lapidot, *The Irgun*.
13 *Skirat iruim kitzoniim be-eretz Israel*, 43.
14 Kaspi, "Batei ha-soar": 148–150.
15 Michniewicz, *Opération Haïfa*, 192.
16 See, for instance: Maunsell to Sir David Petrie, June 14, 1941, TNA, KV 2/517_6, 24; a top secret report titled "The Paluchowicz Case," copy no. 1, July 18, 1941, TNA, HS 4/213.
17 "Code names used by the Skupień, Kaczmarek, and Vogel intelligence stations," an undated document, USHMM, RG-59.047, KOL-25-13_7.

communications.[18] In his book, Michniewicz, speaks of a "defective connection" between the Middle East branch and the London headquarters.[19] Szarkiewicz was well aware of these circumstances and decided for his own reasons to deny his colleagues even fragmentary radio communications with London.

In June 1941, a high-ranking British intelligence officer in Cairo reported Szarkiewicz's puzzling behavior to London, stating that Polish military counter-intelligence officer had asked the British to withhold intelligence of Mikiciński's exact location and the circumstances of his arrival from Polish military intelligence.[20] We can find an echo of this request in a report from the Istanbul branch of the Polish Interior Ministry, according to which there was no connection whatsoever "between the scandalous behavior of Szapiro-Szarkiewicz in Palestine and the head of the local military intelligence station" as of August that year.[21] In practice, this meant that neither arm of the exiled Polish intelligence community, neither the military nor the Interior Ministry, had any influence on Szarkiewicz's conduct vis-à-vis the Mikiciński affair.

What did Szarkiewicz hope to achieve by usurping total control over the investigation of the P. affair? Was he acting solely at his own discretion? It seems reasonable to assume he was primarily driven by his loyalty to the pro-Sanation camp. With the backing of the leaders of that camp (and possibly even without it), the zealous second lieutenant of the Dwójka hoped to create the impression that there were traitors among Kot's supporters, thereby neutralizing Mikiciński and his patron. Sosnkowski, whom Szarkiewicz idolized, would benefit greatly from this development.

Three decades ago, Roman Buczek advanced a different explanation for the behavior of the baptized Jew from Wybranówka: according to his data, Szarkiewicz, slick opportunist that he was, had already found a new patron in Major General Izydor Modelski. Until July 1940, Modelski was second deputy war minister and in charge of military counterintelligence. More importantly, he was rightly regarded as the key person to establish the Polish armed forces in exile, which lent him considerable political clout. According to Buczek, of all the high-ranking Poles staying in the British capital, Modelski was the only one whom Szarkiewicz updated regularly on his progress. And it was Modelski who

---

18 Chief of the Dwójka, Colonel Mitkiewicz-Żółłtek, to General Sikorski, an untitled report; January 20, 1941, HIA, 800/41/0/-/141 Folder 7, Scan 001022.
19 Michniewicz, Opération Haïfa, 200.
20 MX in a letter to M, Cairo, June 1, 1941, TNA, HS 4/213.
21 An extract from a secret report by the Polish Interior Ministry representation in Istanbul, August 26, 1941, PISM, PRM. 50, 10.

told MI5 chief David Petrie that Mikiciński was not to be moved from Acre to Britain, contrary to the wishes of the Kotowcy.[22]

Documents of MI5 and the British Foreign Office from the period 1942–1943 give clear evidence that, at this time, Szarkiewicz was indeed a confidant of Major General Modelski.[23] A fellow native of Lviv, the senior officer enjoyed the backing of the British and was aiming for the top spot in the Polish military establishment. This ambition brought him into open conflict with Minister Kot, who was promoting his own protégé, Marian Kukiel—a longtime opponent of Modelski—to this coveted post.[24] Modern Polish historiography adds that back in the first half of 1940, Kot had tried to assert control over the military counterintelligence apparatus under Modelski.[25]

It is crucial to note that unlike Kot's conflict with Sosnkowski, this confrontation was not a political clash between the Sikorski camp and the Piłsudchiks, but, rather, one of the deepest and most harmful splits among the followers of the émigré Polish leader. This split will be covered in greater detail below because of its decisive impact on Szarkiewicz's career after Mikiciński's death. For now, we may assume that even before Mikiciński's abduction —most probably after the pro-Sanation camp's failed attempt to oust Sikorski from power in July 1940—Szarkiewicz had realized that it was time to look for a new patron on the winning side. It was probably then that he concluded the secret alliance with Modelski—as a favorite of the British, he was regarded by many as a rising star in the Polish political firmament.[26] Szarkiewicz could very well have offered to help the ambitious general neutralize Kot, by eliminating and discrediting Mikiciński. To carry out this plan, Szarkiewicz and Modelski may have colluded to usurp the investigation of Mr. P. in order to convince the Polish government-in-exile, including Sikorski and the Dwójka headquarters, of Mikiciński's treachery and thereby ensure the defeat of Kot and his entourage. This usurpation was presented to the relevant Polish organs as a demand on

---

22 Buczek, *Człowiek do złotych interesów*, 170.
23 A secret document by MI5 titled "E. Szarkiewicz," February 6, 1942, TNA, KV 2/517_4, 5.
24 Frank Savery, Consul at the British Embassy to the Polish Government-in-Exile, to Sir Frank Roberts, head of the Central Department of the British Foreign Office, November 30, 1942, TNA, KV 2/517_4, 12; a report by the source Brit titled "Professor Stanisław Kot," September 27, 1943, TNA, KV 2/3429_5, 48.
25 Rutkowski, *Stanisław Kot*, 156–157.
26 Roman Buczek asserts that the meeting between Szarkiewicz and Modelski took place as early as the spring of 1940, and that it was the General who facilitated Szarkiewicz's recruitment by the Dwójka and his posting to Romania; allegedly, Modelski also personally advised his new protégé to contact the British intelligence. This assertion is not corroborated by any of the British or other documentary sources at our disposal. See: Buczek, *Człowiek do złotych interesów*, 75.

the part of the British, who supposedly wished to keep the investigation under wraps; in reality, it was an initiative by the Modelski-Szarkiewicz duo.

The Invention of a Nazi Superspy

Nowadays, we know precious little about the course of the investigation into the Mikiciński affair. The Polish and British archival sources available to us indicate that Szarkiewicz interrogated him in Polish and he spoke to British operatives in French. Szarkiewicz appears to have been absent from the latter sessions. The protocols of the interrogations he conducted—thirteen in total—are the only ones to have come down to us. As for the work of his British counterparts, we can read about it in just one of the surviving British references to the P. affair.[27]

According to the SOE summary report from July 1941, during his six-month incarceration in Palestine Samson was interrogated at least five times. Alas, the report fails to specify whether this number refers only to the British-led interrogations or whether the meetings between Mikiciński and his Polish investigator also count toward the total. One thing is perfectly clear: in addition to the inmate's connections with the Germans, the British were also interested in "illegal immigration," by which they meant the desperate attempts of Jewish refugees from Europe and North Africa to find shelter from the Holocaust in their historical homeland.[28] According to scholars who have investigated the struggle of the British Mandatory authorities against the Zionist movement, this migration was very high on the agenda of all the British intelligence and counterintelligence services active in the Middle East. One reason for such priority was a sincere belief that the Nazi enemy was flooding the region with agents posing as Jewish refugees.[29]

The most notorious and tragic consequence of this misconception was the disgraceful behavior of the British in the *Struma* affair of late 1941. *Struma*, a Bulgarian vessel, was sailing from Romania to Palestine under the flag of Panama, carrying hundreds of Jewish refugees. After a high-ranking official in the British Colonial Office had described the *Struma* as "a Gestapo spy ship," the Turks

---

27 MX in a letter to M, Cairo, June 1, 1941, TNA, HS 4/213. In 2021, the Polish historian Kapera wrote that Mikiciński had been interrogated in Palestine by "representatives of the Polish counterintelligence" (reprezentanty polskiego kontrwywiadu). See: Kapera, *Niemieckie świadectwa*, 65. However, the Polish and British sources known to us today refer to Szarkiewicz alone as Samson's interrogator.
28 A top secret report titled "The Paluchowicz Case," copy no 1, July 18, 1941, TNA, HS 4/213.
29 Jeffery, *MI6*, 421.

intercepted and anchored it in quarantine in the Istanbul harbor. Two months later, under British pressure, they sent the ship back to Romania; while traveling over the Black Sea, it took fire from a German or Soviet submarine and sunk.[30]

Szarkiewicz's interrogation reports consist of sheets of paper covered in crowded typewritten text containing only the detainee's alleged answers (the interrogator's questions were omitted in most cases). This method of documentation was the antithesis of the standard procedure of recording investigations used at the time by the security and intelligence services of many countries, including Poland. What is worse, only three of Szarkiewicz's reports were dated: the earliest on March 6, 1941, two others nine days later. However, it is quite possible that every report, dated or not, recorded the contents of earlier interrogations that took place from late January to early March. Therefore, we are unable to determine exactly when the Szarkiewicz-Mikiciński sessions began and how long they lasted. Roman Buczek claims that Mikiciński was first interrogated immediately upon his arrival in Palestine, and his second interrogation took place on February 14.[31] However, this assertion, like many others that appear in Buczek's book, is not supported by the archival sources at our disposal.

That said, Buczek does offer one fully accurate observation about the biased attitude of Second Lieutenant Szarkiewicz on the subject of the investigation. This bias is palpable in the aforementioned protocols. After subjecting Mikiciński to a brief and utterly perfunctory questioning about the particulars of his prewar biography—the most glaring lacunae was his unexpected wealth and contacts with the Soviet embassy during the Warsaw period—the investigator moved to the subject of Mikiciński's relationship with the Germans in an attempt to extract a confession of collaboration with Nazi spy agencies. Mikiciński, a man of keen intelligence and considerable bravery, gave plausible answers to all questions and accusations on this subject, explaining away his contact with the Abwehr officers and von Papen. He claimed to have acted at the behest of Sikorski, Kot, and other senior Polish figures, while categorically denying the charge that he was a Nazi agent out to harm Polish interests.

Certain details of Mikiciński's account of his dealings with Scholz—meetings in the safe house in Breslau, sharing general information about the goings-on in Polish émigré circles—could indeed be perceived as a virtual admission of spying for the Third Reich. And, as we shall soon see, Szarkiewicz and others who hated Mikiciński would come to interpret these statements in just this way. However, the interrogation protocol containing this admission was not signed

---

30 Aharonson, *Hitler, ba'alot ha-brit ve-ha-yehudim*, 167–168.
31 Buczek, *Człowiek do złotych interesów*, 157–158.

by the accused in his own hand. Instead of his signature, the bottom of the page bears the name Mikiciński with no way to determine who actually typed it.[32] Thus, it is quite possible that Szarkiewicz retroactively amended the text in order to convince the Polish High Command, the Dwójka, General Sosnkowski, and the general's followers that Mikiciński and Kot were traitors. If that were the case, why did the Szarkiewicz not simply rewrite all the protocols from scratch to add and remove details as he saw fit? We do not know the answer to that and probably never will, but one possible reason involves the presence of stenographers or British officers at some or all of his interrogations, which would have made it impossible to distort Mikiciński's statements at will.

Apparently, Szarkiewicz—or maybe his new patron, General Modelski—realized at a fairly early stage that the information his prisoner had yielded was too meager to support an ambitious scheme to topple Stanisław Kot. ekspozytura T records provide evidence of this realization. The Istanbul-based Polish operatives who had helped the Little Man orchestrate Mikiciński's abduction received an assignment in February 1941: they were to surreptitiously enter his apartment to search for incriminating evidence against him. The operatives succeeded in their task, but because Turkish police had already examined and sealed the apartment, their pickings were slim indeed. A random collection of Mikiciński's correspondence and business records, for some reason left untouched by the Turks, was meticulously packed and shipped to Szarkiewicz in Palestine. However, it failed to yield any insights into Mikiciński's alleged betrayal or collusion with the Nazi intelligence apparatus. Needless to say, neither the British nor Polish legal authorities would accept these documents as sufficient proof of Samson's crimes, so they offered no way forward in the investigation of the P. affair. The prisoner refused to admit to any wrongdoing.[33]

According to Ladislas Michniewicz, Mikiciński realized fairly early on that his abductors had no proof to back up their accusations against him and ergo no solid basis for continuing to detain him. Thus, he demanded that they release him at once if they could not present the incriminating evidence they had gathered or give him the opportunity, with a lawyer, to exonerate himself before a court of law.[34]

According to Buczek's version, Mikiciński insisted that his trial be held not in Palestine (where, as stated above, the Piłsudchiks were much more

---

32 An undated protocol of the interrogation of Samson Mikiciński, HIA, 800/41/0/-/141 Folder 7, Scans 000967-74.
33 Buczek, *Człowiek do złotych interesów*, 154–156.
34 Michniewicz, *Opération Haïfa*, 194–196.

influential than the Kotowcy), but in London, the permanent seat of the Polish government-in-exile.[35] However, Szarkiewicz and Modelski had very different plans for him. Mr. P. remained locked up behind the thick walls of the Acre prison while his captors began a concerted campaign of doctoring their investigation results and presenting them in this distorted form.

The first to lay eyes on Szarkiewicz's fabrication was Colonel Iranek-Osmecki, who greeted it with instant approval. After Bucharest, the colonel had done stints as chief of the intelligence section of the Paris headquarters of the Union of Armed Struggle, head of the intelligence and information section at the London headquarters of the High Command of the Polish Armed Forces in Exile, and Sikorski's special envoy to occupied Poland. In early February 1941, he was sent back to Britain by General Stefan Rowecki, commander of the Polish underground. On his way there, the colonel passed through the Middle East, making stopovers in Istanbul and Palestine. Many years later, in his memoir, he would assert that the timing of his visit to the region and the beginning of Mikiciński's interrogation was sheer coincidence.[36] However, we have at least two substantive reasons to take this assertion with a grain of salt. First, it was Iranek-Osmecki who, back in the Romanian capital, had initiated a thorough counterintelligence check on Mikiciński; so it would have been quite natural for him to show up in Palestine for a close look at his suspect from Bucharest. Secondly, given his status as a high-ranking counterintelligence officer in the Polish underground—the very underground Mikiciński had so grievously damaged, apparently—Iranek-Osmecki had a professional duty to travel to the Holy Land at once in order to learn the true extent of that damage.

And indeed, according to that same postwar memoir, immediately upon arriving in Palestine, Iranek-Osmecki met with Szarkiewicz and his nominal commander, the former chief of ekspozytura R in Bucharest, Major Józef Bińkowski. In December 1940, Bińkowski left Bucharest for Turkey and was then almost instantly posted to Jerusalem, where he led the local branch of ekspozytura T and continued to oversee Romanian affairs, including the intelligence operations against the Soviet Union conducted from Romanian soil.[37] According to Iranek-Osmecki, he, Szarkiewicz, and Bińkowski compared

---

35 Buczek, *Człowiek do złotych interesów*, 169.
36 Iranek-Osmecki, *Wspomnienia oficera*, 196–197.
37 Dubicki, *Sprawozdanie ppłk. dypl. Stanisława Orłowskiego*, s. 370n12. See the following piece of evidence of the continuing engagement of the former ekspozytura R with Romanian affairs during its Palestinian period: Binkowski to the leadership of the Dwójka in London, a code cable sent via the Polish Consulate-General in Jerusalem, January 18, 1941, USHMM, RG-59.036, A-12-53-35N_0012.

the protocols of Mikiciński's interrogations with the incriminating materials the Polish underground had gathered, noted the similarities, and concluded unanimously that "Mikiciński was an instrument in the hands of the Abwehr." Allegedly, the strongest pieces of evidence against him were the amazing voyages from France to occupied Poland at Kot's behest and the abovementioned admission that he had met Scholz repeatedly in Breslau during those trips.[38]

Quite obviously, this evidence was no different from that which Polish and British intelligence and counterintelligence services had gathered back in 1940. It could not possibly have contained any "smoking gun" (a metaphor still used by many intelligence bodies around the world), a piece of irrefutable evidence that the suspect had spied for another country. And yet this lack of proof did not prevent Iranek-Osmecki from claiming many years later that

> Carrying out Professor Kot's assignments and sending money to Poland were merely a cover for the services rendered by Mikiciński to the Abwehr. He was a double agent, loyal only to the strongest side.[39]

The esteemed colonel, nowadays still regarded as one of the most important intelligence officers of the Polish anti-Nazi underground, almost certainly failed to realize that this conclusion of his was based on a deliberate hoax, one perpetrated in order to strengthen the political standing of General Modelski—not only by weakening that of Minister Kot, but also by marginalizing General Sosnkowski, Iranek-Osmecki's own patron. The ease with which the colonel fell for this ploy could have resulted from several factors. The first of these was the poisonous atmosphere of total suspicion that suffused the Polish underground throughout the German occupation and made Polish operatives wary of people like Mikiciński who could enter and leave the occupied country at will. The second factor was the bitter ideological and political enmity between the pro-Sanation camp and the Sikorski faction. Thirdly, Iranek-Osmecki was naturally convinced that Szarkiewicz was a loyal Piłsudchik foot soldier whose actions were motivated by the desire to reestablish the prewar Polish regime.

The Dwójka headquarters in London also took Szarkiewicz's insinuations at face value. In addition to the protocols of the interrogations and reports related to the Mikiciński affair we know of today, Colonel Mitkiewicz-Żółłtek and his staff may also have received additional Mikiciński-related information from

---

38 Iranek-Osmecki, *Wspomnienia oficera*, 196–197, 199.
39 Ibid., 199.

Szarkiewicz not accessible to present-day scholars. This is the impression given by the summary of the Mikiciński affair that Mitkiewicz-Żółłtek's underlings gave as early as March 13, 1941, while the investigation in Palestine was still ongoing. In this document, we find a unique detail absent from all other materials pertaining to the investigation—namely, the assertion that the suspect had supplied the Abwehr officer Nobis with military and political information and had given him free access to the contents of secret correspondence between the Polish government-in-exile and the resistance movement in occupied Poland.[40]

Remarkably, the details of Mikiciński and Nobis's interactions are missing from a similar summary created three weeks later by the Jerusalem branch of ekspozytura R of the same Dwójka. Instead, it echoes the baseless claim cited repeatedly above that Mikiciński and Scholz's meetings in Breslau attest to the intelligence-gathering nature of their relationship. In the same context, it mentions Mikiciński's contacts with von Papen in Turkey, as well as certain "trips he undertook with Volokhov to Bulgaria and Romania" (such trips are not mentioned in any of the interrogation records that have come down to us). This mishmash of old suspicions and new accusations (probably invented whole cloth) led the Dwójka officers in Jerusalem to conclude that "the spying nature of Mikiciński's activity is quite obvious from his own admissions."[41]

The widespread acceptance of this expert opinion among the Polish military intelligence and counterintelligence officers and the subsequent (planned or spontaneous) growth of the narrative of Mikiciński's betrayal to truly mythical proportions are clearly evident in the Brooklyn report, written after the end of World War II. According to its anonymous author, Mikiciński fully confessed to all crimes during Szarkiewicz's interrogation. Among other things, he allegedly stated that he was recruited as a Nazi spy by the Abwehr officer Scholz from Breslau, who was subsequently promoted to general. The anonymous author goes on to say that following Mikiciński's relocation from Bucharest to Istanbul, Scholz moved from Germany to Bulgaria and was reluctant to lose touch with his exceptionally valuable agent so gave him "espionage assignments in the Middle East."[42]

We must reiterate that the foregoing account is a jumble of easily debunked nonsense. The creators of this hoax were only partially successful in achieving their goal: while Mikiciński was effectively neutralized, his removal did not do

---

40 A report by the Dwójka titled "Mikiciński—information," March 13, 1941, HIA, 800/41/0/-/141 Folder 7, Scan 000999.
41 Major Binkowski, head of the Jerusalem branch of ekspozytura R, "Summary Report on the Mikiciński Affair," April 2, 1941, HIA, 800/41/0/-/141 Folder 7, Scans 000942-944.
42 An undated report titled "Mikiciński Samson," JPIA, Archiwum Osobowe, NZ 154, Sygn. 658.

any harm to Stanisław Kot, as will be shown below. However, it must be admitted that the falsehoods Szarkiewicz circulated and their subsequent mutations had a very negative long-term impact on Mikiciński and Kot's legacies in the Polish historiography of World War II, and in the Poles' collective memory of the events of this war.

The Intelligence Analyst Crying out in the Wilderness

British documents pertaining to the P. affair show that even those officially in charge of Mikiciński's Istanbul abduction and Palestine interrogations—the counterintelligence arm of SIME, the security service of the British Military Administration in the Middle East—failed to obtain conclusive proof of his espionage for the Nazis. In a summary of this affair dated March 24, 1941, the analysts of SIME wrote that his trips to occupied Poland were conducted "undoubtedly with the connivance of the Germans" allegedly trying "to enhance P's prestige with the Poles."[43] The use of the word "undoubtedly" without reference to any specific treasonous act shows that even after several rounds of interrogation, neither Szarkiewicz nor the British agents had acquired any firm evidence. Hence, the SIME analysts had no choice but to ratiocinate on the basis of circumstantial evidence, a method evident also in a high-ranking SIME officer's letter to a colleague at MI5 London headquarters dated June 1, 1941. According to him, the "Inmate P" had carried out his daring exploits in Poland with "the connivance of the German SIS [secret intelligence service]." He did not bring up any concrete facts, either.[44]

Moreover, it turns out that, as of July 1941, the SOE was still basing its conclusions about the Mikiciński affair on the distorted narrative that had led to his arrest. The organization believed that it was the testimony Mikiciński gave in his Palestinian interrogations that pointed to Viktor Kutten and Bronisław Stefanowski-Syrokomla as Nazi collaborators.[45] In reality, this was utterly false, since, as we have already seen, it was Szarkiewicz who brought the evidence against Kutten and his partners in the autumn of 1940. The information Mikiciński allegedly gave half a year later was not necessary to get Kutten behind bars, and we know for certain that no firm evidence against him materialized after that point, either. Nowadays, it is hard to come up with a plausible

---

43 "The P. Affair," a synopsis by D.S.(E) P2446, 24.03.41, TNA, HS 4/213.
44 MX in a letter to M, Cairo, June 1, 1941, TNA, HS 4/213.
45 A top secret report titled "The Paluchowicz Case," copy no 1, July 18, 1941, TNA, HS 4/213.

explanation for this glaring distortion of reality in the SOE report. It may have stemmed from Szarkiewicz's usurpation of the right to conduct simultaneous interrogations of Kutten, Stefanowski, Kąsinowski, and Mikiciński; from the poor communication between the British agencies involved; or even from simple negligence on the part of the SOE analysts who circulated this strange account of events.

At least one British intelligence functionary—apparently an analyst at the SOE headquarters in Cairo—realized shortly after Mikiciński's arrest that the P. affair was based on charges "inconclusive, or unsubstantiated by any real evidence," and he wrote a report to this effect for his superiors. In his opinion, the British had not a shred of factual evidence to prove that Mikiciński had been in charge of a Nazi spy ring, facilitated the mass arrests and executions of Polish resistance fighters, or supplied his alleged handlers in the Abwehr with blank Polish passports. Regarding this last accusation, the author of the report added sarcastically, and very perceptively: "Whatever the Germans may be short of, I doubt whether they could possibly suffer from any shortage of Polish passports." Commenting on Mikiciński's detractors' firm belief that his contacts with shady characters like Volokhov sufficiently proved his involvement in espionage, the author concluded that although such encounters were undisputable fact, they did not seem to prove anything. He supplied several potential explanations, including "innocent smuggling or swindling." The SOE analyst also reminded his addressees that the Polish High Command had given Mikiciński no access to classified information and thus no real power to harm Polish interests; that he had successfully carried out money transfers into occupied Poland; and that his Polish patrons' repeated appeals for real proof of his treachery had gone unanswered for the simple reason that no such proof existed.[46]

The archival research upon which this book is based has yielded no reactions to this candid report from its author's colleagues in the SOE or from any other British intelligence service. But it was possible to establish that Szarkiewicz interrogated Mikiciński until at least mid-March of 1941. We may therefore deduce that SOE and SIME completely ignored the anonymous analyst's very reasonable doubts. Szarkiewicz continued to set the tone of the affair. This ultimately cost Mikiciński his life.

---

46 "Comments on the report by A/H.2 from Istanbul," February 1, 1941, TNA, HS 4/213.

Futile Interventions

While in Palestine the prisoner Mikiciński was fighting for the right to a fair trial, the London-based Minister Kot was actively trying to locate and assist his loyal and invaluable protégé. He refused to credit the official statement released by the Turkish criminal police, according to which Samson had been robbed and murdered by some unknown criminals.[47] Nowadays, it is very hard for us to gauge Kot's motives. Did he have genuine concern for his employee's welfare? Such altruism has always been a rare commodity among politicians. Was he reluctant to lose such a reliable channel of communication with the occupied homeland? Or was he afraid that Mikiciński would lose all hope of rescue and curry favor with his captors by disclosing compromising details about Kot's own contact with the Nazi regime?

Kot first attempted to help Mikiciński by appealing to the Polish public prosecutor's office, which, like Polish military intelligence earlier, immediately agreed to drop all suspicions against Samson and not share them with the British. SOE would later admit that this move deprived them of the ability to try Mikiciński in front of a Polish civil court. Court-martialing him was also out of the question: like the members of Kutten's group, Mikiciński was long past the legal age of conscription, and was not subject to the draft. As for handing him over to the British justice system, that possibility was never even considered—earlier accusations of circulating counterfeit banknotes notwithstanding, the British had no firm proof that Mikiciński had worked against their national interests.[48]

After this important tactical triumph, Kot instructed his supporters in the Middle East to make a concerted effort to discover Mikiciński's fate and whereabouts. "Kot's people in Istanbul and the Middle East bent over backwards in their attempt to find out what had befallen Mikiciński," claimed the author of the Brooklyn report. Kot's confidant in Istanbul, Dr. Karol Alexandrowicz, "questioned everyone he could find, begging, threatening, cajoling," in hopes of finding at least a smidgen of information.[49] Michał Sokolnicki's *Ankara Diary* corroborates this testimony. The Polish diplomat wrote that Alexandrowicz, a representative of the rival political camp, had shown up in Ankara as early as January 20, 1941—four days after Mikiciński's abduction—and that his behavior "made it perfectly clear that he was trying to pick up the trail of Mikiciński, either on his own initiative, or at the behest of Kot." The diarist made no attempt

---

47 A top secret report titled "The Paluchowicz Case," copy no 1, July 18, 1941, TNA, HS 4/213.
48 Ibid.
49 An undated report titled "Mikiciński Samson," JPIA, Archiwum Osobowe, NZ 154, Sygn. 658.

to conceal his anger at Alexandrowicz's behavior: Sokolnicki had an "admonitory conversation" with him, exhorting him not to exceed his official powers and to always remember that the Ankara embassy alone represented the Turkish interests of the Polish government-in-exile.[50]

However, Sokolnicki's warning did not deter Stanisław Kot and his Middle Eastern confidants from tracking and saving Mikiciński. According to Ladislas Michniewicz, who presented himself as a Dwójka veteran in the region, Kot went so far as to use his official status as deputy prime minister to summon Colonel Mitkiewicz-Żółtek, chief of military intelligence, to a private conversation. The irate professor demanded a report on Mikiciński's condition and the reasons for his arrest. The colonel claimed to have learned of Mikiciński's disappearance in the papers and that his diminished ability to communicate with his people in the Middle East had prevented him from receiving any further details. Michniewicz found these explanations mendacious and openly mocked them.[51] However, we now know that communications between the London headquarters of the Dwójka and its Middle Eastern stations, including the one in Palestine, were indeed very poor, and that Szarkiewicz had tried to prevent information about Mikiciński's interrogations from reaching Britain. Thus we may assume with a great deal of confidence that the Polish intelligence chief was not lying, and in all likelihood was truly ignorant of Mikiciński's circumstances at this point in time.

Finally, after searching for some time (according to Michniewicz, two weeks), Witold Korsak, the Polish consul in Jerusalem, told Kot that the British were holding Mikiciński in a Palestinian jail. The encouraged Kot sprung to action. First, he reached out to his friends in the British leadership, and the British ambassador in Cairo, asking them for help securing Mikiciński's release. Next, using his people in Turkey as intermediaries, he notified Hector Briones Luco, who quickly activated his diplomatic channels to rescue his partner and employee.[52] Finally, Kot sent several especially trusted persons directly to Jerusalem with orders to move heaven and earth in service of their goal—releasing Samson from custody. The first of these to set foot in the Holy Land was Polish consul general Karol Bader—the same Bader that Mikiciński had out of occupied Warsaw only a year previously. In the intervening period, he served a stint in Lebanon before transferring to Istanbul. In Jerusalem, Bader met with every Palestine-based Polish functionary he thought might be able to help. To his bitter disappointment, he failed to learn much new information aside from

---

50 Sokolnicki, *Dziennik Ankarski*, 165.
51 Michniewicz, *Opération Haïfa*, 201.
52 Ibid., 201–204.

the fact that Mikiciński had been arrested as part of a "confidential investigation of an espionage affair."[53]

The second Polish official to arrive in Jerusalem was Władysław Kański, the former deputy Polish consul in Bucharest, who had previously taken part in the shuttle diplomacy between Kot and von Papen. Kański's attempted intervention in the Mikiciński affair was also intended to help Kutten and his associates languishing at the Latrun camp. However, his efforts, too, were doomed to failure: British counterintelligence operatives worried that his alleged ideological accord with the Third Reich had prompted him to become a full-fledged Nazi spy.[54]

Nevertheless, Kot had no intention of giving up. Hoping to spring Mikiciński from prison and allow him to come to London, he enlisted the help of his colleague, the exiled Polish foreign minister August Zaleski, to issue Mikiciński a Polish diplomatic passport and pass it on to him through the British authorities in the Middle East.[55] While available information sheds no light on how the British reacted to this peculiar move, we know Mikiciński never got the passport. In fact, it may still be gathering dust in some MI5 archive with a mass of other documents that have yet to be declassified.

The most interesting and still unanswered question this context provokes concerns the possible involvement of exiled Polish leader, Władysław Sikorski, in the persistent efforts by Stanisław Kot—his deputy minister and good friend—to free Mikiciński. The author of the postwar Brooklyn report claimed with obvious self-satisfaction that Szarkiewicz was able to "liquidate" Samson (as the report's text bluntly puts it) not only because the British supported his efforts, but because Sikorski was reluctant to back Kot on the matter of Mikiciński's innocence. "The evidence against Mikiciński was so convincing that only Professor Kot could have ignored it," wrote the report's anonymous author, sarcastically wondering if Kot himself could have been a German spy. He went on to state that even if the professor were innocent of this charge, the "court of history" should still render a guilty verdict against him for his blind endorsement of a man who had done so much harm to Poland.[56]

However, testimonies that have since come to light cast doubt on the claim that Sikorski was indifferent to the efforts to save Mikiciński. First, as Michniewicz wrote back in the 1960s, after Mikiciński had been traced to Palestine, the Polish leader allowed his interior minister to demand explanations from Dwójka chief

---

53 An undated report titled "Mikiciński Samson," JPIA, Archiwum Osobowe, NZ 154, Sygn. 658.
54 An undated draft of a top secret "Memorandum on the Kot organisation in the Middle East," TNA, HS 4/213.
55 An undated report titled "Mikiciński Samson," JPIA, Archiwum Osobowe, NZ 154, Sygn. 658.
56 Ibid.

Mitkiewicz-Żółłtek.[57] Next, we have the June 1941 admission of a trustworthy SIME officer that very prominent Poles obliged to Paluchowicz had "certainly made every effort to protect him."[58] Since British secret correspondence explicitly references Kot and his colleagues in the Polish émigré cabinet, we may assume with a great deal of confidence that the SIME officer meant Sikorski, who did owe Mikiciński a debt of gratitude for rescuing his wife and daughter from Nazi-occupied Poland.

The possibility that Sikorski endorsed Kot's efforts to secure Mikiciński's release may shed new light on the Polish leader's attempts to visit the Middle East, including Palestine, in early 1941. He submitted an official request to Churchill on January 31, two weeks after Mikiciński disappeared in Istanbul, possibly after receiving word from Jerusalem that Mikiciński had been located in Palestine. Sikorski explained his desire to visit the Holy Land by an urgent need to support General Kopański, then stationed there, "in political matters."[59] Quite possibly, these matters involved the unruly behavior of the Sanation supporters who had set up shop in Palestine; Sikorski and Kot regarded the Mikiciński affair as one of the most blatant and outrageous manifestations of this unruliness. We may recall a statement from Jerzy Kurcyusz, one of Kot's closest confidants in the Middle East, claiming Samson's abduction had done "the maximum damage to Polish interests and to the activities sanctioned by the Polish government."[60] Thus, there may be some merit to the conjecture that Sikorski and Kot intended to use the requested Sikorski's trip to the Middle East to free the famous abductee from captivity. When Churchill finally banned the Polish leader from leaving Britain in early 1941, perhaps the last chance to save Mikiciński from the jaws of certain death was lost.

Stanisław Kot, greatly frustrated by this failure, took his anger out on the Polish citizens who abducted Mikiciński and transported him to Palestine. "Some of them lost their jobs in the official institutions subordinated to the Polish government," the anonymous author of the Brooklyn report would later recall.[61] Apparently, this is why Szarkiewicz told the British as early as the

---

57 Michniewicz, Opération Haïfa, 201–204.
58 MX in a letter to M, Cairo, June 1, 1941, TNA, HS 4/21.
59 Sikorski to Churchill, January 31, 1941, PISM, A.XII.1/52A, 21–23.
60 An extract from a secret report by the Polish Interior Ministry representation in Istanbul; August 26, 1941, PISM, PRM. 50, 10.
61 An undated report titled "Mikiciński Samson," JPIA, Archiwum Osobowe, NZ 154, Sygn. 658.

summer of 1941 that he was afraid the members of the ruling Polish cabinet would seek revenge for the things he did in Palestine.[62]

An Anonymous Grave in the Land of the Forefathers

As Michniewicz saw it, Kot's frantic efforts to save Mikiciński instead harmed the latter. The inspector that Colonel Mitkiewicz-Żółłtek dispatched to Jerusalem in mid-February 1941 (Iranek-Osmecki claims this was Colonel Gano, deputy chief of the Dwójka)[63] admitted no legal basis for Mikiciński's abduction and detention. Nevertheless, in a private conversation with Szarkiewicz, he hinted that, in these highly unpleasant circumstances, it behooved him to try to salvage the honor of his organization and his own career. Shortly thereafter, according to Michniewicz, prison guards shot Mikiciński dead. In a report, the guard commander claimed to have witnessed Mikiciński taking part in the prisoners' routine daily walk in the prison yard and then suddenly bolting after a truck and calling for help; after ignoring the guards' warning shouts, he was struck by five bullets, which killed him instantly. In Michniewicz's pithy summation, Mikiciński's life was cut short on February 21, 1941—with no justification whatsoever.[64] In his memoirs, Iranek-Osmecki likewise cites a failed escape attempt as the cause of Mikiciński's death. In this version, Mikiciński tried to escape the guards escorting him to another detention facility. "[In] light of his well-known courage, which bordered on recklessness, he was quite capable of such an act,"[65] he added.

According to Buczek, Mikiciński's life ended not in late February 1941, but a month later on March 28. His killer: none other than Edward Szarkiewicz, afraid that Mikiciński would seek revenge on those who abducted and interrogated him. Szarkiewicz's British counterparts shared this fear and were, moreover, eager to avoid the diplomatic scandal they believed would erupt if Inmate P. were to be released. Apparently, Szarkiewicz contacted MI5 leadership via General Modelski to demand silence: "this affair must not be allowed to get out of Palestine," he wrote. London enthusiastically endorsed his view. Encouraged by their favorable response, Szarkiewicz staged Mikiciński's transfer to a different prison and shot him in the back of the head. He then buried the body on

---

62 Room 055 of the War Office [the secret address for MI5 during WWII] to Sir David Petrie, G.L. 1657/41, August 13, TNA, KV 2/517_6, 26.
63 Iranek-Osmecki, *Wspomnienia oficera*, 196–197, 199.
64 Michniewicz, *Opération Haifa*, 203–206.
65 Iranek-Osmecki, *Afera Mikicińskiego*, 197–200; Iranek-Osmecki, *Wspomnienia oficera*, 199.

sandy ground near Haifa without bothering to mark the spot. By way of later justification, he would claim that Mikiciński tried to escape from the car taking him to his new detention facility.[66]

Unfortunately, the archival sources accessible to us at present do not conclusively confirm or refute Michniewicz, Buczek, or Iranek-Osmecki on the circumstances of Mikiciński's death, nor can we pinpoint the exact spot on the map of the present-day Israel where the death occurred. Quite possibly, because of the exceptional sensitivity of the affair—it has retained explosive potential to this day—the information about it might have been removed from the MI5 and SOE documentary collections. A telegram dated June 14, 1941, suggests such a removal. Writing to Sir David Petrie, Director General of MI5, SIME chief Maunsell discusses writing a letter of recommendation for Szarkiewicz and mentions a telegram sent from Cairo to London the previous week containing a professional evaluation of his work in Palestine.[67] The latter telegram is absent from Szarkiewicz's personal file, which MI5 declassified and turned over to the Kew Archives for safekeeping. Given its timing, this missing telegram could quite plausibly have contained details of the Mikiciński affair, including a reference to Samson's unofficial detention and mysterious death. This may explain why it was subsequently removed, and possibly even destroyed, by concerned British officials.

The summary of an MI5 interview with Szarkiewicz in London in mid-August 1941 bears similar signs of self-censorship. If this document is to be believed, British intelligence officers never bothered to ask their subject about Mikiciński's fate—possibly because it was already known to them—and limited themselves to the observation that "the case of Samson Mikiciński, a notorious German agent... was handled with great skill by Capt. S. during his service in the Middle East."[68] More than a year later, in November 1942, the same MI5 called the Mikiciński affair "the most important case" Szarkiewicz had handled in Palestine, without saying anything about how it came to end.[69] The same is true of the original Polish documents. Thus, while the author of the Brooklyn report did admit that Mikiciński "did not leave [Palestine] for England

---

66 Buczek, *Człowiek do złotych interesów*, 170–171. The date of Samson's death given by Buczek (March 28, 1941) was later echoed by several other Polish and Western historians. See: Dubicki, Nalecz, Stirling, *Intelligence Cooperation*, 229; footnotes 57 and 200 in the collection of documents compiled by Jan Ciechanowski: Ciechanowski, *Polsko-Brytyjska współpraca*, 118, 155.
67 Maunsell to Sir David Petrie, June 14, 1941, TNA, KV 2/517_6.
68 "Cooperation with the Polish Security Services," December 15, 1941, TNA, KV 2/517_5, 28.
69 "Our Relations with the Polish Security Services," November 12, 1942, TNA, KV 2/517_4, 15.

or anywhere else" and that Szarkiewicz had killed him, s/he remained silent on the causes and circumstances of this act.[70]

Today, we can assert with a high degree of confidence that both Michniewicz and Buczek were wrong about the date of Mikiciński's death. A telegram that Polish consul general Bader sent from Istanbul to his superiors in London on May 1, 1941, seems to indicate Samson was still alive at this time. It reports that Colonel Gano had assured Bader that he would arrange a meeting between Mikiciński and the representatives of the Polish consulate general in Jerusalem in order to discuss the situation Mikiciński's Polish and Romanian clients had found themselves in after his arrest. Before leaving their countries to escape war, famine, violence, and the rapidly escalating genocide, many of these people had entrusted Mikiciński to ferry their savings and valuables out of Europe (naturally, in exchange for a certain fee). However, his disappearance put the fate of their precious cargo in doubt, and the refugees petitioned official Polish representatives in Turkey and Palestine to get their money and property back. Bader had hoped to use their predicament as a pretext for setting up the meeting with the prisoner from Acre.[71]

Of course, we cannot discount the possibility that Gano's promise to Bader was just a ploy intended to conceal Mikiciński's true fate from Kot and his people and thereby prevent the Polish government-in-exile and its official representatives from learning that the British had collaborated with other Poles against them. However, some of the British intelligence documents touching on Inmate P. seem to bear out the conclusion Bader's telegram suggests—namely, that Mikiciński was still alive in the beginning of the summer of 1941. The June 1 telegram discussing Szarkiewicz's letter of recommendation and signed by a high-ranking SIME officer mentions "the present whereabouts of P.," implying he was still among the living at this time (or so the writer believed).[72] The SOE report from July 18 states quite plainly that Mikiciński "languished in the Citadel for nearly six months."[73] This information enables us to calculate by simple arithmetic that Samson, who had been brought to Palestine in late January 1941, lost his status as a prisoner (and presumably his life) sometime about the first half of July that year, certainly not in February or March as Michniewicz and Buczek claimed.

---

70 An undated report titled "Mikiciński Samson," JPIA, Archiwum Osobowe, NZ 154, Sygn. 658.
71 A secret telegram by Karol Bader to the Polish Foreign Office in London, May 1, 1941, HIA, 800/41/0/-/141 Folder 7, Scan 001098.
72 MX in a letter to M, Cairo, June 1, 1941, TNA, HS 4/21.
73 A top secret report titled "The Paluchowicz Case," copy no 1, July 18, 1941, TNA, HS 4/213.

Minister Kot's people in the Middle East could not have learned of Mikiciński's death in real time because of the strict secrecy Szarkiewicz and his British colleagues maintained. In late August 1941, the Istanbul station of the Polish Interior Ministry reported to London (quite nonchalantly) that "it is an open secret, known to everyone in Jerusalem, that Mikiciński is being held in some Palestinian jail."[74] Furthermore, according to the anonymous author of the Brooklyn report, Kot would not learn of his devoted and efficient confidant's death until the autumn of 1942, when he paid a brief visit to the Polish consul general in Jerusalem Witold Korsak. Upon hearing the sad news, Kot allegedly cried out, "A hero has been murdered! Monuments will be erected in his honor in Poland!" The Brooklyn author appears to have been particularly incensed by this last phrase and could not resist making a remark: "So the Poles were expected to erect monuments in honor of a German agent!"[75]

When this sarcastic comment appeared in print in the USA, Poland had just been cleared of Nazis, and chances that Mikiciński's homeland might honor him grew dim. The country's new Communist leaders and their patrons in Moscow had their own heroes. In the postwar period, the erstwhile Polish functionaries who still remembered Samson, even those who thought highly of him, were too preoccupied with their own physical and spiritual survival to glorify a Jewish compatriot who had vanished back in January 1941—an eternity ago by the standards of the time. (Besides, it was beyond their modest capabilities.)

Forgotten by the world, the bones of Inmate P. lie in a nameless, sandy grave in the land of his Jewish forefathers somewhere between ancient Acre and Haifa, where local occupants have their own tumultuous history to contend with and their own heroes to commemorate. The amazing biography of the mysterious prisoner of the Acre citadel has thus remained a closed book.

A Polish Domestic Affair

Even after Mikiciński's "neutralization," the British remained deeply concerned about how personally involved Minister Kot and Prime Minister Sikorski had been in their dealings with the Third Reich. Although British investigation failed to furnish any concrete proof of classic espionage, it did confirm the preliminary findings of a series of operational checks that Polish intelligence had carried

---

74 An extract from a secret report by the Polish Interior Ministry representation in Istanbul; August 26, 1941, PISM, PRM. 50, s. 10.
75 An undated report titled "Mikiciński Samson," JPIA, Archiwum Osobowe, NZ 154, Sygn. 658.

out in occupied Poland, Romania, and Turkey: Kot's confidants, both with and without Mikiciński, had interacted with prominent Nazi diplomats, and the Polish deputy premier and interior minister—Sikorski's right-hand man—had supported these meetings. In light of this truly sensational discovery, back in late December 1940 (about three weeks before Samson's abduction), the SOE representative in Istanbul sent a report to his superiors calling the possible personal involvement of Kot and Sikorski in the Mikiciński affair a "very serious" aspect of the whole business.[76]

Three months later, in late March 1941, after Mikiciński confessed that he reached out to the Germans on Kot's orders, a nameless functionary working at SIME headquarters in Cairo concluded that the highest Polish authorities, especially Kot, must bear some responsibility for allowing Mikiciński to dupe them so easily.[77] Another document the SOE drafted in the summer of 1941 spoke openly of Sikorski's attempts to cover up the scandalous activities Kot and his people had been up to in southeastern Europe and the Middle East, including their meetings with the Germans. According to its author(s), the Polish side had intentionally misled the SOE by asking them for granting the Kotowcy access to the British radio transmitters and diplomatic mail while failing to disclose the true purpose of using these means.[78]

Undoubtedly, this was a grave accusation that should have reached the attention of the highest circles in London, even Churchill himself, and caused a major breakdown in the relationship with the Sikorski cabinet. But none of that happened! Instead, in a remarkable diplomatic move, the British averted a looming grave crisis in the British-Polish relationships by designating Kot's contacts with the German's, including the role played by Mikiciński, as "essentially a Polish domestic affair." This approach was first introduced in the already cited March 1941 SIME report, in its paragraph discussing the Polish leadership's responsibility for Mikiciński's actions;[79] and it was later echoed in the SOE's abovementioned draft dating from that summer. An anonymous editor blotted out the draft's most crucial passage directly blaming Sikorski for Kot's problematic behavior, leaving intact the document's final part which contained only a modest wish to fix the SOE's relationship with Kot and his people. It was proposed to subject "the Kot organization"—the entire international operational network of the Polish Interior Ministry—to constant close

---

76 D/H.2 in a telegram to D/H.1, Istanbul, December 26, 1940, TNA, HS 4/213.
77 "The P. Affair," a synopsis by D.S.(E) P2446; March 24, 1941, TNA, HS 4/213.
78 An undated, top secret draft of a memorandum by SOE, titled "Note on the Kot organisation in the Middle East," TNA, HS 4/213.
79 "The P. Affair," a synopsis by D.S.(E) P2446; March 24, 1941, TNA, HS 4/213.

monitoring by British and Polish security services. Their most crucial objects of interest, as the draft explained, were to be radio communications between the "organization" and its contacts in occupied Poland and elsewhere, as well as bags of British diplomatic mail, which Kot's people had been permitted to use by special arrangement between Sikorski and the British. Finally, the draft suggested that the British demand (only demand, not impose!) an immediate cessation of contact between Kot's people and the enemy. "An organiser such as Kurcyusz . . . should never be in direct touch with enemy agents," sounded the British document.[80]

This British intelligence community's indulgent attitude toward the Sikorski-Kot duo and the people who contacted the Nazis "on behalf of the Polish government" may seem incredible to us in the present day. "Should never be in direct touch with enemy agents" is not the kind of reaction that one might have expected from the British, who had just made the horrifying discovery that their closest military ally was flirting with the enemy. Each of these developments—the secret negotiations, their exposure, and the British's decision to treat them as an internal Polish affair—took place against the backdrop of the German air war's heavy toll. Any British or foreign citizen MI5 arrested for aiding the Nazi regime would be sent to prison immediately, and sometimes put to death.[81] Although the British fully understood the danger of Polish-German relationships and had just carried out a logistically and diplomatically complex operation to eliminate the key middleman between the two nations, they ultimately settled on keeping a closer watch of Kot's men in Europe and the Middle East. British authorities did not even bother to issue a tacit reprimand to Sikorski, which would have been fully appropriate under the circumstances. Could they have exhibited such amazing restraint without the intervention of the top echelon of British political leadership?

At present, we have no answer to this crucial question, since the relevant British organs never bothered to give one. No explanation can be found in British studies of World War II, either—for some reason, their authors never discuss how local political leaders and the security and intelligence organs under them felt about the contacts between the fugitive Polish politicians and Nazi Germany. British analyses of the relationship between Winston Churchill and David Petrie, a veteran of the Indian Imperial Police who assumed leadership of

---

80 An undated, top secret draft of a memorandum by SOE, titled "Note on the Kot organisation in the Middle East," TNA, HS 4/213.
81 Andrew, *The Defence of the Realm*, 241–262; Cobain, "Secrecy and Firing Squads."

MI5 in 1941,[82] indicate that Petrie did not share the minutiae of his operational activities with the prime minister. Thus, for two whole years at the height of World War II, Churchill learned nothing of the large-scale "Double Cross" operation to unmask, arrest, and convert Nazi spies active in British territory.[83] We may conclude that Petrie, guided by professional considerations of his own, could very well have tried to keep his boss in the dark about the details of the Mikiciński affair, and even about the contact Kot (and possibly Sikorski) had with the Nazis. However, it seems that in this case, any such attempt at concealment would have failed, since the whole operation—Mikiciński's neutralization, his transport to Palestine, and his subsequent interrogations there—required three distinct British intelligence organs. Furthermore, these events occurred in a region far removed from the British Isles, where Petrie's control was less stringent. This is the reason why, as early as February or March of 1941, information about Mikiciński's condition leaked to interested parties, including the supreme Polish leadership in London. Hence, it would be more reasonable to assume that Churchill and his entourage were aware of the preparations for the abduction in Istanbul from the very start, and that it was carried out with their blessing. In that case, though, why did the British refrain from taking the next logical step of neutralizing the overreaching Polish minister and harshly rebuking his boss and personal friend?

The answer to this puzzle might be very simple. The British's amazing reticence could have stemmed from a genuine desire to stay out of the interminable and mind-bogglingly tangled political feuds happening within the Polish elite. An MI5 report from late 1942 titled "Our Relations with the Polish Security Services" gives evidence of this desire;[84] as does another MI5 document produced around the same time that mentions the author's revulsion at "the eternal squabbles and political intrigues which are characteristic of the Polish nature and which can never be eliminated."[85]

However, the British's reaction to the Polish leader's behavior could have had a more complex motivation, one dictated by the military-diplomatic situation in Europe in the summer of 1941. On July 12, three weeks after the Nazi invasion of the Soviet Union, London and Moscow famously turned the page in their diplomatic relationship and signed an Anglo-Soviet agreement on cooperation in the war against Nazi Germany.[86] And as early as July 30, almost immediately

---

82 Jeffery, *MI6*, 427.
83 Andrew, *The Secret World*, 651–652; Aldrich and Cormac, *The Black Door*, 114.
84 "Our Relations with the Polish Security Services," November 12, 1942, TNA, KV 2/517_4, 15.
85 Captain F. Derbyshire to Major S. Alley from E2, December 5, 1942, TNA, KV 2/517_4, 14.
86 Reynolds, Pechatnov, *The Kremlin Letters*, 25.

after the presumed date of Mikiciński's assassination in Palestine, Churchill forced Sikorski to officially reestablish diplomatic relations with the Soviet Union,[87] a very difficult move for the Poles. It might not be too much of a stretch to assume that to convince the notoriously headstrong Polish leader, the British used compromising materials about the Kot group's contact with the Nazis. In other words, Sikorski may have been blackmailed.

Moreover, we must not forget that his forced reconciliation with Moscow occasioned an outpouring of protest in occupied Poland and the diaspora from various political factions and individuals opposed to it, including members of Sikorski's entourage. And yet, the Polish leader overcame the political crisis gripping his government and the Polish parliament-in-exile by pushing through the unpopular decision to make peace with the Kremlin.[88] The perspicacious Churchill may have foreseen this outcome all along, that only Sikorski was willful enough to impose the hateful reconciliation upon the Poles; this may be the reason why the British leader refrained from creating a public scandal from the revelations about Minister Kot and his employees. Besides, the subject of backroom dealings lost its sting, at least for a little while, when the Polish lost their key middleman. At present, this is merely a working hypothesis for future historical study. Unfortunately, we have no facts to confirm it.

That said, if Churchill did indeed decide to avoid a confrontation with the Polish national leadership in order to focus on Britain's more important strategic goals, this decision offered Stanisław Kot no protection from British revenge. As the next part of the book will show, the historical role of Edward Szarkiewicz did not end with Mikiciński's elimination. Shortly after concluding their strategic alliance with Moscow, the British transferred him to London. Once in the capital of the British Empire, he was to become a key figure in a complex, multistage scheme that MI5 and Polish General Izydor Modelski plotted to engineer a backstage coup first against the Polish state security apparatus, and ultimately against the Polish army as a whole. It seems that the end goal of this stunning British maneuver was establishing full political control over the exiled Polish political leadership, expelling the prominent Kotowcy from its ranks, and weakening (or possibly even neutralizing) the all-powerful Minister Kot.

---

87 Tusiewicz, *Historia Polski*, 380; Wieczorkiewicz, *Historia polityczna Polski*, 227–239.
88 Kochanski, *The Eagle Unbowed*, 164–169; Wieczorkiewicz, ibid.

Part Two

A COUNTER-INTELLIGENCE ACE OR A DESPICABLE SADIST?

Chapter 7

A Plot Hatched in London under the Auspices of MI5

Terrified Poles in Palestine

"Tel Aviv is a thoroughly modern city, and, on the whole, a pleasant one," gushed a Polish soldier who had found himself in the Holy Land in 1940. "All the local residents are Jews, overwhelmingly Polish ones, and one can hear Polish being spoken everywhere. This language is quite sufficient to get by, because, even if the person whom you address happens not to know Polish, he will be sure to fetch you some native of Poland at once."[1] For his part, Dr. Henryk Rozmarin, the Polish consul general in Tel Aviv, noted in August that year: "As for the Jewish community of Palestine, it shows a positive attitude to Poland and its most vital interests."[2]

This historical reality emerged as a result of the large numbers of Polish Jews who immigrated to the land of their forefathers in the interwar period. In 1931, there were more than sixty thousand natives of Poland living in Palestine. Throughout the 1930s, and especially on the eve of World War II, the stream of Polish-speaking immigrants to the Land of Israel increased greatly, and their

---

1   Koper, *Polskie piekiełko*, 335–336.
2   An untitled report by Henryk Rozmarin to the Polish Foreign Office in London, August 6, 1940, USHMM, RG-59.036, A-12-3-2_0083.

number surpassed 150,000. After September 1, 1939, several thousand more Polish citizens, Jews and non-Jews, arrived in Mandatory Palestine as legal or illegal refugees, passing through Romania or Hungary and then through Turkey or Cyprus. They were joined by some seven thousand soldiers and officers of the Polish Carpathian Riflemen Brigade who had left Syria when local French authorities swore allegiance to the collaborationist Vichy government. This sizeable contingent of Polish speakers was concentrated in the three large cities of Tel Aviv, Jerusalem, and Haifa. There, they quickly established an infrastructure of various services, educational and recreational establishments, media outlets, and even some light industry.[3]

The wave of new arrivals in Palestine included former high-ranking officials in the prewar Sanation regime. One of these was General Felicjan Sławoj Składkowski, prime minister and interior minister of the Second Polish Republic from 1936 to 1939. He lived with his family in Tel Aviv, where he worked odd jobs at Polish NGOs, corresponded with American President Roosevelt in his spare time, and was known in the local Polish community as the most zealous devotee of the late Marshal Piłsudski. Sławoj Składkowski and his many compatriots—supporters of the Sanation, draft dodgers unwilling to serve in the Polish army in exile, real and imaginary German and Soviet agents, and ordinary criminals—were under constant Dwójka surveillance. (The service established its station in the Holy Land in December 1940 as a branch of ekspozytura T based in Turkey.)[4] These activities did not go unnoticed by the underground Jewish organization Irgun. Its counterintelligence arm kept an eye on the Polish operatives gathering information on Jewish deserters from the Polish military units stationed in Palestine and even exposed some agent, probably a Jew and a former Polish serviceman, who communicated regularly with the Polish diplomats in Jerusalem.[5]

These circumstances helped greatly to smooth the professional acclimatization of Edward Szarkiewicz in Palestine. As noted above, upon his arrival in the

---

3   Koseski, *Emigracja żydów*, 34–35; Patek, *Polska emigracja niepodległościowa w Tel Awiwie*, 99–110; Pietrzak, *Polscy uchodźcy na Bliskim Wschodzie*, 19; Sroka, *Emigracja żydów polskich*, 109–122.
4   Koper, *Polskie piekiełko*, 152–155, 335–341; Pietrzak, *Polscy uchodźcy na Bliskim Wschodzie*, 16. See also on the activities of ekspozytura T in Palestine: The Ministry of Information and Documentation, Overview of the Jewish Press No. 12, March 6, 1941, London, USHMM, RG-59.034, A-10-2-25_0032; The Polish Foreign Office in London to the President of Poland in Exile, the Chairman of the Council of Ministers, the Polish Interior Minister, and the Ambassador of the Republic of Poland to the UK, a top secret report on the basis of telegram o. 91 from Jerusalem, USHMM, RG-59.036, A-12-53-39L_0006.
5   AE, report no. 26/43, February 10, 1943, file no. Kaf-4-3/1/31,34.

country in the autumn of 1940, he immediately established close ties with the criminal investigation department of the Mandatory police. Apparently, his relationship with the Cairo headquarters of SIME dates to the same time, and his patron in that body was none other than its boss, Chief Brigadier Raymund John Maunsell. Both sides classified the sphere of Szarkiewicz's activities as "general security intelligence work."[6] This vague designation concealed Szarkiewicz's prosecution of the Kutten and Mikiciński affairs and his intense and ruthless behavior among the local Polish expatriates, both Jewish and not. Szarkiewicz suspected many of them of having contact with Soviet and Nazi enemies, and of acting against Polish and British interests as they were understood by Szarkiewicz himself, his fellow Sanation supporters, and eventually by his new patron, General Izydor Modelski.

Kot's people in Turkey would later complain that Edward behaved in Palestine "like the Nazi Gestapo and the Soviet GPU, put together."[7] They alleged that he arrested dozens of completely innocent people on a personal whim under the pretext that they were involved in suspicious activity and jailed them in prisons and penal camps, side by side with real spies and criminals. His interrogation methods were said to be based on physical and psychological violence, and included threats to shoot detainees on the spot. The station of the Polish Interior Ministry in Istanbul meticulously collected information on Szarkiewicz's behavior from his former detainees and their wives, who would also occasionally find themselves behind bars with criminals. One of the station's reports to London asks why Szarkiewicz's interrogations had physically and psychologically wrecked so many young patriots who had volunteered to serve their suffering homeland in the ranks of the Polish army in exile, and then answers its own question: the man, inspired by the scandalous Mikiciński affair, was trying to advance his career by making others suffer while indulging his sadistic tendencies.[8]

Direct confirmation of this accusation can be found in a letter of complaint against Szarkiewicz, intercepted and translated by British counterintelligence in February 1942. Its author, the Polish officer Józef Poznański, who was in Chile at the time and wrote to his friend in the UK, claimed that back in September 1940, upon disembarking in the port of Haifa, Dwójka representative Szapiro-Szarkiewicz had detained him and put him in a jail cell with five

---

6 Szarkiewicz to Sir David Petrie, July 26, 1945, TNA, KV 2/518_1, 24–25.
7 An extract from a secret report by the Polish Interior Ministry representation in Istanbul, August 26, 1941, PISM, PRM. 50,10.
8 Ibid., 10–11.

other Polish officers who had likewise been arrested for seemingly no reason. His only "crime" was that en route to Santiago from London, he had made a stopover in Istanbul to visit the Chilean embassy, where Consul Mikiciński gave him a bottle of French perfume and asked to bring it to South America as a gift for the wife of the Chilean chargé d'affaires. After spending almost half a year in custody, Poznański and his five Polish cellmates went on a hunger strike and managed to contact a Polish general stationed in Palestine asking for help. In their plea, they claimed to have fallen victim to "persecution on the part of the Jew Szapiro." Poznański's 1942 letter sums up the story thusly: "A multitude of suspicious types and troublemakers have flooded the ranks of the Polish military intelligence in the Middle East . . . Their only concern is to eat their fill, loot the state treasury to the best of their ability, and put innocent people behind bars."[9]

Szarkiewicz's victims' protests made no impression on the Mandatory Police in Palestine, nor on the SIME in Egypt. The British were glad that Szarkiewicz was able to handle "the case of Samson Mikiciński, a notorious German agent . . . with great skill."[10] At this time, Edward had just been promoted to captain, bypassing the rank of lieutenant, and took a "special course in the Middle East." While the course's exact nature is unknown to us, we may assume that the fresh graduate never got the chance to put his new knowledge to use: in mid-July of 1941, as soon as his training concluded (and apparently shortly after Mikiciński's death), Szarkiewicz was summoned to London to take up a new post at the Headquarters of the Supreme Command of the Polish army in exile.[11] Buczek claims Szarkiewicz's rapid advancement was the handiwork of his new patron, General Izydor Modelski.[12]

The Mystery of Room B at the Westminster Hospital

Having received the summons from Britain, Szarkiewicz set out on a long journey to his new place of service.

---

9 Poznański to Walkowski, February 12, 1942, TNA, KV 2/517_4, 30–31.
10 Captain F. Derbyshire, "Co-operation with the Polish Security Service," December 15, 1941, TNA, KV 2/517_5, 28–31.
11 Room 055 of the War Office [the secret address for MI5 during WWII] to Sir David Petrie, G.L. 1657/41, August 13, 1941, TNA, KV 2/517_6,26; Szarkiewicz to Sir David Petrie, July 26, 1945, TNA, KV 2/518_1, 24–25.
12 Buczek, *Człowiek do złotych interesów*, 171. See also: Ciechanowski, *Polsko-Brytyjska współpraca*, 118.

From early 1941, the British sea and air lanes in the Mediterranean basin were under constant attack by the Nazi navy and air force.[13] Hence, all those wishing to travel from Palestine to the British Isles had to make a huge detour via Egypt, Sudan, and Nigeria, where they would board a ship and sail north through the Atlantic to their final destination, accompanied by a British naval escort; British security officials stationed in Africa would closely monitor each trip.

Szarkiewicz's case was no different. On July 15, 1941, the Cairo headquarters of the British Middle East Land Forces Command notified the office of the commander of the British garrison in Lagos that the previous day, a group of British subjects and foreigners left Egypt for Nigeria en route to the UK; among them was Edward Szarkiewicz, owner of Polish diplomatic passport no. 81/66/40.[14] About three weeks later, on August 7, each passenger reached British shores of Britain, an outcome far from certain in those days. Soon after, Szarkiewicz began his appointment as the liaison between the headquarters of the Supreme Command of the Polish Army (what the Poles called the Headquarters of the Supreme Leader) and MI5.[15]

On August 13, Captain Edward Szarkiewicz showed up at MI5's London headquarters, a cache of offices hidden behind the large "To Let" sign at 57–58 St. James Street.[16] MI5 officials rolled out the red carpet for their Polish-Jewish guest, and Chief Sir David Petrie granted him a personal audience. Earlier that day, Petrie had read a highly complementary profile of Szarkiewicz written by SIME chief Maunsell:[17]

> Szarkiewicz has been working during the last 12 months in close touch with our security authorities in Istanbul, Palestine, and here, and has won golden opinions from all of them. He was personally responsible for the removal from Istanbul of X . . . an operation which required the highest resource and courage. He has been 100% co-operative with us in all security matters relating to Poland, and in addition, has been most helpful,

---

13 Gruchman, *Die verpassten strategischen Chancen*, 471–474; Porch, *The Path to Victory*, 217–218.
14 The Office of the Supreme Commander in Cairo to the Office of the Commander in the Lagos Region, July 15, 1941, TNA, KV 2/517_6, 29. See also: Room 055 to Sir David Petrie, G.L. 1657/41, August 13, 1941, TNA, KV 2/517_6,26.
15 Major Alley to the head of the MI5 Department of Foreign Citizens, March 12, 1945, TNA, KV 2/518_1, 7; Szarkiewicz to Sir David Petrie, July 26, 1945, TNA, KV 2/518_1, 24–25.
16 See on the location of the MI5 Headquarters at this time: MI5 in World War II; Andrew, *The Defence of the Realm*, 231. However, from October 1940 most of the departments of this agency were housed at Blenheim Palace near Oxford. See: Andrew, ibid., 217, 231.
17 Room 055 to Sir David Petrie, G.L. 1657/41, August 13, 1941, TNA, KV 2/517_6, 26.

particularly in Palestine, in dealing with general security matters concerning Balkan countries. He has an intimate knowledge of Polish politics and we have found that his advice can be accepted without reserve on any matters concerning them.[18]

Maunsell and Petrie had a very simple reason for their enthusiastic approval: Szarkiewicz was willing to cooperate closely with the British in operational matters. To their great chagrin, tensions between Churchill and Sikorski had limited the cooperation between the security and intelligence organs of the United Kingdom and the Polish government-in-exile. A special MI5 report from December 1941 captures a general sense of indignation on the matter: "There appears to be no doubt that the Polish 2nd Bureau [of the Dwójka] feels reluctant to give us information that might involve well-known [Polish] persons or persons holding important Government Posts."[19] Against this backdrop, Szarkiewicz's demonstrated readiness for close cooperation would have come as a pleasant surprise to those stationed in Jerusalem, Cairo, and London, and they seemed thankful for his appearance. At headquarters, he soon became known as "Our Friend Sz." Just as soon as he arrived, the British started making plans to tighten their control over the Polish intelligence community. They took full advantage of Edward's Anglophilia, his many skills, and his close familiarity with the British security apparatus. They intended to position him behind the scenes to sway the Polish government in favor of the official London and its directives. General Izydor Modelski, the only high-ranking Polish official at that time who knew the Mikiciński affair inside and out, would protect the Little Man from his many foes within London's Polish military elite. MI5's "independent sources" univocally portrayed the general as "genuinely pro-British and really anxious to bring about closer cooperation between the Poles and the British."[20]

Like his protégé, Modelski was also despised by many in the Polish army in exile. To mock him, they turned his first name into the diminutive-derogatory nickname "Izya." However, Modelski was an experienced combatant, a harsh commander, and a very ambitious man. Before the outbreak of World War I, he had joined the anti-Austrian underground in his home city of Lviv and went on to fight the Bolsheviks and the Ukrainian nationalists. He held several command posts in the infantry of the independent Polish Republic and quickly rose

---

18 Maunsell, SIME Cairo Headquarters, to Sir David Petrie, G.S.I. 18/4/1(b), June 14, 1941, TNA, KV 2/517_6, 24.
19 Captain F. Derbyshire, "Co-operation with the Polish Security Service," December 15, 1941, TNA, KV 2/517_5, 28–31.
20 Ibid.

to colonel. When he was discharged from the army in the late 1920s, he became one of the most vocal political opponents of the ruling Sanation regime. In the autumn of 1939, Sikorski arranged for Modelski to travel unimpeded from Romania to France, and shortly thereafter appointed him to the prestigious and influential post of second deputy war minister in the rank of major general. His new responsibilities included vetting and recruiting new cadres for the Polish armed forces being reestablished in exile. He made a name for himself as an implacable foe of the representatives of the prewar Polish government and their supporters by doing everything in his power to keep them out of the military units under Sikorski's command. It was upon his orders that the Polish military attaché in Bucharest, Colonel Tadeusz Zakrzewski, carried out a thorough political screening of the Polish soldiers and officers who expressed a desire to join Sikorski in France.

Overnight, this behavior won Modelski many enemies in the Polish émigré circles and in Sikorski's new cabinet. One of these was his colleague/rival General Marian Kukiel, the first deputy minister of war. Modelski's highly negative reputation remained unchanged even after July 1940, when during the evacuation of Polish troops from defeated France to Britain, his clear and decisive actions helped save many thousands of Polish soldiers from certain captivity and death. When Kukiel arrived on the "Island of the Last Hope," he lost his high ministerial post and was sent to Scotland to command the First Polish Corps stationed there. In 1941, then languishing in "Scottish exile," he begged one of Sikorski's confidants to "find a way to have Modelski removed from the army."[21] However, the demoted general's pleas, went unheeded. In February 1942, the Supreme Leader would announce Modelski's appointment as the sole deputy head of the Ministry of War.[22] Since Sikorski had become war minister alongside many other pressing duties, Modelski could exercise almost total control over the Polish army in exile.

For Szarkiewicz, this dramatic upswing in his patron's military and political status in 1941 and early 1942 was very auspicious; as was the sudden removal of his archenemy, Stanisław Kot, from Britain. In September 1941, only a month after Szarkiewicz arrived in the British capital, Sikorski ordered Kot's dismissal from his position as minister of the interior. His new appointment was far less prestigious and influential. He became the ambassador to the embattled Soviet

---

21 Cichoracki, *Sprawcy klęski wrześniowej*, 350.
22 Hułas, *Goście czy intruzi?* 115.

Union just two months after Churchill browbeat the Poles into reestablishing diplomatic relations with Moscow.[23]

Immediately, on Szarkiewicz's advice, MI5 launched an effort to persuade Sikorski to turn the Dwójka over to Modelski and relinquish his formal control of the internal security system of the entire Polish army in exile. On September 11, 1941, the de-facto master of the Polish armed forces and would-be controller of its counterintelligence unit accepted an invitation to the Travellers Club on London's Pall Mall street, a prestigious, renowned, and highly exclusive gentlemen's club that has survived to the present day. There, Modelski met two emissaries of MI5, Major Stephen Alley[24] and Captain F. Derbyshire, for a private meeting.[25] After the war, Derbyshire would set up an extensive network of agents within British Zionist organizations suspected by David Petrie's people of aiding the anti-British Jewish underground in Palestine.[26]

The contents of that tripartite secret meeting at the Travellers Club are a mystery to us. Nevertheless, it is quite obvious that its participants reached an agreement on the format of their future cooperation. A month later, Szarkiewicz informed his new partners/handlers in the leadership of the British security service that Sikorski had finally agreed to subordinate Polish military counterintelligence to Modelski and would soon sign the relevant order. He went on to explain that counterintelligence was to be fully separated from the Dwójka, transferred from the Rubens Hotel in London (the permanent base of operations of the Supreme Command of the Polish army in exile), and—most crucially in this context—headed by Modelski's confidant. Izya intended to act on his own with no interference on the part of the "people from the Rubens." He would handpick a new staff of official and unofficial employees and monopolize control over all the counterintelligence affairs that touched on British interests.[27] Szarkiewicz gave what was essentially a blueprint for a backstage coup in the security and intelligence apparatus of the Polish army. From now on, this system was to operate under the watchful eyes of MI5, giving the British full control over the Sikorski government.

However, as early as the end of October 1941, Modelski suddenly informed his sympathizers in British counterintelligence that Sikorski had unexpectedly reneged on his support for the impending reform. This change of heart, which

---

23 Rutkowski, *Stanisław Kot*, 223.
24 A veteran of MI5, during World War II he served in E Division (Alien Control), 2 Section (Nationals of Baltic, Balkan and Central European countries).
25 Major S. Alley, a memorandum, September 11, 1941, TNA, KV 2/517_6, p. 2.
26 Andrew, *The Defence of the Realm*, 354.
27 Captain F. Derbyshire to Major S. Alley, October 8, 1941, TNA, KV 2/517_6, 11; Major S. Alley to Sir David Petrie, October 9, 1941, TNA, KV 2/517_6, 9.

boded ill for the conspirators, was apparently the handiwork of those "people from the Rubens." An MI5 official commented on this development:

> Party intrigues have always played a prominent part in Poland's political life. Party strife broke out with extreme violence after the signing of the Polish/Soviet Agreement. The anti-SIKORSKI elements, especially the National Democrats sized the opportunity to accuse SIKORSKI of betraying Poland in the interests of Britain and the international Jewry. Unfortunately SIKORSKI himself is a weak and vain man. He surrounded himself with members of the Polish aristocracy as well as with persons known to be schemers and adventurers, out of their own personal gain.[28]

But this unpleasant surprise did nothing to dampen Szarkiewicz's spirits. In mid-December, he personally leaked some compromising materials about his own organization to MI5, an apparent attempt to force the British to push through his desired Dwójka reforms. Szarkiewicz claimed that Polish military intelligence had deliberately refrained from sharing important information about the unseemly behavior of high-ranking Polish officials and had made no attempt to put a stop to it, either. According to Szarkiewicz, the reason for this reluctance was the fear of the "Dwójka" chief, Colonel Gano—the same Gano whose wife was rescued from occupied Poland with Mikiciński's help—that "drastic action on his part might involve persons in high places who would either use their influence against him with General Sikorski or in the event of a prosecution would bring disgrace on other persons surrounding the C. in C. [Sikorski]."[29]

The British security service, which now believed Szarkiewicz to be "an excellent intelligence officer,"[30] greenlit his complaint at once. Internal MI5 correspondence asserted that Gano's behavior, as described by Szarkiewicz, did become an urgent "security matter" for the United Kingdom. David Petrie was advised to quickly meet Sikorski and persuade him to implement the planned reform that would remove the military counterintelligence from Dwójka's purview. Alley and Derbyshire, the aforementioned MI5 emissaries at the Travellers

---

28 F. Derbyshire, "Cooperation with the Polish Security Service," December 15, 1941, TNA, KV 2/517_5, 29.
29 Ibid., 30.
30 Ibid., 32.

Club, met with Modelski and Szarkiewicz to work out a concrete plan of action;[31] shortly thereafter, Modelski visited Petrie in his office for the same purpose.[32]

Thus, by the end of 1941, an unofficial British-Polish taskforce—Alley, Derbyshire, Modelski, and Szarkiewicz—had activated under the auspices of MI5 chief David Petrie. The apparent goal of this highly secretive body was to subordinate the whole of the Polish intelligence and security apparatus, and through it the Polish government-in-exile, to Churchill's interests. It remained active even when, in late December, at the height of the taskforce's campaign to persuade Sikorski to back the proposed Dwójka reform, Szarkiewicz suffered a sudden heart attack and was hospitalized at Westminster Hospital in central London. Thanks to MI5's intervention, he got a private room marked B on the hospital's second floor, an extraordinary luxury for relatively low-rank officer in wartime. Reporting to Alley, a hospital representative described his accommodations: "I have arranged for the transfer of Captain Edward Szarkiewicz to a single room to-day as I understood from you that the nature of his work is such that those people who come to interview him must have privacy."[33]

Hence, Edward's hospital room became the site where the fate of the Sikorski government would be decided. As the patient's condition improved, he moved to a private apartment outside London. However, even there, instead of submitting to the rest cure often recommended in such cases, Szarkiewicz remained active in the Modelski/MI5 conspiracy, regularly traveling to the British capital in the general's private car.[34] This detail clearly demonstrates the importance and urgency of his duties to his patrons/handlers in the British intelligence community.

The Grey Eminence of the Polish Army in Exile

Apparently, in the second half of January 1942, Alley, Derbyshire, Modelski, and Szarkiewicz finished drawing up their plans for the Dwójka. On January 23,

---

31 Ibid., 30-32.
32 F. Derbyshire, "The Reorganization of the Second Polish Desk," February 23, 1942, TNA, KV 2/517_5, 13.
33 Major S. Alley to Officer of the Medical Service G. Mcknab, the Westminster Hospital, December 30, 1941, TNA, KV 2/517_5,25; Officer of the Medical Service G. Mcknab to Major S. Alley, December 27, 1941, TNA, KV 2/517_5, 26.
34 A telegram from the MI5 Department of Foreign Citizens to the Cairo branch of the organization, February 17, 1942, TNA, KV 2/517_5,16; Major S. Alley to Miss I. Smith, March 7, 1942, TNA, KV 2/517_5, 4; Captain F. Derbyshire of the MI5 Department of Foreign Citizens, a memorandum, March 17, 1942, TNA, KV 2/517_5, 10.

Modelski sent Sikorski a written proposal on intensifying the struggle against "defeatist and corrupting elements" in the ranks of the Polish army in exile. The "necessary steps" he recommended included gathering incriminating information against those elements, creating a special catalogue of their dossiers, and—most crucially—ejecting at once any officer who objected to these policies from the headquarters of the Supreme Command.[35]

Exactly one month later, on February 23, Sikorski would appoint Izydor Modelski his sole deputy in the War Ministry and essentially give the ambitious general power over all the Polish armed forces in a huge area that stretched from the British Isles to the Middle East. As a result, Petrie's underlings and their Polish counterparts could start enacting their plan of taking over the Polish military counterintelligence apparatus and bringing the government-in-exile to heel. In these conditions, the British counterintelligence unit in charge of the affairs of foreign citizens staying in UK territory denied SIME leadership in Cairo a request to have Szarkiewicz returned to the Middle East. "His services will be required here for most important work,"[36] telegraphed MI5 headquarters to Egypt.

One of the key aspects of this work was reorganizing the mechanism of cooperation between the Polish War Ministry and the British security service. For Captain Szarkiewicz, who only recently had been responsible for just one element of the complex relationship between the Dwójka and MI5, this presented a major expansion of powers and a corresponding increase in status. He now oversaw all the correspondence between the offices of Sikorski and Petrie, including those who answered to them. As a result, his colleagues/handlers at MI5 started sending him letters intended for Sikorski for advance review. Whenever MI5 sent messages directly to Sikorski without Szarkiewicz's approval, Szarkiewicz would complain enthusiastically, claiming they had breached some "private agreement."[37] Moreover, beginning in March 1942, Szarkiewicz started a campaign to assume power over all the procedures and decisions pertaining to the day-to-day security of the Polish military forces in Britain and the Middle East.[38]

Sikorski soon learned of these activities and was likely well aware that they could destroy the independence of his government. In a confidential and highly emotional letter to Modelski on March 20, 1942, the Polish leader accused him of

---

35 Modelski to the Chief of Staff of the Supreme Command and to Sikorski, January 23, 1942, PISM, A.XII.1/66A, 138.
36 A telegram from the MI5 Department of Foreign Citizens to the Cairo branch of the organization, February 17, 1942, TNA, KV 2/517_5,16.
37 Captain F. Derbyshire to Major S. Alley, March 18, 1942, TNA, KV 2/517_5, 3.
38 Major S. Alley to General Modelski, March 13, 1942, TNA, KV 2/517_5, 6.

staffing key posts in the War Ministry with dubious characters like Szarkiewicz. Sikorski considered Edward "a man of pathological tendencies, utterly devoid of any moral inhibitions, whose behavior in the Middle East antagonized all the local Polish military and civilian circles; who has been spreading scurrilous rumors to the effect that my wife was rescued from Poland by the German spy Mikiciński, and that the latter has also discredited Prof. Kot." This fiery tirade ended with the blunt verdict: "I do not approve of the appointment of . . . Szarkiewicz to a post in the Honorable General's ministry, and I also forbid the Honorable General to use the services of this man in any way."[39]

As unbelievable as it may seem, Modelski simply ignored his boss' instructions. By this time, he may have fully embraced the idea that British patronage would enable him to climb to the top of the Polish political Olympus in exile. Accordingly, his status grew by leaps and bounds. This newfound political clout can most clearly be seen in Szarkiewicz's role in the fate of the so-called Anders's Army, a Polish unit of eighty thousand troops that started in the Soviet Union under the command of Polish general Władysław Anders in the second half of 1941 and early 1942.[40] In March 1942, on the night before this large military force was expected to arrive in the Middle East, Sikorski petitioned the British government for permission to transfer as many as 15,000 of Andres's soldiers and officers to the British Isles. Petrie's people, tasked with looking into this request, sought professional counsel from none other than Szarkiewicz, who advised them to reject Sikorski's plan categorically. By way of justification, he offered the weighty professional opinion that the Polish military counterintelligence apparatus would be unable to give security clearances to so many servicepersons at such short notice. Without them, the Soviets could flood the UK with intelligence agents recruited from among the Poles who had found themselves in USSR territory.[41]

However, it is possible that the real motive behind his decision was Modelski's fear that the arrival of heavy reinforcements from Russia would improve the standing of his rival, General Kukiel. About a month later, on April 24, parts of Anders's Army had already crossed the Soviet-Iranian border and were on their way to Palestine when Sikorski told Churchill of "his decision" to leave

---

39 Iranek-Osmecki, *Postscriptum II*, 549–550.
40 The Anders's Army is also known as the "Polish Armed Forces in the East" (*Armia Polska na Wschodzie*, or *APW*). For more about it, see: Brio, *Pol'skie muzy*, 43–59; Koskodan, *No Greater Ally*,118; McGilvray, *Anders's Army*, 41–79; Wieczorkiewicz, *Historia polityczna Polski*,257.
41 Major S. Alley to Theodore Turner, chief of E Branch for Foreign Citizens, March 11, 1942, TNA, KV 2/517_5,7; Alley to Turner, March 26, 1942, TNA, KV 2/517_5, 1–2.

the majority in the Middle East.[42] Churchill thanked his Polish counterpart cordially, remarking that the Polish forces in the Middle East would defend the common interests of the Allies.[43] This was a real victory for Szarkiewicz against the leader of his country, whose political standing was then on the wane. However, he decided not to advertise it, and MI5 respected his decision. "It is, of course, essential that Szarkiewicz's name should on no account be mentioned in any official correspondence on this matter," Alley wrote to his colleagues.[44] Accordingly, the British would keep silent for decades about Szarkiewicz's important role in determining the fate of Anders's Army. As a result, this episode in his biography remained hidden from friend and foe alike, eluding the attention of historians for the better part of a century before finally coming to light while gathering materials for this book.

On May 9, 1942, Szarkiewicz's co-conspirators, encouraged by their successes, took the next crucial step in their plan. On that day, General Izydor Modelski finally separated the counterintelligence function from the Dwójka and officially subordinated it to his own office. Thus, control of this indispensable and powerful instrument in the Polish state security system transferred from the hands of the government-in-exile into those of the Modelski, Szarkiewicz, and their British counterparts. After changing its name to the Department of Control in the Security Field, the unit at once began to improve its methods of cooperation with the British.[45] Four days later, on May 13, Modelski informed Petrie that Szarkiewicz had officially quit the Dwójka and joined the new department.[46] There, he became responsible for cooperation with MI5 and for conducting exceptionally complex and politically sensitive investigations, at last assuming de facto control over the entire reform of the Polish military counterintelligence apparatus.[47]

Without a doubt, this was the peak of Szarkiewicz's counterintelligence career. A forty-two-year-old, baptized Polish Jew who had joined the Dwójka

---

42 Sikorski to Churchill, top secret, April 24, 1942, PISM, A.XII.1/52A, 91–92.
43 Churchill to Sikorski, May 5, 1942, CHAR, 20/53C/226-227.
44 Alley to Turner, March 26, 1942, TNA, KV 2/517_5, 2.
45 Captain K. Czechowicz, acting head of the Department of Control in the Security Field, to Major S. Alley, May 9, 1942, TNA, KV 2/517_4, 33.
46 Modelski to Sir David Petrie, May 13, 1942, TNA, KV 2/517_4, 36.
47 Major S. Alley to Squadron Commander W. S. Cheney, May 16, 1942, TNA, KV 2/517_4,15; "Our Relations with the Polish Security Services," November 12, 1942, TNA, KV 2/517_4,28; Sir David Petrie to Modelski, May 13, 1942, TNA, KV 2/517_4, 35; Modelski to Sir David Petrie, May 13, 1942, TNA, KV 2/517_4, 36.

only two years earlier now had a permanent pass to MI5 headquarters.[48] The British praised him effusively. "I believe that this collaboration was productive of great benefit to the Polish cause as well as to ourselves," wrote Petrie to Modelski in early June 1942.[49] At the very same time, Petrie told Maunsell in Cairo that Szarkiewicz was "just as keen" to assist the British in their home country as he had been to help them in the Middle East."[50] About a month later, Alley notified the MI5 director that Szarkiewicz had begun "investigating certain channels of suspected leakage, which it is most essential to have cleared up."[51] Meanwhile, MI5 headquarters denied yet another of SIME's requests to have Szarkiewicz returned to Egypt, seeing as he was "in charge [of] most important investigations which will necessitate his stay here."[52]

Was this a reference to the effort to expose and terminate Kot's contacts with the Nazis? Or did it refer to a contemporaneous incident involving a recently appointed Polish air attaché in Washington, D.C., who had plotted to blow up Sikorski's plane as it flew from the UK to the USA?[53] At present, we cannot answer these questions, nor can we determine the extent to which MI5 took advantage of the secret contacts Szarkiewicz had established with a group Alley called the "Jabotinsky-Jews in Palestine,"[54] possibly referring to representatives of Vladimir (Ze'ev) Jabotinsky's Revisionist Zionist movement or its military wing, the Irgun, fighting against the British presence in Palestine. Three years later, in March 1945, Alley would summarize that, in this period, Szarkiewicz proved himself extremely useful to the British, although his frail health and frequent mood swings made it hard to work with him on a regular basis.[55]

Cast Down from the London Olympus

Three months after Modelski's appointment to deputy war minister and just one month after the new Department of Control came under his auspices, Modelski

---

48 Major S. Alley to E. N. Ashby, Secretary of the Head of the Department, an undated document, TNA, KV 2/517_4, 34.
49 Sir David Petrie to Modelski, June 3, 1942, TNA, KV 2/517_4, 24.
50 Sir David Petrie to Maunsell, June 4, 1942, TNA, KV 2/517_4, 23.
51 Major S. Alley to Sir David Petrie, July 22, 1942, TNA, KV 2/517_1, 10.
52 Maunsell to Sir David Petrie, July 20, 1942, TNA, KV 2/517_4, 22; a telegram from MI5 Headquarters to Maunsell, July 22, 1942, TNA, KV 2/517_4, 21.
53 Iranek-Osmecki, *Postscriptum II*, 543–547.
54 Major S. Alley, a memorandum, August 17, 1943, TNA, KV 2/517_3, 9.
55 Major S. Alley to the head of the Foreign Citizens Department, March 12, 1945, TNA, KV 2/518_1, 6–7.

and Szarkiewicz advanced their plans of establishing total control over the Polish government-in-exile's military and intelligence systems. In early June of 1942, Szarkiewicz told his friends at MI5 headquarters that Modelski would soon replace Sikorski as war minister.[56] However, by this point, the British security chiefs had already realized that this prospect stood little chance of becoming reality. Two months earlier, after Modelski's appointment, they warned Petrie of extreme discontent among the Polish units stationed in Scotland under Kukiel's command and their talk of assassinating the general and his patron. Following this report, security at the Rubens Hotel in London tightened greatly, while the Polish units in Scotland were confined to their bases and put under the close watch of Polish military counterintelligence.[57]

Modern Polish historians have determined that the unrest among the Polish soldiers and officers sent to Scotland began as early as 1940, shortly after the Polish government-in-exile and its remaining armed forces evacuated to the British Isles. Discontent arose because of appalling living conditions, woeful pay, and harsh political control that threatened the worst troublemakers with imprisonment in one of the camps the Polish had set up, with British approval, near Glasgow. Perhaps most crucially, Sikorski rarely visited Scotland, which underscored his general indifference to their suffering.[58] When Modelski took control of the Polish military in the spring of 1942, conditions at Polish bases only worsened, especially when it came to the persecution of dissidents and malcontents. He enjoyed gathering incriminating materials against his subordinates, often fake ones, then using this evidence to send them to prison before submitting his verdict to Sikorski for formal approval, thus presenting his boss with a fait accompli.[59]

Many Polish soldiers and officers stationed in Britain—especially Modelski's sworn enemy, General Kukiel—wanted rid of the deputy war minister as soon as possible, through whatever means necessary. Less clear is how Kukiel and his supporters managed to engineer the downfall of a general in Sikorski's good graces. Only four months after Szarkiewicz told MI5 about Modelski's imminent appointment to war minister, Sikorski suddenly announced his resignation from the ministerial post in favor of . . . General Marian Kukiel![60] Several weeks after that, the new war minister used the draft ministerial reform Modelski had

---

56 A memorandum titled "General I. Modelski," June 3, 1942, TNA, KV 2/517_4, 25.
57 The Foreign Citizens Department to Sir David Petrie, an undated report from the spring of 1942, TNA, KV 2/517_7, 6.
58 Koper, *Polskie piekiełko*, 183–198.
59 Wagner, *Torturowani, bici i głodzeni*.
60 Wieczorkiewicz, *Historia polityczna Polski*, 265.

submitted to Sikorski as a formal pretext for expelling his rival from the Rubens Hotel.[61] "I have no desire to work in this man's company!" he declared.

The Polish government-in-exile heeded his call and eliminated Modelski's post at once. To rid itself of his legacy, the Polish War Ministry changed its name to the Ministry of National Defense and underwent thorough structural and functional changes. Modelski, a would-be Polish military strongman, was forced to resign and go on paid sick leave. He remained stranded in this limbo until March 1945, when he finally went into official retirement.[62] As might be expected, the victorious Kukiel proceeded to carry out a purge in the ranks of his ministry, the Polish army in exile, and its intelligence/counterintelligence apparatus, removing or intimidating all those whom he regarded as opponents of the Sikorski government and of himself.[63]

Although we have no evidence that might explain the great speed with which Modelski's enemies cut short his career, we can speculate on the reason for these developments. The simplest explanation is that Sikorski's entourage managed to convince him of the need to eliminate Modelski; each of the military and political factions represented within Sikorski's leadership knew about his authoritarian streak and questioned his loyalties and decisions that prioritized British interests over Polish ones. At that time, an MI5 agent using the alias Brit—in all likelihood, a Polish subject of Jewish origin, possibly even Szarkiewicz himself—remarked that "Kukiel and his cabal" had cooperated closely with Stanisław Kot.[64]

A more complicated explanation would consider the strategic interests of the UK in 1942. The British historian Evan McGilvray addresses these in his book, *Anders's Army*. In late 1941, Churchill began a series of negotiations hidden from Kot and Sikorski. With approval of General Anders, he petitioned Stalin to transfer the new Polish army being created in the USSR to the Middle East under British command, a move that would boost Egypt's defenses against the mounting German threat. McGilvray has discovered that by gaining control of Anders's Army, Churchill hoped to restrain the Sikorski government, which had become too independent for his tastes. He could not allow Anders's Army to

---

61 See the project of the reform of the War Ministry, which was submitted by Modelski to Sikorski in May 1942: USHMM, RG-59.045, A-XII-3-16_0327-0374.
62 Captain F. Derbyshire to Major S. Alley, December 5, 1942, TNA, KV 2/517_4, 13; Hułas, *Goście czy intruzi?* 116, 166.
63 See, for instance, the case of the officer Aleksander Narbut-Luczynski, who was severely reprimanded, at Kukiel's personal order, for publicly supporting the high-ranking officers who had spoken out against Sikorski's policies: Secret order no. 5, April 6, 1943, HIA, A.XII.1/82, 18.
64 A report by the agent Brit, "Professor Stanisław Kot," September 27, 1943, TNA, KV 2/3429_5, 48.

influence the relationship between London and Moscow by fighting alongside the Red Army on the Eastern Front. Indeed, after Anders's Army left Soviet territory in the spring and summer of 1942, Sikorski lost his status as the supreme Polish military and political leader in the war against Nazi Germany. In the eyes of the British and many of his own compatriots, he became a marginal player in global politics.[65]

McGilvray's Polish colleague, Sławomir Koper, adds that following General Anders's departure from the Soviet Union, the relationship between him and Sikorski deteriorated into barely concealed enmity. The General, who enjoyed the favor of the British, felt free to criticize the decisions of the Polish Supreme Leader openly, and in February 1943, he went so far as to send Sikorski a written suggestion (and de-facto demand) to resign from his post. "Such behavior cannot be considered an example of a soldier's loyalty to his commander," Koper concludes. He goes on to wonder: "Might Anders have coveted the post of Supreme Leader for himself?"[66]

This dramatic clash in the upper echelons of the exiled Polish leadership may explain the role MI5 played in the Modelski-Szarkiewicz duo's meteoric rise in late 1941, as well as the British's muted response to their unexpected downfall in the autumn of 1942. Although impossible to prove, there is a possibility that supporting Modelski-Szarkiewicz—including their takeover of the Polish military counterintelligence apparatus—would have remained the centerpiece of Churchill's plan to sideline Sikorski and his cabinet if Stalin had refused to release General Anders and his troops. But as soon as the latter, much more popular and influential than Modelski in Polish emigrant circles, was at Churchill's disposal outside the USSR, London's interest in Izya's services immediately evaporated. If this conjecture is correct, then Captain Szarkiewicz inadvertently helped strengthen Anders's position at Sikorski's expense when, on the night before thousands of Polish soldiers and officers were to depart from the USSR, he gave the British a legitimate excuse for keeping them stationed in the Middle East.

Modelski's removal resulted in an immediate and painful diminution in Szarkiewicz's status. It was only the first of the many cruel strokes of fortune he was to suffer over the next several years, leading to a profound professional and physical crisis. From the moment he arrived in the British Isles in August 1941,

---

65 McGilvray, *Anders's Army*, 41–88; see also on Churchill's desire to use the Polish troops arriving from the USSR to defend British interests in the Middle East: Kochanski, *The Eagle Unbowed*, 191.
66 Koper, *Polskie piekiełko*, 333.

his innumerable enemies in the Polish military, diplomatic and political circles waged a tireless campaign to harm him. The most active among them was Stanisław Kot, who, having already been moved to the USSR for his ambassadorship, worked hard to get Edward expelled from the Dwójka.[67] At some stage, Szarkiewicz himself informed his MI5 contacts that he feared retaliation from influential figures in the Polish leadership.[68] Reporting on this development, British counterintelligence noted that Kot had never forgiven Szarkiewicz for the role he played in the "Mikiciński and Kutten affairs,"[69] and that Polish Foreign Ministry officials' antipathy toward him was partly rooted in their antisemitic views.[70]

At the same time, despite Szarkiewicz's overt alliance with Modelski, residents of the Rubens Hotel in London—now headed by General Kukiel—continued, for some obscure reason, to consider him a representative of the Sanation camp.[71] He was especially pressed to ease the sanctions the Department of Control, while still under Modelski, imposed on Polish soldiers and officers who vocally opposed Izya's grip on the Polish military.[72] Edward's erstwhile colleagues from the Dwójka particularly loathed him. It was because of his and Kukiel's reform that they not only lost control over military counterintelligence, but now became one of the objects of its surveillance.[73]

Antisemitism may also have colored the Polish officers' view of Szarkiewicz, as it was the case with Polish diplomats. Official documents of the Polish army in exile use his dual Jewish-Polish surname Szapiro-Szarkiewicz as late as 1943 despite his renunciation of his Jewish first and last names, his baptism, and his self-identification as a full-blooded Pole.[74] None of this should surprise us. Throughout the war, anti-Jewish sentiment was widespread in Polish émigré military units despite sincere attempts by the High Command to stamp out this pernicious and shameful prejudice. We have already cited the blatantly antisemitic remarks made by one of Sikorski's underlings to the British *Catholic Herald* in June 1941. Another example of this phenomenon, dating to the time when Szarkiewicz was already fighting tooth and nail for his professional future, is a written statement from Colonel Aleksander Idzik, the commander of a Polish

---

67 A top secret memorandum titled "E. Szarkiewicz," February 6, 1942, TNA, KV 2/517_4, 5.
68 Room 055 to Sir David Petrie, G.L. 1657/41, August 13, 1941, TNA, KV 2/517_6,26.
69 A top secret memorandum titled "E. Szarkiewicz," February 6, 1942, TNA, KV 2/517_4, 5.
70 Captain F. Derbyshire to Major S. Alley from E2, December 5, 1942, TNA, KV 2/517_4, 13.
71 Ibid.
72 "Our Relations with the Polish Security Services," November 12, 1942, TNA, KV 2/517_4, 16.
73 Maunsell to Sir David Petrie, a secret personal letter, July 24, 42, TNA, KV 2/517_4,20.
74 See, for instance: Justice Minister Professor Wacław Komarnicki to the Commander of the Polish Navy, December 18, 1943, PISM, A.XII.1/104, 161.

military unit in South Africa: "Jews will always be Jews, full of violent hatred for all things Polish. They pursue only their own interests, and care nothing for Poland."[75]

Quite obviously, deprived of the support of the disgraced General Modelski, Szarkiewicz could not keep his job at the Department of Control in such a hostile atmosphere. The new department's head, Colonel Stanisław Orlowski, had previously served at the Romanian and Middle Eastern Dwójka stations, oversaw some of Edward's activities there and allegedly even valued his professional skills.[76] Nonetheless, in new circumstances, he fairly quickly stripped Szarkiewicz of the powers he had acquired under Modelski. Although the Little Man was never fired formally from his post (probably because MI5 asked Sikorski not to in early November 1942),[77] the department he had established simply squeezed him out.[78] According to the testimony of Major S. Alley, Szarkiewicz's work for Polish military counterintelligence came to an end sometime in late February or early March 1943.[79] On April 1, 1943, Colonel Orlowski told the office on St. James Street that Captain Szarkiewicz had gone on a long vacation.[80] Szarkiewicz himself indicated on an official British form that he quit working for the Polish security apparatus for good on April 13, 1943.[81] He would later explain to Petrie that he was officially put on a two-year-long paid leave that was, in practice, a dismissal.[82]

Thus, at the tender age of forty-three, Captain Edward Szarkiewicz's brilliant and meteoric career in the intelligence and counterintelligence community of the Polish army in exile came to an end. It had lasted all of three years. To explain

---

75 An extract from a report by Colonel Aleksander Idzik, commander of the Johannesburg transit point of the Reserve Officers Department of the Headquarters of the Supreme Command of the Polish Army in Exile, to the Ministry of National Defense. Cited by: "Remarks and Conclusions concerning Minorities," October 1942, USHMM, RG-59.045, A-XII-3-21_0017. See also in this connection: an extract from a report by the Intelligence and Counterintelligence Department of the Headquarters of General Anders, touching on relations between ethnic Polish soldiers and their Jewish comrades, and trying to justify the manifestations of antisemitism: The Second Department of the Command of the Polish Armed Forces in the Middle East, "A Counterintelligence Report for March 1943," April 15, 1943, USHMM, RG-59.045, A-XII-3-23_0024-0025.
76 Dubicki and Suchcitz, *Oficerowie wywiadu WP i PSZ*, 227–234; Iranek-Osmecki, *Postscriptum II*, 547.
77 "Our Relations with the Polish Security Services," November 12, 1942, TNA, KV 2/517_4, 18.
78 O. Alan Harker to Maunsell, May 15, 1943, TNA, KV 2/517_3, 31.
79 Major S. Alley to Sir David Petrie, March 23, 1943, TNA, KV 2/517_1, 12.
80 Orlowski to the MI5 Headquarters, May 17, 1943, TNA, KV 2/517_3, 30.
81 An undated, filled request form for permission to leave the United Kingdom, April 1943, TNA, KV 2/517_7, 21–22.
82 Szarkiewicz to Sir David Petrie, an undated letter, August 1944, TNA, KV 2/518_2, 36.

the causes of this fiasco, Szarkiewicz hinted at the "geopolitical duplicity" of key figures in the Polish émigré leadership. By his account, these figures doubted the prospect of a decisive Allied victory, tried to keep on good terms with both London and Berlin in case of a future British-German pact, and did everything in their power to neutralize the Modelski-Szarkiewicz duo because the latter was aware of and working against these secret diplomatic maneuvers.[83] This explanation may have been an echo of the Mikiciński affair, in which Szarkiewicz and his colleagues in the Dwójka brought to light Kot's close contact with senior Nazi diplomats.

Later, at the end of the war, Major S. Alley presented MI5 leadership with an explanation that completed Szarkiewicz's account of his dishonorable discharge from the Polish army. In Alley's view, Edward's attempts to "clean up certain departments of the Polish General Staff" (apparently from the same advocates of a middle course between London and Berlin) had earned him a host of enemies who got him removed from his post.[84] Whether on purpose or out of ignorance, Alley's belated report did not discuss the likely connection between Szarkiewicz's downfall and the Churchill government's decision to prefer General Anders to General Modelski as a military-political counterweight to Sikorski.

---

83 "Our Relations with the Polish Security Services," November 12, 1942, TNA, KV 2/517_4, 17.
84 Major S. Alley to the head of the MI5 Department of Foreign Citizens, March 12, 1945, TNA, KV 2/518_1, 7.

Chapter 8

Egyptian Exile, Professional Fiasco, and Disappearance in the Mists of History

The Best Investigator in the Middle East

In April 1943, Edward Szarkiewicz, just fired from his beloved job, decided to return to the Middle East, the place where he had reached the apogee of his career as an operational counterintelligence officer two years earlier. His doctors had made clear that he needed to get away from the damp British weather if he stood a chance of recovery. In his official request for permission to leave the United Kingdom, he stated that he had spent the last eighteen months in British territory, was currently unemployed, and intended to travel to Palestine, where he would stay at the King David Hotel in Jerusalem.[1] In late April, his last boss in the Polish military counterintelligence, Colonel Orlowski, notified Major S. Alley from MI5 that Szarkiewicz was planning to leave for the Middle East very soon, and asked the major to help him with filing the necessary paperwork and organizing passage to his destination.[2] About three weeks later, the office on St. James Street informed Maunsell in Cairo by telegraph that Szarkiewicz wished

---

1 An undated, filled request form for permission to leave the United Kingdom, April 1943, TNA, KV 2/517_7, 21–22.
2 Colonel Orlowski to Major S. Alley, April 21, 1943, TNA, KV 2/517_7, 19.

to serve at SIME. However, to avoid losing his military pension, he was trying to secure the official blessing of the Polish military authorities.[3]

For Maunsell, who held Szarkiewicz's professional skills in the field of counterintelligence in very high esteem, this was joyous news indeed. In the summer of 1941, he had requested that Petrie send Szarkiewicz back to Cairo as soon as possible.[4] He continued pestering Petrie with additional requests over the next several months.[5] A year later, in November 1942, Maunsell made yet another attempt to get his hands on the talented Polish officer, stressing that Szarkiewicz would be indispensable in Cairo because of Kot's frenzied activities in the Middle East.[6] Kot had already completed his diplomatic mission to the USSR, was staying in Palestine as the minister of state in the Middle East,[7] and, as it turns out, proving to be a great nuisance to the British. This request, like all those previous, failed to have the desired effect. The SIME chief made one final attempt in the spring of 1943 after Szarkiewicz went on extended paid leave. This time, Maunsell got Petrie's support. Together, they lodged an official appeal to the new boss of the Polish army in exile, General Marian Kukiel, who agreed in principle to Szarkiewicz's transfer.[8]

Edward's career change was further endorsed by Baron Victor Rothschild, a scion of the famous family and one of Britain's most talented and influential security officers then in charge of the Investigative Department of MI5, tasked with preventing and investigating acts of terror and sabotage.[9] In a profile of Szarkiewicz he forwarded to Petrie, Rothschild stated that he was extremely satisfied with Szarkiewicz's professional cooperation and deeply impressed by his investigative skills, talents he displayed while handling an investigation into a certain Soviet agent's suspected efforts to make an attempt on Sikorski's life. Szarkiewicz was "very unhappy and no doubt unpopular" in London, Rothschild wrote, strongly recommending that he be allowed to leave for the Middle East, where "Szarkiewicz would be a tremendous asset in interrogation

---

3 O. Alan Harker to Maunsell, May 15, 1943, TNA, KV 2/517_3, 31.
4 Maunsell to Sir David Petrie, June 14, 1941, TNA, KV 2/517_6, 24.
5 Maunsell to Sir David Petrie, September 13, 1941, TNA, KV 2/517_6, 19; Section E2 (territories outside the UK) of the MI5 Department of Foreign Citizens to the Cairo branch of MI5 (DSO), September 20, 1941, TNA, KV 2/517_6, 17; the Cairo branch of MI5 to Section E2, telegram no. 851, October 17, 1941, TNA, KV 2/517_6, 8; Major S. Alley to the head of the MI5 Department of Foreign Citizens, March 12, 1945, TNA, KV 2/518_1, 7.
6 "Our Relations with the Polish Security Services," November 12, 1942, TNA, KV 2/517_4, 18.
7 McGilvray, *Anders's Army*, 48; Rutkowski, *Stanisław Kot*, 294–328.
8 Szarkiewicz to Sir David Petrie, an undated letter, August 1944, TNA, KV 2/518_2, 36.
9 The original designation of this office was: B Branch/B.1.C section—explosives and sabotage.

work with his excellent knowledge of languages and his particular knack at the work of interrogation."[10]

However, it quickly became clear that Edward's dreams of joining SIME could not be realized on such short notice. First, because of his insistence on preserving his right to a military pension: he demanded assurances that the Poles would not seize his money the moment he left for the Middle East. Further delaying his departure were the fears of the Polish top brass who probably knew (or, at least, could guess) the true nature of Szarkiewicz's relationship with the British, and suspected that once he arrived in Cairo, he would begin to act against the interests of the Polish government.[11]

The archival data at our disposal provides no insights as to the ultimate resolution of the pension question. However, we know that as early as July 1943, Szarkiewicz submitted an official request to leave his post for health reasons;[12] and that two years later, when the war ended, he received no financial benefits from the Polish government-in-exile. We may therefore conclude that Szarkiewicz decided to waive his military pension rights in the summer of 1943 in spite of his misgivings so as to speed up his transfer to Cairo. An April, 1945 announcement from the Polish Ministry of National Defense bears out this conclusion:

> Infantry Reserve Second Lieutenant [sic] Edward Szarkiewicz has been granted, at his own request, an unpaid leave of absence and discharged from the Ministry of National Defense, in order to begin to serve in the British Army.[13]

Mutual distrust between the Polish and the British complicated Szarkiewicz's future role in Egypt. To allay the serious fears of the Polish military chiefs, Petrie personally intervened with a July 27, 1943 letter to Kukiel in which he explained that SIME was interested in Szarkiewicz solely as an experienced investigator with a knowledge of Arabic[14]—an odd justification, since Szarkiewicz had spent less than a year in Palestine and would not have had enough time to master Arabic given his extensive involvement in the Mikiciński and Kutten affairs and the demands of his day-to-day counterintelligence work. And yet, two weeks later, on August 12, Kukiel signed Edward's discharge papers, telling

---

10 The chief of B.1.C to Sir David Petrie, March 20, 1943, TNA, KV 2/517_1, 11–12.
11 A secret telegram from the MI5 Headquarters to Maunsell, July 1, 1943, TNA, KV 2/517_3, 25.
12 Ibid.
13 Iranek-Osmecki, *Postscriptum II*, 548.
14 Sir David Petrie to Kukiel, July 27, 1943, TNA, KV 2/517_3, 18.

Alley that he could not decline Petrie's personal request and would not obstruct Szarkiewicz's transfer any further.[15]

Less than a week after Szarkiewicz's discharge, Petrie sent Kukiel a second message claiming that the British needed Szarkiewicz as an expert in the espionage activities of the Axis countries in the Middle East, as both MI5 and SIME had observed these activities intensifying in Egypt, Palestine, Syria, and Turkey.[16] We now know for certain that Petrie was sincere: on July 10, the Cairo office of SIME asked MI5 headquarters about the possibility of having Szarkiewicz brought to Egypt at once in order to interrogate some German paratroopers captured in Iraq.[17] Correspondence on the matter shows that the Poles remained concerned about the nature of Szarkiewicz's new role and that the British attempts to allay these concerns continued into the autumn of 1943: on October 12, Maunsell sent Orlowski a letter reassuring him that Szarkiewicz would never work against Polish interests in the Middle East.[18]

As it turns out, Edward did not consider himself bound by any obligations to the Poles: when he left the Department of Control, he took valuable information about Polish counterintelligence. On August 17, a day when Petrie sent one of his calming messages to the Polish minister of national defense, Szarkiewicz informed Maunsell, via Alley, that upon arriving in Egypt, he would tell the British about "a man who is au courant with all the arms smuggling in Palestine;"[19] and three weeks later, on October 5, when the SIME head came to London to meet with the Little Man, the latter confessed his intention to take a sealed suitcase full of "materials concerning Polish activities" on his trip to Cairo.[20] We do not know how Maunsell reacted to a revelation that violated his promises to the Polish leadership. However, we know for certain that he took personal care of the final preparations for Szarkiewicz's journey to the Middle East.[21]

And so, in the last week of October 1943, after twenty-five months on British soil, Edward Szarkiewicz, retired captain of the Polish army in exile and former conspirator in an attempted backstage coup of the Polish military and intelligence

---

15 Major S. Alley to Sir David Petrie, August 12, 1943, TNA, KV 2/517_1, 18–19.
16 Sir David Petrie to Kukiel, August 17, 1943, TNA, KV 2/517_3, 10.
17 An urgent code cable, July 10, 1943, TNA, KV 2/517_3, 21.
18 Derbyshire, a memorandum, October 12, 1943, TNA, KV 2/517_1, 23.
19 Major S. Alley, a memorandum, August 17, 1943, TNA, KV 2/517_3, 9.
20 An unknown correspondent (the signature is illegible) to Major S. Alley, "A Memorandum on the Contents of the Conversation between Colonel Maunsell and Captain Edward Szarkiewicz from October 5, 1943," October 6, 1943, TNA, KV 2/517_2, 31.
21 Major S. Alley to the head of the MI5 Department of Foreign Citizens, March 12, 1945, TNA, KV 2/518_1, 7.

apparatus, left his modest apartment at 23 Collingham Road in Kensington and headed for Liverpool. There, at the local port, a ship waited to take him to the coast of North Africa, now fully liberated from German-Italian occupiers.

The Survivor from the KMF 25-A Convoy

In October 1943, Liverpool had already suffered seriously from the German aerial bombing campaign, the Blitz, the intensity of which here was only marginally inferior to the barbaric Luftwaffe raids on London. Some three thousand Liverpudlians perished. Nevertheless, the renowned Port of Liverpool, the largest of its kind on the British west coast and the key link between the United Kingdom and North America, operated without interruption.[22]

Szarkiewicz arrived in the city on October 24. He was not set to depart until October 27, so he had plenty of time to spare, which he used in part to write farewell letters to his friends/handlers from MI5, Sir David Petrie and Major S. Alley. His letter to the director general of the British security service begins:

> My Dear Sir David,
> I am already on board of ship. Before leaving this country, I would like again to thank you for all you have done for me. I am leaving the shores of this beautiful island with regret. I admire your Country and your Great and fine Nation. You may rest assured that I will do all I can to satisfy and help the war effort.[23]

His letter to Alley was written in a more confidential tone:

> My Dear Major Alley,
> Before leaving England, I feel I must once again thank you for all your kindness and friendship given to me during my stay in England. You will probably remember how many times I expressed my will to go back to [the] Middle East. But today I am rather a little bit sad when I am leaving you. I realise I am leaving behind friends whom you can't so easy find. But I hope my work will be to the benefit of the war effort and once again as so many times before I have to say: "Kismet." Fate! Who knows

---

22 Oakley, "The Luftwaffe Over Liverpool."; *Spirit of the Blitz*.
23 Szarkiewicz to Sir David Petrie, October 24, 1943, TNA, KV 2/517_2, 20.

your secrets? It might happen that I will never see you again! But please remember it is going to be something big now! And if I will come back alive I will first of all look for my friends. Please convey all my best wishes to Derbyshire and Mr. Boyce. I will miss them! I am happy, because I know today that our work has been successful.[24]

These lines show an unexpectedly sensitive, almost sentimental side of Szarkiewicz; his lyrical prose is borderline histrionic. It is difficult to reconcile the letter with Szarkiewicz's merciless abuse of his compatriots and ability to murder in cold blood. Of course, his sentimentality may be nothing but the clever ruse of a cynical manipulator thinking only of his future career prospects in British counterintelligence.

Szarkiewicz was to board the MS *Marnix*. Built shortly before the war, the *Marnix* was originally a Dutch cruise liner for ferrying tourists along the sea lanes of Southeast Asia. In May 1941, it was drafted into the Royal Navy and used to transport Australian troops to the shores of Asia and Africa; later, it participated in the Anglo-American operations to liberate Algeria, Morocco, Sicily, and southwestern Italy. On this occasion, the *Marnix* was to sail from Liverpool to Egypt as part of an Anglo-American naval convoy of twenty-six passenger ships and seven military vessels and assigned the code number KMF-25A.[25]

The *Marnix* sailed out of the Port of Liverpool on October 27 with some 3,500 passengers and crewmembers. The first leg of the journey, from Britain to the Strait of Gibraltar, turned out to be completely uneventful. The crew of the *Marnix* even had time to flirt with British nurses onboard. But when the convoy passed into the Mediterranean along the Algerian coastline, things took a radical turn for the worse. On November 6, at about six in the evening, just as the passengers were finishing their supper, KMF-25A came under a massive attack from thirty German bombers, and a torpedo hit the engine room. Although passengers and crewmembers were unharmed, the former cruise liner, utterly unequipped for naval warfare, began to founder. Fortunately, other ships in the convoy were able to rescue everyone aboard.

Soon the shipwrecked travelers came safely ashore in Algeria near the French town of Philippeville and received medical treatment. Three weeks later, the battered convoy resumed its journey to Egypt. After two days of calm sailing, it was again attacked by German planes flying in from Crete. This time, the British

---

24 Szarkiewicz to Major S. Alley, October 24, 1943, TNA, KV 2/517_2, 21–22.
25 Morison, *The Atlantic Battle Won*, 261.

and Americans decisively repelled the assault and stayed the course to Egypt. Finally, on December 2, 1943, some five weeks after setting out from Liverpool, Szarkiewicz and his fellow passengers arrived in the Egyptian Port of Suez, then traveled by train to Cairo.[26]

Upon his arrival in the capital of Egypt, Edward drew up a scathing report on the first German attack. Without mincing words, he described the crew's criminal negligence during the assault, their flight from the ship's deck when the torpedo hit, and their unpreparedness to rescue passengers; there was even some looting. He submitted the report to the SIME department responsible for the security of seaports, who forwarded it to the London headquarters of MI5, who sent it to gather dust in their archives. This document would not come to light until eight decades later, during research at Kew Archives that preceded the writing of this book.[27] We should not marvel at the fact that the disgraceful behavior aboard the sinking *Marnix* as described by Szarkiewicz is not addressed in any subsequent publications; the participants, their contemporaries and descendants preferred to gloss over unsightly reality, embracing instead a narrative of heroic struggle for survival in the waters of the Mediterranean.

Captain Dunlop Refuses to Rewrite Reports

In late 1943, Cairo was a burgeoning metropolis spreading lazily on both banks of the ancient Nile. It was an urban kaleidoscope of sorts, presenting a unique, colorful mélange of Middle Eastern, African, and European ethnicities, languages, cultures, beliefs, clothes, architecture, food, and music. Local markets, shops, and posh hotels, along with diverse entertainment venues (including even an opera house built in the nineteenth century), offered both locals and foreign visitors a rich panoply of life's pleasures, beyond the wildest dreams of the people of war-torn Europe. And nearby, noisy, thronging, colorful squares and thoroughfares, alongside narrow and dusty lanes, meandering through agglomerations of crumbling masonry, swarmed with clamorous peddlers, shoe

---

26 The First Department of Port Security of SIME to the Director General of MI5, December 11, 1943, TNA, KV 2/517_2, 6–10; report about the assault on Convoy KMF-25A at the US National Archives, December 11, 1943, NARA, USS MCLANAHAN, Act Rep, Attack on Convoy KMF-25A, 11/6/43; Lubeski, *Linebackers of the Sea*, 84–85; Wolf, *German Guided Missiles*, 22–23.

27 The First Department of Port Security of SIME to the Director General of MI5, December 11, 1943, TNA, KV 2/517_2, 6-10; report about the assault on Convoy KMF-25A at the US National Archives, December 11, 1943, NARA, USS MCLANAHAN, Act Rep, Attack on Convoy KMF-25A, 11/6/43.

cleaners, and porters all jostling with modern automobiles and streetcars for a place under the scorching Egyptian sun.[28]

This city was home to the headquarters of the British civilian and military administrations. Their sphere of responsibilities included the gargantuan geographic triangle between the Persian Gulf, the Somali Peninsula, and Libya. The military administration, or Middle East Command, had been established a couple months before the outbreak of World War II and was quartered in the southern section of the city center in a large and ungainly concrete building on 10 Tolambat Street[29] that the locals called Grey Pillars. It lay in the heart of the upscale Garden City neighborhood, which commanded an excellent view of the Nile and the river islands of Gezira and Rhoda. Until July 15, 1943—the official date of the Axis Powers' defeat on the African continent—Grey Pillars housed the control center of regional British military operations, where the commander in chief directed the valiant fight against the military forces of the Third Reich, Fascist Italy, and Vichy France deployed to North Africa. It was there, too, in late June and early July of 1942, that the British lived through the period of fear, verging on panic, occasioned by the prospect of the Nazi Field Marshal Erwin Rommel's capture of Cairo and thus Egypt as a whole. For years afterward, local residents would recall the ashes of the secret documents burned in Grey Pillars and in the nearby British embassy that blanketed the verdant neighborhood.[30]

However, in early December 1943, when the retired Polish army captain Edward Szarkiewicz showed up at the gates of the building on Tolambat Street, ready to begin the new stage in his career as an employee of Security Intelligence Middle East, Grey Pillars' centrality to the British military was a thing of the past. After the Dodecanese campaign, coordinated from Cairo, failed in the fall of 1943,[31] and a Cairo summit of UK, US, and China leadership was held that same November,[32] the Middle East Command sank into the drudgery of London's Sisyphean efforts to maintain the British military and political presence in North Africa and the Middle East. Many of its employees were much less enthusiastic about the new nature of their work. Despite an increasing focus on religious and nationalist anti-British organizations, including the Muslim Brotherhood and the Zionist underground in Palestine, Grey Pillars no longer required the enormous staff it had recruited while fighting on

---

28 Cooper, *Cairo in the War*, 26, 253, 259, 267–268, 293.
29 Nowadays, 10 Etehaad El Mohamyeen El Arab Street.
30 Jacobs and Richardson, *The Rough Guide to Cairo*, 70–71.
31 Ball, *The Mediterranean and North Africa*, 376; Porch, *The Path to Victory*, 473–474.
32 Cooper, *Cairo in the War*, 289.

the North African Front. The disappointed officers yet to find posts elsewhere resented their forced idleness and channeled their pent-up energy into bitter infighting around promotion and career advancement.[33] Needless to say, the noxious atmosphere at the Middle East Command did nothing to facilitate the integration of new employees like Szarkiewicz: foreigners with an imperfect grasp of English, without British citizenship and prior professional experience in British military intelligence.

Further complicating Szarkiewicz's integration was the fact that his new patron, Raymund John Maunsell, stepped down from his post as head of SIME in January 1944, one month after Szarkiewicz arrived at Middle East command headquarters. Maunsell's successor, Major Douglas Roberts, the former commander of MI5 Beirut station and future chief of MI6 internal security, had no need of Szarkiewicz's knowledge or experience in the field of counterintelligence, least of all his insight into Soviet espionage: a native of Odesa, Roberts was fluent in Russian and considered a leading expert on Russian affairs in the Middle East. According to some people who knew him, he had even met Vladimir Lenin in person.[34] In all likelihood, Roberts was not happy to learn that Maunsell, on the eve of his resignation, had allowed a Pole of Jewish origin to infiltrate SIME and entrusted him with the highly sensitive task of combating foreign espionage, including Soviet spies. Does this explain why Szarkiewicz's official entry into his new position was postponed for two months, until February 4, 1944? Roberts would later report to the MI5 chief that Szarkiewicz's frail health had caused the delay; and a British military-medical commission would assign Szarkiewicz to the third category of civil servant, permitted to work only in a sitting position.[35]

Be that as it may, in early February, Szarkiewicz began his duties in the security service of the British forces in the Middle East. Designated an "investigator for highly sensitive affairs" and granted access to top secret files, he used the British-sounding alias Dunlop. In consideration of his last rank in the Polish army in exile, he received the equivalent British rank of captain and a monthly salary of 70 GBP, roughly three times the average monthly income in the British Isles.[36] While we know nothing of the nature or contents of the investigations that he undertook in early 1944, the British documents at our disposal indicate

---

33 Ibid., 269–270.
34 Horne, *But What Do You Actually Do?* 47–48; O'Sullivan, *Espionage and Counterintelligence in Occupied Persia*, 16, 248.
35 Roberts to Sir David Petrie, May 4, 1945, TNA, KV 2/518_2, 8.
36 Szarkiewicz to Sir David Petrie, July 26, 1945, TNA, KV 2/518_1, 24–26, 36.

that, initially, his superiors were more than satisfied with his successes in this area. In late August, Douglas Roberts wrote to Petrie in London:

> I am happy to say that SZARKIEWICZ is doing excellent work and as far as I can judge at the time of writing, there is every prospect of our continuing to employ him to the advantage for a considerable period of time. Though he sometimes requires delicate handling, I regard him as a first-class security officer and I am delighted that his services have been made available to SIME.[37]

Whether Roberts's praise for Szarkiewicz was sincere or given for the benefit of his London bosses, it was not to last. In October 1944, just two months after delivering a panegyric to Edward's professionalism, Roberts cut his salary.[38] A month later, on November 17, Alley reported to his higher-ups at MI5 headquarters that the Little Man's current employers were less than pleased with his investigation methods and recommended transferring him somewhere like Palestine, where he would be of more use.[39]

MI5 headquarters convened a special meeting to discuss the future of their professional relationship with Szarkiewicz, where it was revealed that he had been outraged by his leaders' criticism and refused to rewrite an investigation protocol. Still, MI5 rejected SIME's suggestion to transfer Szarkiewicz to Palestine under the dubious pretext of his Jewish origins; the British were apparently afraid that when he arrived in his historical homeland, Szarkiewicz would be reluctant to take harsh measures against other Jews. (If their apprehension was sincere, it ran counter to everything they knew about Szarkiewicz's actual behavior in Palestine in 1940 and 1941.) At the meeting's close, the participants concluded that Szarkiewicz no longer had a place in British counterintelligence in the Middle East.[40] Thus, only nine months after SIME recruited Szarkiewicz, the new stage in his career ended with an abrupt crash.

We may assume that this downward turn resulted not only from the unhealthy atmosphere at Gray Pillars and Roberts's desire to get rid of his predecessor's protégé, but also from the wave of antisemitism sweeping British administrative bodies in the Middle East. Its manifestations became particularly apparent in

---

37 Roberts to Sir David Petrie, August 22, 1944, TNA, KV 2/518_2, 35.
38 Szarkiewicz to Sir David Petrie, July 26, 1945, TNA, KV 2/518_1, 26.
39 Major S. Alley, a memorandum, November 17, 1944, TNA, KV 2/518_1, 5.
40 Major S. Alley. "A meeting dedicated to Captain Dunlop/Szarkiewicz, November 22, 1944," November 23, 1944, TNA, KV 2/518_2, 23.

November 1944, when fighters of Lehi, a Zionist militant group, gunned down Sir Walter Edward Guinness, First Baron Moyne, the British minister resident for the Middle East and an ardent opponent of Jewish immigration to Palestine.[41] It is possible that, in his capacity as a SIME investigator for highly sensitive affairs, Szarkiewicz was tasked with elucidating the circumstances of this sensational political murder, and that Roberts and his staff thought he would go too soft on his ethnic kin.

"A Super-Intriguer Who Has Fallen out with This Department"

Szarkiewicz's exile landed as a painful blow. He suffered a heart attack in December 1944. His condition was so severe that doctors at the Scottish military hospital in Cairo found it difficult to estimate his chances of recovery.[42] Having learned this, the restless patient dictated from his hospital bed farewell letters to Petrie and Maunsell that subjected SIME leadership to withering criticism. Sadly, these two documents were not included in Edward's file in the MI5 archives. Fortunately, though, we have access to comments on them from two British counterintelligence officers. A certain Major Forrest, stationed in Cairo, claimed in a conversation with his superiors in London that Szarkiewicz had "behaved in such an impardonable manner, slandering his superiors etc., that . . . there is no probability of his being used again by S. I. M. E. when he leaves hospital."[43]

The second commentator, Alex Kellar, was a high-ranking MI5 officer who would succeed Roberts as SIME chief and later become the prototype of Maston, "the man in the cream cuffs," of John le Carré's famous counterespionage novella *Call for the Dead*.[44] Kellar informed Petrie that Roberts had become aware of the contents of Szarkiewicz's farewell letters and was infuriated, declaring that the latter had become clinically paranoid—a possibility British doctors in Cairo categorically rejected[45]—or had decided to undermine the authority of his superiors. Kellar assured Petrie that Roberts had no intention of reinstating Edward at SIME and intended to get him booted from the British

---

41 Charuvi, *Ha-boleshet chokeret*, 149, 244.
42 Roberts to Sir David Petrie, April 4, 1945, TNA, KV 2/518_2, 8.
43 Major S. Alley to the chief of the MI5 Department of Foreign Citizens, March 12, 1945, TNA, KV 2/518_1, 7.
44 Andrew, *The Defence of the Realm*, 350; O'Sullivan, "Joe Spencer's Ratcatchers."
45 Major S. Alley to Sir David Petrie, April 21, 1945, TNA, KV 2/518_1, 8–9.

military establishment. This worried Kellar: if Roberts carried out his threat, Szarkiewicz would become even more resentful, and his close familiarity with the British intelligence community and their work would thus endanger British interests. Kellar proposed having the Little Man transported from Egypt to the UK, where he would be easier to control, and given his fluency in German, could even work as an interpreter when Allied forces occupied Germany.[46]

Maunsell envisioned a similar prospect. After finishing his service in Cairo, he had been assigned to a key post in the counterintelligence service of the Supreme Headquarters of the Allied Expeditionary Force in Europe.[47] The former SIME chief informed Petrie's subordinates that, although "he doubted the qualifications of Szarkiewicz as an interrogator,"—an extremely odd statement from a man who praised the accomplishments of the Polish officer in the field of counterintelligence—he still "might be prepared to consider giving him employment if he were to receive a medical report certifying that Szarkiewicz's physical and mental conditions—particularly the latter—are good enough to ensure his continued usefulness as an intelligence officer."[48]

Meanwhile, Szarkiewicz himself, having learned that his physical condition would not kill him immediately, expressed a desire to terminate his professional relationship with the British and retire to Palestine—as it turned out, he had already purchased an apartment in the vicinity of Tel Aviv. However, at the apparent behest of Douglas Roberts, the British denied him permission and demanded the return to London to complete a formal discharge from SIME and receive an alternative post in some other part of the world.[49]

One might have expected that MI5 headquarters would endorse Roberts's demand to have Szarkiewicz removed from Cairo and Kellar's and Roberts's suggestion to shunt him off to some job in Germany; far from Britain or the Middle East, Szarkiewicz could have continued to serve British interests under Maunsell's watchful gaze. But Stephen Alley from St. James Street objected to the plan. The same Alley who knew Edward in person, was well aware of his significant efforts to defend the British interests and was even considered by Szarkiewicz himself a good friend. On March 12, 1945, he recommended that MI5 oppose the proposal to return Szarkiewicz to London because the move would endanger the relationship between British and Polish counterintelligence. "Szarkiewicz is a super-intriguer," Alley wrote, "and since he has fallen out with

---

46 Alex J. Kellar from the BIB Department of MI5 to Sir David Petrie, March 21, 1945, TNA, KV 2/518_1, 8.
47 Dorril, *MI6*, 814.
48 Major S. Alley to Sir David Petrie, April 21, 1945, TNA, KV 2/518_1, 8–9.
49 Szarkiewicz to Sir David Petrie, July 26, 1945, TNA, KV 2/518_1, 26.

this department may cause considerable trouble as he has access to influential Polish circles."⁵⁰ Alley had essentially demanded to have the ailing Szarkiewicz kept in Cairo for an indefinite period of time, leaving him unemployed, incapable of moving to Palestine or Europe, and most crucially, unable to take a break from the psychological stress of war.

Petrie's official reaction to Alley's recommendation is not preserved in the British archives. However, we know for certain that Szarkiewicz was still in Cairo several weeks after Petrie received it. On April 12, in response to an inquiry British authorities in Palestine made on the subject of Kutten and the other inmates of the Latrun camp, the London headquarters of the Polish Interior Ministry suggested Egypt-based Szarkiewicz as the most knowledgeable source of the reasons for the arrests.⁵¹ Nine days later, on April 21, when Alley contacted— apparently, by phone—the doctor monitoring Szarkiewicz's health, the latter reassured him that the patient was still ill and needed to remain at the Scottish military hospital in Cairo for at least a few more months.⁵²

A Life without Aspirations

On May 1, 1945, less than two weeks after the communication between Major Alley and the hospital in Cairo, the British officer realized that he had underestimated Szarkiewicz's tenacity and craftiness: suddenly news came that the "Cairo patient" had appeared in Britain the day before, despite all the precautions taken by British counterintelligence and Alley himself.⁵³ A little later, it became known that back on April 22—shortly after Egyptian physicians promised to keep him under care for several months—Edward had freely boarded a British hospital ship sailing to England. Just a week later, he was admitted to Whittingham Hospital, near Preston in Northwest England. Alley soon called him on the phone. According to a report on this conversation submitted to Petrie, Szarkiewicz indicated that his health had greatly improved by the time he returned to Britain. He firmly intended to set out for London in two or three days and asked Alley to remind the MI5 director general of his existence.⁵⁴

---

50 Major S. Alley to the chief of the MI5 Department of Foreign Citizens, March 12, 1945, TNA, KV 2/518_1, 7.
51 The Polish Consul in Jerusalem to Minister Kuźniarz in London, a code cable, April 12, 1945, HIA, 800/42/0/-/325 Folder 2, Scan 000319.
52 Major S. Alley to Sir David Petrie, April 21, 1945, TNA, KV 2/518_1, 8–9.
53 Major S. Alley to Sir David Petrie, May 1, 1945, TNA, KV 2/518_1, 10.
54 Ibid.; Szarkiewicz to Sir David Petrie, July 26, 1945, TNA, KV 2/518_1, 24–25.

Most probably, SIME chief Douglas Roberts, who wished to be rid of the Little Man, turned a blind eye to his flight from Egypt. He hastened to reassure Petrie in the "fugitive's" complete harmlessness. Allegedly due to his poor physical condition, Edward had lost his job in the British Middle Eastern security service back in February 1945 and was now a pale shadow of his former self, who only dreamed of leading a quiet life far from those who once knew him.[55] Indeed, the information Alley gathered on Szarkiewicz's first days in the UK confirmed that he shunned all contact with his compatriots and kept a very low profile.[56] Nevertheless, on May 5, Alley sent Szarkiewicz a message insisting that he better focus on restoring his health and refrain from involving himself in the political activities of Polish émigrés. The message also informed the Little Man in no uncertain terms that British doctors had assigned him to medical category E, leaving him with no hope of continuing his career in the British armed forces.[57]

In all likelihood, Szarkiewicz managed to get his "friend" Alley to "remind Petrie of his existence." On Saturday, May 12, 1945, the major brought the Little Man to the MI5 headquarters, for a tête-à-tête with his chief. In spite of the fact that he had been discharged from the Polish army two years earlier and the war in Europe was over, Edward came to Petrie's office in his old Polish military uniform. This outfit underscored his ruined health, Petrie noted in his minutes. Throughout the conversation, the head of MI5 made no mention of his guest's past contributions to the security of the United Kingdom, since at this point, the British had largely become indifferent to this matter.[58] Instead, the talk revolved largely around Szarkiewicz's present condition and plans for the future. When the guest declared his intention to obtain British citizenship, Petrie repeated the advice to keep a distance from Polish politicians—preferably by settling outside London—and gave a very nebulous assurance that MI5 would endorse Edward's request for the naturalization "when the time came [and] assuming nothing untoward happens in the meantime."[59]

To Szarkiewicz's bitter disappointment, it was apparent that his former patrons and handlers in British intelligence were in no hurry to help him settle down in his adopted homeland despite his key role in severing Kot's secret contact with Nazi Germany and his subsequent, heavy involvement in the pro-British coup of the Polish army in exile. Another major source of disappointment was his new

---

55 Roberts to Sir David Petrie, May 4, 1945, TNA, KV 2/518_2, 8.
56 Major S. Alley. Szarkiewicz's address, May 4, 1945, TNA, KV 2/518_2, 11.
57 Major S. Alley. A letter to Szarkiewicz, May 5, 1945, TNA, KV 2/518_1, 10–11.
58 A certain Hale to Major S. Alley, August 18, 1945, TNA, KV 2/518_1, 15.
59 Sir David Petrie on the meeting with Szarkiewicz, May 14, 1945, TNA, KV 2/518_1, 11.

salary: he now subsisted on a meager monthly allowance of twelve pounds.[60] In an attempt to improve his financial situation, Szarkiewicz appealed to the London headquarters of MI5, requesting that this organization instruct SIME to pay him a sum of 280 pounds, the gap between the salary to which he was officially entitled in Egypt and what he was actually paid. His former patron and first boss in Cairo, Raymund Maunsell, unequivocally took his side. Yet, Maunsell's successor in SIME, Douglas Roberts, categorically refused to acknowledge the debt. Petrie took up the cause and tried to force Roberts to pay; only if this attempt failed would MI5 settle Szarkiewicz's claim.[61] Finally, on August 29, after three months of extreme poverty, Szarkiewicz received his 280 pounds, the majority of which he used to cover debts.[62] Hence, his twelve-pound allowance remained the retired Polish captain's primary source of income.[63]

Meanwhile, the question of Szarkiewicz's British citizenship turned out to be much thornier: MI5 leadership categorically refused to help him, save for Alley. Apparently sharing Alex Kellar's view that Szarkiewicz was still capable of doing considerable damage to British security should he wish to, Alley sought help from a high-ranking official of the MI5 Department of Foreign Citizens, notifying him that Szarkiewicz's naturalization was of British interest. Allegedly, this was the only way to forestall Szarkiewicz's arrest and interrogation by Polish émigré authorities, who could extract from him and publicize highly embarrassing information. The official disregarded these arguments, invoking the dry letter of the British naturalization law, according to which, "to qualify for British naturalization Szarkiewicz should either have been in H. M. [His Majesty's military] Service or have been in H. M. Dominions [the UK and its colonies] for five years."[64] Edward officially enlisted with the United Kingdom when he joined SIME in late 1943, and there was no legal way to convince the British Home Office that he had served King and Country earlier. The official instructed Alley to keep Szarkiewicz "as happy as possible," giving him the vague assurance that "D. G. [the director general of MI5] will do what he can WHEN it becomes possible."[65]

---

60 Major S. Alley. A memorandum, August 22, 1945, TNA, KV 2/518_1, 19.
61 Hale to the chief of the MI5 Department of Foreign Citizens, August 2, 1945, TNA, KV 2/518_1, 14.
62 A declaration by Szarkiewicz about the receipt of 280 pounds and the absence of any further financial claims on his part, August 29, 1945, TNA, KV 2/518_1, 17–18.
63 Major S. Alley. A memorandum, August 22, 1945, TNA, KV 2/518_1, 19.
64 Hale to Major S. Alley, August 18, 1945, TNA, KV 2/518_1, 15.
65 Ibid.

Alley apparently carried out this injunction on August 22 at another personal meeting with Szarkiewicz. According to the protocol, the latter tried to convince Alley—and ultimately MI5 leadership—to help him for humane reasons, as his extended stay in the British Isles had further undermined his already frail health and ruined his plans to improve his precarious financial situation by joining a friend's business venture in Egypt.[66] At the same time, the erstwhile Captain Dunlop sent a personal message to Sir David Petrie: "I would very much like to see you in the near future on several matters. Perhaps you would be good enough to let me have an appointment with you at some time and date convenient to yourself."[67]

This quote concludes Szarkiewicz's file, which gathered dust at the MI5 archives for many years before moving to the national archives in Kew; we do not know if British counterintelligence officials bothered to reply to the persistent Polish petitioner. But a notice published in the British press in October 1946 states that the Interior Ministry had granted British citizenship to a foreign subject named Edward Szarkiewicz in September, and we can assume, with a great deal of confidence, that this was our protagonist.[68] This may also indicate that Szarkiewicz spent a little over a year in the British Isles after his last known meeting with Alley. Just four years earlier, he had acted as the right-hand man of one of the leaders of the Polish émigré elite and wielded enormous power over many of his compatriots. Now, at the age of forty-six, he was gravely ill and friendless; had no family, homeland, or steady job; eked out a pauper's existence on a tiny allowance; and rented a small apartment on Collingham Road in London.[69]

Was British citizenship Petrie's parting gift? (He stepped down from his post in the spring of 1946.)[70] Impossible to say. Szarkiewicz's life after he became a British subject is yet another mystery. For some reason, none of the Polish historians who have written about the Mikiciński affair—not even Roman Buczek, who wrote a monograph on the subject—have taken an interest in the subsequent fate of Mikiciński's presumed assassin.

In the late 1990s, Jerzy Iranek-Osmecki—son of Kazimierz Iranek-Osmecki, the legendary intelligence chief of the Polish national underground—commented

---

66 Major S. Alley. A memorandum, August 22, 1945, TNA, KV 2/518_1, 19.
67 Szarkiewicz to Sir David Petrie, August 18, 1945, TNA, KV 2/518_1, 20.
68 "List of aliens to whom Certificates of Naturalization have been granted by the Secretary of State, and whose Oaths of Allegiance have been registered in the Home Office during the month of September 1946," *London Gazette*, Tuesday, October 22, 1946, 5214.
69 Major S. Alley. Szarkiewicz's address, May 4, 1945, TNA, KV 2/518_2, 11.
70 Andrew, *The Defence of the Realm*, 319.

on his father's memoirs, claiming that Szarkiewicz settled in London after World War II, ran a small movie theater in the Kilburn area called the envoy, and died in the late 1950s or early 1960s.[71] An online search yielded the recollections of longtime Kilburn residents who confirmed the envoy's existence; it was open from the mid-1930s to the mid-1950s, when it was sold to a cinema chain that changed its name.[72] This information seems to bear out Jerzy Iranek-Osmecki's testimony: perhaps Szarkiewicz, foreseeing his death, decided to sell the property.

It is much harder to verify the assertions of some Polish historians, who do not bother to cite their sources, that, after the end of World War II, Szarkiewicz went to Communist Poland and vanished behind the Iron Curtain without a trace.[73] It is of course possible that, after receiving British citizenship, Szarkiewicz, like many of his compatriots including Modelski, became disillusioned with life in the West and chose to return to his homeland. However, the archives of the Polish Ministry of Public Security, the agency that would have been responsible for monitoring Szarkiewicz if he had returned from Britain, yield not a single reference to a baptized Polish Jew who worked for the British against the exiled government of his own country. Thus, the final chapter in the life of this fascinating individual will remain shrouded in the mists of history until new archival evidence comes to light in the United Kingdom, Poland, or even Israel.

---

71 Iranek-Osmecki, *Pułkownik Kazimierz Iranek-Osmecki*, s. 530–531; Iranek-Osmecki, *Postscriptum II*, 538.
72 Kilburn Classic; Ken Roe, *Classic Kilburn*.
73 See, for instance: Gulbicki, *Tropem zabójcy generała*.

Part Three

THE WORLD AFTER SAMSON AND EDWARD

Chapter 9

The Battle Over the Legacy of "Lis"

A Tiny Army in a Large Leather Suitcase

Dr. Gad Franco, one of the leading Jewish legal minds in Turkey, must have been very surprised when one day in April 1941, the municipal court of Ankara suggested he take custody of the property of a certain Samson Mikiciński, a missing Chilean diplomat and Polish citizen. This unexpected offer resulted from an official appeal to the Turkish justice system from Franco's Polish colleague, Karol Bader, a doctor of law. In March 1941, Bader was appointed to consul general in Istanbul—and, as the reader may recall, was a close associate of the influential Polish minister Stanisław Kot.[1] Franco agreed to make a thorough inventory of the personal effects, valuables, and money Mikiciński left in Turkey, then try to identify and locate potential heirs to his estate.

Polish diplomats in Turkey learned of Mikiciński's estate's existence on February 8, 1941, some three weeks after Szarkiewicz abducted him, when Istanbul police published a summary of its investigation into the circumstances of his disappearance. According to the Turkish detectives, Mikiciński had been murdered by person(s) unknown with criminal motives, probably robbery, a

---

1 Karol Bader served as the Polish consul general in Istanbul from April to October 1941. See: Jaskulski, *Embassy of the Republic of Poland in Ankara*, 32.

commonplace crime in the former Ottoman capital before and during the war. And yet, Héctor Briones Luco, the Chilean chargé d'affaires in Turkey, must have realized that the mysterious disappearance of his business partner was the handiwork of powers that had nothing to do with the criminal underworld. For this reason, he hurried to get rid of Mikiciński's belongings that remained at the Chilean legation, untouched by Turkish police. To help him, Luco turned to the Polish consul in Istanbul, Wojciech Rychlewicz—a supporter of the Sanation camp and probably an officer of the Dwójka[2]—and one Captain Pilecki, an official representative of Polish military intelligence. Together, they smashed in Mikiciński's door and spent several hours drawing up a detailed inventory. They found a large leather suitcase containing a veritable treasure trove: about a thousand gold coins from assorted countries and time periods, wads of American and European banknotes, gold jewelry, platinum, diamonds, and a host of other valuables. The Poles would later estimate the total value at about two million British pounds sterling, equivalent to more than 100 million pounds in 2024. In the early 1940s, such a sum would have bought about 150 British Spitfire fighter aircraft, or a roughly equal number of American Sherman tanks (in other words, a small army).

Four days later, on February 13, Consul Rychlewicz personally transported the suitcase from the Chilean representation in Istanbul to the Polish embassy in Ankara. Rychlewicz and Sokolnicki, who would omit this incident from his *Ankara Diary*, gave another inspection and description of the valuables with two other embassy employees serving as witnesses. They sealed the suitcase and turned it over to the embassy accountant for safekeeping, storing the key in the embassy's safe deposit box in a special sealed envelope marked "For the Ambassador only."[3]

The treasures Rychlewicz and Pilecki brought to light consisted of Mikiciński's personal property and the money and valuables Polish and Romanian citizens fleeing war-torn Europe had entrusted to him for transfer to Turkey and Palestine. One of the estate's was none other than Ludwig Buchwald, the colorful character from the Turkish criminal underworld flourishing during the war. Shortly after

---

2 Wojciech Rychlewicz served as the Polish consul general in Istanbul from November 1937 to March 1941. See: Jaskulski, *Embassy of the Republic of Poland in Ankara*, 32. See *also* on Rychlewicz's activities in Turkey, including his membership in the Polish military intelligence and the aid he rendered to Jewish refugees from occupied Poland: Bek. Ha-matsil' me-istanbul; see also on Rychlewicz's allegiance to the pro-Sanation camp: Alexandrowicz, Kurcyusz, Kuźniarz, and others to Sikorski; November 20, 1940, PISM, PRM. 50, 16–16/16.
3 Protocol, February 15, 1941, copy for the Second Department of the Supreme Command Headquarters, HIA, 800/41/0/-/141 Folder 7, Scans 000956-000961.

Turkish officials published the notice of Mikiciński's death in a robbery gone wrong, Buchwald demanded his rightful portion of the inheritance. As Buczek noted five decades later, after his claim was rejected, he sought redress from the local justice system,[4] prompting Karol Bader, Rychlewicz's successor in the post of Polish consul in Istanbul, to appeal to the Turkish courts, leading ultimately to Franco's appointment to custodian of Mikiciński's estate.[5]

Bader may not have been motivated by an altruistic desire to help Buchwald and the others wronged by the Mikiciński affair. Buczek explains that Bader violated two Polish laws: a prohibition on giving foreign citizens custody over the property of Poles who died abroad and Polish espionage law dictating that all Mikiciński's property rightfully belonged to the exiled government in London.[6] Hence, Bader's attempt to involve foreign authorities in the resolution qualified as professional misconduct. Bader, who was certainly aware of this, must have had ample grounds to act as he did. Quite possibly, he and Kot hoped to use the Turks to liberate Mikiciński's abandoned property from the Polish embassy in Ankara controlled by the Sanation camp and appropriate it for their own uses. If this was indeed their intention, they must have been sorely disappointed by the stance Turkish authorities took on the contents of Mikiciński's large leather suitcase.

A Polish-Turkish Diplomatic Crisis around the Division of Jewish Property

Ludwig Buchwald's appeal to the Ankara court aroused the curiosity of the Turkish authorities—up until that moment, they had no inkling of the fabulous wealth Mikiciński had left behind. Very soon, they determined that the leather suitcase Rychlewicz had smuggled into the Polish embassy was not the only treasure that had slipped through the Turks' fingers. They learned of a bulky parcel containing a large sum of money, gold, diamonds, and other valuables that apparently had arrived at the Chilean embassy in Bucharest, then delivered to Istanbul by an unidentified British courier and handed over to Whitehall, the local representative of MI6, then shipped in secret to Palestine with the help of

---

4   The contents of radio message no. 174 (May 9, 1941) from the Polish Consul General in Istanbul, transmitted on May 19, 1941, by the Head of Referat (Department) "West" of the "Dwójka," Major Zichoń, to the leadership of the "Dwójka": HIA, 800/41/0/-/141 Folder 7, Scan 001014.
5   Buczek, *Człowiek do złotych interesów*, 174.
6   Ibid.

Whitehall's confidant, a Jew named Izak (Yitzhak) Stern. Another portion of the inheritance, thirteen suitcases crammed with valuables and several Persian rugs, had gone into storage at the Port of Istanbul; the Chilean representative had hurriedly shipped it to the Polish consulate in Jerusalem as soon as he learned of Mikiciński's disappearance. The Turks managed to grab only a few crumbs, namely the unnamed contents of Mikiciński's safe deposit box at the Istanbul branch of Banca Commerciale Italiana (one of fascist Italy's largest banks) and valuables, worth about 250,000 US dollars, that police had found at Mikiciński's last residence before his abduction, a room at the upscale Park Hotel near Taksim Square.[7]

In early May of 1941, Turkish authorities—equally determined to lay their hands on the contents of the leather suitcase—sent identical, strongly worded protests to Chilean and Polish representatives in Istanbul and Ankara. Their message stated that Luco's decision to involve the Poles in the matter of Mikiciński's legacy was incompatible with his obligations to his host country and hampered the Turkish police investigation into the circumstances of Mikiciński's disappearance.[8] Cowed, the Chilean diplomat switched sides immediately and sent the Poles a letter requesting they hand over the suitcase to the Ankara court.

When he mailed a copy of the letter to the Turkish Foreign Ministry, officials unleashed the full brunt of their anger on Ambassador Sokolnicki and his colleagues. On May 13, Turkish foreign minister Mehmet Şükrü Saracoğlu shared the details of the growing diplomatic scandal around Mikiciński's inheritance with Prime Minister Refik Saydam, urging him to let the Poles know in no uncertain terms that they had to respect Ankara's position. (Soon, Saracoğlu would sign a friendship treaty with the Third Reich that would enable his country to sit out the European war.) While Saydam's response is unknown to us, we know that the Turkish cabinet refrained from harsh measures against the Poles. The likely reason for this lenience was their desire to expand cooperation with the Polish government-in-exile in the aviation realm. In the autumn of 1940, the Poles, with British consent, started training Turkish pilots and aircraft mechanics and broke ground on a large airplane manufacturing plant in central

---

7 An undated report titled "Mikiciński Samson," JPIA, Archiwum Osobowe, NZ 154, Sygn. 658; Consul Poninski, Istanbul, to the Polish Minister of Foreign Affairs, London, December 23, 1941, HIA, 800/42/0/-/312, Box 1, Folder 1, Skans 000646-647; Buczek, *Człowiek do złotych interesów*, 172–173.

8 Ambassador Sokolnicki, Ankara, to the Polish Foreign Office in London, code cable, July 8, 1942, HIA, 800/42/0/-/312, Box 1, Folder 1, Skans 000610-611; Buczek, *Człowiek do złotych interesów*, 175.

Turkey, far from prying eyes.⁹ The facility became operational in May 1941, the very moment Saracoğlu was to intervene in the dispute over Mikiciński's inheritance. Undoubtedly, Saydam prioritized the continuous operation of a plant with Polish advisors over the contents of some suitcase.

Meanwhile, dozens of Mikiciński's customers now in Israel established a public committee in Tel Aviv to negotiate the return of their property. In the spring of 1941, the members of the committee appealed to Bader, who reached out to the deputy chief of the Dwójka, Stanislaw Gano, in an attempt to find out what had happened to Mikiciński and whether he could be reached to discuss the rights of his customers to a share of his legacy. On May 1, Bader informed his bosses in London that Gano had promised to set up a meeting between the Polish consulate in Jerusalem and Mikiciński.¹⁰ This promise remained unfulfilled and quite possibly had been only a ruse to deceive Kot and his people in the Middle East about Mikiciński's actual condition. Gano's inaction hurt and disappointed the members of the Tel Aviv public committee, and on July 24, some of them (including an Eiger, probably Karol Eiger, whom Mikiciński had rescued from a concentration camp in Poland the year before) sent a telegram to the Polish Foreign Office in London:

> In October 1940, the Polish government empowered the Chilean representation in Bucharest to extend [diplomatic] protection to the Polish citizens [in Romania]. We, as Polish citizens, handed over our property to the secretary of this representation, whose present whereabouts are unknown, and our property is being kept mostly at the Polish embassy in Ankara, and partly at the Polish consulate in Jerusalem. Both institutions refuse to return the money and property to their rightful owners, who are currently in Palestine. These persons are in desperate straits since those are their last possessions. In light of this, we ask the [Polish] Ministers of Foreign Affairs and Justice to give instructions to have the property that has been detained [in Turkey] shipped to Palestine, and to have it returned [to its rightful owners], along with the portion that is already in Jerusalem.¹¹

---

9   Czulda, *Pod tureckimi skrzydłami*.
10 A secret telegram from Karol Bader to the Polish Foreign Office in London, May 1, 1941, HIA, 800/41/0/-/141 Folder 7, Scan 001098.
11 A telegram from Tel Aviv to the Headquarters of the Polish Foreign Office in London, July 24, 1941, HIA, 800/41/0/-/141 Folder 7, Scans 000095-000097.

The Polish government-in-exile found itself between a rock and a hard place, the Turks on the one side, the Jews in Palestine on the other. While Turkish authorities did not deny in principle the right of the Jewish refugees to some of the contents of the leather suitcase, they insisted on receiving all the contents first and holding onto them until their provenance had been determined and the investigation into Mikiciński's whereabouts had concluded. Conversely, the Jews made no claim to Mikiciński's private property, but demanded that their personal assets be immediately returned, citing a dire financial situation.

In response to these conflicting demands, the Polish Foreign Office doubled down on its original position: the suitcase would remain at the Polish embassy in Ankara. In the second half of 1941, Sokolnicki's people initiated a dialogue with the Turks in hopes of convincing them of their position, but failed. In December, the mayor of Istanbul sent the Polish embassy a written ultimatum, expressly demanding that the "suitcase of discord" be handed over to the Turkish authorities in the next twenty-four hours. In parallel, their Turkish-appointed custodian, Gad Franco, urged the Poles to agree to a compromise: he would hold Mikiciński's treasures for safekeeping until diplomatic and legal channels clarified their status. But the Poles dug in their heels, and half a year later, in May 1942, the Turks warned the Poles that "the activities of the Polish consul in Istanbul might run into certain difficulties" if they maintained their stance on Mikiciński's possessions.[12]

And indeed, the relationship between the Turkish and Polish governments somewhat cooled in the second half of 1942 and early 1943. At this time, Ambassador Sokolnicki kept reporting to London on Turkish leaders' "boundless sympathy" for the Polish cabinet in exile;[13] but the Polish military advisors and aviation engineers stationed in Turkey noticed an attitude shift in their local colleagues, trainees, and employees at the airplane manufacturing plant they had helped build.[14]

This change might be attributable to the death of Turkish Premier Saydam in July 1942. His successor, the aforementioned Saracoğlu, felt more fealty to London and Moscow, which was bound to affect Ankara's attitude toward Sikorski and his cabinet (among other things).[15] Shortly after assuming the

---

12 The Turkish Foreign Office to the Polish Foreign Office, a copy, May 7, 1942, HIA, 800/42/0/-/312, Box 1, Folder 1, Scans 000628-629; Menemencioğlu to Sokolnicki, June 18, 1942, HIA, 800/42/0/-/312, Box 1, Folder 1, Scan 000592; Buczek, *Człowiek do złotych interesów*, 172–184.
13 Sokolnicki, *Dziennik Ankarski*, 399.
14 Czulda, *Pod tureckimi skrzydłami*.
15 Sokolnicki, *Dziennik Ankarski*, 395–396.

premiership, the nationalist introduced a new high tax allegedly to increase the military budget. All Turkish residents were supposed to pay this task, but in practice, it became an effective instrument of economic oppression against the country's ethnic and religious minorities, including the Jews. A Turkish Jew whose family suffered greatly under Saracoğlu's new policy would recall many years later that: "They knew what to take, so as to leave not a single penny for survival; those unable to pay were sent to work camps."[16] The Ankara lawyer Gad Franco was among these insolvents sent into forced labor.[17] It may be assumed that his removal from the Turkish capital—and subsequent loss of contact with the Poles—did nothing to help smooth over the hard feelings about Mikiciński's treasures.

The Lawyer Florin Writes to General Gürsel

Only in June of 1943 were the Poles finally ready to compromise with the Turks. Władysław Sikorski had recently spent several weeks in the Middle East inspecting Polish military forces and underwent a change of heart; after more than two years of multinational, intercontinental conflict, Sikorski settled the matter of the suitcase in a moment of desperation for Ankara's support in the rapidly accelerating Polish-Soviet conflict. Sokolnicki was nearly able to arrange him a meeting with Turkish foreign minister Hüseyin Numan Menemencioğlu in Baghdad,[18] but the confab was not to occur, as Menemencioğlu had the presence of mind not to wave the red Polish flag in front of the Soviet bull. Nevertheless, Polish officials had already settled the terms of the treasures' disbursement. Thus in February 1944, all formalities dispatched, the contents of the large leather suitcase moved from the Polish embassy in Ankara into permanent storage at the Istanbul headquarters of Osmanlı Bankası, one of Turkey's oldest and largest banks.[19]

Concurrently, London gave the Polish consulate general in Jerusalem permission to distribute what had arrived of Mikiciński's legacy in Palestine to local Polish and Romanian Jews able to prove their claims to inheritance. These refugees would get all their property back, but those with a share of the treasure

---

16 Testimony of David Kimchi, born in Istanbul, Turkey, 1930, regarding his experiences in Istanbul and the attitude of the Turkish government toward minorities before the outbreak of the war and during the war, Tel Aviv, January 2, 1982, YVA, Record group: O.3, File No. 4280.
17 Bali, *Devlet'in Yahudileri ve 'Öteki' Yahudi*, 109–160.
18 Sokolnicki, *Dziennik Ankarski*, 529–530.
19 Buczek, *Człowiek do złotych interesów*, 184.

that remained in Turkey—a larger number of beneficiaries entitled to a far bigger portion of Mikiciński's estate—never saw a penny. This discrepancy can be traced to a July 1942 decision of the Polish Ministry of Justice that made official the Polish government's lack of obligation to petition the Turks to return of the property to its rightful owners. As the Polish officials saw it, Jewish refugees had availed themselves of Mikiciński's services in Bucharest at their own risk, without the knowledge of the Polish government, and with no guarantees of any kind; hence, it was now their responsibility to fight for their rights in whatever manner they saw fit.[20]

Apparently, the shafted clients soon became convinced that they would never be able to reclaim their lost property—for almost two decades, nothing appears in any publication about any attempt to appeal to the authorities in Ankara. Finally, in late January 1961, just after Turkish general Cemal Gürsel had carried out a military coup and assumed the presidency, a report appeared in the Israeli daily newspaper *Maariv*: Haifa-based attorney Alfred Florin had written to Gürsel requesting the return of a jewelry box he had given to Mikiciński for transfer to Palestine. The newspaper describes the motives behind Florin's unusual letter to the head of the junta:

> The story of this jewelry box goes back to 1940, when Mr. Florin handed it over to a foreign diplomat, who was to ship it from Bucharest to Tel Aviv. The diplomat, one Mikiciński, combined the roles of Chilean representative and *chargé d'affaires* of the Polish government-in-exile in Bucharest. He left the Romanian capital in 1940, intending to travel to the Land of Israel. At that very time, Mr. Florin ... handed him an iron box containing 133 gold coins and twenty-three pieces of jewelry, some of them set with large diamonds. One of the two keys to the box was entrusted to Mikiciński, while the other was retained by Florin. The box also contained a list of its contents, written in its owner's hand. As Florin would learn many years later, in January 1941 Mikiciński was found dead in his car, in a street in Istanbul. His murderers have never been found. During the subsequent investigation by the Turkish police, the aforementioned jewelry box was found among the deceased's effects in the Polish

---

20 Mieczysław Sędzielowski, head of the Consular Referat (Department) of the Polish Foreign Office, top secret memorandum, July 15, 1942, HIA, 800/42/0/-/312, Box 1, Folder 1, Scans 000606-607.

representation building. The box, along with all the other items found there, was handed over to the local court, and remained for many years in the custody of the Turkish legal authorities. In accordance with Turkish law, when no lawful heirs could be found, all this property ended up being deposited in the Turkish treasury. . . . Following a lengthy investigation by Attorney Marco Cohen from Tel Aviv, Mr. Florin was able to determine the fate of his missing valuables. Now, he has appealed to the Turkish head of state, asking him to instruct the Turkish treasury to return the lost box to its rightful owner.[21]

Attentive readers of this book already well-versed in the minutiae of the Mikiciński affair will have noticed the errors and inaccuracies that crept into the article's text, a reflection of the press' limited knowledge and a testament to the success of the disinformation campaign Szarkiewicz had launched with the British two decades earlier to conceal the true story of Mikiciński's abduction in Istanbul and subsequent imprisonment and execution. We do not know today if Gürsel ever sent Florin a response, nor do we know if any other Holocaust survivor or their descendants ever appealed to Ankara. Essentially, Florin's letter is the final chapter in the long saga of Mikiciński's estate. In the many years between now and then, all traces of the money and valuables in his possession at the time of his death have disappeared for good from the memory of those living in the country where Mikiciński found his final resting place.

---

21 "Israeli tove'a mi-turkia lehachzir lo tevat tachshitim."

Chapter 10

The Fates of the Secondary Characters in this Drama, against the Backdrop of the Processes That Shaped Its Course

The Chronicle of a National, Political, and Personal Fiasco

"'Kismet.' Fate! Who knows your secrets?" wrote Edward Szarkiewicz in his farewell letter to Major Stephen Alley. Fate dealt cruel blows to Szarkiewicz and to his victim, Samson Mikiciński, first by cutting short the careers and lives of both men, then stripping their struggles and personal suffering of any historical significance. Their political masters in the Polish government-in-exile and the supporters of the prewar Sanation were reduced to bit players in European and global geopolitics even before the end of the hostilities in Europe in May 1945 and denied the ability to return to their homeland; and neither Kot's nor Modelski's once powerful factions made it past the end of the war, and were relegated to the darkest and dustiest shelves of the warehouse of history as soon as the Nazis were defeated.

Sikorski lost his place at the apex of the Polish military-political pyramid as early as the summer of 1942, a year after Mikiciński's death, when the hand of fate (or more accurately, Stalin and Churchill) moved Anders's Army and its tens of thousands of troops from frozen Russia to the Middle East and General Anders became the most popular military and political leader of the Polish diaspora.¹ Attentive readers might recall that MI5 regarded Sikorski as a weak man, and despite all his efforts to reverse their opinion, the British (including Henry Hopkinson, a private secretary to the minister of state in the Middle East posted permanently to Cairo) zealously defended Anders from what they recognized as Sikorski's attempts to unseat him.²

In the spring of 1943, Germany announced the discovery of a mass grave in occupied Soviet territory containing the remains of the Polish officers killed in what became known as the Katyn massacre. The Polish government-in-exile was reluctant to dismiss it out of hand as a German provocation, and Sikorski endured a profound crisis in his relationship with Churchill, demanding verification of German claims about Moscow's involvement in the massacre. Having promised Stalin to "discipline the Polish press,"³ Churchill was incensed that the Polish politicians and journalists staying in his country were unwilling to "shut up" on the subject of Katyn, and he insistently demanded that Sikorski calm "these unwise people." When Sikorski requested a trip to the Middle East in 1943, Churchill made suppressing Polish public opinion a requisite for his approval.⁴ Flying home to Britain in July, a few months later, Sikorski's airplane crashed into the Strait of Gibraltar, killing him and his daughter Zofia, whom Mikiciński had rescued from occupied Warsaw in early 1940.⁵

Since the crash, a great number of Poles, respected historians among them, have been convinced that their fugitive leader fell victim to a British conspiracy,

---

1 McGilvray, *Anders's Army*, 41–88; see also on Anders's political promotion upon his arrival in the Middle East: Rutkowski, *Stanisław Kot*, 323–328.
2 Hopkinson to Churchill, April 6, 1943, CHAR, 20/109/89-92.
3 Churchill to Stalin, sent April 28, 1943, received April 30, 1943, in Reynolds and Pechatnov. *The Kremlin's Letters*, 244; Churchill to Stalin, sent May 12, 1943, received May 13, 1943, Ibid., 251.
4 Marian Kukiel, Minister of War, to the members of the Polish government-in-exile, an untitled report about Churchill's conversation with Sikorski and Raczyński, April 27, 1943, USHMM, RG-59.045, A-XII-3-21_0181; the Intelligence Department of the Headquarters of the High Command of the Polish Armed Forces in Exile to the head of the Political Department of the War Ministry, "An Extract from a Report on the Military-Political Situation in the Middle East from April 15, 1943 to May 15, 1943," London, June 16, 1943, USHMM, RG-59.045, A-XII-3-22_0156; Churchill to Foreign Secretary Eden, May 10, 1943, CHAR, 20/128/12; Churchill to Eden, May 16, 1943, CHAR, 20/128/20; see also: a report by the Polish Foreign Office about the efforts by the British censors in Cairo and Jerusalem to prevent publications about the Polish-Soviet relations in the Polish press: the Polish Foreign Office in London to the President of Poland, Polish Prime Minister, and Minister of Information, an untitled secret report based on telegram no. 228 from Jerusalem, April 13, 1943, USHMM, RG-59.036, A-12-53-38L_0020; the Polish Foreign Office in London to the Minister of Information and Documentation and to the Polish ambassador to London, an untitled secret report based on telegram no. 72 from Jerusalem, February 7, 1944, USHMM, RG-59.036, A-12-53-39L_0005.
5 Foot, *The Death of General Sikorski*, 457–458.

or maybe a Russian one, or maybe one orchestrated within the opposition circles of the Polish diaspora.[6] One occasionally encounters the claim that Edward Szarkiewicz was behind this event. Jerzy Iranek-Osmecki, the son of Kazimierz Iranek-Osmecki, first advanced the hypothesis. His father and Szarkiewicz had served together for several months in the Bucharest ekspozytura of the Dwójka in 1940 and remained friends for many years afterward. Jerzy Iranek-Osmecki claims that shortly before he passed in the late 1950s or early 1960s, Edward confessed to his former commander that it was he who organized the crash in Gibraltar. According to Jerzy, his father was convinced that Szarkiewicz was telling the truth because he had carried out Mikiciński's assassination. Jerzy did not doubt this version of events, either. He postulates that at the time of Sikorski's death, Szarkiewicz was working for British counterintelligence in the Middle East in a high-ranking position equivalent to brigadier, and thus enjoyed free access to Sikorski's aircraft when it stopped over in Cairo before continuing to Gibraltar.[7]

However, the historical research that preceded the writing of this book uncovered evidence that decisively refutes all allegations of Szarkiewicz's involvement in Sikorski's death, whether Szarkiewicz truly confessed or was framed by one or both Iranek-Osmeckis. We know for certain that Edward was still in London in July 1943, stranded in professional limbo. He left the British Isles in the fall and started work at the Cairo branch of British counterintelligence in a fairly low-level job no earlier than February 1944. At the moment Sikorski's airplane crashed into the coast of Gibraltar, Szarkiewicz would have been powerless to affect the course of events; at most, he could have brought down some flying insects in Hyde Park...

Szarkiewicz's rival Stanisław Kot proved to be an amazing political survivor right up to the end of the war. However, not even Kot could avoid the merciless fate of the Polish émigré elite and was barred from returning to his Soviet-liberated homeland as an important government official. In September 1941, at the height of his bitter struggle against the pro-Sanation camp, while trying desperately to learn of Mikiciński's fate, after Churchill had all but forced Sikorski to reestablish diplomatic relations with the USSR, Sikorski dispatched (read: banished) Kot to Russia to serve as the first ambassador of the Polish government-in-exile. As a result, Kot became permanently disqualified from serving as the minister of the interior, a position that had enabled him to closely

---

6 Wieczorkiewicz, *Historia polityczna Polski*, 277–280.
7 Jerzy Iranek-Osmecki, *Postscriptum II, Wspomnienia oficera*, 538; see a reprint of this assertion by the Polish historian Sławomir Koper: Koper, *Polskie piekiełko*, 538.

monitor the Polish émigré community and the secret channels of communication with occupied Poland. After assuming his ambassadorial duties, he tried to build a new network of secret informants from the Polish military officers and civilians in Soviet territory, but his attempt was a resounding failure. The Soviets easily uncovered the network and unceremoniously expelled the hapless ambassador from the country.[8]

According to the report in the Brooklyn archives, Kot's abortive attempt to play at spycraft led to the December 1941 arrest of two renowned Polish politicians and Jews, Wiktor Alter and Henryk Ehrlich, who had found themselves in the Soviet Union after the Nazis invaded Poland.[9] Both men died under interrogation by Stalin's NKVD. For decades afterward, their loved ones—along with Western, Russian, and Israeli historians—tried to puzzle out the Soviet secret service's reasoning for arresting and killing them at the very moment other Soviet organs were intending to use them for propaganda purposes abroad. In the end, the prevailing view became that Alter and Ehrlich had gotten too close to the Polish embassy and became victims of their own recklessness when they presumably used their contacts to try to learn the fate of the Polish officers taken prisoner by the Soviets in the autumn of 1939.[10] The Brooklyn document fully confirms this supposition, clearly fingering Kot as the culprit whose actions led to Alter's and Ehrlich's arrests by the NKVD. According to the report, both were members of an improvised network of informants that Kot planned to seed in Soviet territory. For this very reason, NKVD counterintelligence operatives identified the pair as foreign spies and dealt with them in accordance with the standard wartime Soviet procedure for such cases.[11]

Kot emerged unscathed from this tragic episode and Sikorski allowed him back into the Polish government-in-exile. Until March 1943, he served as the minister of state in the Middle East and was then recalled to London and appointed minister of information and documentation. In this post, he was

---

8   An undated report titled "Mikiciński Samson," JPIA, Archiwum Osobowe, NZ 154, Sygn. 658.
9   Alter and Erlich were members of the so-called Bund, or the "General Jewish Labor Bund in Lithuania, Poland, and Russia." This socialist party was established in the 1890s, reached the peak of its influence in the first half of the twentieth century, and withered away after World War II. See on Alter and Erlich's membership in the Bund: Wieczorkiewicz, *Historia polityczna Polski*, 247.
10 Al'tman, Anderson and Redlich, *War, Holocaust and Stalinism*, 13–14, 171; Rutkowski, *Stanisław Kot*, 274–275.
11 An undated report titled "Mikiciński Samson," JPIA, Archiwum Osobowe, NZ 154, Sygn. 658. See also the British sources that corroborate the position of the Brooklyn report: McGilvray, *Anders's Army*, 48, 245, footnote 21.

responsible, inter alia, for supervising the Polish émigré and underground press, and official Polish propaganda.

Just a month after returning to the UK, Kot played a key role in formulating the official Polish response to the Katyn affair, thereby contributing to the acute crisis in Polish-Soviet relations. Moscow reacted to Sikorski's stance by cutting off all diplomatic contact with the exiled Polish leadership. At the height of this crisis and for a little while later, the Kremlin sent numerous messages to the Sikorski government demanding the dismissal of Kot and several other high-ranking officials.[12] The growing Polish-Russian schism resulted in the almost complete marginalization of Sikorski and his entourage in the eyes of Britain and the US. Both countries began to drift toward accepting the Soviet position on the borders of postwar Poland and its political structure.

After Sikorski's death, Kot continued to hold the post of minister of information and documentation under new premier Stanisław Mikołajczyk. However, Kot's political career had passed its zenith, and the overall status of the London-based Polish government-in-exile declined precipitously in 1944 and 1945. In the words of a contemporary Polish official, the British still tolerated it, but completely ignored its input.[13] Hence, after hostilities ended on the European continent, the soldiers and officers of the Polish army in exile—what Churchill had described "80,000 excellent fighting men under our operational command"[14]—were not invited to the victory celebrations taking place all over the United Kingdom. Meanwhile, Kot quietly packed his belongings and returned to Poland, now under Communist control. He hoped to join the so-called Provisional Government of National Unity, which allegedly intended to admit certain prominent representatives of the Polish diaspora into its ranks alongside openly pro-Soviet figures. However, Kot's political U-turn ended in bitter disappointment. After spending two years in honorary exile as the ambassador of the new Poland in Rome, he returned to Britain to lead the typical life of an aging political émigré. He remained one of the leaders of the exiled Polish People's Party, which rapidly devolved into a totally powerless social club of world-weary and misanthropic elderly exiles and a convenient

---

12 Rutkowski, *Stanisław Kot*, 294–338, 356–357.
13 The Department of Political Work with the Press [originally named the "Press-Political" Department], "Information for the Honorable Minister Professor St. Kot," London, May 5, 1944, USHMM, RG-59.045, A-XII-3-22_0365.
14 Churchill to Stalin, sent December 3, 1944, received December 3, 1944, in Reynolds and Pechatnov, *The Kremlin's Letters*, 506.

platform for the activities of the intelligence organs of Communist Poland in the West.[15] Stanisław Kot died in 1975.

General Izydor Modelski, Edward Szarkiewicz's former patron and co-conspirator, lost his political clout even faster than Kot did: in late 1942, Izya was dismissed as deputy war minister and lost access to Sikorski. He spent the rest of the war on forced sick leave. Shortly after his official discharge in March 1945, like Kot and many other prominent Polish émigrés, Modelski packed his belongings and returned to the homeland. There, he enjoyed a surprisingly warm reception, which may have been the result of his dealings with the Polish Communists in Britain. He was even posted in London for a time to help organize his countrymen's repatriation to Communist Poland. As early as 1946, General Modelski was sent to Washington, DC to take the once-prestigious post of military attaché at the Polish embassy. With Warsaw's foreign policy now completely subordinate to Moscow, this job was a sinecure with no practical influence, a reality of which he soon became aware.

Two years later, having at last burned his bridges with his superiors in Warsaw and fired for reasons of incompetence, Modelski announced his desire to stay in America. He spoke to Congress and the local press, claiming that he had been sent to the US to set up a Communist spy network. In response to Modelski's "disgraceful" behavior, the Polish authorities held a court martial, at which the "despicable renegade" was charged with high treason and sentenced in absentia to fifteen years' imprisonment. Modelski died an American citizen in 1962. At the time, few of his compatriots could recall that only two decades earlier, this unassuming seventy-four-year-old man had been a vigorous, power-hungry, and high-ranking Polish officer who most likely aspired to replace Sikorski as supreme commander of the Polish army in exile.[16]

Nowadays, the name of Izydor Modelski has all but vanished from the pages of both Polish and Western publications on the subject of World War II. Quite possibly, he was the anonymous author of the report on the Mikiciński affair held at the Piłsudski Institute in Brooklyn: it contains some singular facts from Mikiciński's biography and Szarkiewicz's investigation in Palestine, so the person who wrote it must have had some firsthand knowledge. As of now, it seems Modelski was the only postwar Polish émigré in the US to have such knowledge. The attentive reader may recall that, as early as 1941, he was closely

---

15 Rutkowski, *Stanisław Kot*, 359–420; Tarka, "Waldemar Sobczyk i 'Nasz Znak'," 321–363.
16 "Lieut. Gen. Izydor Modelski, 74, Polish Spy Who Defected, Dies," *New York Times*, September 28, 1962, 25; Korowicz, *I Escaped to Speak for the Enslaved*, 103–112; Łukasiewicz, *Przesłuchania generała Modelskiego*, 413–496. See the section titled "Sources and Bibliography."

involved with Szarkiewicz, who regularly updated him on the progress of his investigation into the Mikiciński affair.

Our knowledge of the subsequent fate of the Polish citizens around Mikiciński from the outbreak of war until his abduction in Istanbul in January 1941 is much patchier. Samson's partner/rival from Romania, Viktor Kutten, and his associates Bronisław Stefanowski-Syrokomla and Stanisław Kąsinowski never came before a British or a Polish judge. Like many other dangerous aliens, they remained in indefinite internment in Palestine until the end of the war. According to the Brooklyn report, the Polish government-in-exile had sanctioned this confinement. In reality, however, their continued detention was the result of Kot's personal intervention, who likely saw it as a means of getting back at Kutten for incriminating Mikiciński while under interrogation in Palestine.[17] Only in early March 1945 did Kutten and company's friends and acquaintances decide to lobby for their release and made the appropriate appeals to the British and the exiled Polish authorities in Palestine and the UK. The letter Stefanowski-Syrokomla's colleagues mailed to the Polish foreign minister, via the Union of Polish Journalists, ends with the following sentence:

> As the Polish legal code does not allow for the indefinite detention of a citizen of the country without trial or verdict, we deem it our duty to demand that the authorities immediately put a stop to this abnormal situation.[18]

At the end of the month, forced by public pressure, the exiled Polish Interior Ministry admitted to its British colleagues that, over the past two years, it had not received any new information that might have led to a breakthrough in their investigation of Kutten's affair.[19] The British reply to this confession is unknown to us, but subsequent events indicate that London instructed the Poles to speed up their release of Kutten, Stefanowski-Syrokomla, and Kąsinowski. Some three weeks later, on April 12, Viktor Kutten was transferred from the prison hospital where he had been held for some time to the British Wilhelmina camp near the city of Lydda (now Lod). This transfer led to a marked improvement in

---

17 An undated report titled "Mikiciński Samson," JPIA, Archiwum Osobowe, NZ 154, Sygn. 658.
18 Members of the Union of Polish Journalists to the Polish Foreign Minister in Exile, March 8, 1945, HIA, 800/42/0/-/325 Folder 2, Scan 000325.
19 A. Tarnowski from the Polish Foreign Office to the British Embassy at the Polish government-in-exile, March 20, 1945, HIA, 800/42/0/-/325 Folder 2, Scan 000323.

his physical condition.[20] On April 24, the British Foreign Office contacted its Polish counterpart with an insistent request to ask the Polish Interior Ministry to speed up their decision on the release of the Latrun inmates.[21] On May 5, Polish general Marian Kukiel decreed that "in light of changing circumstances, there is no longer any need to hold Kutten, Stefanowski-Syrokomla, and Kąsinowski in detention;"[22] finally, on May 24, the Polish consul in Jerusalem, Zdzisław Szczerbiński, telegraphed his superiors in London that Kutten, Stefanowski-Syrokomla, and Kąsinowski had been released.[23] The subsequent fate of the three men is, as of yet, lost to history. However, a few references to Bronisław Stefanowski-Syrokomla exist: he and his family may have remained in Palestine (and, later, in the new State of Israel) until 1950, whereupon he moved to Australia; he supposedly died there in 1996, at the age of eighty-nine.[24]

The Polish Foreign Office continued to insist that Kutten and his comrades had been guilty of treason even after their release. According to a reply telegram sent to Consul Szczerbiński from London, Kutten was acting in Bucharest at the behest of both the Gestapo and the Abwehr, and the Polish government-in-exile agreed to release him and his accomplices only under pressure from the British, including the High Commissioner for Palestine.[25]

Relatedly, in the spring of 1945, the Dwójka continued for some reason to search for Mikiciński's and Kutten's partners in crime among the Polish refugees stranded in Bucharest and Istanbul during the war. Thus, a report submitted to the Polish cabinet in exile, apparently derived from Dwójka reports, when discussing the activities of the Provisional Government in Warsaw noted that Henryk Bydgoszcz, a renowned Polish cinematographer from the interwar period and an alleged candidate for a post in Communist Poland, had been

---

20 The Polish Consul in Jerusalem to Minister Kuźniarz in London, code cable, April 12, 1945, HIA, 800/42/0/-/325 Folder 2, Scan 000319.
21 The British Embassy at the Polish government-in-exile in London to the Polish Foreign Office, an untitled reminder of the British request from April 24, 1945, and a demand to speed up the decision about the release of Kutten, Stefanowski-Syrokomla, and Kąsinowski, May 15, 1945, HIA, 800/42/0/-/325 Folder 2, Scan 000303.
22 A document signed by Kukiel, "Viktor Kutten and Comrades—Information," May 5, 1945, HIA, 800/42/0/-/325 Folder 2, Scan 000308.
23 Szczerbiński, the Polish Consul in Jerusalem, to the Polish Foreign Office in London, an untitled telegram, May 24, 1945, HIA, 800/42/0/-/325 Folder 2, Scan 000296.
24 "Bronislaw Stefanowski Syrokomla"; Lee, "Obituary."
25 The Polish Foreign Minister in London to Polish Consul Szczerbiński in Jerusalem, regarding the release of Kutten, Stefanowski, and Kąsinowski, May 24, 1945, HIA, 800/42/0/-/325 Folder 2, Scans 000299-000300.

Mikiciński's confidant in the Romanian capital from 1939 to 1941.[26] In reality, none of the Polish or British documents dealing with Mikiciński or Kutten available to us mention Bydgoszcz by name. Romanian authorities arrested him at the very end of the war and deported him to Poland, where he was imprisoned until July 1946. He went on to spend the last twenty-five years of his life as a seller of medicinal herbs in Kraków.[27] The reason the exiled Polish secret service came to suspect him of collaboration with the Polish Communists and went so far as to portray him as a partner in Mikiciński's imaginary crimes remains a mystery to this day.

Another man to suffer grievously because of the Mikiciński affair was Stanisław Schwarzstein, the Polish citizen regarded as Mikiciński's right-hand man in Istanbul. As the attentive reader may recall, his arrest by Turkish police in late 1940 or early 1941 was a ploy likely by Szarkiewicz and the British to establish personal contact with his boss, Mikiciński. According to the Polish documents, the Turks released Schwarzstein after Mikiciński disappeared, and he immediately left Turkey to join his brother Adam in Buenos Aires through British-controlled Karachi. There, local colonial authorities detained and summarily imprisoned him in the Dehradun jail in northern India, notorious for its terrible conditions. The official cause of Schwarzstein's arrest was his connection to the Kutten affair—in other words, his imaginary collaboration with the Nazi enemy.[28]

In late 1944, when the Dwójka finally took an interest in Schwarzstein's fate, they found out he was still locked up in Indian jail, in a cellblock reserved for Germans, Austrians, and Italians, some bona fide Nazis and Fascists. Furthermore, it transpired that Schwarzstein had been arrested in Karachi in 1941 at the request of the Polish War Ministry (meaning the Dwójka itself), probably at Szarkiewicz's instigation. Adam Schwarzstein, who had no inkling of the causes of the misfortune that had befallen his brother, repeatedly petitioned the Polish embassy in Buenos Aires to have Stanisław released.[29] We do not know if the two brothers ever got to meet in Argentina or elsewhere.

---

26 "The Policies of the 'Provisional Government,' Which Is Acting at the Behest of Moscow," top secret, March 3, 1945, PISM, PRM. 173/5, 93.
27 Sołtysik, *Szumowiny Kinematografii*, 116–121.
28 A notification by the Polish representative in Bombay, B. Weidemeier, about Schwarzstein's arrest, April 18, 1941, HIA, 800/42/0/-/325 Folder 2, Scan 000290.
29 A query by Consul General Karol Poznański to the Polish Foreign Office in London regarding the fate of Stanisław Schwarzstein, November 24, 1944, HIA, 800/42/0/-/325 Folder 2, Scan 000295; a report by Colonel Miniewski, head of the Intelligence Department at the Headquarters of the Ministry of National Defense, titled "Stanisław Schwarzstein—Information," December 9, 1944, HIA, 800/42/0/-/325 Folder 2, Scan 000292.

The Desperate Search for a Polish Quisling

None of this book's sources contain any information about the fate of Samson Mikiciński's patrons/curators, Scholz and Nobis, besides a statement that Major Fabian, aka Scholz, passed away in Breslau in 1944.[30] The same is true of agents Volokhov and Bobajewski, who had been in close contact with Mikiciński in 1939–40. In the autumn of 1945, Soviet intelligence reported the arrest of a forty-five-year-old man named Volokhov in Western Ukraine. Prior to the Nazi invasion of the USSR, this Volokhov had been an agent for both the Germans and the Soviets; after June of 1941, he worked as a resident agent for German military counterintelligence (i.e., the same Department III of the Abwehr in which Scholz served) in occupied Lviv.[31] Is this the same Volokhov who had been Mikiciński's partner in occupied Warsaw, working under the auspices of the Breslau branch of the Abwehr in 1939–40? This is not clear, and we are unlikely to ever settle the question.

As for Scholz, the Polish historian Roman Buczek claims that the high-ranking Abwehr officer did not fall "hook, line, and sinker" for the Turkish press reports about Mikiciński's "mysterious disappearance" and "murder." To make certain that Samson was truly no longer available for cooperation, Scholz dispatched his Russian agent, Feodor Bobajewski, to Bucharest, Sofia, and Istanbul to look for him. When Bobajewski's search concluded several months later, he reported that the British had smuggled Mikiciński out of Turkey and shipped him to Cairo, where he was murdered. Scholz refused to believe the enemy would liquidate so valuable a prisoner on such short notice and dispatched to Turkey another envoy, Leonid Volokhov. The Ukrainian managed to establish secret contact with a certain employee of the Polish consulate and obtain valuable information about the activities of the Dwójka. However, the conclusion Volokhov reached proved equally disappointing for Scholz: the British had indeed captured Mikiciński and, therefore, he was no longer available for dealings with the Germans. The nature of those dealings was allegedly disclosed to the British by another Abwehr agent, the Polish citizen Ryszard Mańczyński. In February 1942, he too went to Turkey to find out what had happened to Samson, but, according to Buczek, immediately surrendered to the British. His interrogations revealed that Abwehr officers in Breslau were

---

30 Bębnik, *Sokoły kapitana Ebbinghausa*, 489.
31 Ivan Grushetsky, First Secretary of the Lviv Regional Committee of the Communist Party of Ukraine, to Nikita Khrushchev, First Secretary of the Central Committee of the Communist Party of Ukraine, November 23, 1945, top secret, USHMM, RG-31.026M.0057.00001099.

chiefly interested in Mikiciński as a unique source of income and pining for the salad days of their lucrative, common enterprise. Scholz was apparently the only one with real aspirations to turn Mikiciński into his super-agent in the Middle East—by early 1942, just a pipe dream.[32]

Since Buczek did not mention his sources, we cannot assess how reliable his account of Scholz's yearlong search for Mikiciński is. If his information is accurate, then it is quite possible that Scholz's true aim was reopening channels of negotiation with the Poles, a goal about which a low-ranking agent like Mańczyński could have had no inkling. The attentive reader will recall that Mikiciński played a key role in maintaining those channels and had even contacted von Papen, the German ambassador to Turkey, to do so. Undoubtedly, his sudden disappearance from the Turkish arena in January 1941 dealt a major blow to the fledgling Polish-German relationships. As soon as it became clear that there was no hope of his return, the Germans began to look for other ways of moving their relationship with the Poles forward. Quite possibly, Berlin's decision to explore alternative channels of communication also stemmed from their heightened suspicions of the Kotowcy after Mikiciński's arrest and Kot's transfer from the European geopolitical arena to Soviet Russia.

Shortly after severing ties with Kot, in May–June 1941, the Germans showed some indication of trying to improve their relations with the occupied Polish population. On June 15, the Polish ambassador to the Vatican, Kazimierz Papée, reported to his superiors in London that, according to information that had reached the Holy See, the Germans were preparing for some kind of activity in Soviet territory and changing their policy vis-à-vis the Poles. "It seems that the political and religious persecution has become less acute [now]," noted the diplomat.[33] Some two months later, on August 18, Papée informed headquarters that following their invasion of the USSR, the Germans had brought former Polish premier Kazimierz Bartel to Berlin for negotiations. Bartel's Nazi hosts proposed establishing of a pro-German puppet government in Poland, with him at the head. After Bartel refused, these nameless Nazi doves of peace apparently

---

32 Buczek, *Człowiek do złotych interesów*, 185–187. Buczek's claim that Scholz and his people learned of Samson's abduction by the British is sharply at odds with the assertion by Scholz's former factotum and driver, Arthur Hermann, who told his American interrogators that Mikiciński had escaped to Turkey thanks to the money of the wealthy Polish Jews he had rescued, and then relocated to the USA, where his mother lived in Chicago. See: CI Consolidated Interrogation Report No. 13, 10 in Mendelsohn, *The Final Solution*. In all likelihood, this is yet another example of Hermann's aforementioned incompetence in all aspects of the Mikiciński affair.

33 The Polish Ambassador to the Vatican, Kazimierz Papée, to the Polish Foreign Office in London, untitled code cable no. 107, June 15, 1941, USHMM, RG-59.036, A-12-53-37P_0076.

made the same offer to Adam Ronikier, a Polish aristocrat and conservative politician, but he too rejected the possibility of becoming a quisling.[34]

The Germans made another diplomatic overture of this kind a year later in the summer and autumn of 1942, at the peak of the German advance in North Africa and Russia, and immediately after the Japanese and Franz von Papen made a failed joint attempt to mediate between Berlin and Moscow. (The two capitals even exchanged views on Poland's fate despite being at war with one another.)[35] In early July that year, the Polish ambassador to the Vatican (the aforementioned Papée) warned his bosses in London that the Nazis were trying to set up a pro-German political faction in Poland and had even called upon the Italians, who enjoyed an excellent relationship with the Polish diaspora, to help them achieve this goal. Italian foreign minister Count Ciano and his representative in Madrid contacted Polish politicians and urged them to agree to establish a Polish-Italian-German alliance, invoking the so-called secret Soviet-British agreement to turn over eastern Polish lands to the Bolsheviks.[36]

And indeed, at the end of July, apparently following the contacts reported by Papée, a high-ranking representative of the Reich Security Main Office named Joachim Dömling arrived in Warsaw. Dömling introduced himself to the Poles as the adjutant of Heinrich Himmler, head of the SS and the Gestapo. The purpose of his visit was to meet with the leaders of Miecz i Pług (or Sword and Plow), a local, clandestine, Christian-nationalist organization. Established in October 1939 shortly after the fall of Poland, Miecz i Pług billed itself as anti-British and anti-Soviet; advocated for the creation of a Slavic empire in Eastern Europe;[37] competed politically and militarily with the Polish underground supporting the government-in-exile; and (most crucially in this context) established a working

---

34 The Polish Ambassador to the Vatican, Kazimierz Papée, to the Polish Foreign Office in London, untitled code cable no. 162, "News from the Homeland," August 18, 1941, USHMM, RG-59.036, A-12-53-37P_0085; see also: Zychowicz, *Opcja niemiecka*, 98.
35 Information about these contacts was obtained by the Polish ambassador to the Vatican from several unconnected sources. See: the Polish Foreign Office in London to the Polish President, Chairman of the Council of Ministers, and his Deputy, an untitled report based on telegram no. 139 from the Vatican, May 18, 1942, USHMM, RG-59.036, A-12-53-37P_0186; the Polish Foreign Office in London to the Polish President, Chairman of the Council of Ministers, and his Deputy, an untitled report based on telegram no. 156 from the Vatican, May 23, 1942, USHMM, RG-59.036, A-12-53-37P_0191.
36 The Polish Ambassador to the Vatican, Kazimierz Papée, to the Polish Foreign Office in London, untitled code cable no. 196, July 8, 1942, USHMM, RG-59.036, A-12-53-37P_0198.
37 See on the dissemination of the idea of the "Slavic empire" in occupied Warsaw as early as December 1941: Reichssicherheitshauptamt, Amt IV, Meldung wichtiger staatspolizeilicher Ereignisse, Nr. 10, vom 22. Dezember 1941, YVA, Record group: O.53-Ludwigsburg, USSR Collection, File No. 130.

relationship with the Gestapo by 1942. As part of this relationship, the members of Miecz i Pług (known as Mieczowcy) received weapons and ammunition from the Germans and used them against the Communist partisans from the east. They refrained from attacking the occupiers, enjoyed immunity from the Gestapo raids, and were even granted relative freedom of movement within the boundaries of the Generalgouvernement. Dömling's visit was the logical continuation of this cordial relationship. His meeting with the Mieczowcy took place in a Warsaw restaurant under heavy guard by local Gestapo agents. There, they agreed that Miecz i Pług leadership, with German assistance, would send a special delegate to London to secure an audience with the leader of the pro-Sanation camp, General Kazimierz Sosnkowski, and offer him the opportunity to return to Poland to establish a Polish-German alliance against Moscow.[38]

The plan swung into action in the first days of September 1942 with the help the Radom Gestapo's leader, Paul Fuchs, one of the top Nazi experts on combating clandestine organizations and an ardent advocate of the German-Polish alliance. Fuchs permitted an emissary of Miecz i Pług to leave the GG and cross the German-Swiss border, easing his travel with Gestapo protection.[39] We do not know whether this delegate of the Polish nationalists ever reached London and met with Sosnkowski, but even if he did, the scheme was a complete fiasco: Sosnkowski remained in Britain, and after the death of his political rival, General Sikorski, he was appointed supreme commander of the Polish army in exile. Fuch's next attempt to send an emissary to Palestine also failed. In July 1943, a Polish-speaking German officer left the GG, arrived in Turkey, and, posing as a businessman, tried to cross illegally into neighboring Syria. After being intercepted by the vigilant British, he was handed over to SIME in Cairo, where he was subjected to the "harsh interrogations" of German-speaking investigators.[40] Edward Szarkiewicz may have been among them, since he was stationed in Cairo and specialized in interrogating enemy spies.

These failures may have influenced the decision by the Nazi leadership to cut off contact with Miecz i Pług in the summer of 1943. A little later, three of its leaders were assassinated, allegedly by the Polish national underground. Latter-day historians of the Polish resistance have theorized that a Soviet agent who had infiltrated the leadership of the Mieczowcy had carried out this action.[41] However, in light of the Gestapo's intense involvement with this nationalist

---

38 Wilamowski, *Honor, Zdrada, Kaźń*; Zychowicz, *Opcja niemiecka*, 204–209.
39 Rodak, "Paul Fuchs"; Zychowicz, *Opcja niemiecka*, 208, 212–217.
40 Rodak, ibid.
41 Zychowicz, *Opcja niemiecka*, 209–211.

organization, it is equally plausible to assume that the Germans controlled the Soviet agent and used him to eliminate would-be allies who had failed to deliver the goods, all the more likely since Polish nationalists were then becoming a significant political and military threat to the occupying authorities.

Despite its failed attempts to meet with Sosnkowski and Anders, Berlin did not abandon hopes of finding willing partners among the Poles. The search for a Polish quisling became even more intense after the catastrophic defeats of the Wehrmacht on the Eastern Front in the spring and summer of 1943 and the approach of the Red Army to the borders of the GG. At this time, Soviet and Polish underground intelligence began to report on a large-scale evacuation of civilian institutions from occupied Soviet territories, and even (as the Home Army claimed) on Russia's alleged plans to continue its triumphant march through Poland into Germany.[42] The Germans tried to convince the Poles that life under Stalin would be much tougher than life under Hitler, so their only hope was to establish a military-political alliance with the Third Reich.[43]

Some Polish circles greeted Germany's attitude shift with enthusiasm. Back in the spring of 1943, Vatican representatives in the GG had reported on the growing local discontent with Britain's willingness to let the USSR annex eastern Polish lands;[44] and the Italian press covered the outpouring of Polish anger at the Katyn affair and support for accepting a German alliance, with Italy acting as mediator.[45] In May and June of that same year, Polish military intelligence informed the British Ministry of Defense that Mussolini had met with Hitler and urged him to improve the behavior of the Germans in occupied Poland; and

---

42 Falkov, *Meragle ha-ye'arot*, 276–280; Bułhak, Raport szefa oddziału II KG AK, 15–77; Chief of Staff of the Supreme Commander Major General Stanisław Kopański, to the President and Chairman of the Council of Ministers of the Polish Republic. An untitled, top secret report about the beginning of the German evacuation from Lviv, October 21, 1943, USHMM, RG-59.043, A-48-4-B1_0024; Chief of Staff of the Supreme Commander Major General Stanisław Kopański, to the President, Chairman of the Council of Ministers, and Interior Minister of the Polish Republic. An untitled, top secret report about the beginning of the German evacuation from Vilnius, October 26, 1943, USHMM, RG-59.043, A-48-4-B1_0026.
43 See one of the most vivid examples of this propaganda line in an interview with Hans Frank by the Nazi newspaper *Deutsche Allgemeine Zeitung* from October 29, 1944: "Statement by Frank on Polish-German Relations (according to "News Digest" no. 1597)," a document with no information about the author or the recipient, November 8, 1944, USHMM, RG-59.036, A-12-73-5_0167.
44 The Polish Foreign Office to the President, Prime Minister, and Foreign Minister of the Polish Republic, an untitled secret report based on telegram no. 105 from the Polish Ambassador to the Vatican, April 6, 1943, USHMM, RG-59.036, A-12-53-38DD_0028.
45 The Polish Foreign Office to the President, Prime Minister, and Foreign Minister of the Polish Republic, an untitled secret report based on telegram no. 138 from the Polish ambassador to the Vatican, April 30, 1943, USHMM, RG-59.036, A-12-53-38DD_0035.

that at a conference of military attachés of the Axis powers in Stockholm, Italian officers had criticized Germany's anti-Polish policies, claiming that Berlin's refusal to reestablish a powerful Polish state frightened Europe's other Slavic nations and pushed them into the Stalin's arms.[46]

The curious headline "Hitler Is Looking For Polish Puppets" appeared in late March 1943 in the Jerusalem-based *Palestine Post*. The story spoke of German plans to establish a pliable government in occupied Poland and a "Polish Legion" that would join the armed struggle against Bolshevist Russia. The Palestine newspaper named Alfred Wysocki—a Polish lawyer and diplomat who had served as ambassador to Berlin and Rome—as a possible head of the future puppet cabinet.[47] According to modern Polish historians, Wysocki made a good impression on the Führer, and in 1941, he met with Nazi governor-general Hans Frank to discuss a possible modus vivendi between the German occupiers and the Poles.[48] The *Palestine Post* claimed that the appointment of the former ambassador to the post of Polish quisling was already a done deal. The Polish consulate in Jerusalem immediately denied these allegations, going so far as to assert that the article was a Soviet provocation aimed at tarring all Poles as Nazi collaborators.[49]

The following weeks and months would prove the Polish diplomats right. Wysocki was not to be appointed to any post in the GG. However the question of the Polish Legion arose again in early June of 1943, when sources within Italian Fascist leadership informed the Polish embassy to the Vatican that the Germans had launched a campaign to recruit legionnaires from concentration camp inmates, including several captive Polish generals. The Italian sources emphasized that Frank was pushing the creation of a pro-German Polish government;

---

46 "Information about the attitudes of the 'Axis' countries to Poland," May 16, 1943, USHMM, RG-59.045, A-XII-3-21_0210; the War Ministry, the Minister's Office, and the Political Department to the Polish Foreign Office, an untitled report about information received from Stockholm, June 30, 1943, USHMM, RG-59.045, A-XII-3-21_0057.

47 The Polish Foreign Office to the Chairman of the Council of Ministers and the Minister of Information and Documentation of the Polish Republic, an untitled secret report based on telegram no. 188 from the Polish consulate general in Jerusalem, March 29, 1943, USHMM, RG-59.036, A-12-53-38L_0014.

48 Zychowicz, *Opcja niemiecka*, 103–105; see also a Polish notice from 1940, where Wysocki is referred to as one of the few Poles who have met with Frank: a "brief notice" sent by Mr. Falterow at the behest/recommendation of Mr. Wachomak (?) through Ms. Elina Zaleska, May 1, 1940, USHMM, RG-59.047, KOL-25-10-A_161.

49 The Polish Foreign Office to the Chairman of the Council of Ministers and the Minister of Information and Documentation of the Polish Republic, an untitled secret report based on telegram no. 188 from the Polish consulate general in Jerusalem, March 29, 1943, USHMM, RG-59.036, A-12-53-38L_0014.

allegedly, his activities in this area were not coordinated with von Ribbentrop, yet fully endorsed by Hitler, who had changed his mind about the Poles.[50]

Moreover, in the autumn of 1943, the Lviv Regional Office of the NKGB published a special report on Polish-German contact intended for Nikita Khrushchev, then first secretary of the Communist Party of Ukraine. Their source was a German, Robert Evgen'evich Rupp, born in 1896. In June 1941, after the Nazis invaded the USSR, Rupp stayed in Lviv. Acting on his own initiative, he reached out to the local branch of the security service and became a close advisor to the chief in charge of GG and Galicia. In July 1944, Rupp fled with the retreating occupiers and, a year later, was arrested in Prague by Soviet military counterintelligence (SMERSH). In his interrogation, the arrestee claimed that, back in November 1942 (i.e., after the Radom Gestapo had dispatched its agent to establish contact with Sosnkowski), his patron had held a "personal consultation" with Prince Karl Radziwiłł to reorient the focus of the Polish national underground from the German occupying authorities to the "Soviet threat."[51]

In addition, Rupp informed the Soviets, the Germans and the Poles had held two rounds of talks in Lviv in September and October 1943. In the first, special delegate Franz von Papen, accompanied by Rupp and the head of the local Gestapo, met with members of the Polish intelligentsia from Lviv. Their discussion revolved around the possibility of reestablishing an independent Poland and creating a Polish government in Kraków to be led by former premier Leon Kozłowski. The Poles sent delegates from the Home Army to the second round of talks, allegedly agreeing to cease all anti-German activity and focus on the Russians. According to the 1943 report the NKGB submitted to Khrushchev, Rupp's testimony about von Papen's participation was corroborated by the information given by another arrestee, an ethnic Pole named Kazimierz Romaszkan.[52]

It is unclear how far we should trust this report in light of its blatant errors. The member of the Radziwiłł family whom the SD chief allegedly consulted

---

50 The Polish Foreign Office to the President, Prime Minister, Deputy Prime Minister, and Minister of Information and Documentation of the Polish Republic, an untitled secret report based on telegram no. 205 from the Polish Ambassador to the Vatican, June 8, 1943, USHMM, RG-59.036, A-12-53-38DD_0056; see also on Frank's appeals to Hitler, from June 1943 on, to soften the attitude of the occupying authorities, and of Himmler's subordinates in particular, to the Polish population: Noakes and Pridham, *Nazism*, 968–974.

51 Ivan Grushetsky, First Secretary of the Lviv Regional Committee of the Communist Party of Ukraine, to Nikita Khrushchev, First Secretary of the Central Committee of the Communist Party of Ukraine, November 23, 1945, top secret, USHMM, RG-31.0 26M.0057.00001093-00001101.

52 Ibid.

was probably not Prince Karl Radziwiłł, but Prince Janusz Radziwiłł, who had indeed contacted the Germans during the early period of the occupation; and the assertion that the Home Army ceased all anti-German activity in the autumn of 1943 is manifestly false. If the report is at least partially true, and von Papen—Mikiciński's former contact in the German administration—did indeed travel to Lviv to discuss reestablishing an independent Poland with Kraków as its capital, it was just another diplomatic fiasco. According to recent Polish historical studies, Leon Kozłowski—who had stayed behind in Poland in September 1939, was arrested by Soviet authorities, escaped into the territory of the GG, and was subsequently taken to Berlin to discuss the future of his country—was ultimately rejected by the Nazis as the Polish quisling. Completely forgotten by the Germans and his own people, he settled in Berlin and died in an Allied air raid in May of 1944.[53]

As for Franz von Papen, his expulsion by the Turks in August 1944, as a gesture from Ankara toward the Allies, brought his career in the German civil service to an abrupt end. He returned to his homeland at the height of the bloody purge that started after a failed attempt on Hitler's life and retired quietly to his estate in western Germany, where he was arrested by American occupation authorities in April, 1945. He was tried at Nuremberg for complicity in the Nazi crimes, acquitted, then convicted by a denazification court and released three years later, in 1949. For the next two decades until his death at eighty-nine, he busied himself writing articles, books, and memoirs about his life and times.[54]

In the nine months that passed between von Papen's (real or imagined) negotiations with the Home Army and the Warsaw Uprising on August 1, 1944, Hans Frank and other GG leaders contacted the commanders of the Home Army, the clergy, local political leaders, and even the Delegatura, the Polish government-in-exile's clandestine representation in the territory of occupied Poland. The Nazis, aware that the Red Army's advance toward the Third Reich's borders threatened their very existence, offered the Poles "good neighborly relations in a new socialist Europe," "a joint struggle against the common Bolshevist enemy," and other, similarly empty slogans aimed at preventing the opening of a "Polish front" in the German rear at the very moment the Wehrmacht needed desperately to hold back the Russian advance to the west. What's more, the

---

53 Zychowicz, *Opcja niemiecka*, 126–133.
54 Rolfs, *The Sorcerer's Apprentice*.

Germans actually urged the Poles to give up on the national uprising they were planning with full knowledge of German intelligence.[55]

But the Nazi's secret diplomatic efforts were in vain, since at this stage of the war, the vast majority of Poles at home or in exile were against any kind of agreement with the Third Reich.[56] The Polish and the German sides would inflict heavy casualties upon one another right up until March 1945, when the last German occupiers were driven out of Poland for good. The Warsaw Uprising alone, which lasted some two months and ended in resounding defeat, claimed the lives of approximately 120,000 Polish soldiers and civilians, while German casualties totaled about ten thousand killed and wounded.[57] In a remarkable coincidence, one of the few buildings in downtown Warsaw that survived the uprising was the elegant house on 2 Frascati Street.[58] Although its famous occupant, the "Chilean diplomat" from the town of Boćki, did not survive the vagaries of war, the house is still intact and serves as a memorial for future generations of Warsaw and visitors to the Polish capital.

The Betrayers Betrayed

Another building to miraculously survive the ravages of war—in this case, the fires of the Blitz—was the former MI5 headquarters at 57–58 St. James Street. Photographs of wartime London show fully destroyed buildings on nearby Duke Street,[59] suggesting that Sir David Petrie's lair had only narrowly avoided a similar fate. Its survival may have been a matter of blind luck or of the inability of the Nazi intelligence to pinpoint its location for the Luftwaffe.

Petrie was similarly fortunate. He remained at the helm of the British state security apparatus for the last four years of the war and the first that followed it,

---

55 Zychowicz, *Opcja niemiecka*, 307–343; the Special Department of the Headquarters of the Supreme Command of the Polish Army in Exile to the President of the Polish Republic, "Sucking the Poles into the Anti-Bolshevist Front," March 27, 1944, USHMM, RG-59.043, A-48-4-B1_0052; the Special Department of the Headquarters of the Supreme Command of the Polish Army in Exile to the Supreme Commander, a demonstration of the contents of report no. 4 about the current situation, from April 12, 1944, received on April 30, 1944, May 1944, USHMM, RG-59.043, A-48-4-B1_0074; the Supreme Commander of the Polish Army in Exile, Lieutenant General Sosnkowski, to the President of the Polish Republic, a demonstration of the contents of report no. 15 about the current situation, from June 28, 1944, received on July 6, 1944, USHMM, RG-59.043, A-48-4-B1_0114.
56 Gąsiorowski, *Polityka niemiecka na ziemiach okupowanych*, 79.
57 Stachnik, "Ilu Niemców naprawdę zginęło"; Wieczorkiewicz, *Historia polityczna Polski*, 435.
58 Joachimczyk, "Fotografia z Powstania Warszawskiego."
59 "WW2—London under fire."

retiring only after Churchill left 10 Downing Street in the spring of 1946. His longevity was probably not an accident of history, but the result of his ability to navigate the tangled world of wartime British politics and security by constantly adapting to the changing domestic and international situation. A vivid example of Petrie's adaptability can be found in his unquestioning acceptance of Churchill's decision to disassociate from the Polish government-in-exile just after the end of the war. This change of course resulted in MI5 quickly and completely severing its relationship with its erstwhile strategic partners in the émigré Polish intelligence and counterintelligence community. The chiefs of MI6 and SOE did likewise.

Among the most severe consequences of this severance was the betrayal of the hundreds—or possibly even thousands—of Polish intelligence agents essential to the British victory, even those like Modelski and Szarkiewicz who had brought their own government to heel. Cut off from all British support, they had to fend for themselves now. Many dropped below the poverty line and left the UK in search of better lives in other countries, including Communist Poland.

Among those who lost everything overnight was Home Army intelligence chief Colonel Kazimierz Iranek-Osmecki, Szarkiewicz's former boss in Romania and the intelligence chief of the Home Army, who had probably also taken part in Mikiciński's interrogations in Palestine. The Germans imprisoned him at the end of the Warsaw Uprising. After surviving Nazi captivity, he arrived in London and found administrative work at the small neighborhood cinema Szarkiewicz ran, living out his remaining years in very modest circumstances.[60] In 1961, Szarkiewicz apparently no longer among the living, Iranek-Osmecki received an unexpected and highly tempting offer from the renowned British film producer Maurice J. Wilson to help turn the Mikiciński affair into a feature spy thriller. (Iranek-Osmecki's acquaintance, who mediated with Wilson on his behalf, told him he "could make a killing out of it.")[61] For some reason, the offer fell through, and Iranek-Osmecki missed the chance to improve his material circumstances.

An even more tragic victim of Britain's betrayal can be found in SOE operative Krystyna Skarbek-Granville. After pulling off a string of truly heroic operations in occupied Poland and France, she remained in the United Kingdom after the war. She received no recognition or financial support and was therefore forced to

---

60 Iranek-Osmecki, *Pułkownik Kazimierz Iranek-Osmecki*, 530–531; Jerzy Iranek-Osmecki, *Postscriptum II*, 538.

61 Fundacja Generał Elżbiety Zawackiej, Toruń, M-199/808 Pom., Witkowski Stanisław, Do Pana Pułkownika Dyplomowanego Kazimierza IRANKA-OSMECKIEGO, 42 Emperors Gate, LONDON S.W.7—ENGLAND, Alhambra, dn. 25.a. 61r, kpbc.umk.pl, Witkowski_Stanislaw_199_808_Pom.pdf, 127.

subsist on odd jobs while living in a hostel for the poor, operated under the auspices of the Polish Red Cross. She was ultimately stabbed to death by a stalker.[62]

General Mieczysław Słowikowski, who during the war was in charge of an intelligence network that played a major role in the 1943 liberation of North Africa, would later harshly criticize the British for betraying him and his colleagues. "A foreigner performing enormous and highly valuable services to this country will get nothing in return, except for some more or less shiny baubles," he complained in his memoirs.[63]

After David Petrie retired from MI5, the British were taught a painful lesson in realpolitik. In a Machiavellian world, countries, individuals, and organizations pursue their narrow interests to the exclusion of everything else and are willing to run roughshod over the principles of humanity, democracy, and liberalism, flouting national and international laws and conventions, breaking promises and oaths, and disregarding personal and collective obligations. This treachery becomes the norm and can easily boomerang against its culprit. In the British case, such a backclash coming seemingly out of nowhere was the highly unpleasant discovery that throughout the war against the Nazis, and for some time afterward, a Soviet spy ring made up of British citizens had been active within the local intelligence community and had managed to get their hands on the most zealously guarded national secrets. The emergence of this network, later known as the Cambridge Five, is often linked to the considerable popularity of Communist ideas in Britain in the 1930s and 1940s. However, any earnest attempt to come to grips with the historical context and direct causes of this phenomenon should consider the Machiavellian spirit that came to dominate British foreign policy before and during World War II. As the fate of Poland and its people demonstrates, the political leaders of the UK and the diplomats who did their bidding were prepared not only to sign treaties with the totalitarian regimes of Nazi Germany and the Soviet Union, but also to sacrifice countries and nations friendly to the British in order to appease those regimes. Likewise, the Cambridge Five betrayed not only their country, but their closest friends, turning their backs on the Western values of humanism, democracy, and liberalism. While these values were not always consistently applied within the UK, even less so in the vast expanses of the British Empire, they would greatly influence how British society developed in the postwar years.

The number five was appended to the name of the Cambridge ring retroactively in the early 1990s, when a Soviet intelligence operative who had defected

---

62 Koper, *Polskie piekiełko*, 424–427.
63 Ibid., 424.

to the West confirmed the involvement of MI6 veteran John Cairncross; until that moment, the ring had been known as the Cambridge Four. However, various persons in Britain and elsewhere have insisted that a much larger number of Englishmen spied on behalf of the Soviets. Among those named as "contenders" for the dubious title of Stalinist spy was none other than Baron Nathaniel Mayer Victor Rothschild. As a high-ranking MI5 officer, he had warmly endorsed Edward Szarkiewicz for a position at SIME in Cairo for his fruitful cooperation in foiling Soviet activities against Britain. The earliest suspicions against the baron surfaced in the 1950s. Shortly thereafter, it transpired that Rothschild had been on friendly terms with the future members of the Cambridge Five while studying at Cambridge University in the thirties, and had even secretly joined the British Communist Party. It was also alleged that, in 1934, Rothschild had been officially recruited by a Soviet intelligence officer operating illegally in Britain; and that later, after becoming a member of the House of Lords and an officer of the Security Service, Rothschild had supplied his Moscow handlers with extensive and highly useful information on matters of policy, diplomacy, and security.[64]

For decades, Rothschild attempted to defend his reputation, going so far as to commission a high-ranking MI5 veteran to prove his innocence in his memoirs.[65] Remarkably, he stayed in the House of Lords, maintained close ties with the British intelligence and counterintelligence community, served as a security advisor to several prime ministers, and held a number of key posts in the British establishment. Additionally, he managed several private commercial ventures, including the famous bank of the Rothschild family, and vigorously supported the young State of Israel.

Baron Nathaniel Mayer Victor Rothschild passed away in 1990, at the age of seventy-nine.[66] Four years later, the Australian historian and journalist Roland Perry published a monograph on the Cambridge Five putting forth a thesis backed by multiple sources, including interviews with Soviet intelligence veterans: Rothschild had facilitated the Soviet spy network's infiltration of the British security and intelligence apparatus and had personally delivered British state secrets to Moscow. Perry's evidence-based hypothesis aroused mixed reactions among his fellow historians in the UK and elsewhere, and so the

---

64 Lekarev, "Baron Viktor Rotshil'd"; Liubimov, *Shpiony*, 222–232; Wright, *Spycatcher*, 272–274.
65 See, for instance, about the aid allegedly rendered by Rothschild to MI5 in unmasking the members of the "Cambridge Five": ibid., 327–329.
66 Aldrich and Cormac, *The Black Door*, 287, 303, 356; Liubimov, *Shpiony*, 222–232; Wright, *Spycatcher*, 147–148.

question of Rothschild's connections with the Soviet intelligence community has remained open.[67]

Even the 2016 publication of the memoirs of the first chairman of the KGB failed to settle the question for good. Ivan Serov, who died in 1990, had allegedly concealed the memoirs in the wall of his garage; they were found by sheer chance many years later. The work contains the brief chapter "On V. Rothschild" that asserts Rothschild had been aware of the Cambridge Five's connections with Soviet intelligence. Serov also alleges that Rothschild used the spy ring to supply Moscow with information about the Palestine question and London's attitude toward a burgeoning Jewish state. Serov complains that Rothschild purposely distorted information for his own Zionist ends and severed his ties with the Russians after the establishment of the State of Israel: unlike many of his contemporaries in Britain and other Western countries who collaborated with Moscow out of solidarity with Communist ideals, Rothschild was just an opportunistic "fellow traveler"[68] willing to "play at spycraft" as long as it advanced the cause of Zionism.

So, was he a spy or not? Even if, as Serov claims, Rothschild managed to be "something in-between"—the tail wagging the Soviet dog—he still harmed Britain's national interests as outlined until 1948. Did he also manage to recruit Szarkiewicz to his cause? After all, Szarkiewicz had a proven track record of switching patrons and a keen insight into the contemporary situation in Palestine, making him an ideal source of information and agent of influence within SIME, this linchpin of British power in the Middle East. Such a scenario seems quite plausible. However, we are unlikely to have a definitive answer unless the equivalent of Serov's diary comes to light in the United Kingdom or Israel.

Keeping a Low Profile

Tucked away in the Neve Sha'anan neighborhood in south Tel Aviv, one of its oldest quarters, is a small, quiet street named after Akiva Eiger, head rabbi of the city of Posen (present-day Poznań) in Poland in the early nineteenth century. Regarded as one of the foremost Torah scholars of the modern era, his influence on Jewish religious legislation and judicial practice in Israel and all around the world remains considerable. Presently, most people who live on Eiger Street

---

67 Leitch, "Rotshild"; Perry, *The Fith Man*.
68 Serov, *Zapiski iz chemodana*.

and in the area that surrounds it are refugees and migrant workers from Africa and the Philippines. However, in the mid-twentieth century, this area housed the Jewish laborers who built Tel Aviv. Celebrated Israeli playwright, poet, and prose writer Hanoch Levin was born on Eiger Street and would go on to write about the unique atmosphere of the neighborhood where he grew up.[69]

Nowadays, nobody left in Tel Aviv (or anywhere else in Israel, for that matter) can recall that while little Levin was playing with his friends in the narrow Eiger Street, another Akiva Eiger—a direct descendant of his illustrious namesake—walked the city streets. Prior to World War II, he had gained a reputation in his native town of Zgierz, and far beyond it, as a prominent Zionist activist, an influential Polish industrialist, and the brother-in-law of one of the leaders of the Polish People's Party. However, by the early 1950s, the most remarkable thing about this man was the mystery of his deliverance from Nazi-occupied Poland in 1940: he was the same Karol Eiger who had managed to avoid certain death thanks to the intervention of Samson Mikiciński and the assistance of Nazi military intelligence officers.

Akiva Eiger, the youngest and most successful son of one of Zgierz's most renowned and wealthiest families, was named after his famous ancestor. His parents owned a large textile company called Eiger and Sirkis consisting of several garment factories serving the Russian and European markets. The head of the family, Moshe Zvi (or Moshel) was a God-fearing Jew with a secular academic education, an outstanding textile engineer, and a poet. He was also the darling of Zgierz's Jewish community, an open-handed philanthropist who financed both religious institutions and the Zionist movement. Under his influence, Akiva-Karol (born in 1890) became a Zionist activist in his twenties and founded sports and cultural clubs for local Jewish youth; meanwhile, he was head of the Jewish Bank, president of the Association of Jewish Industrialists. He was active in his native city, collaborating closely with his Polish and Germans neighbors.[70]

Throughout the 1920s and 1930s, right up to the outbreak of World War II, the young Eiger remained fully engaged with these manifold commitments. For some reason, he remained in Poland until September 1939. Shortly after the German occupation began, he and other distinguished residents of Zgierz were incarcerated in the Radogoszcz prison in Łódź. A total of about forty thousand people—Jews, Poles, and even some Germans classified as dangerous elements—passed through the gates of this terrible facility until it was destroyed

---

69 Yakobson, "Sivuv."
70 Fisher and Malchieli, *The Industrialist—the Poet*, 428–432.

in January 1945. Many of them were shot in a forest nearby.[71] Akiva's brother, Shlomo Salomon Eiger, was deported to the Warsaw Ghetto with his wife Charlotte; neither survived the war. Their sister, Rozalia Levenson-Eiger, was murdered in Auschwitz.[72]

Only one other sibling survived the war. Dorota, the second sister, had violated family traditions, religious precepts, and national principles when in 1923 she married Polish politician Zygmunt Graliński, then a young, successful lawyer. Right after the war broke out, the couple left Warsaw for Paris, where Graliński became deputy foreign minister in the Sikorski cabinet. (A year later, while he was sailing to Canada on a Polish diplomatic mission, a U-boat sunk his ship and killed him.)[73] After arriving in France, Dorota Gralińska established contact with Mikiciński and asked him to help extricate her brother Akiva-Karol from occupied Poland. Did she also intercede on behalf of the other Eigers? And if she did, why didn't Mikiciński rescue them? We will probably never know the answer.

Mikiciński's interrogation protocols and Buczek's book reveal that one of the Abwehr officers helping Mikiciński located Eiger in the Radogoszcz prison. After being released on some pretext, Eiger was taken to Breslau. From there, he and Mikiciński traveled to Bucharest via Berlin. (The lucky survivor did not go to France at once to thank his sister; perhaps he was shunning Dorota for her decision to marry a non-Jew.) Buczek reports that Eiger did a stint as Mikiciński's assistant and may even have interacted with Abwehr officer Erich Nobis. Shortly thereafter, he left for Cyprus.[74] What happened next? As stated above, in July 1941, a man with the same last name—probably Akiva-Karol—signed a petition drawn up in Tel Aviv by the public committee representing the victims of the Mikiciński affair, demanding the return of their property being held at the Polish consulate in Jerusalem. Essentially, this is the last fact of Eiger's fascinating life verifiable by archival sources. At the age of fifty-one, after decades of extensive business and public activities in his native Poland, he seemingly went off the grid.

A compendium of short biographies of prominent Jews in Zgierz (published in Israel between 1975 and 1986) attempts to shed some light on what happened to Eiger after he left Cyprus. The authors of Eiger's entry dispatch his release from a Nazi prison in one sentence: "He was miraculously able to sneak

---

71 "Radogoszcz. Police Prison."
72 Fisher and Malchieli, *The Industrialist—the Poet*, 428–432.
73 "Graliński Zygmunt."
74 Buczek, *Człowiek do złotych interesów*, 62.

outside and, after a series of dangerous escapades, reach Romania and Cyprus." Once in Cyprus, he volunteered to join Anders's Army and was assigned to the third Carpathian Riflemen Brigade, where he became a cultural-educational officer and moved to the Libyan city of Tobruk to fight against the Germans. Later, Eiger and his fellow servicemen were redeployed to Iraq via Palestine; he eventually returned to North Africa, then left for Italy to join the famous Battle of Monte Cassino as an intelligence officer.[75] The biography claims that Eiger greatly improved working conditions for his fellow Jews by fighting against antisemitism in the Polish military units, even managing to convince Polish supreme command to allow Jewish soldiers to restore their original Jewish names from the Polish ones they had adopted to avoid persecution.[76]

The biography concludes with the assertion that sometime around 1952, Eiger returned to the land of his forefathers and died in Israel about a year later, after a grave illness, at the age of sixty-three. From his hospital bed, he allegedly managed to send a letter to a group of Zgierz natives who had gathered at some unknown location to commemorate their relatives who had died in the Holocaust:

> I regret being unable to join you on this day of mourning for our murdered loved ones. However, my heart is with you . . . May this memorial ceremony bind us, the survivors, with the bonds of brotherhood and mutual aid. Be strong![77]

Quite obviously, this account is highly problematic: it draws on unknown sources, distorts well-known historical facts, and contradicts already established details of Eiger's life story. The first notable incongruity is the assertion that Eiger, born in 1890, joined the Polish army around age fifty. (After all, he must have left Romania and arrived in Cyprus at the time when the Polish embassy in Bucharest was closing down in the autumn of 1940.) Polish citizens of such advanced age without prior military training were not called to serve. As the attentive reader will recall, the forty-five-year-old Mikiciński could not be legally drafted into the army to be tried by a court martial.

The second significant incongruity is the reference to Cyprus as the place where Eiger was drafted into General Anders's Third Carpathian Riflemen Brigade. As far as we know, no Polish army units were stationed on that island,

---

75 See on the Battle of Monte Cassino: Brio, *Pol'skie muzy*, 59–63; McGilvray, *Anders's Army*, 115–130; Wieczorkiewicz, *Historia polityczna Polski*, 359–362.
76 Fisher and Weinstein, "Akiva (Karol) Eiger": 432–436.
77 Ibid.

and none of them recruited Polish citizens to their ranks there. Moreover, the Third Carpathian Riflemen Brigade did not actually exist. There was a real Polish unit called the Separate Carpathian Riflemen Brigade, formed in Syria in April 1940 and redeployed to Palestine two months later. In August 1941, it went to Tobruk, Libya, to fight under British leadership; in May 1942, they returned to Palestine to join with General Anders's troops arriving from the USSR to become the Third Carpathian Riflemen Division. When Eiger came to Cyprus in the autumn of 1940, he could not have possibly joined a non-existent brigade of the not-yet-born Anders's Army. And contrary to what this biography says, he could not have traveled directly from Cyprus to Tobruk, since in July 1941, he was almost certainly in Palestine, as shown by his signature on the aforementioned petition to the Polish government-in-exile.

A final incongruity is Eiger's alleged transfer from the ranks of the Carpathian Riflemen to the intelligence department of Anders's Army, and his subsequent intense efforts to defend its Jewish soldiers and officers. None of the available sources about Anders's Army mentions Akiva-Karol Eiger or his heroic exploits on behalf of the Jews.[78]

Setting aside these incongruities and blatant errors, the biography's biggest puzzle remains its laconic description of Eiger's miraculous escape from the Radogoszcz prison. Why did he conceal that his sister had interceded on his behalf and that he had received help from a Nazi officer? The answer to this question may be very simple: fear. Quite possibly, right up to his death in the early 1950s, Eiger feared that the real circumstances of his miraculous rescue would come to light: that an active Zionist, the scion of a revered Jewish religious dynasty, had evaded the Nazi murder machine that had swallowed millions, including many of his relatives and almost the entire Jewish community of Zgierz, with the help of a sister who had married outside the faith and the middleman she had hired to negotiate with the Nazis. Fear may also explain the fantastic story about the Third Carpathian Riflemen Brigade and Anders's Army: a stirring tale of fighting against Nazis and Polish antisemitism makes for an excellent smokescreen.

Many of the dozens if not hundreds of wealthy Jews Mikiciński helped escape from Austria, Germany, Poland, and Romania made similar efforts to obscure their pasts. It became even harder for them to tell the truth after August 1950, when the Israeli Knesset passed the Nazis and Nazi Collaborators (Punishment)

---

78 In an attempt to find references to the service of Akiva-Karol Eiger in Anders's Army, the author of this book made a thorough search of the document collections from the Sikorski Archive pertaining to the service of Jews in the Polish Army in Exile, see: USHMM, RG-59.044-59.045.

Law. At this time, the Israeli press was awash with stories about "Jews suspected of grave crimes against the Jewish people, who now live in the State of Israel," while upstanding citizens swamped the police and the justice system with reports about relatives, acquaintances, colleagues, neighbors, and others who had allegedly collaborated with the Nazis before moving to Israel.[79]

In 1952, Israeli public interest in collaboration peaked once more as a result of a scandal involving a doctor, Israel (Rudolf) Kastner, accused of collaborating with the Nazis in the last year of the war while trying to save Hungarian Jews from extermination. From 1954 to 1957, the citizens of the Jewish State were riveted to Kastner's unfolding trial, initially conducted at the Jerusalem District Court before moving to the Supreme Court of Israel. Kastner was assassinated in early 1957, before the court could reach a final verdict. He was posthumously acquitted, albeit by a slim majority of one vote. The decision to acquit aroused considerable public opposition, reflecting the Israeli's extremely negative views on contact between the Jewish leaders of occupied Europe and the Nazi authorities, even what that contact was motivated by legitimate concerns.[80] It seems that at this point in time, it was completely impossible for those Mikiciński rescued with the Nazi Abwehr to come clean about their pasts, even to their own families. These survivors, both in Israel and abroad, kept a low profile and remained tight-lipped until their deaths. We may wonder if they ever felt guilty about their decision to save their own lives through their wealth and useful connections.

Only Alfred Florin, the attorney from Haifa, went to the press when in January 1961, he demanded his share of Mikiciński's legacy. As stated above, Florin's revelations did not arouse any response, and the Israeli public would never learn whether his appeal to the Turks had any effect. There were more pressing issues at hand: on May 23, 1961, Israeli Premier David Ben-Gurion announced that Adolf Eichmann had been abducted from Argentina and brought to Israel. Shortly thereafter, Eichmann's historic trial began in Jerusalem, reviving the public debate about the collaboration of individual Jews with the Nazis.[81] Against this backdrop, Florin would have been wise to sink back into obscurity and avoid drawing scrutiny to the circumstances of his own evacuation from fascist Romania.

---

79 Levi, "Ha-edim ma'ashimim ve-dorshim": 95–118.
80 Segev, *Medina be-chol' mehir*, 505–506.
81 See on the assertions made during the trial, to the effect that, in many places, Jews made efforts to save at least part of their community from extermination by negotiating with the local police or the Nazi occupying authorities; furthermore, the Jewish negotiators would occasionally offer bribes to save only their own relatives and loved ones: Bach, "Machshavot": 6.

Afterword

A Perfect Tragedy of Imperfect Heroes

As Stanisław Jerzy Lec wrote, "He who has lived through a tragedy was not its hero." Lec, a veteran of the Polish Communist underground and partisan movements and a globally renowned philosopher, poet, and satirical writer, was awarded Poland's highest honor, Polonia Restituta, like Samson Mikiciński before him.[1]

The story told in this book is a capital-T Tragedy.

It is the tragedy of Poland, which fell to the onslaught of external forces, fought against a brutal occupation, was betrayed by foreign friends and comrades-in-arms, and forced to submit to the hated Moscow regime.

It is the tragedy of the Polish political and military elites (including the intelligence community) who had rebuilt themselves away from their crushed and occupied homeland and made an enormous contribution to liberating Continental Europe from the scourge of Nazism, but became mired in internecine feuds. Suppressed by their British allies, denied their dream of a triumphant return to their beloved Warsaw, these men and women were forced to fight, often in vain, for their collective and individual survival in the harsh postwar reality.

---

1 Quoted from: Brodsky, *On "September 1, 1939" by W. H. Auden*, 314.

It is the tragedy of Polish Jewry, which despite its heroic resistance, was almost annihilated by the Nazis, their local collaborators, and even some who fought against Nazism, including the Polish Communists.[2]

And, finally, it is the tragedy of two Polish Jews, Samson Mikiciński and Edward Szarkiewicz. Having left their ancestral religion and occupied homeland behind; having wandered the length and breadth of a European continent hurtling into the abyss of the most terrible war in human history; having joined rival factions of the Polish diaspora; having acted under the aegis of powers teetering on the brink of a clash, the two men finally came face-to-face in the Middle East in a duel that claimed one of their lives. Both would go down in their compatriots' collective memories as the embodiment of absolute evil.

What have we learned about this tragic pair? We can confidently say that Mikiciński deserves to be included in the pantheon of the most fascinating personalities of World War II. He was a typical transnational product of his era: a polyglot who could easily assimilate into different cultural milieus, assume and discard any persona at will, and cross war-torn Europe's political borders as though he was traveling around the twenty-first-century European Union. Mikiciński may also be regarded as the prototype for the modern Russian-Jewish oligarchs. Like them, he exploited the geopolitical and economic upheavals of his time and the suffering of his own people to amass enormous personal wealth; was on friendly terms with big shots on multiple continents; casually flouted national and international laws; and played fast and loose with human lives. Mikiciński's most brilliant operations—and his most controversial—were his rescue transactions. To ensure the success of this enterprise, he secured the cooperation of politicians, diplomats, intelligence officers, émigrés, and criminal bosses from various (and occasionally mutually hostile) countries. While he made these transactions for money (and sometimes quite a lot of it), he saved the lives of dozens, maybe even hundreds of people—and certainly would have saved many more if he had not been abducted from Istanbul in January 1941.

Was the price Samson paid for his extraordinary achievements his transformation into a Nazi spy and traitor to his homeland? In this book, I have shown that Polish counterintelligence officers and their British counterparts were unable to prove his supposed treason. The evidence they brought against him was wholly circumstantial and hence woefully inadequate to substantiate the allegations of betrayal. This circumstantial evidence includes Mikiciński's meetings with the

---

2   See the accusations of having massacred Polish Jews, which were leveled at Stefan Kilanowicz (AKA Grzegorz Korczyński), one of the most prominent commanders of the Polish Communist partisans: Gontarczyk, *Z genealogii elit PZPR*, 214–229.

high-ranking Abwehr officer from Breslau and vague indications of the latter's desire to turn Mikiciński into his super spy in the Middle East; Mikiciński's several trips to occupied Poland in the company of other German officers; his uncanny successes in evacuating people to France and Romania; and, finally, his dealings with the Kutten group and Bulgarian diplomats with suspected links to the Nazis.

All the evidence against Mikiciński is based on fragmentary facts taken out of context and often purposefully twisted, as well as on details from Abwehr driver Arthur Hermann's highly problematic testimony.[3] I have gone over each item of the "prosecution's case" and presented my own counterarguments. Hopefully, my readers have found them convincing. Among other things, I have described the indications of the possible geopolitical underpinnings of Samson's rescue transactions, including Admiral Wilhelm Canaris's personal involvement in at least one of them. I have shown that my protagonist made no attempt to keep his connections with his alleged Nazi handlers secret, and that at least some of these connections were purely businesslike in nature. I have adduced evidence of the full postwar rehabilitation of the Kutten group and the Bulgarians, who even went on to become heroes in their homeland. My investigation has shown that some of British intelligence officers held doubts about Mikiciński's betrayal and the damage he caused the Polish underground. Most crucially, I have been able to locate and present Mikiciński's personal card from the files of the Frankfurt Gestapo that describes him not as a German agent, but as a person with suspected ties to Western intelligence agencies. Thus, we can conclude with a great deal of confidence that all allegations of Mikiciński's Nazi espionage activities are utterly baseless.

Polish and British intelligence operatives should have investigated Mikiciński's connections with Soviet intelligence instead: his enviable financial situation at the time he left Russia for Germany in the early 1920s; his dealings with Soviet diplomats in Warsaw and with a pro-Soviet banker in Paris a decade later; and the possibility that his close associate in occupied Poland, Leonid Volokhov, had been connected to the NKVD before the war. Taken together, they may indicate a close, decades-long relationship with Soviet Russia and its intelligence agencies. It is unclear why this aspect of Mikiciński's biography was not scrutinized at the time, not even during his incarceration in Palestine. Polish and British counterintelligence operatives, Szarkiewicz in particular, could have been so fixated on the idea of getting their prisoner to confess he was a Nazi spy

---

3   See about Hermann and his postwar highly problematic testimony to the Americans in the Chapter 1 of this book.

that they elected to ignore any unrelated wrongdoings. More than eight decades after the fact, we cannot solve this mystery without access to the Soviet intelligence archives in Moscow, still closed to both Russian and foreign historians.

The same can be said of Samson's nemesis, Captain Edward Szarkiewicz. Even more amazingly, he managed to avoid a single background check, no matter how superficial, while being recruited by Polish and British counterintelligence. For this reason, we are currently unable to confirm or refute the allegations of his contemporary rivals and later Polish historians that before World War II, Szarkiewicz had spied for Germany, or maybe even Russia.

We know for certain that from a young age, Szarkiewicz dreamed of a big career. This was why he moved from Lviv to the Polish capital, was baptized, and tried to join the ranks of the Polish elite. His actions after the war broke out were the logical continuation of this strategy of self-advancement: by serving in Polish military counterintelligence, which had probably hired him because of his connections in the pro-Sanation camp, Szarkiewicz would be able to meet the right people among the exiled Polish political and military leadership. And indeed, a brilliant opportunity presented itself to curry favor with the British security bosses and General Izydor Modelski, whom the British were grooming to replace Sikorski. The name of that brilliant opportunity was Samson Mikiciński. Mikiciński's idiosyncratic personality and behavior made it easy for Szarkiewicz to paint him as the most dangerous Nazi spy while obscuring his own sources of information. Szarkiewicz then staged a truly theatrical abduction (described here in unprecedented detail) and orchestrated Mikiciński's transfer to Palestine for interrogation. When the prisoner persistently refused to admit his treason, Szarkiewicz apparently killed him outright and buried his body in the sands near Haifa. In this way, the Little Man with the grandiose ambitions was able to preserve his reputation—and his future career prospects—with the British.

That said, it is also possible that Szarkiewicz and his commander (and later close friend) Kazimierz Iranek-Osmecki were genuinely convinced that Mikiciński was a traitor. Undaunted by their failure to formally prove his guilt, they decided, in clear conscience, to liquidate him. We must not forget that these were the darkest days of the war and the brutal occupation of Poland. Iranek-Osmecki and his colleagues in the Polish underground would unhesitatingly eliminate their compatriots by the sackful for far slighter offenses than the charges brought against Mikiciński.

A much more perplexing mystery in the present context is why the British sanctioned the liquidation (or at minimum, refrained from reacting to it) despite their full awareness that no proof of Mikiciński's Nazi loyalties existed, to say nothing of the lack of evidence of any direct or indirect damage he caused the security of the United Kingdom or the British Empire. It is possible that the British were desperate to close the channel of negotiations Mikiciński had opened between Polish deputy prime minister Stanisław Kot and high-ranking Nazi diplomats, the existence of which Mikiciński confirmed in his interrogation. Needless to say, Churchill's government could not have been pleased by this news. Kot's defection (to say nothing of Sikorski's) from the British Isles and the creation of a pro-German government in Warsaw would have dealt a serious blow to the legitimacy of the war effort in the eyes of British and the world. After all, defending Poland and reestablishing its sovereignty were among the weightiest arguments London used to justify declaring war on Germany, and after France fell in the summer of 1940, its decision to see the war to the bitter end. If the British consented to Mikiciński's assassination (and possibly even encouraged it) for geopolitical reasons, then it stands to reason that Churchill was involved in sealing Mikiciński's fate. However, the reader should keep in mind that this is merely a hypothesis that needs to be substantiated with a thorough analysis of the relevant archival materials if and when such materials come to light.

Szarkiewicz's success in Palestine became a springboard for his counterintelligence career. My discovery of this fact is a significant achievement of my research. The historians and journalists who have previously tackled the Mikiciński affair did not bother to reconstruct Szarkiewicz's life trajectory after the death of his victim. My attempt has yielded a stunning new finding in the existence of a previously unknown conspiracy: MI5, Modelski, and Szarkiewicz carried out a plot to establish control over Polish military counterintelligence, and through it, all Polish armed forces from the British Isles to the Middle East. As the conspirators' enthusiasm reached a fever pitch, they decided to appoint the ambitious Modelski as head of the Polish War Ministry, instead of Sikorski. The first stage of this plan turned the Little Man into the big man of the Polish military and intelligence apparatus, an éminence grise of sorts. For several months in the spring and summer of 1942, he was the arbiter of the fate of the whole Polish army in exile. Thus, according to an archival testimony I brought to light, Szarkiewicz supplied MI5 with a legitimate professional reason to deny Sikorski's request to station Anders's Army in Britain. This refusal seems to have been part and parcel of Britain's general effort to weaken the increasingly intractable Sikorski's influence on Polish émigré circles, especially the Polish military units that fought under British leadership.

However, neither Szarkiewicz nor Modelski (who had already envisioned his rise to the summit of the exiled Polish military Olympus under British auspices) had any inkling that London was playing bridge, as was its wont, while they themselves could barely play poker. And, in this British game, Modelski, loathed by many Polish soldiers and officers, seems to have played a supporting role. If Stalin had not allowed Anders to arrive in the Middle East at the head of a large Polish military contingent, Modelski was likely to have replaced Sikorski and taken center stage. However, fate (and Stalin) decreed otherwise, and the British were able to create a military-political counterweight to the Sikorski government within the Polish diaspora, far from the British Isles. Therefore, Modelski's professional fortunes of took a rapid turn for the worse. Thus did Modelski and Szarkiewicz exit this historical drama. Both men were thrown to the lions to be devoured by the furious Sikorski and his entourage before being forced to leave the British capital altogether.

Over the next several years, Szarkiewicz experienced a terrible personal fall: the shameful expulsion from the ranks of SIME in Egypt; the attempt by his erstwhile friends/handlers to prevent his return to Britain and their petty haggling over his modest due; and, finally, his lengthy stay in the UK without citizenship, basic rights, or any support. Such was the reward MI5 and His Majesty's Government gave the man who had placed himself at the service of the United Kingdom back in the summer of 1940 and who had played a key role in stopping contact between the Polish deputy premier and the Nazi regime—an event shown above to be of crucial importance to the continuation of the British war against the Third Reich. That said, this book has also made it clear that Szarkiewicz's case was typical of London's attitude toward the Polish citizens who had aided the British intelligence community in its struggle against the Nazis and stayed in British territory after the war.

Then, after Szarkiewicz's untimely death in the late 1950s or early 1960s, blind fate dealt a final, posthumous blow when Kazimierz Iranek-Osmecki blamed him for orchestrating the airplane crash near Gibraltar that had claimed the life of Władysław Sikorski. This allegation has become deeply entrenched in the Polish historiography of World War II, turning Szarkiewicz into one of the most odious figures of that terrible conflict in the eyes of many of his compatriots. I am happy to have been able, in the course of my study, to clear Szarkiewicz of the completely unjustified charge of assassinating the Polish national leader. This spurious accusation had nothing to do with the actual facts of his life. Mojżesz Szapiro-Szarkiewicz was a very complex man whose attempts to get ahead in life caused many people much pain, and who was apparently willing to murder a compatriot. However, as has been conclusively proven above, he could not possibly have harmed Sikorski and ought to be fully cleared of this particular charge in the "verdict of history."

Open Ranks

This book has thoroughly demolished yet another historiographic myth: that the Poles closed ranks while fighting against the Nazi occupation of their homeland. This myth was kept alive by Polish émigrés in the West and their sworn enemies, the Communists, who had come to power in Poland after World War II; it reappeared in the post-Communist Poland of the early twenty-first century. In fairness, Polish historians like Paweł Wieczorkiewicz and Piotr Zychowicz were the first to cast doubt on this narrative. However, I believe that their arguments need to be bolstered with a number of important historical facts—what I set out to do.

First, look at the Poles who stayed in German-occupied territory after the September defeat of 1939. We can confidently assert that their response to the occupation was far from monolithic. Some Poles called for an immediate settlement with the enemy and even took practical steps in this direction; their aim was to bring life back to normal. Some aristocrats, city mayors like Warsaw's Stefan Starzynski, and members of the Polish intelligentsia like Prince Janusz Radziwiłł and certain professors from Kraków University endorsed this accommodationist policy. At the same time, there were also Poles, mostly members of the prewar far right, who actively courted an alliance with the Nazis in order to counter the Russian-Bolshevist threat from the East and liberate the eastern Polish lands from the Red Army.

The willingness of certain players to negotiate and even cooperate with the Nazis did not vanish after the Generalgouvernement was established, nor after the terrible wave of Nazi terror between late 1939 and the first half of 1940. Instead, it deepened in 1942 and 1943. This collaborationist sentiment produced the symbiosis between the Gestapo and the Polish fascist organization Miecz i Płog. If we are to believe the Soviet counterintelligence reports, it also spurred Polish civilian and military leadership to attempt to work out a modus vivendi with the authorities of the Generalgouvernement in response to the threat of the approaching Red Army. That various Polish political factions engaged in dialogue with the Germans on the eve of the Warsaw Uprising of 1944 (as described by Zychowicz in his book) underscores this desire to cooperate.

Even more important in the historical context analyzed here was the idea of reaching a compromise with the occupiers among Polish émigré circles in the West, including the Polish government-in-exile. My research has shown clearly that Sikorski's fellow exiles were ambivalent toward his decision to continue the war against the Third Reich side by side with the British after France fell. This is one of my most significant findings. In 1940 and 1941, émigrés who regarded themselves as Polish patriots, who had fought the Nazis from the very beginning of the war until the remnants of the Polish army evacuated to Britain, spoke openly of coming to terms with Europe's new geopolitical reality and prioritizing the Poles suffering in the occupied territories by collaborating with Nazi leadership and its delegates in Poland. This collaborationist spirit peaked with Sikorski's deputy Stanislaw Kot's secret contact with the Nazis in the second half of 1940 and early 1941. While the content of these meetings is unknown, the very fact of their existence should put to rest the myth that the Poles acted together as one. Historical reality is much more complex. From now on, historians writing about the Poles' relationship with their German occupiers cannot ignore this crucial fact.

Moreover, British intelligence assumed that Sikorski was aware of Kot's tentative flirtation with the Germans and was even trying to conceal it from his allies in London. Clearly, this was a far-reaching assumption that contradicts everything we know about Sikorski's refusal to engage in any dialogue with Berlin. Hence, it requires further research of Polish, British, and other relevant historical sources. If the British intelligence operatives are proven right, this will upend our traditional view of the Polish government-in-exile from the fall of France to the Nazi invasion of the Soviet Union. Perhaps Kot, allegedly driven by narrow and selfish political interests, was not acting alone. Sikorski, disappointed in Churchill's dismissive attitude toward him and his cabinet, could have countenanced reaching a settlement with the Nazi occupiers that would have allowed him to return to Poland as the head of a pro-German government.

Sane Realists in the "European Jungle"

In light of all the above, we are bound to ask ourselves one crucial question: What are those of us living in the twenty-first century to make of the fact that many Poles, both at home and in exile, advocated for a temporary accommodation with the Nazi invaders, some even calling for a Polish-German alliance in the geopolitical and military spheres? The national narratives of the heroic struggle against the occupation that have prevailed in postwar historical literature and the public discourse in both the Communist East and the capitalist West have led us to believe that steadfast armed resistance, often involving self-sacrifice, was the only viable option to the occupied. In reality, however, apart from political factions that prioritized national or class struggles over individual lives, most inhabitants of the European continent under the Nazi jackboot found for other strategies to survive, from full capitulation and collaboration to passively resisting the occupiers' policies and orders.⁴ Thus in France, La Résistance was initially dominated by ideological Communists, while the great majority of the French refrained from struggling against the occupiers and instead confined their activities to quiet sabotage of the Germans' directives.⁵

It is for this reason that Paweł Wieczorkiewicz, Piotr Zychowicz, and other modern Polish historians assert that it would have been far better for World War II-era Polish leadership to follow the example of the French and place less emphasis on lofty notions like national pride, territorial integrity, and loyalty to western allies. As the mentioned historians see it, dogmatic adherence to these principles at the expense of the lives and well-being of flesh-and-blood Poles led to the destruction that leveled Polish cities, caused the deaths of millions of Poles, and brought about the genocide of the Polish Jews. This terrible outcome might have been averted if Poland had been more like the French Vichy government.⁶

Without getting bogged down in a long and wearying discussion of what might have been, let us try to elucidate one question: Did the German option as described by Wieczorkiewicz, Zychowicz, and their supporters actually exist? Did the Nazi occupiers themselves countenance the possibility of any agreement with the occupied Poles or reestablishing Polish statehood in the territory of prewar Poland? In other words, was there a viable alternative to the political and humanitarian catastrophe that befell the Poles during World War II? In my opinion, we can now answer this crucial question in the positive. My research has brought to light evidence that shows figures in Nazi Germany (including Hitler himself), as well as fascist and conservative European leaders in alliance with the Third Reich, endorsed the idea of creating a rump Polish state that would have been able to join a Berlin-led, anti-Bolshevik bloc. Thus, in my opinion, at least during the first year of the occupation, leading politicians in Poland and in exile had a real window of opportunity to mitigate the horrors of the occupation in territory not yet annexed to the Third Reich or under the control of the USSR.⁷

---

4   British historian Evan Mawdsley has noted that "realists on the continent" often understood that collaboration was the only rational strategy under the circumstances. See: Mawdsley, *Fifth Column*, 14–15.
5   See, for instance: Vast, "Résistance intérieure française."
6   Wieczorkiewicz, "Wojna polska"; Zychowicz, *Opcja niemiecka*, 421–431; see also on the difficulties that the Germans ran into when implementing their anti-Jewish policies in Vichy France: Kershaw, *Hitler*, 594.
7   At this point, I would like to refer the reader to the thesis advanced by the famous American historian Timothy Snyder, according to which the Nazis committed their greatest atrocities against the local population, both Jewish and non-Jewish, in those regions of Eastern Europe where the local state structures and ruling elites had been destroyed, either by the Third Reich or by the Soviet Union. See, for instance: Snyder, "The Origins of the Final Solution."

As I see it, this discovery inevitably leads us to the following conclusion: Polish politicians and community leaders like Władysław Studnicki who stayed behind and tried to establish a relationship with the Germans during the initial phase of the occupation should not be regarded as despicable traitors, but sane realists and patriots. They saw their chance and tried to exploit it for the good of their suffering country. Although they failed—Nazi leadership in Berlin, despite being generally interested in cooperation, considered them unfit to lead the Poles—it is worth stressing again that these people were realists and good patriots. Needless to say, this judgment excludes the Polish fascists, who did not only disregard the welfare of all their fellow citizens but attacked those they considered aliens and ideological enemies.

I am fully aware that this conclusion will be very hard to swallow for many people in Poland and elsewhere. However, I encourage all my potential opponents to acknowledge that, by anathematizing these Polish "traitors," we unfairly discriminate against them: there were similar traitors in France, Czechoslovakia, and many other European countries. We should recall that Paris and Prague—pearls of European tourism so beloved of us today—avoided Warsaw's bitter fate thanks largely to local politicians who chose to collaborate with Nazi occupiers.

I believe that a similar rehabilitation should be extended to Stanisław Kot's secret diplomatic contact with the emissaries of the Third Reich. Like many of their compatriots at home and abroad, Kot and his associates (and possibly Sikorski himself) saw a window of opportunity to negotiate with the enemy and decided to take advantage of it, both to ameliorate their people's suffering and satisfy their own political ambitions. Their geopolitical maneuvers happened in a context of profound disillusionment. The exiled Polish leadership held little faith that they could achieve their aims through their alliance with Britain and France, which had already fallen. They had experienced the shocking realization that the hospitable British, for all their high-flown rhetoric, cared only about their own narrow interests and were more than willing to reach a settlement with Berlin or Moscow behind the Poles' backs and at their expense.

I foresee a possible objection to my thesis: despite the British leaders' behavior, the members of the Polish government-in-exile in secret contact with the Nazis should have realized that in a war that had already swallowed their country and was spreading across the European continent, such interactions with the enemy were completely out of place, and that even if their initiative

---

If Snyder's thesis is correct, then, by consenting to the creation of a "rump Polish state" in 1940–1941, the Polish politicians might indeed have saved many of the citizens of their occupied homeland from the terrible suffering and death that lay in store for them.

had been successful, it would have bound them to the criminal regime in Berlin and strip them of their legitimacy in the eyes of the West. In response to this objection, I would like to point out that until the German invasion of the Soviet Union and the Japanese assault on Pearl Harbor, no one knew that humanity had just become embroiled in a new, terrible, and lengthy world war. This ignorance extended even to world leaders. When Hitler was about to invade Poland, he still hoped to avoid a major European conflict and tried to dissuade the British from responding with force; and at the end of the Polish Campaign, when he learned the Wehrmacht was nearing a logistical collapse, he reassured his political and military entourage—and through them, all of Germany—that the Reich had no intentions of getting involved in a protracted military conflict.[8]

Stalin, for his part, regarded the pacts that he signed with Hitler in 1939 as an opportunity to keep his country out of the large-scale European conflict, which he feared greatly. At the same time, he did not believe that Germany and Britain would engage in a life-and-death struggle.[9] Sumner Welles, the United States undersecretary of state, visited London, Paris, Berlin, and Rome half a year after the fall of Poland and was told by Mussolini that, unlike in 1914, neither side involved in the current conflict wants a "real war" and therefore the chances of achieving a lasting peace between them are high.[10] When he returned home, Welles reported that Europe was "nearing a diplomatic and political catastrophe,"[11] which shows he felt the situation there was not yet catastrophic.

Neville Chamberlain was well aware that Italy and Japan were not eager for war and tried until May 1940 to convince Rome and Tokyo to stay out of the German-French-British conflict or possibly even join London and Paris.[12] Meanwhile, British intelligence reported that the Italian government remained on good terms with London, and His Majesty's ambassador to the Italian capital even established a cordial personal relationship with Foreign Minister Count

---

8 Adamthwaite, *The Making of the Second World War*, 93; Bock, *The War Diary*, 79; Herbert von Dirksen, *Moscow, Tokyo, London*, 286; Frieser, *The War in the West*, 289–290; Kroener, *Der Kampf um den Sparstoff Mensch*, 402–417. See also on the weakness of the German war industry in September 1939: Mueller-Hillebrand, *Das Heer 1933–1945*, 23–29.
9 Gorodetsky, *Bein ashlaya le-tarmit*, 343; see also the assertion, by British historian Evan Mawdsley, that, in the summer of 1940, the USSR and the USA watched the British-German clash from the sidelines, showing not the slightest desire to get involved: Mawdsley, *Fifth Column*, 14.
10 Miller, "The Welles Mission to Rome."
11 The Polish ambassador to London to the Polish Foreign Office in Angers, "The Voyage of Sumner Welles," secret, April 8, 1940, USHMM, RG-59.036, A-12-1-8_0112.
12 Mee, *The Foreign Policy of the Chamberlain Wartime Administration*.

Ciano.¹³ Thus, when they started negotiations with Berlin in the second half of 1940, the Polish émigré leaders could not possibly have known that they were in a world war for the simple reason that nobody recognized it as such. Hence, they did not necessarily believe they had missed their last chance to close a deal with the leaders of the Third Reich.¹⁴

Moreover, the notion of not negotiating with the enemy was not widely held in this period. This may seem surprising to us nowadays, but even after the Wehrmacht's string of stunning victories in the spring and summer of 1940, continental Europe remained a hotbed of diplomatic maneuvers, occasionally quite daring ones, to forge bonds between warring camps. Thus, the British reaped great successes on the Spanish diplomatic front, convincing Generalissimo Franco's pro-German fascist regime to reject Berlin's demands to occupy Gibraltar.¹⁵ Likewise, the officials of Vichy France, who had allegedly thrown in their lot with the Germans, exchanged intelligence with London and even maintained secret relationships with the British to prevent the Wehrmacht from using French colonies in North Africa.¹⁶ Stalin, Hitler's partner in the partition of Poland, worked with the British behind Hitler's back to prevent a possible German-British rapprochement and secure Churchill's formal approval of the Soviet territorial acquisitions in Eastern Europe. At the same time, the Soviet leader also discussed partitioning the Balkans with the Italian Fascists.¹⁷ As for Mussolini, he made overtures to the Americans and even signaled his willingness to cancel Italy's state of war with Britain.¹⁸

As we can see, everyone talked to everyone else in hopes of improving their own diplomatic and military standing in the midst of the rapid and enormous geopolitical changes happening in Europe. "What we see in Europe today is a jungle"—this is how Ivan Maisky, then Soviet ambassador to London, described the frantic diplomacy sweeping the continent;¹⁹ and his chief, the

---

13 Weekly Political Intelligence Summary No. 1 (Covering the Period from the Outbreak of War to October 3, 1939), October 3, 1939, USHMM, RG-59.006.M-FO371/24054, Scan 00022.
14 This position—namely, that, until the second half of 1941, the European military conflict was not yet a "big" world war—is now the mainstream view in the historiography of World War II, both in the West and in Russia. See, for instance: Kershaw, *To Hell and Back*, 348–352; Noakes and Pridham, *Nazism*, 812; Torkunov, *Istoriia velikoi pobedy*, 606.
15 Smyth, *Diplomacy and Strategy of Survival*, 110–132.
16 Kitson, *The Hunt for Nazi Spies*, 78–79; Thomas, *Britain and Vichy*, 75–82.
17 Gorodetsky, *Bein ashlaya le-tarmit*, 47–49, 113–114.
18 An untitled secret report by the Polish embassy in Bern to the Polish Foreign Office in London, on the contents of a conversation with an unnamed citizen of some neutral country, about the situation in Switzerland and Italy, December 29, 1940, USHMM, RG-59.036, A-12-1-8_0115-0116.
19 Gorodetsky, *Bein ashlaya le-tarmit*, 114; Maisky, *Vospominaniia*, 478.

notorious Andrey Vyshinsky, stated that "international relations are fluid, and may develop."[20] Thus, we can conclude that the Poles' decision to open a secret channel of negotiations with the Nazis was in full accord with the zeitgeist and conformed to the general practices of contemporary European diplomacy.

Finally, we must not lose sight of the fact that global geopolitical actors, including the Polish government-in-exile, were not yet concerned about becoming tainted by their association with the criminal Nazi regime. The Third Reich was not universally associated with crimes against humanity until 1941.[21] In the second half of 1940, the international community still regarded the Nazi state as quite legitimate: its representatives in the Generalgouvernement had not yet prohibited the local population from contacting the outside world via ordinary mail nor banned them from leaving.[22] Most crucial in this context, German atrocities committed during the first year of Polish occupation had not yet eclipsed "ordinary" crimes against civilians, which had featured in every major war of the first half of the twentieth century, from the Boer War to the Second Sino-Japanese War. Many Poles—as well as British intelligence, for that matter—believed that the German's crimes paled in comparison to the atrocities, real or alleged, taking place in the USSR-controlled eastern Polish territories.[23]

Germany's crimes against Polish Jews had yet to evolve into the wholesale extermination of an entire people. Neither Kraków nor Warsaw nor any other Polish city had large Jewish ghettos; these would emerge only in the autumn of 1940 and spring of 1941.[24] For this reason, sources of the Polish Ministry

---

20 Gorodetsky, ibid.
21 Breitman, *Intelligence and the Holocaust*, 17–47; Gilbert, *Churchill and the Holocaust*.
22 See the list of rules for those wishing to leave the borders of the Generalgouvernement: the Polish consulate general in Jerusalem to the Polish Foreign Office in Angers, "Francopol, the Polish Tourism Bureau, Rules," April 11, 1940, USHMM, RG-59.047, KOL-25-47A_9-10; a document without signature or addressee, titled "Traveling out of Warsaw," December 15, 1939, USHMM, RG-59.047, KOL-25-47A_116; a document without signature or addressee, titled "Rules for Traveling out of Warsaw," January 6, 1940, USHMM, RG-59.047, KOL-25-47A_117-18.
23 As early as October 1939, the British intelligence assumed that the fate of the Poles in the territories annexed by the USSR would be worse than the fate of their compatriots who had found themselves under German rule. See: Weekly Political Intelligence Summary No. 1 (Covering the Period from the Outbreak of War to October 3, 1939), October 3, 1939, USHMM, RG-59.006.M-FO371/24054, Scan 00022. See also a Polish document without signature or addressee, titled "The Behavior of the Poles Following the Bolshevik Invasion," secret, December 9, 1939, USHMM, RG-59.036, A-12-73-2_0051.
24 See, for instance: a document without signature or addressee, titled "The Jewish Ghetto in Warsaw," September 15, 1940, USHMM, RG-59.036, A-12-73-A2_0187-88. See also a detailed description of the situation of the Polish Jews from September 1939: Aharonson, *Hitler, ba'alot ha-brit ve-ha-yehudim*, 61–65. Although Professor Aharonson states in his book

of Information and Documentation in occupied Poland claimed in October 1940 that, "despite the prevailing impression, the situation of the Jews is not so bad."[25] The president of the German Red Cross, Charles Edward, the Duke of Coburg, was able to convince the Americans that the reports about the horrible mistreatment of Jews in the GG were baseless exaggerations;[26] and some Polish Jews who had managed to leave their occupied homeland—among them Marcus Maliniak, who had witnessed the arrival of the Red Army in Lviv before returning to Palestine in early 1940—testified that the Polish-Jewish refugees who had found themselves in Soviet territory "often returned to the German occupation zone."[27]

Hence, by attempting to negotiate with the Germans in the second half of 1940, Polish leaders did not believe they were binding their country to a criminal Nazi regime, nor that their attempts would delegitimize the Sikorski government, or any other government that might have been established in Poland with the Germans' consent. After all, at that moment, many governments in Europe and elsewhere—including Italy, Spain, Finland, Romania, Hungary, Japan, France, and the USSR—maintained more or less close relations with Germany and did not lose their legitimacy in the eyes of London or Washington. The Americans were in no hurry to burn all bridges with Berlin until the Germans declared war on them in December 1941, more than two years after Germany

---

that the treatment of Jews in the territory of the Generalgouvernement was extremely brutal, he admits that, in 1939–1941, it did not yet amount to a genocide.

25 The *expozytura* of the Ministry of Information and Documentation in Lisbon, report no. 5, October 21, 1940, USHMM, RG-59.047, KOL-25-10-A_333. See a similar assertion recorded two months later, after the establishment of the Warsaw Ghetto: the source "Nur," "Addition to Report no. 21," December 20, 1940, USHMM, RG-59.047, KOL-25-10-A_361.

26 Büschel, *Hitlers adliger Diplomat*, 227–228; see also the highly concerned report by Raczyński, the Polish ambassador to London, according to which the British had allegedly learned from Washington that the Americans believed the Germans' assurances about the supposedly low mortality rate among the Polish civilian population, and about the ability of the German side to cope with the challenge of feeding this population on its own, with no need for American help: Raczyński to the Polish government in Angers, code cable no. 112, December 22, 1939, USHMM, RG-59.036, A-12-53-28_0058.

27 The testimony of Marcus Maliniak, a resident of the city of Kiryat Motzkin, at the Polish Consulate in Tel Aviv, February 10, 1940, USHMM, GK_159_228cz2, 33; see a similar testimony by a Polish Jew about the flight of Jews from Soviet territory into the German occupation zone, because of Bolshevik terror and food shortages: [Protocol of the interview] with Mr. C. Ch., April 20, 1940, USHMM, GK_159_228cz2, 152; and the statement of an American businessman of Jewish origin who returned from the USSR in October 1940 and told a correspondent of the American Jewish newspaper *Yidisher Courier* that most of the Jewish refugees who had arrived in Soviet territory from European countries expressed a desire to return to Nazi-controlled areas: the Ministry of Information and Documentation: Jewish Press Overview no. 7, January 30, 1941, London, USHMM, RG-59.034, A-10-2-25_0009.

occupied Poland. So why do we hold Sikorski and Kot to a higher standard, expecting them to refuse to change their stance on the Third Reich in the second half of 1940?

The perception that the Polish government-in-exile's contact with Nazi emissaries was fundamentally unproblematic is reflected clearly in Kot's refusal to accept Szarkiewicz's, Iranek-Osmecki's, and other pro-Sanation operatives' attempts to paint Mikiciński as a despicable Nazi spy and a traitor to his homeland. Jerzy Kurcyusz, Kot's highly placed representative who met personally with the Germans, declared that he and Mikiciński had acted in the interests of the exiled government. Kot would later claim that Mikiciński's acts on behalf of his government should have been rewarded with monuments all over liberated Poland, not a bullet in the brain and an unmarked grave in the desert. I fully endorse Kot's view. My long journey through the labyrinth of the Mikiciński affair has convinced me that the man who acted under the alias Lis played a rare historical role. Despite his status as a secondary actor in the world-historical drama that would shape the subsequent fate of humanity, thanks to his extensive connections and remarkable talent for mediation, he was able to give the star players a real opportunity to change their political-military strategy on a fundamental level and pivot from an alliance with now-useless Britain to one with Germany.

The Legacy of Thucydides

Unfortunately (or fortunately), we will never know how the situation in Europe and the rest of the world would have developed had the Polish government-in-exile succeeded in realigning its geopolitical priorities in late 1940 and early 1941. The change was prevented by the actions of another secondary actor, Edward Szarkiewicz, who gave his British patrons a real opportunity to prevent the Poles from exercising their real opportunity to switch to Hitler's camp.

Were the British right to cut off the diplomatic connection between Kot's people and the Germans? This question is highly uncomfortable for those whose view of World War II was shaped by its classic historiography. As we have established, the dramatic encounter between Szarkiewicz and Mikiciński occurred when World War II was not yet a world war, when Nazi Germany had not yet become the embodiment of absolute evil, and when diplomatic relations with the Nazi regime were not yet taboo for most of the international community. It is highly tempting to conclude that, paradoxically, Kot's and Mikiciński's actions on the German front presented a real opportunity for London, too: an honorable exit from its deadlock with Berlin. After all, as stated above, without the need to defend the Poles, Britain would have lost much of its legitimacy to pursue the war. From this, it is but a short step to accuse Churchill of neglecting this opportunity, contrary to the interests of his own country, Europe, and the whole world. Actually, such accusations against the legendary British leader have already been voiced by some of my Western colleagues. According to them, in 1940–1941, Churchill rejected all of Hitler's peace initiatives in order to pursue what they call an unnecessary war.[28]

However, I am inclined to accept the position of the historiographical school which asserts that Churchill's uncompromising stance vis-à-vis the Third Reich was fully justified by Britain's long-term national interests. While, as stated above, the Poles' actions were quite reasonable from their own point of view, the British were under no obligation to accept it—indeed, they could not possibly accept it. In the opinion of many senior British officials, the behavior of the Nazi regime in the domestic and foreign arenas that began in 1933 and peaked in 1938–1939 clearly proved it espoused and practiced dictatorship and nationalism, was willing to commit extreme violence, and strived to secure hegemony on the European continent and spread its power beyond its borders. Most crucially, the British became convinced that Hitler was pursuing a consistent policy aimed at stripping them of their superpower status, as Churchill noted in his speech at the British Parliament on May 28, 1940.[29] In this situation, as the official London saw it, the most vital long-term interest of the United Kingdom and the British Empire was not another temporary settlement with Berlin along the lines of the Munich Agreement, but "a real hard punch in the stomach" of the Third Reich, as Chamberlain put it in the letter to his sister quoted above.[30]

Quite obviously, Britain's consistent pursuit of this basic interest made it impossible for Poland to pursue its own national interests as conceived by the member of Sikorski's cabinet who had initiated contact with the Germans.

---

28 Buchanan, *Churchill, Hitler, and the Unnecessary War*; Charmley, *Churchill: The End of Glory*. See also an assertion in a similar vein in a recent publication by Cambridge University Press: Ferris and Mawdsley, *The War in the West*, 329; and an account of the events preceding the "Blitz," which suggests that it was Churchill's decision to reject the German peace overtures and prosecute a destructive bombing campaign against Berlin that led to the escalation of the German-British military conflict in the autumn of 1940: Napier, *Churchill*, 66–70.

29 Ansel, *Hitler Confronts England*, 149–153; Rees, *Behind Closed Doors*, 71; see also the speech by the Archbishop of York in October 1939, which has been cited above: Archbishop of York, The Spirit and Aim of Britain in the War, October 2, 1939, USHMM, RG-59.006.M-FO371/22949, Scans 00236-243.

30 See the explanation of the position of the British leadership vis-à-vis Germany in 1940: Best, *Churchill*, 150–159.

Once these channels of communication had been severed and their key middleman, Mikiciński, eliminated, the British ruthlessly subordinated the Polish government-in-exile to its strategic logic in the diplomatic and military realms. Their actual enslavement of the weak Polish ally remained in force until the very end of World War II, largely due to the confinement of the exiled Polish government to London, strict censorship of all of Poland's statements and actions, and total control of Anders's Army, the largest and most powerful Polish military force.

This development was not likely to have surprised the famous ancient Greek historian Thucydides. Back in the fifth century BCE, in his celebrated *History of the Peloponnesian War*, he wrote that the freedom of states and nations was a direct function of their political and military might. "The strong do what they can and the weak suffer what they must"—this is how, according to Thucydides, Athenian envoys admonished the inhabitants of the Isle of Melos, who were unwilling to submit to Athenian rule. "And it is not as if we were the first to make this law, or to act upon it when made," they added. "We found it existing before us, and will leave it to exist forever after us."[31]

The geopolitical effect of the Mikiciński affair clearly demonstrates that this ancient law of nature governing the system of international relations has remained valid for the last 2,500 years. Even now, in the third decade of our own century—especially in the view of the current wars in Ukraine and the Middle East—there are no grounds to believe that it will not exist forever, as the ancient Athenians promised.

---

31 Quoted from: Donelly, *Realism and International Relations*, 23.

Sources and Bibliography

Archives and Collections of Documents

AGH—General Historical Archive of the Chilean Ministry of Foreign Affairs (Archivo General Histórico—Ministerio de Relaciones Exteriores de Chile).

CHAR—The Chartwell Papers at the Churchill Archives Center, Churchill College, Cambridge, England.

FGEZ—The General Foundation of Elżbieta Zawacka in Toruń, Poland (Fundacja Generał Elżbiety Zawackiej).

HIA—The Hoover Institution Archives, Stanford University, USA.

JPIA—The Józef Piłsudski Institute of America. New York City.

NARA—The National Archives and Records Administration, Washington, DC, USA.

PISM—The Polish Institute and Sikorski Museum, London.

TNA—The National Archives of the UK, Kew.

USHMM—The United States Holocaust Memorial Museum, Washington, DC

XNC—The Papers of Neville Chamberlain, Cadbury Research Library Special Collections, University of Birmingham.

YVA—The Archives of the Yad Vashem Holocaust Memorial Complex, Jerusalem.

Published Collections of Documents

Ciechanowski, J. S., comp. *Polsko-Brytyjska współpraca wywiadowcza podczas II wojny światowej*. Vol. 2. Wybór dokumentów. Warszawa: Naczelna Dyrekcja Archiwów Państwowych, 2005.

Felshtinsky, Y., comp. *TSRS-Vokietija 1939. TSRS ir Vokietijos santykių dokumentinė medžiaga 1939 m. balandžio-spalio mėn*. Vilnius: Mokslas, 1989.

Friedrich, K.-P., bearb. *Die Verfolgung und Ermordung der europäischen Juden durch das nationalsozialistische Deutschland 1933-1945*. Band 4, *Polen September 1939–Juli 1941*. München: Oldenbourg Wissenschaftsverlag, 2011.

Mendelsohn, J., ed. *The Final Solution of the Abwehr*. Vol. 13. New York: Taylor & Francis, 1989.

Naumov, V., ed. *1941 god*. 2 vols. Moscow: MF "Demokratiia," 1998.

Noakes, J., and G. Pridham, eds. *Nazism 1919-1945*. Vol. 2, *Foreign Policy, War and Racial Extermination*. A Documentary Reader. Exeter: The University of Exeter Press, 1991.

Pechatnov, V. and D. Reynolds, eds. *The Kremlin Letters. Stalin's Wartime Correspondence with Churchill and Roosevelt*. New Haven: Yale University Press, 2018.

Sotskov, L., comp. *Agressiia. Rassekrechennye dokumenty Sluzhby Vneshnei Razvedki Rossiiskoi Federatsii 1939-1941*. Moscow: Ripol Klassik, 2011.

Sweet, P. R., H. M. Smyth, et al., eds. *Documents on German Foreign Policy 1918-1945* (Series D, 1937-1945). Vol. 7, *The Last Days of Peace, August 9–September 3, 1939* Washington, DC: Government Printing Office, 1956.

_____. *Documents on German Foreign Policy 1918-1945* (Series D, 1937-1945). Vol. 8, *The War Years, September 4, 1939–March 18, 1940*. London: Her Majesty's Stationery Office, 1954.

_____. *Documents on German Foreign Policy 1918-1945* (Series D, 1937-1945). Vol. 9, *The War Years, March 18–June 22, 1940*. Washington, DC: Government Printing Office, 1956.

_____. *Documents on German Foreign Policy 1918-1945* (Series D, 1937-1945). Vol. 10, *The War Years, June 23–August 31, 1940*. London: Her Majesty's Stationery Office, 1957.

Biographies, Autobiographies, Memoirs, and Diaries

Armitage, D., and J. Pitts, eds. *C. H. Alexandrowicz. The Law of Nations in Global History*. Oxford: Oxford University Press, 2017.

Bobrowski, C. *Wspomnienia ze stulecia*. Lublin: Wydawnictwo Lubelskie, 1985.

Bock, F., v. *The War Diary 1939-1945*. 1st ed. Atglen, PA: Schiffer Publishing, 1996.

Buczek, R. *Człowiek do złotych interesów*. Warszawa: Oficyna Literatów "Rój," 1991.

Carol II. *Însemnări zilnice. 1937-1951*. Vol 2, *13 martie–15 decembrie 1939*. Bucharest: Scripta, 1997.

Charmley, J. *Churchill: The End of Glory. A Political Biography*. San Diego, CA: Harcourt, 1993.

Chivulescu, N. *Armand Călinescu, om de stat și conducător de țară*. Bucharest: Lucman, 1998.

Cikar, J., comp. *Türkischer Biographischer Index*. Band 1. Berlin: De Gruyter, 1993.

Danielsson, S. K. *The Explorer's Roadmap to National-Socialism: Sven Hedin, Geography and the Path to Genocide*. London: Routledge, 2012.

Dilks, D. *Churchill and Company. Allies and Rivals in War and Peace*. London: I.B. Tauris, 2015.

Dirksen, H. v. *Moscow, Tokyo, London. Twenty Years of German Foreign Policy*. London: Hutchinson, 1951.

Feiling, K. *The Life of Neville Chamberlain*. London: Macmillan, 1947.

Fraenkel, H., and R. Manvell. *Hermann Göring*. London: Heinemann, 1962.

Giedroyc, J. *Autobiografia na cztery ręce*. Warszawa: Towarzystwo Opieki nad Archiwum Instytutu Literackiego w Paryżu, 2006.

"Graliński Zygmunt Stanisław Cyprian 1897-1940." Parlamentarzyści, Biblioteka Sejmowa. Accessed February 20, 2024, https://bs.sejm.gov.pl/F?func=find-b&request=000000491&find_code=SYS&local_base=ARS10.

Halder, F. *Kriegstagebuch. Tägliche Aufzeichnungen des Chefs Generalstabes des Heeres 1939-1942*. Herausgegeben vom Arbeitskreis für Wehrforschung in Stuttgart, bearbeitet von Hans-Adolf Jacobsen. Band 1: *Vom Polenfeldzug bis zum Ende der Westoffensive*. Stuttgart: Kohlhammer Verlag, 1962.

―――. *The Private War Journal of Generaloberst Franz Halder, Chief of the General Staff of Supreme Command of the German Army (OKH)*. Vol. 2, Historical Division, SSUSA, 11 Sep–6 Dec 39. N.p.: n.p. 1950.

Hesse, F. *Das Spiel um Deutschland*. München: List Verlag, 1953.
Hunt, Sir David KCMG OBE. *A Don at War*. Rev ed. London: Routledge, 2013.
Iranek-Osmecki, K. *Powołanie i Przeznaczenie. Wspomnienia oficera Komendy Głównej AK 1940-1944*. Warszawa: Państwowy Instytut Wydawniczy, 1998.
Jenkins, R. *Churchill: A Biography*. London: Picador, 2012.
Karski, J. *Story of a Secret State. The Testimony of the Man Who Tried to Stop the Holocaust*. Tel Aviv: Yediot Sfarim, 2014.
Kershaw, I. *Hitler: A Biography*. New York: W.W. Norton & Company, 2010.
Klee, E. *Das Personenlexikon zum Dritten Reich. Wer war was vor und nach 1945*. 2nd ed. Frankfurt am Main: Fischer Taschenbuch Verlag, 2005.
Koeves, T. *Satan in a Top Hat: The Biography of Franz Von Papen*. Whitefish, MT: Literary Licensing, LLC, 2011.
Kowalski, W. T., and J. W. Sosnkowska. *W kręgu mitów i rzeczywistości*. Warszawa: Interpresss, 1988.
Kurcyusz, J. *Na przedpolu Jałty: wspomnienia z tajnej służby w dyplomacji*. Katowice: Societas Scientiis Favendis Silesiae Superioris, Institut Górnośląski, 1995.
Lockhart B. *The Diaries of Sir Bruce Lokhart 1939-1965*. Basingstoke: Palgrave Macmillan, 1973.
Longerich P. *Hitler: A Biography*. Oxford: Oxford University Press, 2019.
Maisky, I. *The Maisky Diaries: Red Ambassador to the Court of St James's, 1932-1943*. Edited by Gabriel Gorodetsky. New Haven, CT: Yale University Press, 2015.
Michniewicz, L. *Opération Haïfa. Les espions ne se pardonnent pas*. Tournai: Casterman, 1969.
Mueller, M. *Canaris. Hitlers Abwehrchef. Biographie*. Berlin: List Taschenbuch, 2007.
Muggeridge, M., ed. *Ciano's Diary, 1939-1943*. London: Heinemann, 1947.
Neville, P. *Appeasing Hitler: The Diplomacy of Sir Nevile Henderson, 1937-39*. Studies in Diplomacy. Basingstoke: Palgrave Macmillan, 1999.
Patterson, A. L. *Between Hitler and Stalin: The Quick Life and Secret Death of Edward Smigly Rydz, Marshal of Poland*. Indianapolis, IN: Dog Ear Publishing, 2010.
Pobóg-Malinowski, W. *Na rumuńskim rozdrożu. Fragmenty wspomnień*. Warszawa: Warszawska Oficyna Wydawnicza GRYF, 1990.

"Ramón Briones Luco." Biblioteca del Congreso National de Chile, accessed March 5, 2024. https://www.bcn.cl/historiapolitica/resenas_parlamentarias/wiki/Ram%C3%B3n_Briones_Luco.

Reuth, R.G., Hrsg. *Joseph Goebbels. Tagebücher 1924-1945*. Band 3: *1935-1939*. München: R. Riper & Co. Verlag, 1992.

Reynolds, D. *In Command of History. Churchill Fighting and Writing the Second World War*. London: The Penguin Group, 2004.

Ritter, G. *Carl Goerdeler und die deutsche Widerstandsbewegung*. München: Dt. Taschenbuch Verl., 1964.

Rolfs, R. W. *The Sorcerer's Apprentice. The Life of Franz Papen*. Lanham, MD: UPA, 1995.

Rutkowski, T. P. *Stanisław Kot 1885-1975. Biografia polityczna*. Warszawa: Wydawnictwo DiG, 2000.

Self, R. *Neville Chamberlain: A Biography*. London: Routledge, 2006.

Serov, I. *Zapiski iz chemodana. Tainye dnevniki pervogo predsedatelia KGB, naidennye cherez 25 let posle ego smerti*. Moscow: Olma Media Group, 2016.

Sokolnicki, M. *Dziennik Ankarski 1939-1943*. London: Gryf Publications Ltd., 1965.

Stevenson, W. *A Man Called Intrepid. The Secret War 1939-1945*. London: Sphere Books, 1976.

Studnicki, W. *Irrwege in Polen. Ein Kampf um die polnisch-deutsche Annäherung*. Göttingen: Göttinger Arbeitskreis, 1951.

Sudoplatov, P. *Raznye dni tainoi voiny i diplomatii. 1941 god*. Moscow: Olma-Press, 2001.

Szafer, W. *Wspomnienia przyrodnika. Moi profesorowie, moi koledzy, moi uczniowie*. Wrocław: Ossolineum, 1973.

Terlecki, R. "'Za sprawę ojczyzny…' Jerzy Kurcyusz 1907–1988." In *Na przedpolu Jałty. Wspomnienia z tajnej służby w dyplomacji*, edited by J. Kurcyusz, 9-25. (Katowice: Instytut Dziedzictwa Myśli Narodowej, 1995).

Tsokoff, K. "Moja droga do Polski i walka u boku polskich przyjaciół." In *Ramię w ramię. Wspomnienia cudzoziemców uczestniczących w polskim ruchu oporu w latach 1939–1945*, compiled by Stanisław Okęcki, 168-206. Warszawa: Chytelnik, 1980.

Weitz, J. *Joachim von Ribbentrop. Hitler's Diplomat*. 1st ed. London: Weidenfeld and Nicolson, 1992.

Zakrzewski, A. *Wincenty Witos: chłopski polityk i mąż stanu*. Warszawa: Ludowa Spółdzielnia Wydawnicza, 1985.

Books and Monographs

Adamthwaite, A. P. *The Making of the Second World War*. London: Routledge, 1989.

Aharonson, Sh. *Hitler, ba'alot ha-brit ve-ha-yehudim*. 2nd ed. Tel-Aviv: Ha-Kibbutz ha-Meuhad and Machon Ben-Gurion, 2009.

Aldrich, R. J., and R. Cormac *Spying and the Crown. The Secret Relationship between British Intelligence and the Royals*. London: Atlantic Books, 2022.

———. *The Black Door. Spies, Secret Intelligence and British Prime Ministers*. London: William Collins Books, 2017.

Al'tman, I., K. Anderson, and S. Redlich. *War, Holocaust and Stalinism. A Documented History of the Jewish Anti-Fascist Committee in the USSR*. London: Routledge, 1995.

Andrew, C. *The Secret World. The History of Intelligence*. New Haven: Yale University Press, 2018.

———. *The Defence of the Realm. The Authorized History of MI5*. London: Penguin Books, 2010.

Andrew, C., and V. Mitrokhin. *The Mitrokhin Archive. The KGB in Europe and the West*. London: The Penguin Press, 1999.

Ansel, W. *Hitler Confronts England*. Durham, NC: Duke University Press, 1960.

Bali, R. N. *Devlet'in Yahudileri ve 'Öteki' Yahudi*. İstanbul: İletişim, 2004.

Bębnik, G. *Sokoły kapitana Ebbinghausa. Sonderformation Ebbinghaus w działaniach wojennych na Górnym Śląsku w 1939 r.* Katowice: LIBRON, 2014.

Berridge, G. R. *British Diplomacy in Turkey, 1583 to the Present. A Study in the Evolution of the Resident Embassy*. Leiden: Martinus Hijhoff Publishers, 2009.

Best, G. *Churchill. A Study in Greatness*. Oxford: Oxford University Press, 2003.

Brio, V. *Pol'skie muzy na Sviatoi Zemle. Armiia Andersa: mesto, vremia, kul'tura (1942-1945)*. Jerusalem: Gesharim and Mosty Kul'tury, 2017.

Buchanan, P. J. *Churchill, Hitler, and the Unnecessary War. How Britain Lost Its Empire and the West Lost the World*. New York: Crown Publishing Group, 2008.

Bungay, S. *The Most Dangerous Enemy. A History of the Battle of Britain*. London: Aurum Press, 2015.

Büschel, H. *Hitlers adliger Diplomat. Der Herzog von Coburg und das Dritte Reich*. Frankfurt am Main: S. Fisher Verlag, 2016.

Carlton, D. *Churchill and the Soviet Union*. Manchester: Manchester UP, 2000.

Ciechanowski, J. *Defeat in Victory. A Firsthand Account of International Developments on the Washington Scene during the War Years.* New York: Doubleday, 1947.

Clark, L. *Blitzkrieg. Myth, Reality, and Hitler's Lightning War—France 1940.* New York: Atlantic Monthly Press, 2016.

Cooper, A. *Cairo in the War 1939–1945.* London: John Murray: 2013.

Ćwięk, H. *Przeciw Abwehrze.* Warszawa: Dom Wydawniczy Bellona: 2001.

Davies, N. *Im Herzen Europas. Geschichte Polens.* München: C.H. Beck, 2006.

Donelly, J. *Realism and International Relations.* Cambridge: Cambridge University Press, 2000.

Dorril, S. *MI6: Inside the Covert World of Her Majesty's Secret Intelligence Service.* New York: Touchstone, 2002.

Dubicki, A. *Dzieje polskiej placówki dyplomatycznej w Bukareszcie (1919–1940).* Łódź: Wydawnictwo Uniwersytetu Łódzkiego, 2014.

Dubicki, T. *Konspiracja Polska w Rumunii 1939–1945.* Tom 1, *1939–1940.* Warszawa: Auditor, 2002.

———. *Polscy uchodźcy w Rumunii 1939–1945.* Warszawa: Gryf, 1995.

Dubicki, T., D. Nalecz, and T. Stirling, eds. *Intelligence Cooperation between Poland and Great Britain during World War II.* Vol. 2. Elstree: Vallentine Mitchell, 2005.

Dubicki, T., and S. J. Rastworowski. *Sanatorzy kontra Sikorszczycy, chyli, Walka o władzę na uchodźstwie w Rumunii 1939–1940.* Warszawa: Adiutor, 1993.

Dubicki, T., and A. Suchcitz. *Oficerowie wywiadu WP i PSZ w latach 1939–1945.* Tom 2. Warszawa: LTW, 2011.

Falin, V. *Vtoroi front. Antigitlerovskaia koalitsiia: Konflikt interesov.* Moscow: Tsentrpoligraf, 2000.

Falkov, Y. *Meragle ha-ye'arot: pe'ilutam ha-modi'init shel ha-parṭizanim ha-Sovyeṭim 1941–1945.* Jerusalem: Magnes Press/Yad Vashem, 2017.

Forczyk, R. *We March against England. Operation Sea Lion 1940–41.* Oxford: Osprey Publishing, 2016.

Gąsiorowski, A. *Polityka niemecka na ziemiach okupowanych.* Warszawa: Biblioteka Otwartej Nauki, 2010.

Gorodetsky, G. *Bein ashlaya le-tarmit. Stalin ve-mivtsa Barbarossa.* Tel-Aviv: Maarachot, 1999.

Gruchmann, L. *Nationalsozialistische Grossraumordnung: Die Konstruktion einer 'deutschen Monroe-Doktrin'.* Stuttgart: Deutsche Verlags–Anstalt, 1962.

Halley, J. J. *The Squadrons of the Royal Air Force & Commonwealth, 1918–1988.* Tonbridge: Air-Britain (Historians) Ltd., 1988.

Haslam, J. *The Spectre of War. International Communism and the Origins of World War II.* Princeton, NJ: Princeton University Press, 2021.

Hassel, A. V., and S MacRae. *Alliance of Enemies: The Untold Story of the Secret American and German Collaboration to End World War II.* New York: Thomas Dunne Books & St. Martins Griffin, 2008.

Held, R. *Kriegsgefangenschaft in Großbritannien: deutsche Soldaten des Zweiten Weltkriegs in britischem Gewahrsam.* München: Oldenbourg, 2007.

Holland, J. *The War in the West—A New History.* Vol. 1. New York: Atlantic Monthly Press, 2015.

Horne, A. *But What Do You Actually Do? A Literary Vagabondage.* London: Weidenfeld and Nicholson, 2011.

Hughes-Wilson, J. *Military Intelligence Blunders.* London: Bonnier Books, 2023.

Hułas, M. *Goście czy intruzi? Rząd polski na uchodźtwie wrzesień 1939—lipiec 1943.* Warszawa: Instytut Historii PAN, 1996.

Israel, U. *Flugboote des zweiten Weltkrieges.* Berlin: Deutscher Militärverlag, 1972.

Jacobmeyer, W. *Heimat und Exil. Die Anfänge der polnischen Untergrundbewegung im Zweiten Weltkrieg.* Hamburg: Leibniz–Verlag, 1971.

Jacobs, D., and D. Richardson. *The Rough Guide to Cairo & the Pyramids.* London: Rough Guides, 2011.

Judas, E. *Rasputin: Neither Devil nor Saint.* Los Angeles: Wetzel Publishing Company, 1942.

Jeffery, K. *MI6. The History of the Secret Intelligence Service 1909–1949.* London: Bloomsbury Paperbacks, 2011.

Kaczorowski, B. *Franco i Stalin. Związek Sowiecki w polityce Hiszpanii w okresie drugiej wojny światowej.* Łódz: Wydawnictwo Uniwersytetu Łódzkiego, 2016.

Kahn, D. *Hitler's Spies. German Military Intelligence in World War II.* Boston: Da Capo Press, 2000.

Kamiński, M. *Edvard Beneš kontra gen. Władysław Sikorski. Polityka władz czechosłowackich na emigracji wobec rządu polskiego na uchodźstwie 1939–1943.* Warszawa: Neriton, 2005.

Kershaw, I. *To Hell and Back. Europe 1914–1949.* London: Penguin Books, 2016.

———. *Making Friends with Hitler. Lord Londonderry and Britain's Road to War.* London: The Penguin Group, 2004.

Kessler L. Wingate J. *Betrayal at Venlo: The Secret Story of Appeasement and Treachery*. London: Leo Cooper, 1991.

Kitchen, M. *British Policy Towards the Soviet Union during the Second World War*. Basingstoke: The Macmillan Press, 1986.

Kitson, S. *The Hunt for Nazi Spies. Fighting Espionage in Vichy France*. Chicago: The University of Chicago Press, 2008.

Kochanski, H. *The Eagle Unbowed. Poland and the Poles in the Second World War*. London: The Penguin Press, 2013.

Koper, S. *Polskie piekiełko. Obrazy z życia elit emigracyjnych 1939–1945*. Warzsawa: Bellona, 2012.

Koper, S., and T. Pawłowski. *Mity polskiego września 1939*. Warszawa: Czarna Owca, 2019.

Koskodan, K. K. *No Greater Ally. The Untold Story of Poland's Forces in World War II*. Oxford: Osprey Publishing, 2009.

Lembke, H. H. *Bankier, Fälscher, Historiker: Der Weg des Isaac Lewin durch die Geschichte seiner Zeit*. Freiburg: Centaurus Verlag & Media UG, 2012.

Lisiewicz, P. M. *W imieniu Polski podziemnej: Z dziejów wojskowego sądownictwa specjalnego Armii Krajowej*. Warszawa: Instytut Wydawniczy Związków Zawodowych, 1988.

Liubimov, M. *Shpiony, kotorykh ia liubliu i nenavizhu*. Moscow: Olimp, 1997.

Lubeski, R. *Linebackers of the Sea*. Bloomington: AuthorHouse, 2010.

Madajczyk, C. *Generalna Gubernia w planach hitlerowskich*. Warszawa: PWN, 1961.

Malzacher, W. M. *Berliner Gaunergeschichten: Aus der Unterwelt 1918–1933*. Haude & Spener, 1970.

McGilvray, E. *Anders's Army. General Władysław Anders & the Polish Second Corps 1941–46*. London: Pen & Sword Books, 2018.

McKay, C. G. *From Information to Intrigue. Studies in Secret Service Based on the Swedish Experience, 1939–1945*. London: Routledge, 1993.

Miner, S. M. *Between Churchill and Stalin. The Soviet Union, Great Britain, and the Origins of the Grand Alliance*. Chapel Hill, NC: The University of North Carolina Press, 2017.

Morison, S. E. *The Atlantic Battle Won. May 1943–May 1945*. History of United States Naval Operations in World War II, Vol. 10. Urbana—Chicago: University of Illinois Press, 2002.

Mueller-Hillebrand, B. *Das Heer 1933–1945*. Band 2, *Die Blitzfeldzüge 1939–1941. Das Heer im Kriege bis zum Beginn des Feldzuges gegen die Sowjetunion im Juni 1941*. Frankfurt: Mittler & Sohn, 1956.

Napier, S. *Churchill. Military Genius or Menace?* Stroud: The History Press, 2018.

Nicoară, T. *Istoria și tradițiile minorităților din România*. Bucuresti: Ministerul Educației și Cercetării, 2005.

Olson, L. *Last Hope Island. Britain, Occupied Europe and the Brotherhood That Helped Turn the Tide of War*. London: Random House, 2017.

Orbach, D. *The Plots against Hitler*. London: Head of Zeus Ltd., 2017.

O'Sullivan, A. *Espionage and Counterintelligence in Occupied Persia (Iran): The Success of the Allied Secret Services*. Basingstoke: Palgrave Macmillan, 2015.

Perry, R. *The Fifth Man: The Soviet Super Spy*. London: Sedgwick & Jackson, 1994.

Pietrzak, J. *Polscy uchodźcy na Bliskim Wschodzie w latach drugiej wojny światowej*. Łódź: Wydawnictwo Uniwersytetu Łódzkiego, 2012.

Porch, D. *The Path to Victory. The Mediterranean Theater in World War II*. New York: Farrar, Straus and Giroux, 2004.

Puchalski, Z., and I. J. Wojciechowski. *Ordery i odznaczenia polskie i ich kawalerowie*. Warszawa: Krajowa Agencja Wydawnicza, 1987.

Ramme, A. *Der Sicherheitsdienst der SS. Zu seiner Funktion im faschistischen Machtapparat und im Besatzungsregime des sogenannten Generalgouvernements Polen*. Berlin: Deutscher Militärverlag, 1970.

Rees, L. *Behind Closed Doors. Stalin, the Nazis and the West*. London: BBC Books, 2008.

Rigg, B. M. *Rescued from the Reich: How One of Hitler's Soldiers Saved the Lubavitcher Rebbe*. New Haven, Connecticut: Yale University Press, 2006.

Rojek, W. *Wojenne losy polskiego złota, Wydanie specjalne*. Warszawa: Narodowy Bank Polski, 2014.

Rossino, A. B. *Hitler Strikes Poland: Blitzkrieg, Ideology, and Atrocity*. Lawrence, KS: Kansas University Press, 2003.

Rothschild, R. *Peace of Our Time*. Oxford: Pergamon Press, 1988.

Salameh, F. *Language, Memory, and Identity in the Middle East: The Case for Lebanon*. Lanham: Lexington Books, 2010.

Sawyer, R. D. *The Tao of Spycraft. Intelligence Theory and Practice in Traditional China*. Boulder, CO: Westview Press, 2004.

Schreiber, G., B. Stegemann, and D. Vogel. *Das deutsche Reich und der Zweite Weltkrieg*. Band 3, *Der Mittelraum und Südoeuropa*. Stuttgart: Deutsche Verlags–Anstalt, 1984.

Scislowski, S. *Not All of Us Were Brave*. Toronto: Dundurn Press, 1997.

Segev, T. *Medina be-chol' mehir. Sipur hayav shel' David Ben-Gurion*. Jerusalem: Keter, 2018.

Shirer, W. H. *The Collapse of the Third Republic. An Inquiry into the Fall of France*. London: The Literary Guild, 1969.

Sierpowski, S. *Studia z Historii Włoch XX Wieku*. Poznań: Wydawnictwo Naukove Uniwersytetu im. Adama Mickiewicza w Poznaniu, 2012.

Smith, B. F. *Sharing Secrets with Stalin. How the Allies Traded Intelligence, 1941–1945*. Lawrence, KS: University Press of Kansas, 1996.

Smyth, D. *Diplomacy and Strategy of Survival. British Policy and Franco's Spain, 1940–1941*. Cambridge: Cambridge University Press, 1986.

Snyder, T. *Bloodlands. Europe Between Hitler and Stalin*. London: Vintage Books, 2011.

Sokolov, B. *Okkupatsiia. Pravda i mify*. Moscow: AST-Press Kniga, 2002.

Sterling, E. J., ed. *Life in the Ghettos during the Holocaust*. Syracuse: Syracuse University Press, 2005.

Strumph-Wojtkiewicz, S. *Piąta kolumna w Paryżu*. Warszawa: Iskry, 1979.

Strzałka, K. *Między przyjaźnią a wrogością. Z dziejów stosunków polsko-włoskich (1939–1945)*. Kraków: Arcana, 2001.

Studnicki, W. *System polityczny Europy a Polska*. Komorów: Antyk Marcin Dybowski, 2010.

Sukenik, Sh., et al., eds. *Kehilat Semiatich*. Tel Aviv: Igud yotzei semiatich be-yisrael u-be-artzot ha-brit, 1965.

Szeremietiew, R. *Siła złego … Niemcy-Polska-Rosja*. Warszawa: Rytm, 2015.

Tamkin, N. *Britain, Turkey and the Soviet Union, 1940–45: Strategy, Diplomacy and Intelligence in the Eastern Mediterranean*. Basingstoke: Palgrave Macmillan, 2009.

Tebinka, J. *Mocarstwa zachodnie wobec Polski w latach 1939–1945*. Warszawa: Biblioteka Otwartej Nauki, 2010.

Terlecki, O. *Szkice i polemiki*. Warszawa: Krajowa Agencja Wydawnicza, 1987.

Thomas, R. T. *Britain and Vichy: The Dilemma of Anglo-French Relations, 1940–42*. London: Macmillan, 1979.

Torkunov, A., ed. *Istoriia velikoi pobedy*. Vol. 2. Moscow: "MGIMO-Universitet," 2020.

Tusiewicz, R. *Historia Polski od A do Z. Repetytorium*. Warszawa: Kram, 2005.

Urbach, K. *Go Betweens for Hitler*. Oxford: Oxford University Press, 2015.

Vallentin, A. *Les atrocités allemandes en Pologne, témoignages et documents*. Paris: R. Denoël, 1940.

Volodarsky, B. *Stalin's Agent. The Life and Death of Alexander Orlov*. Oxford: Oxford University Press, 2015.

West, N. *Double Cross in Cairo. The True Story of the Spy Who Turned the Tide of War in the Middle East*. London: Biteback Publishing, 2015.

Wette, W. *The Wehrmacht. History, Myth, Reality*. Cambridge, MA: Harvard University Press, 2006.

Wieczorkiewicz, P. *Historia polityczna Polski 1935–1945*. Warszawa: Książka i Wiedza, 2010.

Wilamowski, J. *Honor, zdrada, kaźń: Afery Polski podziemnej 1939–1945*. Warszawa: Agencja Wydawnicza CB, 1999.

Williamson, D. G. *The Polish Underground 1939–1947*. Campaign Chronicles. Barnsley: Pen & Sword Books, 2012.

Wolf, W. *German Guided Missiles: Henschel Hs 293 and Ruhrstahl SD 1400X (Fritz X)*. Bennington, VT: Merriam Press, 2006.

Wright, P. *Spycatcher. The Candid Autobiography of a Senior Intelligence Officer*. New York: Dell Publishing, 1988.

Zdanovich, A. *Pol'skii krest sovetskoi kontrrazvedki. Pol'skaia liniia v rabote VChK-NKVD, 1918-1938*. Moscow: Kraft+, 2017.

Zimmerman, J. D. *The Polish Underground and the Jews 1939–1945*. Cambridge: Cambridge University Press, 2015.

Zürcher, E. J. *Turkey. A Modern History*. London: I. B. Tauris & Co Ltd Publishers, 1994.

Zychowicz, P. *Opcja niemiecka. Czyli jak antykomuniści próbowali porozumieć się z III Rzeszą*. Warszawa: Rebis Dom Wydawniczy, 2014.

Chapters in Edited Collections

Ball, S. "The Mediterranean and North Africa, 1940-1944." In *The Cambridge History of the Second World War*, vol. 1, edited by J. Ferris and E. Mawdsley, 358-388. Cambridge: Cambridge University Press, 2017.

Breitman, R. "Intelligence and the Holocaust." In *Secret Intelligence and the Holocaust*, edited by D. Bankier, 17-47. New York: Enigma Books and Yad Vashem, 2006.

Breitman, R., P. Brown, and N. J. W Goda. "The Gestapo." In *US Intelligence and the Nazis*, edited by R. Breitman et al., 137-164. Cambridge: Cambridge University Press, 2005.

Brodsky, J. "On 'September 1, 1939' by W.H. Auden." In *Less Than One; Selected Essays*, edited by J. Brodsky, 304-356. New York: Farrar, Straus and Giroux, 1986.

Bułhak, W. "Raport szefa oddziału II KG AK ppłk. dypl. Mariana Drobika 'Bieżąca polityka polska a rzeczywistość' i sprawa jego arzestowania (listopad-grudzień 1943)." In *Wywiad i kontrwywiad Armii Krajowej*, edited by W. Bułhak, 15-77. Warszawa: IPN, 2008.

Ciechanowski, J. S. "Polski wywiad wojskowy w Portugalii podczas drugiej wojny światowej." In *Wywiad i kontrwywiad wojskowy II RP. Z działalności Oddziału II SG WP*, edited by T. Dubicki, 237-251. Łomianki: Wydawnictwo LTW, 2012.

Dilks, D. N. "The British Foreign Office between the Wars." In *Opinion publique et politique extérieure en Europe. Vol. 2, 1915-1940*. Actes du Colloque de Rome (16-20 février 1981), 165-186. Rome: École Française de Rome, 1984.

Dubicki, T. "Sprawozdanie ppłk. dypl. Stanisława Orłowskiego z likwidacji Ekspozytury 'R' Oddz. II Szt. NW w Bukareszcie." In *Wywiad i kontrwywiad wojskowy II RP. Z działalności Oddziału II SG WP*, vol. 2, edited by T. Dubicki, 365-395. Łomianki: Wydawnictwo LTW, 2012.

Engel, D. "'Ve-ba'arta ha-r'a mekirbecha'—le-birur ha-musag 'shituf pe'ula' be-tkufat ha-shoa be-aspaklaria shel' mishpatei Michael Vaichert." In *Ha-Shoa—historia ve-zikaron, sefer yovel'*, edited by Israel' Gutman, 1-24. Jerusalem: Yad Vashem, 2002.

Ferris, J., and E. Mawdsley. "The War in the West, 1939-1940: The Battle of Britain?" In *The Cambridge History of the Second World War. Vol. 1, Fighting the War*, edited by J. Ferris and E. Mawdsley, 315-30. Cambridge: Cambridge University Press, 2015.

Fisher, W., and Y. L Weinstein. "Akiva (Karol) Eiger of Blessed Memory." In *Memorial Book Zgierz (Poland), Translation of Sefer Zgierz, mazkeret netsal le-kehila Yehudit be-Polin*, edited by D. Shtockfish (Sztokfisz), Sh. Kanc, and Z. Fisher, 432-436. Tel-Aviv: Zgierz Society, 1975-1986.

Fisher, Z., and Y. A Malchieli. "The Industrialist–the Poet." In *Memorial Book Zgierz (Poland), Translation of Sefer Zgierz, mazkeret netsal le-kehila Yehudit be-Polin*, edited by D. Shtockfish (Sztokfisz), Sh. Kanc, and Z. Fisher, 428-432. Tel-Aviv: Zgierz Society, 1975-1986.

Förster, J. "Hitlers Entscheidung für den Krieg gegen die Sowjetunion." In *Das deutsche Reich und der Zweite Weltkrieg*, Band 4, edited by H. Boog, J. Förster, et al., 3-37. Stuttgart: Deutsche Verlags-Anstalt, 1983.

Frieser, K.-H. "The War in the West, 1939-1940. An Unplanned Blitzkrieg." In *The Cambridge History of the Second World War*. Vol. 1, *Fighting the War*, edited by J. Ferris and E. Mawdsley, 287-314. Cambridge: Cambridge University Press, 2015.

Gorodetsky, G. "Introduction." In *The Maisky Diaries. Red Ambassador to the Court of St. James's 1932-1943*, edited by G. Gorodetsky, xvi–xvii. New Haven: Yale University Press, 2015.

Graml, H. "Resistance Thinking on Foreign Policy." In *The German Resistance to Hitler*, edited by H. Graml, H. Mommsen, H. J. Reichhardt, and E. Wolf, 14-29. Berkeley, CA: University of California Press, 1970.

Iranek-Osmecki, J. "Postscriptum II: Śmierć gen. Władysława Sikorskiego." In *Powołanie i Przeznaczenie.Wspomnienia oficera Komendy Głównej AK 1940-1944*, edited by K. Iranek-Osmecki, 538-56. Warszawa: Państwowy Instytut Wydawniczy, 1998.

———. "Pułkownik Kazimierz Iranek-Osmecki. Wspomnienie syna." In *Powołanie i Przeznaczenie.Wspomnienia oficera Komendy Głównej AK 1940-1944*, edited by K. Iranek-Osmecki, 503-535. Warszawa: Państwowy Instytut Wydawniczy, 1998.

Kroener, B. R. "Der Kampf um den 'Sparstoff' Mensch. Forschungskontroversen über die Mobilisierung der deutschen Kriegswirtschaft 1939-1942." In *Der Zweite Weltkrieg. Analysen, Grundzüge, Forschungsbilanz*, edited by W. Michalka, 402-417. München and Zürich: R. Piper, 1989.

Modsley, E. "Fifth Column, Forth Service, Third Task, Second Conflict? The Major Allied Powers and European Resistance." In *Hitler's Europe Ablaze. Occupation, Resistance, and Rebellion During World War II*, edited by Ph. Cooke and B. H. Shepherd, 14-32. New York: Skyhorse Publishing, 2014.

Oltmer, J. "Prekäre Duldung und aktive Intoleranz. Das Schicksal jüdischer Flüchtlinge in der Weimarer Republik." In *Berlin Transit. Jüdische Migranten aus Osteuropa in den 1920er Jahren*, edited by I. Bertz et al, 34-36. Berlin: Wallstein Verlag, 2012.

Pepłoński, A. "Funkcjonowanie i efekty działań polskiego kontrwywiadu ofensywnego w latach 30. XX wieku." In *Sekretna wojna. Z dziejów kontrwywiadu II RP*, vol. 1, edited by Z. Nawrocki, 194-210. Warszawa: Agencja Bezpieczeństwa Wewnętrznego. Centralny Ośrodek Szkolenia, 2013.

Reynolds, D. "Churchill in 1940: The Worst and Finest Hour." In *Churchill*, edited by D. Blake and W. R Louis, 241-56. Oxford: Clarendon Press, 1996.

Sikorski, T. "'Wyznajemy zasady narodowe polskie i uniwersalne katolickie', Stronnictwo Narodowe na emigracji (1939–1992): zarys działalności i myśli politycznej." In *Angielski łącznik. Albin Tybulewicz (1929–2014)*, edited by K. Niewiadomski and M. Jaworski, 11-82. Warszawa: Muzeum Historii Polski, 2016.

Slutsch, S. "Die deutsch-sowjetischen Beziehungen im Polenfeldzug und die Frage des Eintritts der UdSSR in den Zweiten Weltkrieg." In *Präventiv-krieg? Der deutsche Angriff auf die Sowjetunion*, edited by B. Pietrow-Ennker, 99-117. Frankfurt am Main: Fischer Taschenbuch Verlag, 2011.

Vast, C. "Résistance intérieure française." In *Encyclopédie de la Seconde Guerre Mondiale*, edited by Jean-François Muracciole and Guillaume Piketty, 1121-1126. Paris: Robert Laffont, 2015.

Articles in Scholarly Journals and Encyclopedias

Adamczyk, A. "Piłsudczycy na emigracji 1939-1944." *Biuletyn Instytutu Pamięci Narodowej*, no. 5-6 (2008): 99-107.

Bach, G. "Machshavot ve-hirhurim 30 shana le-achar mishpat aichman." *Be-shvil' ha-zikaron, Yad Vashem*, no. 41 (2001): 4-51. Accessed March 5, 2024. https://www.yadvashem.org/odot_pdf/Microsoft%20Word%20-%201410.pdf.

Brügel, J. W. "Eine zerstörte Legende um Hitlers Aussenpolitik." *Vierteljahrshefte für Zeitgeschichte*, no. 5 (1957): 385-387.

Chimiak, L. "'Adam Tarnowski–nasz poseł w Sofii'. Przyczynek do dziejów współpracy polskobułgarskiej w latach 1939–1941." *Pamięć i sprawiedliwość. Pismo naukowe poświęcone historii najnowszej* 2, no. 24 (2014): 227-251.

Cichoracki, P. "Sprawcy klęski wrześniowej przed sądem historii, red. Mieczysław Adamczyk, Janusz Gmitruk, Oficyna Wydawnicza ASPRA-JR, Muzeum Historii Polskiego Ruchu Ludowego, Wszechnica Świętokrzyska,

Warszawa 2005, ss. 317." Recenzja, *Pamięć i Sprawiedliwość. Pismo naukowe poświęcone historii najnowszej*, no. 5 (2006): 350.

Foot, M. R. D. "The Death of General Sikorski." *Intelligence and National Security* 21, no. 3 (2006): 457–458.

Gontarczyk, P. "Z genealogii elit PZPR. Przypadek Stefana Kilianowicza vel Grzegorza Korczyńskiego." *Glaukopis*, no. 1 (2003): 214-229.

Gruchman, L. "Die 'verpassten strategischen Chancen'. Der Achsenmächte im Mittelmeerraum 1940/41." *Vierteljahrshefte für Zeitgeschichte* 18, no 4. (1970): 456-475.

Henke, J. "Hitler un England Mitte August 1939. Ein Dokument zur Rolle Fritz Hesses in den deutschbritischen Beziehungen am Vorabend des Zweiten Weltkrieges." *Vierteljahrshefte für Zeitgeschichte* 21, no. 2 (1973): 231-242.

Hułas, M. "Wrogowie naszych sojuszników. Kwestia (nie)istnienia stanu wojny między Polską a Włochami. 1940." *Białostockie Teki Historyczne* 15 (2017): 205-228.

Iranek-Osmecki, K. "Afera Mikicińskiego." *Zeszyty Historyczne* (Paryż), no. 32 (1975): 198.

———. "Szkodliwa książka (Władysław Michniewicz, Operation Haifa)." *Zeszyty Historyczne* (Paryż) 18, no. 192 (1970): 221-229.

Jaskulski, W. "Embassy of the Republic of Poland in Ankara in the Period of September 1939–July 1945." *International Journal of Humanities and Social Science Invention* (IJHSSI), 2nd ser., 8, no. 1 (2019): 26-33.

———. "Bogusław Miedziński." *Przegląd bezpieczeństwa wewnętrznego*, no. 5 (2011): 229-230. www.abw.gov.pl/download.php?s=1&id=10.

Kania, L. "Kolejny świadek wrześniowego dramatu na Kresach. Odnaleziony memuar przodownika Sobieralskiego ze Śniatyna." *Zeszyty Naukowe Uniwersytetu Przyrodniczo-Humanistycznego w Siedlcach*, no. 112 (2017): 117-139.

Kapera Z. J. "Niemieckie świadectwa o Samsonie Mikicińskim." *Scripta Historica*, no. 27 (2021): 59-78.

Kaspi, Y. "Batei ha-soar be-eretz israel' be-tkufat ha-mandat ha-briti." *Katedra* 32 (1984): 141-174.

Koseski, "Emigracja żydów z ziem polskich w XX wieku." *Studia z Nauk Społecznych* 14, no. 7 (1999): 27-40.

Krausnick, H. "Legenden um Hitlers Außenpolitik." *Vierteljahrshefte für Zeitgeschichte*, no. 2 (1954): 217-239.

Kunicki, M. "Unwanted Collaborators: Leon Kozłowski, Wladyslaw Studnicki and the Problem of Collaboration among Polish Conservative Politicians in World War II." *European Review of History* 8, no. 2 (2001): 203-220.

Lampe, J. R. "Interwar Bucharest and the Promises of Urbanism." *Journal of Urban History* 9, no. 3 (1983): 267-290.

Lebedeva, N. "'Sentiabr' 1939: Pol'sha mezhdu Germaniei i SSSR." *Vestnik MGIMO-Universiteta*, Special Issue (2009): 231-249.

Levin I. "Ha-e'dim maashimim ve-dorshim—skira rishonit shel' yehudim she-nichshedu be-israel' be-shituf pe'ula im ha-natsim ve-she-lo hu'amdu le-din." *Katedra* 162 (2017): 95–118.

Łukasiewicz, S. "Przesłuchania generała Modelskiego przed komisjami Izby Reprezentantów i Senatu USA wiosną 1949 roku," *Pamięć i Sprawiedliwość: biuletyn Głównej Komisji Badania Zbrodni przeciwko Narodowi Polskiemu Instytutu Pamięci Narodowej* 1, no. 15 (2010): 413-496.

Macdonald, K. "The Evolution of W. H. Smith's Bookselling Strategies and Responsibilities, from the Edwardians to a More Permissive Age." *Logos* 29, no. 2-3 (2018): 26-36.

Machniak, A. "Polski wywiad i kontrwywiad wojskowy w latach 1918–1939 wobec Związku Sowieckiego. Charakterystyka działalności zawarta w dokumentach Głównego Zarządu Informacji Wojska Polskiego." *UR Journal of Humanities and Social Sciences* 1, no. 2 (2017): 27-43.

Martin, B. "Britisch-deutsche Friedenskontakte in den ersten Monaten des Zweiten Weltkrieges. Eine Dokumentation über die Vermittlungsversuche von Birger Dahlerus." *Zeitschrift für Politik*, no. 19 (1972): 206-221.

Misgav, T. "Machane ha-ma'atzar be-latrun be-tkufat ha-mandat ha-briti." *Alei zait ve-cherev* 9 (2009): 158-185.

Miszewski, D. "Polska polityka zagraniczna i rola wojska w geopolitycznych rozważaniach podpułkownika Tadeusza Zakrzewskiego, skierowanych do premiera, gen. Władysława Sikorskiego." *Studia z Dziejów Rosji i Europy Środkowo-Wschodniej* 51, no. 2 (2016): 151-166.

Młynarczyk, J.A. "Pomiędzy współpracą a zdradą. Problem kolaboracji w Generalnym Gubernatorstwie—próba syntezy." *Pamięć i Sprawiedliwość: biuletyn Głównej Komisji Badania Zbrodni przeciwko Narodowi Polskiemu Instytutu Pamięci Narodowej*, no. 1 (2009): 103-132.

Paszkiewicz, L. B. "Komitet dla Spraw Kraju. Zarys działalności Adama Ciołkosza w latach 1940-1942." *Archiwum Emigracji* 1-2, no. 12-13 (2010): 158-173.

Patek, A. "Polska emigracja niepodległościowa w Tel Awiwie po drugiej wojnie światowej (1945-1948)." *Studia Środkowoeuropejskie i Bałkanistyczne* 24 (2016): 99-120.

Schöllgen, G. "'Another' Germany: The Secret Foreign Contacts of Ulrich von Hassel during the Second World War." *International History Review* 11, no. 4 (1989): 648-667.

Seydi, S. "The Intelligence War in Turkey during the Second World War: A Nazi Spy on British Premises in Istanbul." *Middle Eastern Studies* 40, no. 3 (2004): 75-85.

Solarski, B. "Bitwa nad Bzurą. W 70. rocznicę (1939-2009)." *Notatki Płockie* 54, no. 2 (2009): 41-49.

Sołtysik, M. "Szumowiny Kinematografii (cz. 3). Kup pan album! Błysk oczu z 'menażerii typów.'" *Palestra*, no. 10 (2014): 116-121.

Sroka, M. "Emigracja żydów polskich w latach 1918-1939. Zarys problematyki." *Państwo i Społeczeństwo*, no. 2 (2010): 109-122.

Świerczek, Marek, "Władysław Michniewicz, *Wielki bluff sowiecki*." *Przegląd Bezpieczeństwa Wewnętrznego* 9, no. 5 (2013): 271-273.

Tarka, K. "Waldemar Sobczyk i 'Nasz Znak'—dywersja w ruchu ludowym na emigracji." *Pamięć i Sprawiedliwość* 2, no. 18 (2011): 321-363.

Tazbir, J. "'Stanisław Kot 1885-1975: biografia polityczna', Tadeusz Paweł Rutkowski, Warszawa 2000: [recenzja]." *Dzieje Najnowsze* 33, no. 4 (2001): 161-165.

Țiu, I. "Terrorism as Political Tool. The Assassination of Romanian Prime Minister Armand Călinescu by Legionnaires: 21st of September 1939." *Cogito: Multidisciplinary Research Journal* 5, no. 3 (2013): 61-69.

Żebrowski, R. "Obóz przejściowy w Zbąszyniu." *Polski Słownik Judaistyczny*, Żydowski Institut Historyczny. Accessed March 5, 2024. https://delet.jhi.pl/pl/psj?articleId=13670.

PhD Dissertations and Lectures

Bines, Jeffrey. "The Polish Country Section of the Special Operations Executive 1940-1946: A British Perspective." PhD diss., University of Stirling, 2008. Accessed March 5, 2024. https://dspace.stir.ac.uk/bitstream/1893/929/1/z%20Thesis.pdf.

Isci, O. "Russophobic Neutrality: Turkish Diplomacy, 1936-1945." PhD diss., Georgetown University, 2014

Miller, R. L. "The Welles Mission to Rome: February–March 1940. FDR's Diplomatic Initiative to Mussolini." Paper presented at the New York Military Affairs Symposium, NYMAS-CUNY, New York City, May 27, 2008. Accessed March 5, 2024. http://bobrowen.com/nymas/Robert%20Miller%20-%20Sumner%20Welles.html.

Mee, R. C. "The Foreign Policy of the Chamberlain Wartime Administration, September 1939–May 1940." PhD diss., University of Birmingham, 1998. Accessed March 5, 2024. https://core.ac.uk/download/pdf/76822.pdf.

Snyder, T. "The Origins of the Final Solution: Eastern Europe and the Holocaust." Paper presented at the London School of Economics and Political Science, March 12, 2014. Accessed March 5, 2024. https://www.youtube.com/watch?v=fxyHV90ESIY.

Nonacademic Publications in Print and Digital Newspapers and Journals

"Air Ministry, 21st February 1941," *London Gazette*, February 21, 1941, 1077. Accessed March 5, 2024. https://www.thegazette.co.uk/London/issue/35083/supplement/1077/data.pdf.

Bek E. "Ha-matsil' me-istanbul: ha-konsul ha-polani she-itsil' yehudim ba-shoah." *Israel ha-yom*, December 10, 2020. Accessed March 5, 2024. https://www.israelhayom.co.il/article/828547.

"British Reply to German Proposals." *Hansard*, October 12, 1939, vol. 352 cc563-603. Accessed March 5, 2024. https://api.parliament.uk/historic-hansard/commons/1939/oct/12/british-reply-to-german-proposals.

Brzeziecki, A. "Zagadka Wilhelma Canarisa. Dlaczego szef Abwehry pomagał Polakom?"

twojahistoria.pl, February 9, 2021. Accessed March 5, 2024. https://twojahistoria.pl/2021/02/09/zagadka-wilhelma-canarisa-dlaczego-szef-abwehry-pomagal-polakom/.

Bulletin of International News (Royal Institute of International Affairs), 16, no. 19 (September. 23, 1939).

"Chilean Chancellor Sought in Istanbul." *Wilmington Morning Star*, January 22, 1941. Accessed March 5, 2024. http://chroniclingamerica.loc.gov/lccn/sn78002169/1941-01-22/ed-1/seq-4/.

Cobain, I. "Secrecy and Firing Squads: Britain's Ruthless War on Nazi Spies." *Guardian*, August 28, 2016. Accessed March 5, 2024. https://www.theguardian.com/world/2016/aug/28/britain-nazi-spies-mi5-second-world-war-german-executed.

Cynk, J. B. "Rewelacje Szarkiewicza—sprawa broni czechosłowackiej." *Skrzydlata Polska* 6, no. 2356 (2009), 53-56.

Czulda, R. "Pod tureckimi skrzydłami." *Polska Zbrojna*, January 1, 2017. Accessed March 5, 2024. http://polska-zbrojna.pl/home/articleinmagazineshow/21585?t=Pod-tureckimi-skrzydlami.

"Documents and Photos of Jewish Pogroms in Rumania Displayed by Chilean Diplomat." *Jewish Telegraphic Agency Daily News Bulletin* 8, no. 200 (August 7, 1941), 2.

"Edward Stanisław Fikus (1895-1971) polanicki fotograf w latach 1946-1971." *Nieregularnik Polanicki*, no. 1 (2018), 25-33.

Finlay, M. "Why Book Shops Are A Popular Feature Of Many Airports." *Simple Flying*, August 8, 2023. Accessed March 5, 2024. https://simpleflying.com/airport-bookshops-popularity-guide/.

Flight, March 6, 1941, 197.

Gulbicki, P. "Tropem zabójcy generała." *Dziennik Polski*, July 10, 2009. Accessed March 5, 2024. https://wiadomosci.onet.pl/kiosk/tropem-zabojcy-generala/kw0qc.

Iranek-Osmecki, K. "Do Kraju przez cztery kontynenty. Powrót do Londynu." *Wiadomości* 14, no. 9 (674) (1959), 2.

"Israeli tove'a mi-turkia lehachzir lo tevat tachshitim." *Ma'ariv*, January 23, 1961, 8.

Kellerhoff, S. F. "Hitler's Milliarden in der Schweiz." *Handelszeitung*, June 27, 2014. Accessed March 5, 2024. https://www.handelszeitung.ch/politik/hitlers-milliarden-der-schweiz-632026.

Klisurova, L. "B'lgari spasiavat polski evrei, a Desi Radeva prenese istoriiata im v muzeia v'v Varshava." *24 Chasa*, October 12, 2017. Accessed March 5, 2024. https://www.24chasa.bg/novini/article/6493602.

Koreś, D. "Tajemnice generała Gano." Biuletyn IPN-Pamięć.pl 7-8, no. 16-17 (2013), 48-53.

Korowicz, M. S. "I Escaped to Speak for the Enslaved." *Life* 36, no. 9 (March 1, 1954), 103-112.

"Ladislav Michniewich. Opération Haïfa." *Information Juive*, November 15, 1970, 8.

Leitch, D. "Rotschild Spied as a 'Fifth Man.'" *Independent*, October 23, 1994. Accessed March 5, 2024. https://www.independent.co.uk/news/uk/home-news/rothschild-spied-as-the-fifth-man-1444440.html.

Lekarev, S. "Baron Viktor Rotshil'd: Istoriia sponsora kembridzhskoi piaterki." *Argumenty nedeli*, February 1, 2007. Accessed March 5, 2024. http://argumenti.ru/espionage/n40/33679.

"Lieut. Gen. Izydor Modelski, 74, Polish Spy Who Defected, Dies." *New York Times*, September 28, 1962, 25.

"List of aliens to whom Certificates of Naturalization have been granted by the Secretary of State, and whose Oaths of Allegiance have been registered in the Home Office during the month of September 1946," *The London Gazette*, October 22, 1946, 5214.

Milmo, C. "MI5 Feared Duke of Bedford Was Nazi Choice for Britain's Leader." *Independent*, May 9, 2002. Accessed March 5, 2024. https://www.independent.co.uk/news/uk/home-news/mi5-feared-duke-of-bedford-was-nazi-choice-for-britains-leader-9241251.html.

Mok, K. "Bookstores continue to flourish in Changi Airport." *Changi Airport Group*, April 2023. Accessed March 5, 2024. https://www.changiairport.com/corporate/media-centre/changijourneys/the-changi-experience/bookstores.html.

"Motywy zabójców generała Sikorskiego." *Salon24*, December 9, 2008. Accessed March 5, 2024. https://www.salon24.pl/u/witas1972/55209,motywy-zabojcow-generala-sikorskiego.

Oakley, F. "The Luftwaffe Over Liverpool." *Commonweal*, January 13, 2016. Accessed March 5, 2024. https://www.commonwealmagazine.org/luftwaffe-over-liverpool.

Oliver, E. F. "Miracle of the Monterey. The Night of Nov. 6, 1943—When Matson Line's Luxury Liner Braved all Odds in World War Two's Greatest Rescue at Sea." *Cruise Travel* (November/December 1983), 48-65.

"Ppłk. Kleczyński, katastrofa w Gibraltarze a tragedia w Smoleńsku." *Bibuła. Pismo Niezależne*, December 8, 2010. Accessed March 5, 2024. http://www.bibula.com/?p=29139.

Rodak, W. "Paul Fuchs zwany 'Lisem z Radoma'. Gestapowiec, który szachował Podziemie." *Polska Times*, May 19, 2016. Accessed March 5, 2024. https://polskatimes.pl/paul-fuchs-zwany-lisem-z-radomia-gestapowiec-ktory-szachowal-podziemie/ar/10012656.

"Samson Mikicinski Ne Oldu?" *Vatan*, January 22, 1941, 1, 5.

Schlögel, K. "Stiefmütterchen Berlin." *Zeit Online*, November 17, 2015. Accessed March 5, 2024. https://www.zeit.de/zeit-geschichte/2015/04/russen-in-deutschland-berlin-charlottenburg-russlanddeutsche-wuensdorf.

Sendek, R. "Południowcy w polskiej konspiracji." *Polska Zbrojna*, no. 5 (853) (May 2017): 118-121. Accessed March 5, 2024. https://zbrojni.blob.core.windows.net/pzdata2/TinyMceFiles/pz5_2017.pdf.

"Sir Arthur Forbes, Earl of Granard, 77." *New York Times*, November 21, 1992.

Stachnik, P. "Ilu Niemców naprawdę zginęło w Powstaniu Warszawskim?" *Ciekawostki historyczne.pl*, July 31, 2017. Accessed March 5, 2024. https://ciekawostkihistoryczne.pl/2017/07/31/ilu-niemcow-naprawde-zginelo-w-powstaniu-warszawskim/#4.

Stańczyk, T. "Dr Cytowska: Dla Roosevelta najważniejszy był Związek Sowiecki." *Polska Agencja Prasowa*, September 10, 2012. Accessed March 5, 2024. https://dzieje.pl/aktualnosci/dr-cytowska-dla-roosevelta-najwazniejszy-byl-zwiazek-sowiecki.

Strachanowski, P. "Guwernantka Zubczewska, czyli ucieczka generałowej." *inowroclaw.naszemiasto.pl*, October 27, 2017. Accessed March 5, 2024. https://inowroclaw.naszemiasto.pl/guwernantka-zubczewska-czyli-ucieczka-generalowej-historia/ar/c1-4291164.

Sunday Dispatch, December 10, 1939. In *Deutschland in der öffentlichen Kriegszieldiskussion Grossbritanniens 1939-1945*, Europäische Hochschulschriften/European University Studies, German ed., edited by H. Fromm, 46. Frankfurt am Main-Bern: Peter Lang, 1982.

Szczepański, J. "Błyskotliwy agent czy zdrajca? Tajenica Samsona Mikicińskiego." *Nasza Historia*, April 29, 2016. Accessed March 5, 2024. https://naszahistoria.pl/blyskotliwy-agent-czy-zdrajca-tajenica-samosna-mikicinskiego/ar/9895157.

Szeremietiew, R. "1939. Ucieczka, której nie było." *Tygodnik Solidarność*, November 7, 2017. Accessed March 5, 2024. https://www.tysol.pl/a12970-Romuald-Szeremietiew-1939-Ucieczka-ktorej-nie-bylo.

Szustakowski, J. "Jak uratowano skarb narodu." *Polska Zbrojna*, December 10, 2016, 2-3.

Wagner, R. "Torturowani, bici i głodzeni. Dramatyczne sceny w polskim obozie. Przemilczana karta naszej historii." *Co za Historia*, September 20, 2018. Accessed March 5, 2024. https://cozahistoria.pl/torturowani-bici-i-glodzeni-dramatyczne-sceny-w-polskim-obozie-przemilczana-karta-naszej-historii/.

Wieczorkiewicz, P. "Wojna polska." *Rzeczpospolita*, September 17, 2005. Accessed March 5, 2024. https://archiwum.rp.pl/artykul/570184-Wojna-polska.html.

Yacobson, M. "Sivuv leyad ha-bait shel' Chanoch Levin, ha-tachana ha-merkazit ha-yeshana ve-dirot ba-i'r." *Chalon achori*, March 14, 2013. Accessed March 5, 2024. https://michaelarch.wordpress.com/2013/03/14/.

Publications on the Official Websites of Various Institutions

Andrew, Christopher. "MI5 in World War II." Security Service MI5. Accessed February 20, 2024. https://www.mi5.gov.uk/mi5-in-world-war-ii.

"Battle of Britain Chronology." Battle of Britain Historical Society, page 21. Accessed February 20, 2024. https://www.battleofbritain1940.net/0021.html.

"Boćki—Historia społeczności," *Wirtualny sztetl*, Muzeum Historii Żydów Polskikh Polin. Accessed March 6, 2024. https://sztetl.org.pl/pl/miejscowosci/b/1908-bocki/99-historia-spolecznosci/137093-historia-spolecznosci.

Gasior, M. "The Polish Pilots Who Flew in the Battle of Britain." *Imperial War Museums*, January 9, 2018. Accessed March 6, 2024. https://www.iwm.org.uk/history/the-polish-pilots-who-flew-in-the-battle-of-britain.

Gilbert, M. "Churchill and the Holocaust." BBC History, February 17, 2011. Accessed March 6, 2024. https://www.bbc.co.uk/history/worldwars/genocide/churchill_holocaust_01.shtml.

Kochanowski, J. "Polen in die Wehrmacht? Zu einem wenig erforschten Aspekt der nationalsozialistischen Besatzungspolitik 1939-1945," Katolische Universität Eichstätt-Ingolstadt. Accessed March 6, 2024. https://www1.ku.de/ZIMOS/forum/docs/kochan.htm.

"Mihail Manoilescu (1891-1950)." *Radio România*. Accessed February 20, 2024. http://www.romania-actualitati.ro/mihail_manoilescu_1891_1950-46362.

"Order Odrodzenia Polski," PREZYDENT.PL. Accessed February 20, 2024. https://www.prezydent.pl/prezydent/kompetencje/ordery-i-odznaczenia/ordery/order-odrodzenia-polski/.

"Spirit of the Blitz. Liverpool in the Second World War." Merseyside Maritime Museum. Accessed March 5, 2024. https://www.liverpoolmuseums.org.uk/whatson/merseyside-maritime-museum/exhibition/spirit-of-blitz.

"Still Keeping the home Fire Burning after 75 years. The Polish Hearth: 1939-2014." Accessed March 5, 2024. http://ogniskopolskie.org.uk/about.aspx.

Other Digital Sources

"Bronislaw Stefanowski Syrokomla." Find a Grave, January 19, 2024. https://www.findagrave.com/memorial/123737282/bronislaw-stefanowski-syrokomla.

Historical Currency Converter. Historicalstatistics.org. Accessed February 20, 2024. http://www.historicalstatistics.org/Currencyconverter.html.

Joachimczyk, J. "Fotografia z Powstania Warszawskiego. ul. Frascati przy Wiejskiej." sierpień-wrzesień 1944, MPW, nr. inwentarzowy MPW-IP/1162. Accessed February 20, 2024. https://www.1944.pl/szukaj-zdjec.html?search=Fotografia+z+Powstania+Warszawskiego.+ul.+Frascati+przy+Wiejskiej.

Tetramesh. "Kilburn Classic." Flickr, 2014. https://www.flickr.com/photos/tetramesh/14060318555.

Lapidot, Y. "The Irgun: The Acre Prison Break." *Jewish Virtual Library*. Accessed February 20, 2024. https://www.jewishvirtuallibrary.org/the-acre-prison-break.

Lee, M. "Obituary: Agnieszka Dorota Syrokomla-Stefanowska." University of Sydney, September 9 2008. Accessed March 5, 2024. https://www.zrobtosam.com/PulsPol/Puls3/index.php?sekcja=4&arty_id=6246.

"Radogoszcz Police Prison. Łódź Ghetto." Holocaust Education & Archive Research Team. Accessed February 20, 2024. http://www.holocaustresearchproject.org/ghettos/Radogoszcz.html.

Roe, K. "Classic Kilburn. 405 Kilburn High Road, London, NW6 7QF." *Cinema Treasures*. Accessed February 20, 2024. http://cinematreasures.org/theaters/18276.

"Shimshon Mikichinski." Forum istoriia ve-te'ud. Accessed February 20, 2024. https://www.fresh.co.il/vBulletin/showthread.php?t=475951.

"WW2—London under fire-bomb damage in Duke Street, St James Date: circa 1941." Alamy, Image ID: G3BXPD. Accessed February 20, 2024. https://www.alamy.com/stock-photo-ww2-london-under-fire-bomb-damage-in-duke-street-st-james-date-circa-105368661.html.

Index

A
Aachen, 79, 86
Abwehr, the, xix, xxi,–xxii, 2, 14, *passim*
Acre (aka Akko and Akka), 182–83, 185, 189, 200–1
Adamsky, Dmitry, xxvi
Africa, 213, 234–36, 280. *See also* North Africa
Agabekov, Georges, 124n4
Aharonson, Sh., 137n38, 297–98n24
A/H.2, agent of SOE, 59, 132
Air Force Cross, order, the, 176–77
Akka (Akko). *See* Acre
Alan Harker, Oswald, 227n78, 230n3
Albania, 123
Alexandrova, Anna (aka Nyusya), 81, 85
Alexandrowicz, Karol, 100n15, 102, 127n10, 128n13, 131n25, 165, 194–95, 250n2
Algeria, 234
Ali (code name). *See* Kurcyusz, Jerzy
Ali (code name). *See* Janssen, Alfred
Alley, Stephen, 149n30, 152n45, 176n130, 204n85, 213n15, 216–19, 220n41, 221–22, 224n62, 226n70, 227–29, 230n5, 232–33, 234n26, 238–44, 258
Allied force, the, xiv, xxv, 18, 123, 228, 240, 274
Allies, the, xv, xxii-xxiii, 8, 16n22, 16n26, 20n43, 35n99, 221, 274
Alter, Wiktor, 261
American Immigration Service, the, 62n21
Amsterdam, 74
Anders, Władysław, xiv, 220, 224–25, 227n75, 228, 258–59, 271, 282, 290
Anders's Army, the, 220–21, 224–25, 227n75, 258, 282–83, 289, 301
Angers, 14, 15n21, 21, 23n51, 42n135, 46n153, 46n160, 59n168, 85n29, 88n37, 92, 100–2, 104–5, 107–8, 110, 128, 140, 146, 295n11, 297n22, 298n26
Ankara, 30–31, 34, 59, 71, 73, 92, 115, 121, 123–24, 126, 128–29, 133–34, 162–69, 174, 194–95, 249–57, 274
Anschluss, the, 54, 65, 67n37

Ansel, Walter C., 50
Antonescu, Ion, 115, 121, 155, 180
APW (Armia Polska na Wschodzie). *See* Anders's Army
Arab Revolt, the, 182
Arciszewski, Mirosław, 99, 100n13, 127–31, 136, 146
Archbishop of York. *See* Temple, William
Argentina, 266, 284
Argetoianu, Constantin, 97
Argos, travel agency, the, 65n29
Arhion Etzel, military organization. *See* Irgun
Armia Krajowa (AK). *See* Home Army
Arthur. *See* Hermann, Arthur
Ashby, E. N., 222n48
Asia, 6, 234
Association of Jewish Industrialists, the, 280
Aston, Adam, 57
Atatürk, Mustafa Kemal, 122
Athens, 106, 177, 301
Atlantic Ocean, the, 176, 213
Atlit, suburb, the, 182
Auschwitz, 281
Australia, 20–21n43, 234, 265
Austria, xviii, 54, 65, 132, 283
Austro-Hungarian Empire, the, xiii, xviii, 42, 54, 148
Austro-Hungarian Parliament, the, 42
Axis countries, xxi, 115, 123, 180, 232, 236, 272
Ayaspaşa district, the, 114
Azis (code name). *See* Kurcyusz, Jerzy

B
Babinski, W., 25n59, 88n37
Bader, Karol, 81, 127, 167, 195, 200, 249, 251, 253
Baghdad, 255
Baginski, Henryk, 77, 79, 87
Balkan region, the, 83–84, 109, 114, 123, 150, 168, 214, 296
Baltic Sea, the, 30, 34
Banca Commerciale Italiana, the, 252
Bank of England, the, 17

Barbarossa, xiv
Baron de Ropp, William, 46–47
Baron Koch, 74
Baron Montagu Collet Norman, 17
Baron Moyne, Sir Walter Edward Guinness, 239
Baron Rothschild, Nathaniel Mayer Victor, 230, 278–79
Baroness Ostrowska-Koch, Krystyna, 74, 76
Bartel, Kazimierz, 268
Battle of Britain, the, xiv, 10
Battle of Monte Cassino (Battle for Rome), the, xiv, 282
Battle of the Bzura, the, 33, 35
Bauer, businessman, 66
Bębnik, Grzegorz, 67n34
Będzin, 85n29
Beirut, 127, 167, 237
Beck, Józef, 16, 29n75, 100, 108, 126–27
Belarus (Belorussia), 15n18, 51, 81n19
Belgium, 4, 82–84, 86, 90, 139–40
Beneš, Edvard, 20
Ben-Gurion, David, 284
Bern, 42n135, 89n47, 296n18
Berlin, 8, 16–17, *passim*
Berlin Opera, the, 50
B.1.C section. *See* MI5 Investigative Department
Białystok, 101
Bielecki, Eugeniusz, 66
Bielsk County, the, 57
Bińkowski, Józef, 189, 191n41
Black Sea, the, 187
Blenau, Zygmunt, 117–18
Blenheim Palace, the, 213n16
Blitz (Blitzkrieg), the, xiv, 10, 32, 33n87, 233, 275, 300n28
Blue Palace, the, 64–65
Bobajewski, Feodor (aka Bobby), 66–67, 80–81, 85, 267
Boćki, xviii, 57–58, 61, 62n21, 70–71, 82, 136, 159, 275
Boer War, the, 297
Bolivia, 132
Bolsheviks, the, 25, 58, 60, 131, 159, 214, 269, 293, 298
Bombay, 266n28
Bomek und Romek, 101–2
Borough of Richmond, 6
Bosporus, the, 114, 122, 124, 132, 174
Bratislava, 32
Brauchitsch, Walther von, 33, 35, 41
Brazil, 107
Breslau (Wrocław), xix, 63n21, 67–69, 80, 82–87, 89n44, 94, 104, 133, 142, 187, 190–91, 267, 281, 287

Briones. *See* Luco
Brit, the agent, 53n182, 185n24, 224
Britain, the, xiv, 6, 10, *passim*
British, the, *passim*
British Empire, the, xxiii, 36, 205, 277, 289, 300
British Isles, the, 16, 18, 23, 26, 46, 127, 136, 204, 213, 219–20, 223, 225, 237, 244, 260, 289–90
British Foreign Office, the, 14, 24, 45, 99, 151, 185, 265
British Middle East Land Forces Command, the, 213
British Military Administration, the, xxiv, 192, 236
British Military Censor, the, 95, 105
British National Archives, xxvii, 6, 62n21, 235n26–27, 302
British Parliament, the, 300
British Security Intelligence Middle East (SIME), the, xx, xxiv–xxv, 152, 169, 172, 192–93, 197, 199–200, 202, 211–13, 219, 222, 230–32, 235–40, 242–43, 270, 278–79, 290
Brocki, Jan, 24n55, 44, 85n29
Brooklyn, 5–6, 59, 62, 65, 82, 88, 90, 100, 104, 106, 111–13, 117–18, 141, 150, 162, 165–67, 170–72, 191, 194, 196–97, 199, 201, 261, 263–64
Brown, Beatrice, 40n124
Brussels, 63, 70n43, 73–74, 86
Brzeziecki, Andrzej, 69, 88n41
Bucharest, xix, 8, *passim*
Buchwald, Ludwig, 132–33, 250–51
Buczek, Roman, 3, 60, 66, 67n34, 166, 175–78, 182, 184, 185n26, 187–88, 198–200, 212, 244, 251, 267–68, 281–82
Budapest, 34, 36n106, 52n180, 85n29, 92n57, 101–2, 109, 126
Buenos Aires, 85n29, 266
Bulgaria, 23, 67n34, 81n19, 107–11, 115, 133, 191, 287
Bund (General Jewish Labor Bund), the, 261n9
Butler, a Colonel, 147n23
Bydgoszcz, Henryk, 265–66
Bzura, 33, 35

C

Cabinet Minister, the, 92
Cadenbronn Salient, 33n88
Cadogan, Sir Alexander, 38
Cairncross, John, 278
Cairo, xx, xxv, 19, 135n36, 152, 158, 169, 171–72, 184, 186n27, 192n44, 193, 195,

197n58, 199, 200n72, 202, 211, 213–14, 218n34, 219, 222, 229–32, 235–36, 239–41, 243, 259–60, 267, 270, 278
California, the, xxvi, 5, 105n30, 263, 302
Călinescu, Armand, 97
Cambridge, 302
Cambridge Five, network, 277–79
Cambridge Four, network, 278
Cambridge University, the, 278, 300n28
Canada, 281
Canaris, Wilhelm, xix, xxi, 33, 34n93, 69, 78–79, 85, 88, 142, 164, 287
Capt. S. (Szarkiewicz), 199. *See also* Szarkiewicz
Carlton, Ernest, 143–44
Carol II, King of Romania, 96–97, 115, 173, 180
Carpathian Riflemen Brigade, the, 155, 157, 210, 282–83
Cat-Mackiewicz, Stanisław, 26
Catholic Herald, The, periodical, 159, 228
Caucasus, the, 124
Chamberlain, Ida, 47
Chamberlain, Neville, 31, 34, 43, 47, 295, 300, 302
Chaplin, Charlie, 67
Charlottenburg, 61
Cheney, W. S., 221n47
Cherbourg, 62n21
Chicago, 63n21, 68n39, 268n32
Chile, xix, 57, 71n46, 104, 211, 302
Chileans (Chilean diplomats or officials), the, xix, 57, 68n39, 70–72, 74, 76–77, 79–84, 87, 114–21, 124, 126, 133–34, 143–44, 158–59, 161–62, 164, 166–67, 174, 180–81, 212, 249–53, 256, 275, 302
China, 236
Churchill, Sir Winston, xiv, 7–8, 12–20, 26, 39, 50, 67, 131, 177, 197, 202–5, 214, 216, 218, 220–21, 224–25, 228, 258–60, 262, 276, 289, 292, 296, 300, 302
CI, the, 63n21, 67n34, 68n37, 68n39, 81n19, 84n28, 87n35, 89n44, 268n32
Ciano, Gian Galeazzo, Count, 23, 29, 38, 41, 269, 296
CID. *See* Criminal Investigation Department
Ciechanowski, Jan Stanisław, 65n29, 107n38, 120n80, 149n33, 150n39, 154n53, 173, 182n9, 199n66
Citadel, prison, the, 182, 200
Claims Conference, organization, the, 164–65
Coburg, 298
Cohen, Marco, 257
Committee of Ministers for Homeland Affairs (Komitet Ministrów dla Spraw Kraju)., the, 76, 101, 125, 167

Communist Party, the, 267n31, 273, 278
Communist Poland, the, 88, 245, 263, 265, 276, 291
Congress, the, 263
Constanța, 97, 118
Convoy KMF-25A, the, 233–34, 235nn26–27
Copenhagen, 22n50, 74
Council of Ministers, the, xxiii, 210n4, 269n35, 271n42, 272n47, 272n49
Council of Seven (K-7), the, 7
Counterintelligence Service, the, xxi, xxiii, 60, 62, 65n27, 68, 71–72, 81n19, 84, 92, 95, 138, 144, 186, 190, 240
Cracow. *See* Kraków
Crete, 20n43, 169, 234
Crimea, the, 58
Criminal Investigation Department (CID), the, xxi, 152, 211
Cripps, Sir Stafford, 13nn11–12, 14–15
Çulu Airport, the, 175
Curzon line, the, 14
Cyprus, xxv, 169, 177, 210, 281–83
Czechoslovakia, 20, 32, 42–43, 50, 294. *See also* Slovakia
Czechowicz, K., 157n67, 221n45

D

Dahlerus, Birger, 37–38, 40–41, 45–47
Daladier, Édouard, 35n99, 98
Damascus, 155
Danzig (Gdańsk), 30–31, 73
Daugavpils (Dvinsk), 61
D.C. *See* California
D/H., agent, 169n106, 169n110, 202n76
de Gaulle, Charles, xxii, 22n49, 152
Dehradun prison, the, 266
Delegatura, the, 274
Delek, 160. *See also* Irgun
Denikin, Anton, 58–59, 66, 94
Denikin's Army. *See* White Army, the
Department of Control (in the Security Field), the, 221–22, 226–27, 232
Department of Foreign Citizen. *See* MI5 Department of Foreign Citizen
Department of Political Work with the Press, the, 262n13
Derbyshire, F., Captain, 106n38, 149n30, 152, 204n85, 212n10, 214n19, 216–19, 224n62, 226n70, 232n18, 234
de Ropp, William, Baron, 46–47
Detroit, 105n30
Dietrich, Marlene, 80
DNB (German News Agency), xxi, 30, 33
Dobrzyński, Wacław Tadeusz, 16n25
Dodecanese campaign, the, 236

Dömling, Joachim, 269–70
Dublin, 16
Duke of Coburg, 298
Dunlop (Szarkiewicz's code name), 235, 237, 238n40, 244. *See also* Szarkiewicz
Dutch officials. *See* Netherlands, the
Dutch territory. *See* Netherlands, the
Dvinsk (Daugavpils), 61
Dwójka (Second Department), the, *passim*
Dziennik Polski, newspaper, the, 105n30

E
Earl of Granard. *See* Forbes
Eastern Europe, the, 5, 29, 269, 293n7, 296
Eastern Front, the, 35, 225, 271
Eden, Anthony, 11n4, 259n4
Educhowski (code name). *See* Fietz-Fietowicz
Edward, Charles, Duke of Coburg, 298
Egypt, xxv, 19, 148n26, 148n29, 171, 176, 212–13, 219, 222, 224, 229, 231–32, 234–36, 240–44, 290
Ehrlich, Henryk, 261
Eichmann, Adolf, 284
Eiger, Akiva (Karol), rabbi, 87–88, 253, 279–83
Eiger, Charlotte, 281
Eiger, Dorota. *See* Gralińska, Dorota
Eiger, Moshe Zvi (Moshel), 280
Eiger, Rozalia. *See* Levenson, Rozalia
Eiger, Shlomo Salomon, 281
Eiger and Sirkis, company, 280
Eighth Army, the, 83
Ellis Island Foundation, the, 62n21
England, the, 38, 47, 199, 233, 241, 302
English Channel, the, 19
ESS13 (Szarkiewicz's code name), 152, 172. *See also* Szarkiewicz, Edward
Europe, xviii, xix, xxi, *passim*
European Union, the, 2, 286
ekspozytura R, Polish military intelligence station in Bucharest, the, 100, 140, 142–47, 150–52, 183, 189, 191, 260
ekspozytura T, Polish military intelligence station in Ankara, the, 59, 62n21, 63n24, 66n32, 67n36, 68n38, 70n43, 74n5, 77nn12–13, 133–35, 166, 188–89, 210
Ethiopia, xxv
Expeditionary Force, the, 176, 240

F
Fabian (Habian), Heinz Heinrich, xix, 67n34, 68n37, 267. *See also* Scholz (code name)
Fietz-Fietowicz, Edmund (aka Educhowski and Piast), 101–2

Fighters for the Freedom of Israel (Lehi), group, xxiii, 239
Fighting France (France combattante), xxii
Fikus, Edward Stanisław, 110
Finland, 22-23, 50, 298
Fitin, Pavel, 51n178
Florin, Alfred, 255–57, 284
Forbes, Sir Arthur Patrick Hastings, the 9th Earl of Granard, 175–77
Foreign counterintelligence section (III F), the, 67n34
Forrest, Major, 239
France, xiv, xviii–xix, *passim*. *See also* Vichy France
Franco, Francisco, 22, 26, 149, 296
Franco, Gad, 249, 251, 254–55
Frank, Hans, xiv, 44, 48–52, 81, 104, 109, 271n43, 272, 273n50, 274
Frankfurt, 164, 287
Free France (France libre), xxii
French army (forces, troops etc.), the, 33n99, 35, 98, 140
French Central Bank, the, 89
French Counterintelligence Service (Sûreté nationale), the, 140
French Resistance, movement, 27, 293
Fritz, a driver of Scholz, 83–84
Fuchs, Paul, 270
Führer, the, 28, 30–31, 34, 38n116, 41, 43, 89, 272. *See also* Hitler, Adolf
Fundacja Generał Elżbiety Zawackiej, 276n61, 302

G
Galicia, 273
Gamelin, Maurice, 35n99
Gano, Bronisława, 88, 160, 217
Gano, Stanisław, 88, 160–61, 198, 200, 217, 253
Gaulle, Charles de, xxii, 22n49, 152
Gdańsk (Danzig), 30–31, 73
George, Prince, 11, 46
General Government (Generalgouvernement, GG), the, xiv, xix, xxii, 43–45, 47–51, 80–84, 85n29, 87–91, 91–94, 102–4, 106–7, 109–10, 113, 136, 270–74, 291, 297–98
General Jewish Labor Bund, 261n9
General Staff of the French Army, the, 98
General Staff of the German Army, the, 28n72, 34, 129. *See also* High Command
General Staff of the Polish Army, the, xxii, 15n19, 17n28, 59, 70, 140n5, 150, 163n85, 228. *See also* High Command
General Staff of the Red Army, the, xxiv, 51n178

Genoa, 114
George VI, King, 12n5, 130, 162, 176, 290, 295
German Army (forces, troops etc.), the, xiv, xxi, 28n72, 31–34, 36, 42–43, 48, 115
German Empire, the, xiii
German Foreign Office, the, 17n27, 22nn46–48, 22n50, 30n80, 31n83, 32, 33n90, 35n98, 36, 37n109, 38, 39n120, 39n122, 47n158, 50n170, 54, 145
German News Agency (DNB), xxi, 30, 33
Germans, the, *passim*
Germany, *passim*
Gestapo (German Secret State Police), the, xxii, 27, 42, 44, 48–49, 81, 84, 85n29, 87–90, 104, 106, 108, 113, 133, 139, 141, 155, 161–65, 186, 211, 265, 269–70, 273, 287, 291
Gezira, island, 236
Gibraltar, Strait of, the, xiv, 234, 259–60, 290, 296
Giedroyc, Jerzy, 51, 74, 100, 103, 116–19, 126, 127n11, 128, 129n19, 130, 155, 158
Giles, Arthur, 152
Glasgow, 223
Goebbels, Joseph, xxii, 25, 27, 40–41
Goering (Göring), Hermann, 22n49, 37n107, 38n112, 45–46, 48, 50
Golovannikov, André (Andrei), 138–39
Gomel, 81n19
GPU, the, xxii, 211
Grabarsky, Alexander, 154n53, 273n51
Grabowski, Józef, 127n12
Graf von der Schulenburg, Friedrich-Werner, 17n27, 33n90, 35n98, 37
Gralińska, Dorota (Dora), née Eiger, 87n36, 281
Graliński, Zygmunt, 87, 281
Grand Orient Lodge, the, 92
Great Britain, the, 35n99
Great Depression, the, 63
Greece, 20n43, 103, 176–77, 301
Group B, the, 109–11
GRU, the, xxiv
Grushetsky, Ivan, 267n31
Gubbins, Colin, 150
Guinness, Sir Walter Edward, 1st Baron Moyne, 239
Gürsel, Cemal, 255–57

H
Habian, Heinz. *See* Fabian, Heinz
Habsburg dynasty, the, 54
Hague, the, 25n59, 38, 88n37
Haifa, 4, 152, 154, 179, 182, 199, 201, 210–11, 256, 284, 288

Halder, Franz, 28n72, 34, 38, 41
Halifax, Lord, 11, 14–15, 29, 40, 50
Hamburg, 71
Hedin, Sven, 38
Heim, Alfred (code name), 132. *See also* Janssen, Alfred
Hemar, Marian (Hescheles), 154
Henderson, Sir Nevile, 29
Hermann, Arthur, 62–63n21, 67–69, 83–84, 86–87, 89n44, 268n32, 287
Hescheles. *See* Hemar, Marian
Hesse, Fritz, 30–32
Heydrich, Reinhard, 25
High Command of the German forces, the, 28n72, 34, 62. *See also* General Staff
High Command of the Polish forces, the, 50n174, 52n180, 82, 188–89, 193, 226, 259n4. *See also* General Staff
Himmler, Heinrich, xxi, 66n31, 84, 87, 141, 269, 273n50
His Majesty. *See* George VI
Hitler, Adolf, xxiv, 8, 12, 14, 16, 19, 21n45, 26, 28–31, 34, 36–46, 48–52, 54, 66, 69, 78, 129, 137, 164, 177, 270–74, 293, 295–96, 299–300. *See also* Führer, the
Höberth, Eugen von, 42
Holocaust, the, xxvi, 111, 136, 137n38, 164, 186, 257, 282, 302
Holocaust Memorial Museum, the, xxvi, 302
Holy See, the, 11n3, 268
Home Army (AK), xx, xxii, xxv, 3, 76, 125, 271, 273–74, 276
Homs, 155
Hoover Institution, the, 5, 302
Hopkinson, Henry, 259
Hotel Alcron, the, 67
Hotel Ambassador, the, 142, 145
Hotel Eden, the, 80
Hotel European, the, 70n43
Hotel King David, 229
Hôtel Majestic, the, 61–62
Hotel Park, the, 173, 252
Hotel Regina, the, 82, 139
Hotel Rubens, the, 216–17, 223–24, 226
Hotel Savoy, the, 75
House of Lords, the, 278
Hungary, xiii, xviii, 23, 35, 42, 54, 85, 98, 100–1, 109–10, 115, 139, 148, 155, 210, 284, 298
Hunt, Sir David, 176–77
Hyde Park, the, 10, 260

I
Idzik, Aleksander, 226, 227n75
Ikonomov, Dimitar, 107, 109, 111, 115

Imperial Russian Army, the, xvi, 58–59
India, xx, xxin41, 266
İnönü, İsmet, 122–23
Interior Ministry, the. *See* Polish Interior Ministry
Iran, xxv, 114, 123, 220
Iranek-Osmecki, Jerzy, 260
Iranek-Osmecki, Kazimierz, xix, 3–4, 60, 140–46, 150, 159, 162, 177–78, 189–90, 198–99, 244–45, 260, 276, 288, 290, 299
Iraq, 124n4, 232, 282
Irgun (Arhion Etzel or AE), military organization, the, xxiii, 4, 160, 182, 210, 222. *See also* Zionist
Iron Cross, order of, the, 67n37
Iron Curtain, the, 245
Iron Guard (Legionary movement), the, 97, 115–16, 129, 165
Isle of Melos (Milos), 301
Israel, xxiii, xxvii, 2, 4, 199, 209, 245, 253, 256, 261, 265, 278–79, 281–84
Istanbul, xix, 2, 8, *passim*
Italian Foreign Office, the, 21
Italians, the, xx, 12, 17–18, 38–39, 168, 266, 269
Italy, xxi, 17, 23, 29, 39, 44, 46, 98, 123, 132, 234, 236, 252, 271, 282, 295–96, 298
Izya. *See* Modelski, Izydor

J
Jabotinsky, Vladimir (Ze'ev), 222
Jagiellonian University in Kraków, the, xix, 42, 52, 102, 105, 109, 156, 291
Janssen, Alfred (aka Heim, Alfred or Ali), 132
Japan, xxi, 17, 21n43, 23, 269, 295–98
Jerusalem, 108n43, 127, 131, 154, 156, 182–83, 189, 191, 195–98, 200–1, 210, 214, 229, 241n51, 252–53, 255, 259n4, 265, 272, 281, 284, 297n22
Jewish Bank, the, 280
Johannesburg, 227n75
Józef Piłsudski Institute of America, the, xxvii, 5, 59, 263, 302
Journal d'Orient, Le, newspaper, 181
Judas, Elizabeth, 171
Jūrmala, 9

K
Kański, Władysław, 127–28, 130–31, 156, 196
Kapera, Zdzisław, 3n5, 65n27, 67n34, 67–68n37, 69, 70n43, 140n7, 141n10, 186n27
Karachi, 266
Karl Radziwiłł, Prince, 273–74
Karski, Jan, 92–93

Kąsinowski, Stanisław, 108n43, 146, 153–54, 157, 193, 264–65
Kastner, Israel (Rudolf), 284
Katyn, xiv, 259, 262, 271
Kaunas, 74
Keitel, Wilhelm, 34n93
Kellar, Alex, 239–40, 243
Kendzior, Alexander, 87
Kensington, 10, 233
Kew, district, xxvii, 6–7, 176, 199, 235, 244, 302
KGB, the, xxiii, 279
Khrushchev, Nikita, 267n31, 273
Kilanowicz, Stefan (aka Korczyński, Grzegorz), 286n2
Kilburn area, 245
Kimchi, David, 255n16
Kiryat Motzkin, 298n27
KLM, airline, the, 50
KMF-25A, Convoy, the, 233–34, 235nn26–27
Knesset, the, 283
Koch, French Baron, 74
Komarnicki, Titus, 42n135
Komarnicki, Wacław, 226n74
Komitet Ministrów dla Spraw Kraju. *See* Committee of Ministers for Homeland Affairs
Kopański, Stanisław, 155, 157, 197, 271n42
Koper, Sławomir, 2–3, 225, 260n7
Korczyński, Grzegorz. *See* Kilanowicz, Stefan
Kornaus, Jan, 16n23, 100n13, 100n15, 101nn17–18, 103n21
Korsak, Witold, 195, 201
Kot, Stanisław (aka Tigris), xix–xx, 5–6, *passim*
Kotowcy, the, 102, 108, 127, 130–31, 134–35, 153, 167, 180–81, 185, 189, 202, 205, 268
Kowalewski, Jan, 26, 28
Kozielewski, Jan Romuald, 92–93
Kozłowski, Leon, 273–74
Kraft, economic advisor, 106
Kraków, xix, xxii, 2, 24, 42, 44n142, 48, 50, 52, 85n29, 102, 105, 109, 141, 156, 266, 273–74, 291, 297
Kraków University, the. *See* Jagiellonian University in Kraków
Kremlin, the, 13, 15, 37–38, 205, 262
Kresy Wschodnie, 13, 20
Krzemieniec, 34
K-7, the, 101
Kukiel, Marian, 146n20, 154n57, 155n58, 185, 215, 220, 223–24, 226, 230–32, 259n4, 265

Kulski, Władysław, 21
Kunicki, Tadeusz, 117–18, 126–27, 159, 161–63, 168
Kurcyusz, Jerzy (aka Ali/Azis/Novina), 100n15, 106, 107n38, 120, 127–28, 130–31, 134–37, 141n10, 165n89, 197, 203, 250n2, 299
Kuśnierz, Bronisław, 146n20, 154n57, 155n58
Kutten, Viktor, xviii, xx, 106–15, 129n17, 133, 145–47, 152–58, 163, 165–66, 168, 172, 183, 192–94, 196, 211, 226, 231, 241, 264–66, 287
Kuty, 96
Kuźniarz, Tomasz, 100n15, 105n30, 127n10, 128n13, 131n25, 241n51, 250n2, 265n20

L

Labour, party, the, 14
Lagos, 213
La Resistance, movement, 27, 293
Latin America, the, xviii, 12, 65–66, 121, 144. *See also* South America, the
Latrun camp, the, 153–54, 157–58, 196, 241, 265
Latvia, 39, 61, 74
League of Nations, the, 76
Lebanon, 89, 132, 195
Łebkowski, Andrzej, 154
Lebrun, Albert, 35n99
Lec, Stanisław Jerzy, 285
le Carré, John, 239
Legionary Movement (Legionaries), the. *See* Iron Guard
Lehi (Fighters for the Freedom of Israel), group, xxiii, 239
Lem, Stanisław, 154
Lenin, Vladimir, 151, 237
Levant, the, 152
Levenson, Rozalia, née Eiger, 281
Leviathan, ship, 62n21
Levin, Hanoch, 280
Leviton, Evser, 62n21
Leviton, Rosa, 62
Libya, 236, 282–83
Lis (Mikiciński's code name), 93, 105n30, 124, 157, 165n89, 249, 299. *See also* Mikiciński
Lisbon, 26, 52n180, 173, 181n6, 298n25
Lisova, Helena, 78n15
Lithuania, 59, 74, 261n9
Little Man (Szarkiewicz's code name), 147, 188, 214, 227, 232, 238, 240, 242, 288–89. *See also* Szarkiewicz, Edward
Liverpool, 233–35
Lockhart, Bruce, 151

Lod (Lydda), 264
Łódź, 63, 80, 87, 166, 280
London, xiv, xxii, xxv, *passim*
London Headquarters, 11n3, 168n103
Loraine, Sir Percy, 46
Lord Forbes, 175–77
Lubavitcher Rebbe. *See* Schneersohn, Yosef Yitzchak
Luco, Héctor Briones, Chilean chargé d'affaires in Brussels, xix, 70–71, 73, 76, 79–80, 82–83, 114, 119–20, 174, 181–82, 195, 250, 252
Luco, Ramon Briones, Chilean Ambassador from Rome, 70n43, 71
Ludyga-Laskowski, Jan Józef, 27–28
Luftwaffe (German Air Force), the, 233, 235
Lupescu, Magda (Elena), 173
Lupian, Edward Marian, 98n6
Lviv (Lwów), xviii, 101, 148, 185, 214, 267, 271n42, 273–74, 288, 298
Lviv Oblast, the, 148
Lydda (Lod), 264

M

Maariv, newspaper, 4, 256
Mackensen, Georg von, 29
Madrid, 22, 173, 269
Maisky, Ivan, 15n18, 17, 45n147, 296
Maisnerova, Maria, 85n29
Makhno, Nestor, 58
Maliniak, Marcus, 298
Mańczyński, Ryszard, 267–68
Mandatory Palestine, the, xxi, 57, 131, 147, 152–54, 157, 169, 172, 182, 186, 210
Mandatory police, the, 152–53, 156, 211–12
Manoilescu, Mihail, 180
Marek, Stefan, 64–65, 82, 139
Marquess of Londonderry, 17
Marquess of Tavistock, 16
Maunsell, Raymund John, xx, 152, 183n16, 199, 211, 213–14, 222, 226n73, 227n78, 229–30, 231n11, 232, 237, 239, 240, 243
Mawdsley, Evan, 293n4, 295n9, 300n28
May Coup, the, xiii
McGilvray, Evan, 224–25
McLaren, Moray, 151
Mcknab, G., 218n33
Mediterranean Basin, the, 123, 176–77, 182, 213, 234–35
Menemencioğlu. *See* Numan Menemencioğlu, Hüseyin
Menzies, Stewart, 172
MGB, the, xxiv
Mia Mia isolation camp, 132
Michael I, King, 115

Michniewicz, Ladislas (Władysław), 4, 58, 60, 141n10, 182–84, 188, 195–96, 198–200
Middle East, the, xiv, xx, xxiv, 4, *passim*
Middle East Command, the, 236–37
Miecz i Pług (Sword and Plow or Mieczowcy), organization, xxiii, 269–70, 291
Miedziński, Bogusław, 49
MI5, counterintelligence agency, xx, xxiii, xxv, *passim*
MI5 BIB Department , 240n46
MI5 Department of Foreign Citizen, the, 147n23, 149n30, 213n15, 218n34, 219n36, 228n84, 230n5, 232n21, 239n43, 241n50, 243
MI5 Investigative Department, the, 230–31
Mikiciński, Samson (aka Shimshon/Solomon/Lis/Fox/Mik/Paluchowicz/Mr. P.), *passim*
Mikiciński, Viktor-Vitaly, 63, 75
Mikołajczyk, Stanisław, 262
Military Museum, the, 122
Menielescu, a refugee. *See* Manoilescu, Mihail
Miniewski, a Colonel, 151, 266n29
MI9, a special service, xxii, 168
MI6, the, xxiii, xxv, 143, 151, 166–67, 169, 172, 175, 237, 251, 276, 278. *See also* SIS
Mitte, district, the, 61
Mitkiewicz-Żółłtek, Leon, 112n53, 112n56, 146n18, 147n21, 156–57, 161n76, 163, 183, 184n18, 190–91, 195, 197–98
Modelski, Izydor (Izya), xx, 150, 184–90, 198, 205, 211–12, 214–16, 218–28, 245, 258, 263, 276, 288–90
Mokotów Prison, the, 110
Molotov, Vyacheslav, 17n27, 37–38, 39n121
Molotov-Ribbentrop Pact, the, xiii, 29, 37, 72, 123, 228, 295
Moltke, Hans-Adolf von, 36
Monte Cassino, xiv, 282
Montevideo, 121
Morka, nickname, 139
Morocco, 234
Morsztyn, Count, 76
Moscow, 2, 12, *passim*
Mr. Boyce, 234
Mr. Hale, 242n58, 243n61, 243n64
Mr. Falterow, 48n161, 272n48
Mr. P. (Mikiciński's code name), 183, 185, 169
Mr. Wachomak, 272n48
MS *Marnix*, ship, 234–35
Munich Agreement, the, 300
Munters, Vilhelms, 39
Museum of the History of Polish Jews, the, 111

Mussolini, Benito, 21–22, 34, 39n120, 49, 271, 295–96
Muslim Brotherhood, the, 236
MX, agent, 172n117, 172n120, 184n20, 186n27, 192n44, 197n58, 200n72

N

Narbut-Luczynski, Aleksander, 224n63
Narew, 37n109
National City Bank, the, 71
National Democrats, party, 217
National Military Organization. *See* Irgun, the
National Radical Organization (NOR), the, xxiv, 43, 48–49
Nazi Germany, xiii, xxiii, xxv, 6, 9, 12, 21, 23, 26, 36n103, 85, 115, 122, 132, 138, 147, 164, 181, 203–4, 225, 242, 277, 293, 299
Netherlands, the, 29, 45, 50, 74–75
Neumann-Neurode, Karl Ulrich von, 42
Neve Sha'anan, 279
New York, xxvii, 5, 9, 62, 71, 90, 302
Nice, 27
Nigeria, 213
Nile, the, 235–36
NKGB, the, xxiii, 273
NKVD, the, xxii–xxiv, 51, 261, 287
Noakes, J., 49n163
Nobis, Erich (Ernst), 67–68, 80, 83, 87, 112–14, 129, 131, 133, 142, 145–47, 191, 267, 281
Norman, Montagu Collet, Baron, 17
North Africa, the, xxi, xxv, 6, 17, 154, 186, 233, 236–37, 269, 277, 282, 296. *See also* South Africa
North African Front, the, 237
North America, the, 19, 233
Northern Ireland, the, 12n5
Northwest England, 241
Nova station, the, 183
Novina (code name). *See* Kurcyusz, Jerzy
Nowiński, Tadeusz, 75, 140n7
NSDAP, the, xxiv, xxv
Numan Menemencioğlu, Hüseyin, 254n12, 255
Nuremberg, 274

O

Obersalzberg Speech, The, 28n72
Odesa, 237 Ognisko Polskie, the, 10–11
Operation Barbarossa, the, xiv
Order Odrodzenia Polski. *See* Polonia Restituta, order
Orłowski, Leon, 34n96, 36n106
Orlowski, Stanisław, 227, 229, 232
Osmanlı Bankası, the, 255

Ostdeutscher Beobachter, newspaper, 181
Ostrowska-Koch, Krystyna, Baroness, 74, 76
Ottawa, 85n29
Ottoman Empire, the, 122, 129, 182, 250
Otto Schmidt und Koch, firm, the, 61. *See also* Koch
Oxford, 9, 213n16

P

Paderewski, Ignacy, 17, 23
Palestine, *passim. See also* Mandatory Palestine, the
Palestine Post, The, newspaper, 272
Paluchowicz (Mikiciński's code name), 183, 197 *See also* Mr. P
Panama, 186
Papée, Kazimierz, 11n3, 268–69
Papen, Franz von, 30–32, 34, 54, 129–31, 134–37, 159, 162, 164, 182, 187, 191, 196, 268–69, 273–74
Paraguay, 65–66
Parsifal, Prague branch of the Abwehr, the, 81n19
Paris, xix, xxii, xxvi, 15, 21, 29, 30, 35n99, 39, 60–62, 73–76, 79, 82–83, 85–86, 88, 90, 92n57, 97–98, 99n7, 104, 123, 138–40, 142–43, 146, 149, 150n37, 189, 281, 287, 294–95
Pearl Harbor, the, 295
People's Party. *See* Polish People's Party
Perry, Roland, 278
Persian Gulf, the, 236
Peruvian consul, the, 71
Pétain, Philippe, 22–23, 25, 52n181
Peter of Yugoslavia, King, 21n43
Petrie, Sir David, xx, 149, 150n39, 151n44, 152n45, 152n48, 168n105, 175n125, 176n132, 183n16, 185, 198n62, 199, 203–4, 211n6, 212n11, 213–23, 226n68, 226n73, 227, 230–33, 237–44, 275–77
Petrograd, 58
Pfeifferova, Mrs., 81, 167
Philippeville, 234
Philippines, the, 280
Philips, company, the, 25n59, 87
Phipps, Sir Eric, 98n4
Piast (code name). *See* Fietz-Fietowicz
Pilecki, captain, 250
Piłsudchiks, the, 100–3, 126–28, 130–31, 149, 157, 161, 167, 178, 185, 188, 190
Piłsudski, Józef, xiii, xxvii, 5, 27, 42, 53, 59, 76, 100, 148–49, 210, 263
Pissa, 37n109
Plesman, Albert, 50
Poles, the, *passim*

Polish Academy of Sciences, the, 42
Polish Armed Forces in the East. *See* Anders's Army
Polish Army (forces, troops etc.), the, xvi–xvii, xix–xx, 12n5, 18, 19, 24n57, 27, 35, 41, 51, 52n180, 62, 76, 98, 109, 117, 148–50, 152, 155, 205, 210–16, 218–19, 221, 224, 225n65, 226–28, 230, 232, 236–37, 242, 262–63, 270, 275n55, 282, 283n78, 289, 292
Polish Campaign, the, 21, 28–29, 34, 36, 39, 295
Polish Corridor, the, 30–31
Polish Foreign Office in Exile, 11n3, 140n6
Polish General Staff, the, xxii, 15n19, 17n28, 59, 70, 140n5, 163n85
Polish Institute and Sikorski Museum (PISM), the, xxvii, 110, 302
Political Intelligence Department, the, 14, 24, 40, 44n142, 46–47, 99
Polish Interior Ministry, the, 66, 106, 120, 127, 131, 134, 136n37, 148n25, 161, 175, 184, 197n60, 201–2, 211, 241, 244, 264–65
Polish Legion, the, 272
Polish Ministry of Justice, the, 90, 154, 146, 256
Polish Ministry of National Defense, the, 151n41, 224, 227n75, 231–32, 266n29
Polish National Bank, the, 105n30
Polish National Democrats, 217
Polish National Party (Stronnictwo Narodowe), the, 131
Polish Parliament, the, 23n51
Polish People's Party, the, 42–43, 52, 54, 101, 262, 290
Political Warfare Executive unit, the, 151
Polizei, 66n31
Polonia Restituta, order, the, 94–95, 285
Poltur, travel agency, the, 65–66, 69, 75
Pomorze, 33
Portugal, 17, 88n41, 173
Posen. *See* Poznań
Potocki, Jaroslaw, Count, 74
PoWs, the, 154
Poznań, 33, 279
Poznańska Street, the, 64, 81
Poznański, Józef, 211–12
Poznański, Karol, 266n29
Poznański, Renée, xxvi
Prague, 66, 80–81, 273, 294
Pravda, newspaper, 37n110, 182n7
Preston, 241
Pridham, G., 49n163
Prince George. *See* George, Prince

Prince's Gate, the, 10, 12
Principal Protective Council (Rada Główna Opiekuńcza), the, 48, 105
Prisoners of War. *See* PoW
Prosser, Colonel, 152
Provisional Government of National Unity, the, xv, 262, 265–66
Prussia, xiii
Pukhlev, Trifon, 109–11

R
Raczkiewicz, Władysław, 12, 140
Raczyński, Edward, Count, 11, 15–17, 29, 48n160, 50–51, 259n4, 298n26
Raczyński, Roger, 51, 71, 99–100, 102–3, 105n64, 115n64, 116, 118–20, 126–27, 129, 159, 162–63, 168
Rada Główna Opiekuńcza (Principal Protective Council), 48, 105
Rada Narodowa, 17
Radogoszcz prison, the, 280–81, 283
Radom, 25n59, 270, 273
Radziwiłłs, the, 48, 273
Radziwiłł, Janusz Franciszek, Prince, 42, 48–49, 51–52, 105, 274, 291
Radziwiłł, Karl, Prince, 273–74
RAF. *See* Royal Air Force
Ramme, Alwin, 28
Rasputin, Grigorii, 171
Red Army, the, xv, xxiv, 14, 33, 51n178, 96, 225, 271, 274, 291, 298. *See also* Russian army
Red Cross, organization, the, 48, 277, 298
Reich, the. *See* Third Reich, the
Reich Chancellery, the, 38n116
Reichsführer SS. *See* Himmler, Heinrich
Reich Security Main Office (RSHA), the, xxi–xxii, 25, 124, 269
Reichstag, the, xxiv, 39, 40n125
Remarque, Erich Maria, 80
Republic of Chile, the, 114. *See also* Chile
Republic of Turkey, the, 122. *See also* Turkey
Revisionist Zionist movement, the, 222. *See also* Zionist movement
Reynaud, Paul, 35n99
Rhoda, island, 236
Ribbentrop, Joachim von, xiii, 28–29, 31–32, 33n91, 34, 36–38, 42n134, 45, 47, 52n181, 54, 129, 273. *See also* Molotov-Ribbentrop Pact, the
Richmond, 6
Riga, 74
Rintelen, Enno von, 21, 54
Rintelen, Emil Otto Paul von, 54, 129–31
Rio de Janeiro, 85n29

Rishon LeZion, 9
Rivera, Miguel A., 116, 121
Romaszkan, Kazimierz, 273
Roberts, Douglas, 147n23, 151n44, 237–40, 242–43
Roberts, Sir Frank, 185n24
Romania, xiv, xviii–xix, 2, 4, *passim*
Romanian counterintelligence service, the, 144–45
Romanov, Konstantin, Prince, 82
Rome, xiv, 17, 21, 29, 34, 39, 49, 54, 70n43, 71, 106, 114–15, 132, 263, 272, 295
Ronikier, Adam, 269
Roosevelt, Franklin Delano, 20, 210
Ropp, William de, Baron, 46–47
Rosen, an agent of MI6, 166
Rosenberg, Alfred, 37, 46
Rostworowski, Stanisław, 101, 142, 144–46
Rothschild, Nathaniel Mayer Victor, Baron, 230, 278–79
Rowecki, Stefan, 189
Royal Air Force (RAF), the, xxiv, 10, 46, 176
Royal Navy, the, 234
Rozmarin, Henryk, 209
RSHA (Reich Security Main Office), the, xxi–xxii, 25, 124, 269
RU, the, xxiv
Rupova, Halszka, 49n166
Rupp, Robert Evgen'evich, 273
Russia, xiv, xxii–xxiv, 14, 21–23, 36, 59, 66, 81n19, 85, 103, 159, 220, 237, 258, 260–62, 268–69, 271–72, 280, 287–88, 291, 296n14
Russian army, the, xvii. *See also* Red Army
Russian Imperial Army, the, xvi, 58–59
Russian Empire, the, xiii, xviii, 54, 58, 61, 131, 171
Russian Foreign Intelligence Service, 32
Russians, the, 13, 50–51, 64–65, 96, 133, 135, 143, 160, 260, 267, 273–74, 279
Rutkowski, Tadeusz, 140
Rychlewicz, Wojciech, 166, 174, 250–51
Ryniewicz, Stefan, 89n47
Rysiewicz, Piotr, 127n12
Rzeczpospolita Polska, xiii. *See also* Second Polish Republic

S
Saar, the, 35n99
Saarbruecken, 33n88
Saarland region, the, 33–35
Saint George, Order of, 58
Saint Petersburg, 171
Salameh, Franck, 1
San, 37n109

Sanation, the, 52–53, 76, 78, 92–93, 98–102, 116-18, 125–28, 130–31, 135, 143, 149, 155–58, 162, 165, 169, 173, 184–85, 190, 197, 210–11, 215, 226, 250–51, 258, 260, 270, 288, 299
Santiago, 70, 116–17, 161–62, 212
Sapiegas, the, 48
Sapieha, Prince, 76–77
Saracoğlu. *See* Şükrü Saracoğlu, Mehmet
Saro London seaplane, the, 176–77
Savery, Frank, 185n24
Saydam, Refik, 252–54
Schmidt, Otto, 61
Schmidt und Koch, firm, the, 61. *See also* Koch
Schmidt, Paul, 22n47, 39n120
Schneersohn, Yosef Yitzchak (Lubavitcher Rebbe), 69
Scholz (code name), an Abwehr officer (Fabian, Heinz Heinrich), xix, 66–69, 71, 80, 82–86, 88, 103–4, 112, 133–34, 141n10, 167, 187, 190–91, 267–68
Schulenburg. *See* Graf von der Schulenburg
Schwarzbart, Ignacy, 159n71
Schwarzstein, Adam, 266
Schwarzstein, Stanisław, 165–66, 170, 266
Scotland, 11, 18, 215, 223
SD, the, xxiv, 42, 45, 52n181, 273
Second Department (Dwójka), the, 15n19, 17n28, 64, 140n5, 146n18, 147n21, 161n76, 163n85, 227n75, 250n3
Second Polish Republic, the, xiii, 2, 35, 45, 67, 97–98, 109, 115n64, 116n67, 118n74, 159, 210, 214, 271n42, 271nn44–45, 272n47, 272n49, 273n50, 275n55
Second Sino-Japanese War, the, 297
Sędzielowski, Mieczysław, 90n49, 256n20
Segal, Sofia, 61
Serov, Ivan, 279
Shirer, William H., 33n88, 35n99, 37n109
Sicily, 234
Siegfried Line, the, 33n88
Siemiatycze, 58
Siguranța, the, 144–45
Sikorski, Władysław, xiv, xix–xx, xxii, xxvii, 2, 7, *passim*
Sikorski Museum, the, xxvii, 110, 302
Sikorski's wife and daughter (Helena and Zofia), xix, 77, 81, 86, 91, 167, 197, 259
Silesia, xv
Sima, Horia, 115, 155, 180
SIME. *See* British Security Intelligence Middle East
Singapore, 21n43
Sir Arthur. *See* Forbes

SIS (Secret Intelligence Service), xxiii, xxv, 4, 14, 133, 192. *See also* MI6
Skarbek-Granville, Krystyna, 159, 276
Składkowski, Felicjan Sławoj, 210
Slovakia, 32, 35, 85, 98. *See also* Czechoslovakia
Słowikowski, Mieczysław, 277
SMERSH, Soviet military counterintelligence organization, 273
Smith, I., 218n34
Smolenski, Józef, 52n180
Smolensk Oblast, the, xiv
Snyder, Timothy, 293–94n7
SOE, the, xxv, 4, 6, 18n30, 59, 79, 85, 107n41, 114, 120n80, 128n16, 129n18, 130n22, 132, 135, 148n24, 150, 152n46, 153n50, 156n64, 157, 159, 167, 168n103, 169, 172, 182, 186, 192–94, 199–200, 202, 203n80, 276
Sofia, 67n34, 107–11, 133, 145, 156, 267
Sokolnicki, Michał, 26n68, 30–31, 34, 59, 71, 73, 92, 102n20, 121, 126–28, 166, 173–75, 180–81, 182n7, 194–95, 250, 252, 254–55
Somali Peninsula, the, 236
Sosnkowska, Jadwiga, 82, 86
Sosnkowski, Kazimierz, 76–77, 79–82, 91, 92n57, 93, 100–2, 108, 125–26, 128, 134, 140–44, 151, 167, 184–85, 188, 190, 270–71, 273, 275n55
SO.2, the, xxv, 172. See also SOE
South Africa, the, 49, 227. *See also* Africa
South America, the, 85, 181, 212. *See also* Latin America
Southeast Asia, the, 234
Soviet Interior Ministry, the, xxiv. *See* NKVD
Soviets, the, xiv, 13, 15, 22n49, 32, 34, 38, 48, 63–64, 138–39, 151, 220, 261, 267, 273, 278
Soviet Union, the, xiii-xv, xxiv, 13, 16n26, 22, 24, 28, 35, 36n103, 37, 48n160, 50, 52n181, 63, 67n37, 136, 139, 189, 204–5, 220, 225, 261, 277, 292, 293n7, 295
Sovpoltorg company, the, 63–65
Spain, 17, 22, 139, 173, 296, 298
Spanish Civil War, the, 149
SS (German Security Service), the, xxi–xxii, xxiv–xxv, 42, 44, 62n21, 66n31, 87, 124, 269
Stalin, Joseph, xiv, 8, 13, 15, 23, 26, 37–39, 63, 177, 224–25, 258–59, 261, 271–72, 278, 290, 295–96
Stanford University, the, 5, 302
Starzyński, Stefan, 42, 291

Stefanowski-Syrokomla, Bronisław, 107, 108n43, 109–10, 146, 153–54, 156–58, 192–93, 264–65
Stern, Izak (Yitzhak), 252
Stockholm, 45, 52n181, 74, 92n57, 272
Stronnictwo Narodowe (Polish National Party), 131
Stroński, Stanisław, 156, 157n63
Struma, ship, 186–87
Studnicki, Władysław, 23–25, 28, 51–52, 100, 294
Sturdza, Mihail, Prince, 115
Suez, 235
Şükrü Saracoğlu, Mehmet, 30, 252–55
Sudan, 171, 213
Sudoplatov, Pavel, 13, 48n160, 124
Sultanov (code name), Soviet agent, 124
Supreme Command (Headquarters), the, xxi, 154nn53–54, 154n57, 155n61, 156n62, 212–13, 215–16, 219–20, 225, 227n75, 250n3, 275n55, 282
Supreme Court of Israel, the, 284
Sûreté nationale, 140
Sweden, 45, 46n148
Świetlicki, Andrzej, 43
Switzerland, 79, 88, 90, 120, 270, 296n18
Syria, xxv, 89, 155, 210, 232, 270, 283
Szafer, Władysław, 105
Szapiro, Aron and Ida, 148
Szapiro, Mojżesz (Moses), 148, 290. *See also* Szarkiewicz, Edward
Szapiro-Szarkiewicz, 184, 211–12, 226, 290. *See also* Szarkiewicz, Edward
Szarkiewicz, Edward (aka ESS13/Little Man/Dunlop), xviii, 7, *passim*
Szarkiewicz's parents. *See* Szapiro, Aron and Ida
Szarska-Potocka, Irena, 74, 76, 86
Szczepański, Jakub, 149
Szczerbiński, Zdzisław, 108n43, 165, 167, 265
Szubert, Zbigniew, 27
Szumowski, Tadeusz, 140n7
Szymańska, Halina, Countess, 79

T

Tarnowski, Adam, 107–10, 145, 156, 264n19
Tătărescu, Gheorghe, 105
Tel Aviv, 95, 105, 181, 183, 209–10, 240, 253, 255n16, 256–57, 279–81, 298n27
Temple, William, Archbishop of York, 40, 300n29
Terlecki, Olgierd, 60
Third Reich, the, xiv–xv, xviii–xix, xxi–xxii, xxiv–xxv, 13, 21–25, 27–28, 30, 33, 36, 43–47, 49, 52–53, 66–68, 78–80, 84–86, 108–9, 124, 132, 134, 137, 140, 145, 164, 187, 196, 201, 236, 252, 269, 271, 274–75, 290–91, 293–97, 299–300
Third Republic, the, 98. *See also* France
Thucydides, historian, 299, 301
Times, The, newspaper, 180
Tito, Josip Broz, 21n43
Tobruk, 282–83
Toruń, 276n61, 302
Tokyo, 23n51, 85n29, 115, 295
Trans-Jordan, 175
Travellers Club, the, 216–17
Trayanov, Petar, 107, 109–11
Trzeciak, Stanisław, 43
Tsarist army (Imperial Russian Army), the, xvi, 58–59
Tsokov, Krum, 107–11, 115
Turkey, xxv, 4, *passim*
Turkish Foreign Office, the, 30–31, 114, 123, 252, 254n12, 255
Turks, the, 30–31, 122–23, 127, 132, 162, 165–66, 170–71, 186, 188, 251–56, 266, 274, 284
Turner, Theodore, 220n41, 221n44
Tymczasowy Rząd Jedności Narodowej, xv

U

Ujazdowski military hospital, the, 82
Ukraine, xviii, 15n18, 51, 58, 148, 267, 273, 301
Ulmanova, Maria, 49n166
Union of Armed Struggle (Związek Walki Zbrojnej or ZWZ), the, xxv, 76, 100, 125–26, 140–42, 189
Union of Polish Journalists, the, 264
United Kingdom, the, xiv, xviii, *passim*
United States of America, the, xxvi, 2, 20, 61, 62n21, 90, 105n30, 136, 201, 222, 268n32, 295, 301–2
Upper Silesia, xv
Uruguay, 121
USSR, the, xxiii–xxiv, 8, 13, 15, 22, 26n68, 37, 43, 49, 51, 63–64, 101, 123, 220, 224–26, 230, 260, 267–68, 269n37, 271, 273, 283, 293, 295n9, 297–98

V

Vane-Tempest-Stewart, Charles Stewart Henry, 7th Marquess of Londonderry, 17
Vatan, newspaper, 179
Vatican, the, 17, 268–69, 271–72, 273n50
Vichy France, the, 22–23, 26–27, 52n181, 155, 210, 236, 293, 296
Vienna, 54, 66, 85n29, 106
Vilnius, 271n42

Vistula, 37n109
Volokhov, Alexander, 81n19
Volokhov, Leonid, 81, 85, 133–34, 191, 193, 267, 287
Vybranivka (Wybranówka), 148, 184
Vyshinsky, Andrey, 13n12, 297

W

Walkowski, 212n9
Warsaw, 1–2, 9, *passim*
Warsaw Uprising, the, xiv, xxii-xxiii, 274–76, 291
Washington, xxvi, 2, 5, 13, 20, 85n29, 105n30, 137, 222, 263, 298, 302
Wehrmacht, the, xxv, 10–11, 25, 27, 32–33, 35–36, 40, 42–44, 48, 67, 84, 104, 114, 123, 271, 274, 295–96
Weidemeier, B., 266n28
Weissauer, Ludwig, 52n181
Weizsäcker, Ernst von, 22n46, 22n48, 32, 36, 38n117, 39n118, 39n120
Welles, Sumner, 295
Wendt Forest, the, 33n88
West, Nigel, 132
Western Belorussia. *See* Belarus
Western Front, the, 40n125, 78
Western Ukraine. *See* Ukraine
Westerplatte peninsula, the, 73
Westminster Hospital, the, 212, 218
Wetulani, Adam, 102
White Army (Denikin's Army), the, 58–59, 66, 94
Whitehall, 251
Whittingham Hospital, the, 241
Wieczorkiewicz, Paweł, 291, 293
Wieniawa-Długoszowski, Bolesław, 23, 29, 34n96, 46, 49n168
Wilhelmina camp, the, 264
Wilson, Sir Horace, 15n18, 31
Wilson, Maurice J., 276
Winterbotham, Frederick, 46
Winter Palace, the, 57
Winter War, the, 22
Witos, Wincenty, 42, 44, 49, 52, 54, 101
Witkowski, Stanisław, 276n61
Wolfson, W., 168, 177
World War I, the, xix, 21, 33, 46, 52, 54, 58, 85, 122, 129, 214
World War II, the, xiii, xvi, xviii–xix, xxii–xxvi, 2, 4–7, 22n49, 23, 24n57, 53, 59, 62, 65, 70, 73, 86, 95, 108, 148–49, 151, 157, 164, 172, 176, 191–92, 198n62, 203–4, 209, 212n11, 213n16, 236, 245, 261n9, 263, 277, 280, 286, 288, 290–91, 293, 296n14, 299, 301
Wrocław (Breslau), xix, 63n21, 67–69, 80, 82–87, 89n44, 94, 104, 133, 142, 187, 190–91, 267, 281, 287
Wybranówka (Vybranivka), 148, 184
Wysocki, Alfred, 272

Y

Yad Vashem memorial complex, the, xxvii
Yemen, xxv
Yeniköy, suburb, 174
Yidisher Courier, newspaper, 298n27
York, 40, 300n29
Yugoslavia, 21n43, 98

Z

Zabieło, Stanisław, 27n69
Zakrzewski, Tadeusz, 98–99, 102–3, 215
Zaleska, Elina, 48n161, 272n48
Zaleski, August, 15nn20–21, 17n27, 23n51, 52n180, 119, 129, 162, 196
Zamojski family, 64
Zbąszyń, 66
Ze'ev. *See* Jabotinsky, Vladimir
Zgierz, 280–83
Zichoń, Major, 154n54, 154n57, 155n61, 251n4
Zigmond, a Soviet agent, 51
Zionist movement, the, 181, 186, 216, 222, 236, 239, 279–80, 283. *See also* Irgun
Żurawski, Zdzisław, 173
ZWZ (Związek Walki Zbrojnej). *See* Union of Armed Struggle
Zychowicz, Piotr, 291, 293

www.ingramcontent.com/pod-product-compliance
Lightning Source LLC
Chambersburg PA
CBHW052044220426
43663CB00012B/2433